1 MONTH OF
FREE
READING

at

www.ForgottenBooks.com

By purchasing this book you are eligible for one month membership to ForgottenBooks.com, giving you unlimited access to our entire collection of over 1,000,000 titles via our web site and mobile apps.

To claim your free month visit:
www.forgottenbooks.com/free894957

ISBN 978-0-266-82484-8
PIBN 10894957

This book is a reproduction of an important historical work. Forgotten Books uses state-of-the-art technology to digitally reconstruct the work, preserving the original format whilst repairing imperfections present in the aged copy. In rare cases, an imperfection in the original, such as a blemish or missing page, may be replicated in our edition. We do, however, repair the vast majority of imperfections successfully; any imperfections that remain are intentionally left to preserve the state of such historical works.

1179 *1179*

No. 3199

United States Circuit Court of Appeals

For the Ninth Circuit

SHIPOWNERS AND MERCHANTS TUGBOAT COMPANY
(a corporation), claimant of the American
Steam Tug "Fearless", her boilers, engines,
tackle, apparel and furniture,

Appellant,

vs.

A. H. BULL & COMPANY, INC. (a corporation),

Appellee.

BRIEF FOR APPELLANT.

WILLIAM DENMAN
McCUTCHEN, OLNEY & WILLARD,
Proctors for Appellant.

Index of Topics.

Table of Authorities.

No. 3199

IN THE

United States Circuit Court of Appeals

For the Ninth Circuit

SHIPOWNERS AND MERCHANTS TUGBOAT COMPANY
(a corporation), claimant of the American
Steam Tug "Fearless", her boilers, engines,
tackle, apparel and furniture,

Appellant,

. vs.

A. H. BULL & COMPANY, INC. (a corporation),
Appellee.

BRIEF FOR APPELLANT.

THE FACTS.

This case arose from a series of misunderstandings
between the captain of the Steamer "Edith" who was
taking the steamer under her own power from pier 46
in San Francisco Bay to the Hunters Point drydock and
the captain of the Tug "Fearless" who was employed
to "assist" the "Edith" in the maneuver. As a result
of these misunderstandings the "Edith" drifted over
2000 feet in the waters of the bay and finally collided

with pier No. 32, sustaining injuries to her starboard side.

There is no dispute in the testimony as to the character of service to the "Edith" for which the tug was employed. The "Edith" was to use her own engines and the tug was to "assist" her in backing from the slip and in turning her round on a maneuver known to the "Edith's" captain and undisclosed to the tug. There is no dispute that the commanding mind as between the two captains was that of McDonald on the "Edith" until at any rate the vessel had backed several hundred feet clear of the slip (McDonald Dep. 75). The primary questions here are whether the "Edith's" captain properly planned and organized for the maneuver with the assisting tug, and whether he ever transferred the controlling authority in the maneuver from himself to the captain of the tug, and whether if he did so, he conveyed the information as to the conditions on the "Edith" to the tug's captain, which was necessary for his guidance on the shifting of the command.

Of the many witnesses on the "Edith", but two were produced and their testimony was taken by deposition. No excuse was offered for not producing all these other witnesses nor any given for the failure to produce the "Edith's" logs which were demanded by the tug's proctor (48).

The two depositions in evidence were those of the captain and second mate, through whose thoughts and actions the planning for the maneuver and the alleged subsequent transfer of authority could alone have been made and if made the proper information as to any changed conditions on the "Edith" given to the new commander. We thus approach this portion of the case, upon which the entire question of causation rests, unembarrassed by any presumptions arising from the adverse decision below. This court is as well able to determine from the captain and second mate depositions whether they had properly planned and organized for the maneuver and whether they had subsequently transferred the command and responsibility and communicated the necessary information to the new chief, as was the trial court. It is as well able to draw inferences so far as they may affect the testimony in the deposition, from the failure to produce the engine room and other logs of the "Edith" and her engineer, her first and third mate and the many members of her crew who handled her tow lines.

On the afternoon of March 4, 1916, the Steamer "Edith", 328 feet long and of about 2700 tons net register, was lying bow in-shore at pier 46 of the San Francisco docks, waiting to start on a trip under her own power and under the dominion of her master, Captain McDonald, from the pier to the drydock at Hunters Point. The voyage was to be in a general southerly direction at right angles to the pier. Pier-head 32, against which the "Edith" finally drifted, was over 2200 feet northerly from her mooring place. Pier 46 is the most southerly of the parallel line of piers projecting at right angles to the San Francisco shore line, which there runs about north and south, angling slightly to the easterly in the north half of the group.

The piers are numbered consecutively to the northerly from pier 46, as 44, 42, 40, 38, 36, 34 and 32, and the maneuvers involved in the case are confined to the waters of the bay off piers 46 to 32. Pier 46 extends into the bay about 800 feet from the water-front line; 44, 42 and 40 extend 650 feet from the water-front line; 38, 667 feet; 36, 721 feet; 34, 662 feet, and 32, 805 feet. On account of the bend in the shore line, pier-head 32 extends to the easterly over 300 feet beyond pier-heads 44, 42, 40 and 38, while it extends over 200 feet beyond pier-head 34.

A clear reach of San Francisco Bay of over thirty miles lies to the southerly of this group of piers, and the tide, which was then well in the ebb, was flowing in the direction from pier 46 to pier 32, and on account of the narrowing of the bay at this point, on towards the shore line. As the uncontradicted testimony shows, close to the heads of the piers, the ebbing tide ran more nearly at right angles to the piers than it did a little further out in the bay.

There was a strong southeasterly wind (18 miles) blowing during the period in question. That is to say, the wind was blowing at an angle of about 45 degrees onto the docks. It is thus apparent, and it is uncontested in this case, that any vessel lying in the waters of the bay, to the easterly of the docks, would be carried by wind and tide in an angle towards them of something less than 45 degrees.

The "Edith" was moved astern out of the slip between piers 46 and 44, into the waters of the bay, a sufficient distance to drift in the wind and the tide, with her stern pointing off shore, and her bow on shore, past all the pier-heads, including pier 34, so that she finally reached a point where her stern was on a line with the easterly end of pier 32, with her bow pointing still towards the shore at nearly right angles. That is to say, at the end of her drift, the entire length of the ship was inside of the extension of the line of pier-head 32 (Captain McDonald, of "Edith", pages 39 and 40). She backed enough just before she struck, to collide with the easterly corner of the pier at a point a third the distance aft from her bow (41). Projecting her angle of drifting back from pier 32, and clearing pier-head 34, she could not have been less than 700 feet from pier 42 when she started to have finished up her drifting in the position which her captain has showed she was in at the end of the drift. The probabilities are that she was still further out in the bay from pier-heads 42 and 44, because of the greater on-shore set of the tide further out in the bay, than at the end of her drift between pier-heads 34 and 32, where the water runs more nearly parallel to the pier-head line.

The following sketch, which is a copy of the exhibit in evidence as far as the outline of the piers is concerned, illustrates these basic facts of the problem.

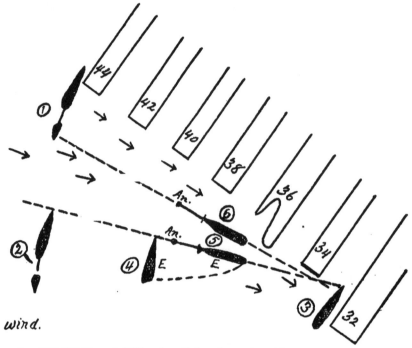

wind.

1. "Edith" and "Fearless" leaving pier 44.
2. "Edith" when "Fearless" dropped line.
3. "Edith" where her captain described her at end of drift.
4. "Edith" if she had dropped anchor.
5. "Edith" if anchored along line of drift; 180 feet chain dropped 50 feet.
6. "Edith" if anchored along any other line of drift taking her clear of piers 36 and 34.
   Small arrows—direction of tide out in bay setting on docks. Parallel to pierhead line closer in.

None of these facts, we understand, are disputed, save that the captain and the mate of the "Edith" asserted that she began her drift with both her own and the tug's engines stopped, when her bow was within fifty feet of the easterly end of pier 42, a condition, which, if true, would have brought her up against pier 40 in the on-shore movement of wind and tide.* We

*The "Edith's" captain had started his engines ahead with a starboard helm to send her on a course ahead towards the docks and curving to port around the time the tug stopped pulling astern (36). He must have been a considerable distance from the docks to have

understand it to have been admitted in the lower court that the captain and mate were in error in their statement as to the distance the "Edith" was off pier 42 at the time she began to drift. The admitted circumstance of the wind and tide and the place of termination of the drift made the greater distance from pier-heads 44 and 42 as the given fact of the problem; and, as to this, all of the other witnesses are substantially agreed. The exact difference is immaterial it being shown that she drifted free of all these intervening pier-heads.

The distance from a point 700 feet off pier 42 to the end of pier 32 is about 1800 feet. The distance from the northerly side of the slip between piers 44 and 46, to pier 32, is about 2100 feet.

On the morning of the fourth, or the afternoon before, the captain of the "Edith" telephoned to the owners of the tug "Fearless" to "assist" him on his trip to the drydock (30). The "Edith's" captain said he did not then expect the tug to help him out of the slip where he was moored (50); but only that he would be assisted in entering the drydock at the end of the trip. Obviously, no plan for the maneuver of backing out and turning to the south could have been communicated by the "Edith's" captain to the tug's through her owners at this time, and it is not so claimed.

When the tug under the command of Captain Sandstrom came alongside the "Edith", Captain McDonald changed his mind and concluded to avail himself of the

thought this maneuver possible. If the vessel had been but 50 feet from pier 42 the tug would have helped the wind and tide drive her against pier 40 as its power pulled her stern to starboard and toward the docks.

tug's assistance in the maneuver he contemplated for backing out of the slip and turning his vessel to the southerly.

The captain's deposition tells us that the "Edith" had forty per cent deeper draft at the stern than at the bow. That is, she was drawing ten feet aft and six feet forward (48). While the failure to produce the logs leaves us without the exact figures, the depositions of the mate and captain agree that the "Edith's" bow was much higher out of water than her stern and hence much easier to swing either by the wind or the tug. Obviously, the place of assistance for a tow boat in swinging the "Edith" after she backed out into the wind and tide, was from her bow. It seems, however, that Captain McDonald's plan contemplated that after the vessel had backed out from the slip the tug would then move from her position astern to a position off the starboard quarter and pull the deeper stern of the vessel to the westerly and starboard while he would endeavor to turn the "Edith's" light and high bow to port into the southeasterly wind as he went ahead on the ship's engines toward the docks on a starboard helm.* He, of course, could have as well gone astern with a port helm and not risked a nearer approach to the docks, while the tug was pulling the bow to starboard.

It is not important which of the three maneuvers was preferable—the first and third were indubitably prac-

*If this really was the "Edith's" captain's intended maneuver he was in clearly admitted fault. After backing out he says he stopped and then started ahead on a starboard helm, when the tug was still straight astern where he could not even see her (Dep 59, 56). The tug of course could not pull the heavy stern around from directly behind nor move to the port side to do so while the steamer was going ahead.

ticable as well as a fourth maneuver; this was that the tug should drop its tow line when the vessel had backed out of the dock and as soon as the line was hauled in the "Edith" should continue backing with her stern turning to the southeasterly away from the docks until the vessel was parallel to them; and then going ahead on a course on a port helm curving to the northerly, easterly and then southerly till pointed to her destination.

It is vitally important that the "Edith's" master, who was in command of the maneuver. not only failed to communicate to the tug which of the four possible maneuvers he contemplated (Dep. pp. 50, 51, 58), but failed to give the tug any code of whistle signals to guide the tug from time to time as the maneuver he chose developed.

He, therefore, must be charged with leaving to the discretion of the master of the tug the determination from the obvious actions of the ship what the next act of the tug was to be and the reasonable expectancy that if the tug started on a maneuver which was not helpful to his plan the "Edith's" captain would advise him *viva voce* through the particular mate who guarded the end of the tow line fastened to the ship, the point to which the eye of the tug master would naturally turn.

The master of the "Edith" being the dominant mind, was therefore solely responsible if this less certain method was productive of any confusion which might possibly arise.

However, not only did the "Edith's" master fail to communicate his plan or arrange for whistle signals, but he also failed to notify the second mate in charge of the after tow line that he was to act as the agent through whom commands would be given to direct the activities of the tug or stop her if she was not acting in coordination.

Captain McDonald's deposition says (55):

"Q. At any rate you didn't arrange any signals.
A. No.
Q. You depended on passing word by the second officer?
A. By the second officer.
Q. What was the second officer's name?
A. Hanson."

Hanson's deposition is (90, 91, 99) as follows:

"Q. You said you expected the tug to get orders from the master? A. Yes.
Q. How were you expecting the master of your ship—he was on the bridge, isn't that right?
A. Yes.
Q. How did you expect the master on the bridge of your ship to give an order to the tug to go ahead. A. By the whistle.
Q. What whistle would he make?
A. That depends on which way they make it out between them.
Q. What?
A. They make that out between them what kind of a whistle they are going to use.
Q. They usually agree on what the signal shall be? A. Yes. (Dep. pp. 90, 91.)

Q. Your duty on the stern is to keep an eye on the towing line?

A. But we are not supposed to watch the tug too; he is supposed to give us a signal what to do.

Q. Who is? A. The tug captain.

Q. What signal did you expect the tug to give?

A. I expected the tug captain to blow a short blast the same as the rest of them do.

Q. Had you ever been towed by that tug before?

A. No.

Q. Did you ever have any conversation with her master before starting out as to what signals he would give you? A. No, sir." (Dep. p. 99.)

The "Edith's" captain expected the communication to be through the second mate; the second mate knew nothing about this, but expected the communication to pass between the two captains by whistles. He neither looked at the tug's captain nor his own but busied himself with other matters about the ship at important moments (99, 98).

In this basic disorganization from which the subsequent confusion and damage arose, the master of the tug had no part. It was not his duty to inform the "Edith's" second mate that his own captain had not advised the tug of the intended maneuver and that he had arranged no code of whistle signals with the tug, and that he, the "Edith's" mate, was the person to whom he was to look for any correction of any action on his part which did not fit into the "Edith's" undisclosed plans. When the second mate gave him the "Edith's" hawser and told him to go ahead, he was entitled to rely on the scheme of communication in both his and Captain McDonald's minds, i. e. through the second mate.

In all this, it must be noted that both the depositions admit the tow line used in assisting the "Edith" in backing from the dock was not over 30 fathoms in length. When we consider that the line had some curve in it down from the ship we see that the mate when standing on the stern and the tow boat captain were not much over 150 feet apart—easy megaphone and visual distance. The tow boat captain knew that his every act was within sight and in calling distance for correction if it did not fit into the "Edith's" plan. It was no fault of his that the "Edith" was both blind and dumb so far as concerned communicating with him while he was assisting off her stern and that he erroneously believed she could both see and speak.

While the "Edith" was lying at the north side of pier 46 a line was passed from her stern to the tug and, through a not to be unexpected misunderstanding, the ship's forward lines mooring her to the dock were not cast off when the tug began to pull and the tow line parted. The forward moorings were then loosened and the vessel drifted in the tide across the slip to the south side of pier 44. No harm came to the ship from this mishap, but the "Edith's" captain was plainly reminded that he should have a clear understanding with his mates as to the method of communication with the tug. He was also warned of a loss in his supply of hawsers and that if he needed any assistance in hawser service from the tug he should have found out what she had and planned for their use.

While the vessel was lying against the south side of pier 44, the other end of the same tow line was passed to the tug, which was lying astern. The line had an eye on its end and it was placed over the towing bits of the tug. Three or four men (89) beside the mate handled the end of the line on the "Edith".

The tug on a signal from the captain through the mate (55) began to pull the ship backward assisting the ship's reversing engines. This continued till the vessel had reached a point out in the bay from which she drifted on the on-setting tide and southeasterly wind till her full length was inside the head of pier 32 (Dep. McDonald, 39, 40). As we have shown, this starting point of the drift must have been where her bow was some 700 feet off pier-head 42.

When at this distance from the docks, the tug captain claims that he saw the "Edith's" propeller stop and concluded that she did not desire to go any further astern and that he would assist at the bow in turning her light head into the wind. He says he stopped his own engine, let the vessels drift towards each other till the line had slackened, then had his crew unfasten the line from his bits and held by hand for an interval when it dropped into the bay. It would take but five minutes for only two men to haul it in (330) and of course a much shorter time with the larger number of men handling it (89).*

All this he was entitled to presume was under the eye of the mate of the "Edith" who could have halted the maneuver at any moment until the line was in the water,

---

*In the lower court the "Edith's" counsel confused the time for two men to haul the line in with that for the three or four men actually there.

or after it was cast off, order the tug to pick up the floating line (with its boat hook from its low stern), refasten it and recommence the towing astern. There is a dispute as to whether the "Edith's" engines were stopped when the line was disengaged from the tug's bits, or when it was dropped into the bay, but this becomes causally immaterial in view of the adoption of the tug's maneuver by the ship without protest.

Instead of attempting to halt the act of the tug or to have it recommence its stern towing, the "Edith's" second mate adopted the tug's maneuver. He had his crew of three or four men (89) commence at once to heave in the 30 fathoms of tow line and continued to do so successfully until the eye on its end reached near the "Edith's" stern where it, in some unknown manner, fouled the propeller, was severed from the rest of the line, and remained attached to one of the propeller blades till the vessel reached the drydock.

The depositions are perfectly clear on this point, namely that the whole length of the line lay in the water, without slack, when the second mate said he saw the tug "leave it go" (Dep. 98); that he heaved "right in" (Dep. 100) "as soon as the tow boat threw it off" (Dep. 73), and that it was the *end* of the line that caught (86).

The second mate says at page 86:

"Q. When you reached drydock did you notice the propeller? A. Oh, yes.

Q. What did you see?

A. I saw the *end* of the line around the shaft, *around the wheel.*"

The "Edith's" captain says at page 60:

"Q. Why do you say that the line fouled the wheel, you didn't see it, did you? A. Yes.

Q. How did you see it?

A. I got the *end* off after when we went into drydock."

The part of the line cut off by the propeller was brought to the court house, but the judge did not inspect it. The superintendent of the dock testified it was in two pieces, including the eye at the end, one 30 and the other 18 feet long.

The captain's deposition says at page 60:

"Q. Did you say that the mate had hauled in the line?

A. Not then, when the engines were stopped, *but before we took time to stop them* the mate was hauling the line in, and it was afoul of the wheel."

Further evidence that it was the *end* that fouled and while the propeller was turning, is the fact that the second mate, who was watching it being heaved in, did not know it was cut till after it was hauled up (100).

Since it lay at length in the water without slack, it must have been hauled for over a hundred feet of its length before it caught in the propeller. Its fouling must have been noticed if it had been caught before this time. The point at which the line was caught in the revolving wheel was off pier 42. The engines were stopped off pier 42 (Dep. 38) and hence the alleged dropping was at or before that time.

Conclusive evidence that the "Edith's" engines were going ahead for some time after the line was cast off is

McDonald's deposition that the "Edith" was going ahead *through the water* at the time her engines were stopped (37). This momentum forward must have been acquired after the tug's lines were cast off or she would have been pulling the tug (lying dead astern, 59) backwards through the water. In other words the engines must have been working for some time while the line was being hauled in.

At this point the unexcused failure to produce the "Edith's" engineer or her engine room log or deck log or the members of the crew hauling the lines, becomes of interest. The logs were demanded on the 20th day of March, 1917, nearly three months before the trial. We may assume that it would have shown the jarring of the propeller shaft as the tow line struck against the stern frame with the propeller twisting it around and that the moment when this occurred bore a causal relationship to the captain's orders to reverse, to stop, and to go ahead (Dep. 58-59). We may infer that the mate's log and men handling the line would emphasize the captain's and mate's testimony that the line had been hauled in to near its end before it was cut off and hence that the engines continued to turn long after they had been hauling it.

However, apart from the missing logs and witnesses, we can see no other conclusion to be drawn from the testimony of the depositions than that the length of the line was hauled in to near its end before it was fouled in the propeller, which was then turning and that in hauling it in at all and not asking the tug to pick it up again the ship adopted and ratified the tug's maneuver

to cease her stern towing before any harm had arisen.
The tug certainly cannot be held at fault if her maneuver is thus adopted without protest from the ship,
and the propeller continued to turn long after the line
had been cast off.

The depositions are equally clear as to *the absence of
any warning to the tug* that the "Edith's" propeller
was fouled and that for the remainder of the period of
the drama from pier 42 until the vessel was in extremis
within 200 feet of pier 32, her captain regarded her as
a "dead ship" with engines out of commission.

In other words, the whole character of the tow was
changed from an "assist" to the engines of the
"Edith", to the duty on the tug to furnish full power
to bring the vessel away from the docks, without the
slightest hint to the tug's captain of the change. The
"Edith's" captain's language in this is clear and specific. He says, deposition pages 61, 67, 68 and 76:

> "Q. As it stands, you were saying that the line
> fouled the wheel because some one else told you so,
> that was the situation at that time?
> A. Yes, sure.
> Q. Did you give the tug any orders after that
> stage of the maneuver? A. No."

In describing the causal responsibility for the loss he
said:

> "Q. I understand that in this position you were
> about 150 feet, the 'Edith' was bout 150 to 200 feet
> from pier 32, is that correct? A. I think so.
> Q. Was it in that position you started your en-
> gines astern (referring to Claimant's Exhibit 'A')?
> A. Yes.

Q. You didn't have any difficulty in operating the engines, did you? A. Not after we started, no.

Q. Was that the first effort that you had made from the time that the line was cast off, as you say, up to the time that the bow-line parted?

A. Yes.

Q. Why was it that you did not make an effort to start your engines before?

A. I was rather afraid when the seven-inch line fouled the wheel, thinking the towboat would have it performed or we would get out without that.

Q. Didn't you think that there was a position of danger there? A. I could readily see it.

Q. When did you first see that?

A. The danger of the line being around the wheel?

Q. No, I mean did you think there was a position of danger from your drifting down, as you have described? A. Yes, I did.

Q. You knew that eventually you must bring up against something, did you not?

A. I surely did.

Q. How was it, I want to know why it was that you did not start your engines before you did? ·

A. Because I didn't want to, I was afraid to attempt that, I was depending on the towboat.

Q. Had you had any communication with the engine room from the time that the second line was cast off up to the time that the third line was cast from your bow to the tug? A. No.

Q. Had not sent any word down to the engineers about this. A. No.

Q. *And yet in that time you had drifted down from off pier 42 to this position between pier 34 and pier 32, is that true? A. Yes.*

Q. Do you know how long that distance is?

A. No.

Q. Didn't you think that the situation there demanded that you take some risk to save your vessel from collision with the pier?

A. *I was expecting the towboat to do something, depending on the towboat.*

Q. You were relying on the towboat?

A. Depending on the towboat.

Q. You did not anticipate that this towboat could handle your steamer in that wind and tide without some assistance from the steamer, did you?

A. No, but it could easily swing us around, though.

Q. As to the fouling of the propeller, you now know, of course, that the propeller, if it was fouled at all, at the time you thought it was, was not fouled sufficiently to have prevented moving the engines, was it?

A. We found that out afterwards.

Q. So that you were acting under a misapprehension of the situation, were you.

A. Apparently, yes.''

Again, Captain McDonald says (p. 78):

"Q. *What do you think was the cause of this disaster?''*

A. *Getting the line in the wheel.*

*   *   *   *   *   *

Q. You concede now that your engines *could* have been moved?

A. *That has the same effect on your mind as if it was not.*

Q. Won't you concede that your engines could have been moved?

A. Anyone would have to concede that because it was done, *but the effect on your mind is just the same, I should judge.''*

The evidence of the depositions as to the absence of the warning to the tug's captain of the change of the character of the "Edith" from an engined vessel to a hulk is in accord with Captain Sandstrom's uncontradicted testimony (f. 300).

"Q. *Did anyone aboard the vessel, aboard the 'Edith', ever suggest to you that the line was in the wheel?*
A. No."

The evidence being clear and specific that the "Edith's" captain believed when off pier 42 (p. 68) that his engines were disabled and did not intend to attempt to use them; and that the tug's captain, in the absence of warning, properly believed that during all this time nothing had happened to the "Edith's" engines, and that she could go astern or ahead under her own power at will, when the line was hauled in, the various maneuvers open to each from *his own view point* therefore became pertinent.

The maneuvers and conduct open to the "Edith's" captain were:

(1) He could drop his anchors at once. They were patent anchors and could be dropped instantly on lifting their brake-bar. The vessel would then have run along till she brought up on her chains and swung round on his head till she was down wind and held in the tide. Since she cleared even pier 36 by a good margin when she drifted down, she would have ridden safely at anchor along this drifting line even with 180 feet of anchor chain out (42). The captain's excuse (64) that he started to drift only forty feet off from pier 42 and would have swung on the pier ends if he anchored is answered by the clearly established fact that she must have started to drift some 700 feet out from pier 42.

He admitted the tide paralleled the pier-head closer in (64) and that her stern was over 40% deeper in the tide than her bow which the anchor would hold while the tide kept her stern away from the docks.

(2) He could have ordered the tug to take another line off her stern by backing up to the "Edith" on a course well around the floating end of the tow line, or, receiving the line from the "Edith's" starboard side to which the tug went (329) and have her tow the "Edith" further away from the docks, straight astern where the pull would have been easy *across the wind* and hence requiring a much lighter hawser. All the tug's power would then have been spent in pulling the vessel lengthwise through the water instead of being wasted in attempting, as he later ordered, to pull the "Edith's" light bow to port against the wind and toward the docks.

(3) He could, if he had so desired (though his owners would never have forgiven him) have called to the tug and frankly resigned the control of the maneuver to her and given *her* the choice as to where *she* should apply her power, with full information that the ship was disabled and could not aid by backing. No doubt, the tug captain would have ordered the "Edith's" anchors down at once and when she had swung around with the tide have taken a bow line from her. When her powerful winches had quickly hoisted the anchors the tug would have pulled her to her destination at the dry-dock; or

(4) He could have made the fatal blunder he did, i. e. of letting the "Edith" drift from 42 to 32 without even trying his engines to see if they would work, permitting the tug to labor under the delusion that he could rely on her power as soon as the tow line was hauled in, and actually giving the tow a line to waste his power pulling the "Edith's" bow parallel with, if not towards, the docks while the wind and tide were taking her on to them.

The tug's captain, ignorant of any engine trouble on the "Edith" (or delusion in her master's mind), and having the dropping of his line accepted by the steamer's mate in hauling it in without protest, could in the absence of command from the "Edith" have entertained either of the two following suppositions:

(1) He could properly believe that the "Edith" was in no danger of any kind; that her tow line had been successfully hauled in and that she could back wherever she pleased at any time; and that there was no *necessity* for any haste on his part or indeed for any further service at all till they reached the drydock; or

(2) He could believe that the "Edith" intended as soon as the tow line was in to back round towards her starboard and northerly out and down the bay and have taken his tug round to help her, if she found it convenient, with a line pulling her head to port. This maneuver would have been as follows:

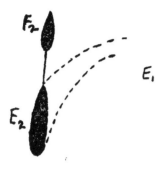

E₁ "Edith" reversing and backing to her starboard eases strain and assists F₁ "Fearless" in swinging head around with minimum strain on towing hawser.

E₂ and F₂ at end of maneuver.

This was an absolutely safe common sense maneuver and he went to the "Edith's" starboard bow (Dep. McDonald 39) where McDonald gave him a line and directed him to pull her head in this direction (Dep. McD. pp. 65, 66) but unhappily without knowledge that he must take the heavy strain on the tow line without help from the ship's engines, and with the result that the tow line broke.

The difference between the strain on the tow line with the help of the ship's engines backing and swinging the stern to starboard and the bow to port and towards the tug, and the dead pull of the vessel's high bow into the wind is obvious. The tug's captain was entitled to believe he would receive the assistance of the ship's engines, but the "Edith's" master knew when he ordered the tug to pull to port (66) that he would not render any such assistance acting under his undisclosed delusion that his engines were disabled.

When we consider the disabled condition of her engines (no less real because imaginary) the order of the

"Edith's" captain to have the tug pull her bow parallel to the pier heads, placed the vessel *in extremis*. His delusion as to the propeller is as much a factor in determining this question as was the on-shore set of the wind or the tide or the greater projection of pier-head 32. No blame can attach to Captain Sandstrom as to any act of his from this point on. Indeed, his permitted belief that the "Edith" could use her engines was one of the gravest factors of danger because it lead to the erroneous conclusion that the strain on the light tow line he received would be lessened by the vessel swinging her bow towards him by backing the "Edith" stern to port.

There is a dispute in the testimony as to whether, after the arrival of the tug at the "Edith's" bow, a demand was made for the tug's heavy 12-inch hawser. It is not claimed that it was before the vessel was well towards the end of her drifting. The tug had no knowledge that the vessel could not use her engines, nor did any of the "Edith's" officers say she was short of lines. The tug's captain does not recall a demand for his heavy line, but says that it would have been much slower to attach to the ship on account of its size and weight.

The District Court made a finding that the vessel was in fault for not giving up this line to the tug, but did not consider it the proximate cause of any damage. If we are correct that the real cause of the loss was the "Edith's" failure to plan and organize for the maneuver, her captain's failure to drop her anchors when he thought her engines disabled, and his permitting the tug to act in ignorance of her inability to use her engines, then the question of furnishing this heavy tow line was immaterial.

The tug captain's act must be judged by *his* knowledge. When out in the stream he was entitled to believe that the vessel was safe without any tow line as she was supposed to have her full engine power to back away from the wharves. When close into the pier 32, the tug was the best judge as to the time it would take to make fast any lines in the emergency. Quite likely, if he had known that the sole reliance of the ship was the hawser and that the full strain of her 2700 tons would pull on it, he would have insisted that the attempt be made to put the heavy tow line aboard the "Edith" for *any* maneuvers, even in an emergency requiring quick action, but no such knowledge was in the tug captain's mind and he cannot be held responsible.

It is interesting to note that Captain McDonald, who knew he had failed to advise the tug of his disabled engines, makes no complaint of any failure to furnish the "Edith" with this hawser, either when questioned as to the third tow line, or even in response to such questions as "What do you think was the cause of this disaster?"

The depositions of the captain and second mate reinforced by the unexplained failure to comply with the demand for the logs and the absence of the other vital witnesses from the "Edith" clearly established the following faults on her part.

1. Although the dominant mind, she failed to disclose her plans to the tug; or, alternatively, she failed to

establish a code of whistles, or a means of *vive voce* communication through the mate between herself and the tug, to control her as the undisclosed maneuvers developed.

2. She accepted the dropping of the tug's line without disclosing that it did not fit into her proposed maneuver.

3. She kept her engines turning ahead for some time after the tug's dropping of the line had been ratified by her hauling it aboard, whereby the line was fouled in the wheel.

4. She failed to drop her anchors off pier 42 when she could safely have done so, although she believed her engines crippled and did not intend to use them.

5. She failed to try her engines after she knew the tow line was hauled in and the end fouled in the blades and while she was drifting past piers 42, 40, 38, 36 and 34, but acted on the theory they were crippled when in fact they were not.

6. She acted on the belief that she had transferred the command of the maneuvers from herself to the tug without advising the tug of this fact so as to give her the discretion to order the "Edith" to anchor, as the tug would undoubtedly have done if knowing of the useless engines.

7. After she began to drift towards the docks she accepted the service of the tug for a maneuver requiring

the assistance of her engines without telling her that her engines could not be used.

8. She relied on the tug's furnishing certain hawsers without arranging for their use in a preliminary discussion.

9. She negotiated for the use of the tug's lines without disclosing to the tug the crippled condition of her engines to enable the tug to determine the character of lines needed.

It is clear that the proximate cause of the loss were these faults of the "Edith".

THE FINDINGS.

The learned District Judge apologizes for the failure to write and file an opinion (354). On an admiralty appeal the opinion performs an important function. It is required by the Rules to be a part of the Apostles.

C. C. A., Rule No. 4;

Benedict Adm., Sec. 581 and note.

Its purpose is to disclose the complete mental process of the judge in arriving at his conclusions. It is not improper to suggest that the haste arising from both sickness and a crowded war calendar, excuses this failure to comply with a practice thus embodied in the rules.

The court's findings are as follows (354):

"Lacking the time to prepare an opinion in this case, I can only state my conclusions from the testimony as follows:

1. The master of the 'Fearless' was at fault in not consulting with the master of the 'Edith' as to the maneuvers intended by him before he undertook to execute them.

2. He was also at fault in casting off the line without warning and while the 'Edith's' wheels were turning.

3. To these faults the accident was due.

4. The 'Fearless' should have passed to the 'Edith', after letting go of her and while she was drifting, a line of sufficient strength to hold her, and should have been prepared to do so. This was not done.

5. The 'Edith' was not at fault for not dropping her anchor, as she was entitled to believe that the 'Fearless' would care for her properly.

A decree will be entered fixing the responsibility of the 'Fearless', and referring the cause to the master to ascertain and report the amount of damage suffered by the 'Edith'."

Two of the four findings are declared causative. The third is distinctly separated from the others as not being causative of the loss. The last decides that the "Edith" was entitled to rely on the tug to extricate her from her position.

As to the first two findings, we have shown conclusively from the *depositions* of the master and second mate:

(1) That the "Edith" was the dominant mind and that it was her duty to disclose her contemplated maneuver to the tug.

(2) That the "Edith" concurred in the dropping of the hawser and gave the tug no notice that dropping it had in any way affected her engines, although the tug was

always within hailing distance. What the effects of this action were on the causal chain is developed in our statement of facts.

As to the last finding that the "Edith" was entitled to "rely" on the tug, the district court's error is similarly shown by the depositions. The "Edith" should have dropped her anchors off pier 42. To rely on the tug, she should first have protested and not quietly accepted the dropping of the tow line; and then disclosed either that she had transferred the dominion over both vessels, or that her engines were (supposed to be) disabled and thus compelled the tug to assume that the dominion was transferred.

As to the third and non-causative finding, before this court can decide that it *was* causative, it must review all the facts in the record.

It thus clearly appears that the court must consider our appeal *do novo* without any hampering inference based on the adverse findings of the lower court.

Specifications of Error Relied Upon.

(4) That the District Court erred in holding, deciding and decreeing that the injury and damage to libelant's vessel, the "Edith", was due to the fault of the American Steamtug "Fearless", the respondent herein, and that there was no fault on the part of the libelant's vessel, the "Edith".

(5) That the District Court erred in not holding, deciding and decreeing that the collision of libelant's

vessel, the "Edith", with pier 32 and the injury and damage to libelant's said vessel were solely due to the fault and negligence of libelant and its said vessel.

(6) That the District Court erred in not holding, deciding and decreeing that the collision of libelant's vessel, the "Edith", with said pier 32 and the injury and damage to libelant's vessel, if due to the fault and negligence of the "Fearless", were, nevertheless, proximately due to the contributory negligence of the "Edith".

(7) That the District Court erred in holding and deciding that the master of the "Fearless" was at fault in not consulting with the master of the "Edith" as to the maneuvers intended by him before he undertook to execute them.

(8) That the District Court erred in holding and deciding that the master of the "Fearless" was at fault in casting off the line without warning and while the "Edith's" wheels were turning.

(9) That the District Court erred in holding, deciding and finding that the master of the "Fearless" cast off the line without warning and while the "Edith's" wheels were turning. [307]

(10) That the District Court erred in holding and deciding that the accident was due to the alleged faults of the master of the "Fearless" in not consulting with the master of the "Edith" as to the maneuvers intended by him before he undertook to execute them and in casting off the line without warning and while the "Edith's" wheels were turning.

(11) That the District Court erred in holding and deciding that the "Fearless" should have passed to the "Edith", after letting go of her and while she was drifting, a line of sufficient strength to hold her and should have been prepared to do so; and in holding and deciding that there was any duty upon the part of the "Fearless" to pass a line to the "Edith" at all.

(12) That the District Court erred in holding and deciding that the "Edith" was not in fault for not dropping her anchor.

(13) That the District Court erred in holding and deciding that the "Edith" was entitled to believe that the "Fearless" would care for her without co-operation from the "Edith" by the latter's dropping her anchor.

(15) The District Court erred in not holding and deciding that if there was negligence and fault upon the part of the "Fearless", nevertheless, there was contributory negligence on the part of the "Edith" proximately causing said accident and the injury and damage to the "Edith" flowing therefrom. [308]

(16) That the District Court erred in not holding, deciding and decreeing that said accident and the injury and damage to the "Edith" were due to the failure of the master of the "Edith" to anchor her on "thinking" his steamer disabled by the line in her wheel.

(17) That the District Court erred in not holding, deciding and decreeing that said accident and the injury and damage to the "Edith" were due to the failure of the first mate of the "Edith" to pass promptly a good

line to the "Fearless" when she was drifting toward pier 32.

(18) That the District Court erred in not holding, deciding and decreeing that the said accident and the injury and damage to the "Edith" were due to the failure of the master of the "Edith" to go astern on the "Edith's" engines instead of allowing her to drift so close to pier 32 before backing that she could not get away from it before colliding.

(20) The District Court erred in not holding, deciding and decreeing that the "Edith" had her own power, that this was an "assist" and not a "towage" and that the duties and responsibilities of the "Fearless" were those of an assisting and not of a towing vessel.

(24) That the District Court erred in not holding, deciding and decreeing that the fouling of the "Edith's" propeller by the line, if there was such fouling, was due to the negligence and fault of the "Edith" in moving her propeller before the line had been taken in.

(27) That the District Court erred in not holding, deciding and decreeing that it was the duty of the "Edith" and not the duty of the "Fearless" to furnish the lines and all the lines required in the maneuver.

THE BURDEN OF PROOF OF GROSS ERROR ON THE PART OF THE TUG.

The burden of proof which the libelant is called upon to sustain in a tug case has found frequent expression in the decisions. It is not enough to show that the proximate cause of the loss is an error of judgment on the tug's part. The evidence must show a *"gross"* error of judgment.

The Czarina, 112 Fed. 541:

"The obligation of a tug is to use ordinary care and diligence with respect to all matters connected with the service she has engaged to perform, and a mere error of judgment on the part of the master will not render her liable for the loss of the tow, unless the error was so gross that it would not have been made by a master of ordinary prudence and judgment."

In

The James P. Donaldson, 19 Fed. 264,

affirmed (21 Fed. 671) (on exemption of the tug from liability for negligence) the writer of the opinion, speaking of two different routes, either of which the master of the tow might have selected, says:

"The disaster which befell him undoubtedly tends to show that he made the wrong selection, but the propriety of his action must not be determined by the result. He can only be chargeable with negligence when he takes a course which good seamanship would deem unauthorized and reckless. 'The owner of a vessel does not engage for the infallibility of the master, nor that he shall do in an emergency precisely what, after the event, others may think would have been the best.' The Hornet (Lawrence v. Minturn), 17 How. 100; The Star of Hope, 9 Wall. 230; The W. E. Gladwish, 17 Blatch. 77, 82, 83; The Mohawk, 7 Ben. 139; The Clematis, 1 Brown, Adm. 499."

The Circuit Court of Appeals for the Second Circuit says in affirming the decision of the District Court in

> *The E. Luckenbach,* 113 Fed. 1017, affirming 109
> Fed. 487:

> "The facts are quite fully stated in the opinion of the district judge. In one respect his statement of them is fairly open to criticism. The testimony hardly warrants the finding that there was a sudden increase of wind; *but we concur with him in the conclusion that the allegations of fault on the part of the tug are supported mainly by the wisdom that comes after the event.* It would have been good judgment to stay in port. It would have been good judgment to turn back at Sewall's Point, when return was feasible and safe· *but we are not prepared to say that in deciding to push on the master of the tug displayed such bad judgment as would amount to recklessness or negligence.* * * * The master made a mistake in pushing on beyond Sewall's Point, but we concur with the district judge in the conclusion that *it was not an error of judgment so gross as to justify a finding of negligence.* The decree is affirmed with costs." (Italics ours.)

Again,

> "Where the master of a tug is an experienced and competent man, much must be left, as occasion arises, to his judgment and discretion in the management of the tow; and a mere error of judgment on his part will not render the tug liable for the loss of her tow, unless the error was so gross that it would not have been made by a master of ordinary prudence and judgment."

> *38 Cyc.* 567.

See, also,

> *The Ivanhoe,* 90 Fed. 510;
> *The Startle,* 115 Fed. 555;
> *The William E. Gladwish,* 196 Fed. 490.

To sustain that burden, the vessel must, in view of the principles laid down by the courts (supra), prove not merely that the master of the tug erred, but that his error of judgment was gross—otherwise negligence is not laid to his door.

These, then, are the rules which apply where the contract is for "towage" with the tug in full charge. *A fortiori* it follows that a tug which has contracted only to "assist", and that only in and about the lighter duties of "assisting", not directing (the master of the vessel retaining the supremacy of command and responsibility) is not an insurer, and can be held only for failure to exercise reasonable (not the highest) care and skill, and that her liability for damages is established not by showing what might be an error of judgment on the part of one charged with the high responsibility of one in full control of tug and vessel and the project in its entirety (which even then must be a *gross* error), but only by showing gross error considering that the duty is only to attend and "assist" a vessel in command of her own master.

> "Of course the relations between the tug and the tow may be modified by express agreement, or the reasonable implication arising from the circumstances and nature of the employment in a particular case" (an "assist" for instance), "so as to make the tug the mere servant of the tow and under its direction; in which case the liability of the tug may be limited to the mere point of furnishing a sufficient motive power for the tow, while the whole responsibility as to the time and manner of making the voyage or transportation will rest with the latter."
>
> *38 Cyc*, 565.

"The owners of a tug are liable for negligence in performing *the special duty they have undertaken, and not otherwise.*" (Italics ours.)

38 Cyc, 566.

What was the "special duty" undertaken by the "Fearless" in this case? To *assist* the "Edith", a vessel with her own motive power and, by her own desire, as indicated by the character of her order for the tug, retaining control of the operation and primary responsibility for it in her own master, from pier 46 to Hunter's Point drydock. The tug was merely in attendance to aid as the "Edith's" captain should expressly direct, or where, for reasons good to himself and on his own responsibility he omitted to direct, by acting as might seem wise and proper according to the exigencies of the occasion. For, while, as heretofore pointed out, the master of a vessel in control may instruct, he often leaves the moves to the judgment of the tugboat captain (Tes. 101), relying on that judgment, and in such event can complain only if that judgment be abused. In other words, the vessel's master may in an "assist" instruct the tug if he choose; that is, indeed, his duty. If he does not discharge it, he can ask only an honest and competent exercise of discretion from the tugboat captain, and, if events do not clearly reveal the intention and program of the "dominant mind" (that of the master of the vessel), no fault attaches to the towboat for misreading it.

THE CASES SHOWING THAT THE "EDITH" IS ESTOPPED FROM CLAIMING DAMAGES ON ACCOUNT OF THE TUG'S DROPPING OF THE LINE, BECAUSE SHE ASSENTED THERE-TO AND AGREED TO THAT PROGRAM WHEN SHE HAD A FREE CHOICE TO REQUIRE THE TUG TO PICK UP THE FLOATING LINE OR TAKE A SECOND STERN LINE OR COULD HAVE DROPPED HER ANCHORS.

When the line was cast off, the "Edith" was a vessel with power. Whatever may have been the situation afterward, her propeller *then* was free. The dominant mind was still her master's. The tug understood him to desire a casting off of the line. He claims now that he desired the tug to hang on. Assuming his claim to be true, the situation resolves itself simply into this:

The tug, having no express instructions from the "Edith", excusably misinterpreted her intent and dropped the line off pier 42, 1800 feet from the colliding point. *It was open to the "Edith" not to acquiesce in the casting off if she wished to persist in her original program,—all that was necessary was for her to signal the tug to pick up the floating line with a boat-hook (the stern of the tug is of course close the water) or take a new line. But the "Edith", having acquiesced—and she did so when, without any suggestion of dissent, her mate began taking in the line, apparently in full accord with the program, and subsequently when he failed to notify the tug of any fouling of the propeller—she estopped herself from thereafter complaining that the casting off of the line was improper, or, at any rate, from asking any damages on account of it.*

The law is well settled that a vessel having free choice to accept or reject a program, by accepting estops

herself from later complaining that it was improper
and indeed obligates herself to co-operate to the fullest
extent in carrying it through. This is especially true in
respect to a vessel not merely having a choice, but being actually, as the "Edith" was, the dominant mind.

The Santa Maria, 227 Fed. 149, at 156:

"With respect to the Mehrer but little need be
said. She as the leading tug was, to the exclusion
of the Santa Maria, the Bristol and Brandywine,
entrusted with the selection of the course of navigation. Knowing that she had in tow a large and
ponderous vessel impossible quickly to be diverted
*the course she was pursuing she was clearly in
fault in assenting to and acting upon the single
blast signal received from the Sweepstakes, instead
of refusing to join in the proposed maneuver and
promptly giving danger signals* and slackening her
speed as far as could be done with safety. Had
she done so it is probable that the Sweepstakes
would not have persisted in pursuing her eastward
swing from the westerly side of the channel, and
the collision might and probably would have been
avoided."

The Luther C. Ward, 149 Fed. 787 at 788:

"As to the first claim, it is sufficient that the
vessels themselves settled the manner of passing
each other, and, considering the distance between
them, the Ward did not act under duress. If the
Ward regarded the maneuver as faulty, her captain
should have blown alarm whistles and stopped
the proposed passing, compelling the Tice to go
about, or otherwise dispose herself."

The Edgar F. Luckenbach, 124 Fed. 947 at 949:

"There was, therefore, ample opportunity for
the vessels to conform to the rule and no adequate
reason has been given for adopting a course at

variance with it. Such course should not have been initiated by the Flint, but having been consented to by the Luckenbach, the latter should have been vigilant to conform to the agreement, in which duty it failed, no change of course having been made by her until the second set of signals when the vessels were in such close proximity that collision was imminent.''

In *The Albermarle,* 1 Fed. Cas. 299 (No. 135), two steamers were meeting nearly head-on, so as to involve risk of collision, and accordingly exchanged signals of one whistle, signifying a port to port passing. Either they did not or could not port soon enough to avoid collision, and so far as the latter was the cause of the collision it was suggested that the giving of the one whistle signal in the first instance was erroneous and the vessel which gave it therefore liable. But in view of the acceptance of that signal, the court held (quoting from the head note):

"That, if it was erroneous and dangerous to port, the vessel giving the signal as a proposition to the other, was not more culpable for doing so, than the vessel which assented, by the response, to the proposed movement, and that both became parties concurring in a hazardous and erroneous experiment.''

In the

Arthur M. Palmer, 115 Fed. 417,

it was held that a vessel which assents by signal that another shall cross her bows cannot urge the attempted maneuver as a fault, though it results in a collision.

And see:

The San Rafael, 141 Fed. 270;

The Electra, 139 Fed. 858;

The Transfer No. 9, 170 Fed. 944;
The Columbia, 195 Fed. 1000.

THE EXTRAORDINARY FAILURE TO PRODUCE THE LOGS OF THE "EDITH" AND THE ENGINEER, FIRST MATE AND OTHER WITNESSES IN VIEW OF THE DELUSION OF HER MASTER AS TO HER ENGINES AND THE CASES ON SUCH NON-PRODUCTION.

Here the "Edith" was the admitted dominant mind in the maneuvers contemplated by her when she left the dock. The registering lobes of that mind are her captain's and engineer's scratch and official logs. They are of peculiar value in showing what went through that mind. The scratch logs are contemporaneous entries of her thoughts and acts; the official logs are her subsequent careful review of the events. Both are of vital interest in reviewing any tragic event through which the vessel has passed.

The Sicilian Prince, 128 Fed. 133, 136;
U. S. Rev. Stats., 4291.

The most important factor in this entire drama laid concealed in this mind of the "Edith's" captain till his deposition, taken long after the pleadings were filed. They were both drawn in complete ignorance of this secret. It was that, although her engines were free to turn, her commander believed that they were not and governed the entire conduct of the "Edith" under this delusion. What he said or signed for in these logs should have been given to the court. The logs were demanded at the taking of the captain's deposition (p. 48).

The penalty for non-production of the witnesses and logs when demanded, is the adverse inference described in the following leading cases:

The Prudence, 191 Fed. Rep. 993, 996:

"The failure of the Prudence either to produce the mate, who was in the pilot house at the time of the collision, or to account satisfactorily for not so doing, is a circumstance which the court cannot fail to observe, in reaching its conclusion. The Georgetown (D. C.) 135 Fed. 855. *Criticism is also made, and not without force, of the failure of the respondent to tender its log for inspection.* The Sicilian Prince (D. C.) 128 Fed. 133, 136. It is fair to say, however, in this connection, that the log was not called for, except in argument, and was then tendered." (Italics ours.)

Corpus Juris, vol. II p. 1186, note 16 (b);

The Santa Rosa, 249 Fed. 160 at 162.

"During the trial the production of these logs was demanded by claimants, and petitioner promised to produce them. This was not done so that it may at least be assumed that their production would not have helped petitioner's case."

The New York, 175 U. S. 187; 44 L. Ed. 126, 134:

"The force of this presumption of a defective lookout is greatly strengthened by the fact that the claimant did not see fit to put upon the stand the officers and crew of the New York, who certainly would have been able to explain, if any explanation were possible, why the lights of the Conemaugh were not seen and distinguished or her signals heard. It was said by this court in the case of Clifton v. United States, 4 How. 242, 246, 11 L. ed. 957, that 'to withhold testimony which it was in the power of the party to produce, in order to rebut a charge against him, where it is not supplied by other equivalent testimony, might be

as fatal as positive testimony in support or confirmation of the charge.' "

The Alpin, 23 Fed. Rep. 815, 816.

"But the claimants knew that the stranding of
their vessel was to be their defense; and tneir
course in relying for proof of the stranding upon
the admissions in the libels and testimony of witnesses, who, while knowing of the stranding, could
not know how it was caused, when the testimony
of those who would be the natural witnesses to
prove such a defense was at command, indicates
the existence of a reason other than that of surprise
for the non-production of these witnesses, *and warrants a presumption that if the officers of the steamer had been called, they would have shown the
stranding to have been the result of negligence in
the navigation of the ship.*" (Italics ours.)

The Santa Rosa, 249 Fed. 160;
Clifton v. United States, 4 How. 242; 11 L. Ed. 957;
The Fred M. Laurence, 15 Fed. 635;
The Bombay, 46 Fed. 665;
The Georgetown, 135 Fed. 854;
The Sandringham, 10 Fed. 556;
The Gladys, 135 Fed. 601;
The Freddie L. Porter, 8 Fed. 170.

and see

Marsden's Collisions, 6 ed., 289.

In considering findings peculiarly based on what was
in the "Edith's" mind, these adverse inferences must
have great force.

In closing this heading of the brief it may well be
remarked that the allegations of an answer drawn in
ignorance of this secret delusion of the opposing ship

cannot have much weight. They could not rationally explain their vessel's interchanges with such an associate for the very good reason that they did not have any clew to her irrational acts.

CONTRIBUTORY NEGLIGENCE.

We believe that we have shown that the chain of proximate causation is made up entirely of the "Edith's" faults which we have enumerated at the end of our statement of facts, and that if any of the tug's acts are faults they did not contribute proximately to the damage.

But, assuming for the moment that they did contribute proximately, can it be said that the faults of the "Edith" are not so interwoven with the tug's that the tug must bear the whole blame?

If the tug, the subordinate agent, was in fault for not participating in the planning for the maneuver, was not the "Edith" the dominant mind at least equally in fault for directing the tug to go ahead in the maneuver, knowing her ignorance?

If the tug erred in disengaging the tow line and dropping it, was not the "Edith", in easy hailing distance, at least equally in fault in accepting this action and hauling in the line without protest or request to have it picked up, or a new stern-line taken?

If the tug (in ignorance of the "Edith's" crippled engines) was at fault for leaving her stern, was not the "Edith" at least in equal fault for concealing the crippling and acting as if all were well?

If the dominant control passed from the "Edith" to the tug was not then the "Edith" squarely in fault for not advising the tug she would not assist with her engines and thus give the tug the chance to order the "Edith" to drop her anchors or to tow from the stern instead of pulling the "Edith's" bow around?

If the tug was at fault regarding the use of its heavy hawser, was the "Edith's" failure to disclose that she could not (or would not) assist with her engines, a material factor in enabling the tug captain to make up his mind what lines he should use?

We submit that the District Court is in plain error here, regardless of what evidence we consider, and that the well established rule for a division of the damage would clearly apply.

> *The Max Morris,* 137 U. S. 1 at 14;
> *J. T. Morgan Lumber Co. v. Coal Co.,* 181 Fed. 271.

For reasons thus set forth, we respectfully urge that the decree of the District Court be reversed and the "Edith" be declared solely in fault.

Dated, San Francisco,
> October 16, 1918.
>> WILLIAM DENMAN,
>> McCUTCHEN, OLNEY & WILLARD,
>>> *Proctors for Appellant.*

United States Circuit Court of Appeals

For the Ninth Circuit

SHIPOWNERS AND MERCHANTS TUGBOAT COMPANY (a corporation), claimant of the American Steam Tug "Fearless", her boilers, engines, tackle, apparel and furniture,

Appellant,

vs.

A. H. BULL & COMPANY, INC. (a corporation),

Appellee.

BRIEF FOR APPELLEE

Upon Appeal from the Southern Division of the United States District Court for the Northern District of California, First Division.

E. S. PILLSBURY,
F. D. MADISON,
ALFRED SUTRO,
OSCAR SUTRO,
Proctors for Appellee.

PERNAU-WALSH PRINTING CO.

Index.

Table of Cases Cited.

No. 3199

United States Circuit Court of Appeals

For the Ninth Circuit

SHIPOWNERS AND MERCHANTS TUGBOAT COMPANY
(a corporation), claimant of the American
Steam Tug "Fearless", her boilers, engines,
tackle, apparel and furniture,

Appellant,

vs.

A. H. BULL & COMPANY, INC. (a corporation),

Appellee.

BRIEF FOR APPELLEE

**Upon Appeal from the Southern Division of the United States
District Court for the Northern District of California,
First Division.**

I.

Statement of the Case.

The case involves liability for damage sustained by
the steamship "Edith" on March 4, 1916, on the San
Francisco water front. She was under her own steam,
backing out of the slip at pier 44 assisted by the
tug "Fearless", preparatory to proceeding to Hunter's
Point. In the course of the ensuing maneuvers she

drifted with the wind and tide in the opposite direction from that which she was to take, colliding with pier 32, and sustaining the resulting damage for which libellant brought this action.

The master of the "Edith" planned to back his ship out of the slip, and intended, with the assistance of the tug, to turn her bow into the wind and tide and thus proceed in a southeasterly direction to Hunter's Point. He expected the tug to hold the stern line and to pull the stern of the "Edith" around to starboard while he turned the bow to port. In other words, he intended to pivot his ship.

At some distance from the slip the tug dropped the line without warning to the "Edith". The operation which the tug intended and attempted was to drop the stern tow line of the "Edith", circle around to her starboard bow, take a bow line, and pull the "Edith's" bow into the tide and wind—a sort of flying switch. This plan was not communicated by the tug's captain to the captain of the "Edith".

As soon as the master of the "Edith" learned that the stern tow line had been dropped by the tug, he stopped the "Edith's" engines, fearing otherwise to foul his wheel in the line. He relied on the tug to take care of the "Edith". The "Edith" drifted rapidly with tide and wind towards the piers. The tug took a tow line, which parted, and the "Edith" crashed against pier 32. The tug captain thought that no line could have kept her from striking the docks (316, 317).

The case for libellant was presented on the depositions of the master and mate of the "Edith".

The claimant, Shipowners and Merchants Tugboat Company, adduced the testimony of the three members of the crew of the tug, of the captain of the tug, of the superintendent of the company, of the general manager of the company, and of another captain in the employ of the claimant.

These witnesses testified orally before the learned District Judge who tried the cause, and who reached the following conclusions:

That the master of the tug was at fault because he failed to consult with the captain of the "Edith" as to the maneuvers intended by him before he undertook them; that he was also at fault because while the "Edith" was backing out and her wheels were turning, he, without warning, cast off a tow line which was fastened to the stern of the "Edith", and which was assisting her out of the slip; and that the accident was due to these faults. The trial court also found that while the "Edith" was drifting, the tug should have been prepared to pass her a line of sufficient strength to hold her, and should have passed such a line, which was not done. Regarding the claim that the "Edith" should have dropped her anchor, the court found that the "Edith" was not at fault in this respect, since she was entitled to believe that the tug would care for her properly. Responsibility for the damage was fixed on the tug (Opinion Hon. M. T. Dooling, Judge (354-5)).

It is the appellant's contention that the service here engaged for and rendered was an "assist" and not a tow, and that the dominant mind in the operation was that of the master of the "Edith". Whatever may have been the purpose and intent of the master of the "Edith" and of the captain of the tug in that regard, when the towage operation was first undertaken, it is obviously not within the functions of a tug performing an "assist" not only to determine the course of the operation, but to undertake it without notice to the tow. It is the appellee's contention that in whatever aspect the conduct of the tug is regarded, it was at fault:

First. If it be regarded as an assisting tug, because it failed to consult with the master, and, on the contrary, took it upon itself to act without instructions from him and in disregard of the "Edith's" proposed maneuver, and because it cast off the tow line without signal to or from the "Edith", thus putting her in danger; and

Second. If the operation be regarded as towage, for attempting a perilous maneuver in dangerous proximity to the piers for which the tug was not equipped and which it failed to accomplish.

II.

THE TUG CAPTAIN DID NOT CONSULT WITH THE MASTER OF THE "EDITH", BUT ACTED ON HIS OWN INITIATIVE WITHOUT NOTICE TO OR ORDERS FROM THE "EDITH". HE CAST OFF THE TOW LINE WITHOUT NOTICE. IN THIS HE WAS AT FAULT.

Counsel for claimant attempt but little explanation of the fact that the captain of the tug violated the first and most obvious duty of an assisting tug—to take and obey the orders of the tow. Indeed, the tug captain violated claimant's own inviolable rule on the subject. Thus Captain W. M. Randall, claimant's superintendent, said that in "assisting" the tug captain "always consults" (266). Clearly the rule which the tug captain failed to observe is merely a dictate of ordinary prudence. He testified on this subject as follows:

"Q. What instructions did you get, if any, from the captain of the 'Edith'?

A. I did not get any instructions from the captain of the 'Edith', except to go ahead.

Q. Did you consult with him before you went out of the slip? A. No.

Q. Did you have a talk with anybody at the office as to what should be done?

A. Captain Randall, at the office, told me what to do.

Q. What did he tell you to do?

A. He told me to go up there and assist the ship to the drydock.

Q. Did he say anything else? A. Nothing else.

Q. When you got up to the 'Edith', did you have any consultation with the captain?

A. No. (307)

*   *   *   *   *   *   *

Q. In an assist, you take the orders of the master of the vessel?

A. Take the orders from the master.

Q. You make the lines fast that he tells you?

A. We generally arrange it, making fast the line ourselves.

Q. You do not wait for his orders about that?

A. When I had enough I told him to make fast.

Q. DID YOU DROP THE LINE WHEN HE TOLD YOU TO?

A. IN THIS PARTICULAR CASE HE DID NOT TELL ME TO. (308)

*   *   *   *   *   *   *

Q. And in those cases in which you are not in charge, you get orders as to how it should be done; is that correct? A. Yes.

Q. Is that correct? A. Correct.

Q. So that in the case of an assist, you would be getting the orders of the captain, would you?

A. I would be getting the orders from the captain, yes. (309)

*   *   *   *   *   *   *

Q. You did not get any instructions from the master to let go? A. No.

Q. You used your own judgment?

A. I used my own judgment; when he stopped his engine, I thought it was time to let go." (313)

And in answer to questions by the court, the witness said:

"Q. Why did you cast off there 700 feet away from the wharf?

A. WELL, WE CAST OFF BECAUSE I INTENDED TO COME UNDER THE BOW OF THE SHIP AND GET A BOW LINE AND PULL HER AROUND.

Q. Did you have room enough for that?

A. I had room enough; if I had got the line I would have had room enough.

Q. You made no investigation or inquiry to find out whether there was a line you could get?

A. I never went aboard the ship; I didn't know what they had there.

Q. You undertook that maneuver without finding out what they had aboard ship?

A. I took the captain's word for that.

Q. What did he tell you?

A. He told me to pull the ship out of the wharf, from the wharf.

Q. *You didn't know what you were going to do, and you did not know what he was going to do?*

A. No." (330-331)

It appears quite clearly from the record that the maneuver which the tug captain had in mind when he left the slip was the one which he unsuccessfully undertook. The claimant's witnesses, Driver, Kraatz and the tug captain himself all so testified. The witness Driver said:

"Q. When you started out on this undertaking, you intended to pull her out here? A. Yes.

Q. And to drop the line? A. Yes.

Q. And to run around the bow and pick her up again and take her to Hunter's drydock?

A. Yes." (144 also 142)

The witness Kraatz testified that the maneuver undertaken by the tug was the way it was done "as a rule" (185); the tug's witness Boster said it was customary (206); the claimant's manager Gray said it was proper (249, 253), and the tug captain testified that he cast off the line in order to perform the operation which he undertook (330, 339).

But Captain Sandstrom's purpose, when the two vessels left the slip, was not disclosed by him to the captain of the "Edith" (327). The "Edith's" master had an entirely different maneuver in mind. If this was an "assist", did the tug captain have the right to undertake an independent maneuver, least of all without advising the captain of the "Edith" to that effect?

If it was an "assist", was the tug justified in pulling the ship out stern first into the wind and tide and dropping the stern line, which was holding the vessel up, without orders of any kind, particularly when such an operation would inevitably force the "Edith" to stop her engines and to drift in the direction of the piers?

Appellant claims that the tug was justified in casting off the line on the tug captain's interpretation of the "Edith's" intent, although the stern line was cast off too near the piers for the safe performance of what the tug captain undertook (see tug captain's testimony 339). But even if the "Edith" had signalled for the dropping of the line at an unsafe distance from the piers, the tug "should object to casting off", if it "thought there was going to be any immediate danger" (testimony claimant's witness Captain Randall 238). Much less was the tug justified in dropping the line at an unsafe point without a signal.

The claimant's witness George W. Driver correctly described the situation:

> "Q. Who took command of this operation?
> A. There were two men in command.
> Q. Two men in command?
> A. Yes." (137)

When he was ready to leave the slip, the master of the "Edith" gave the signal.

> "Q. Who gave the signal to the tug that time to go ahead?
> A. That time, you know, she was on Pier 44 and I told him to go ahead, waived my hand to the third officer and told the towboat to go ahead." (55)

He expected the towboat to swing the "Edith" around.

He said:

> "We wished our head to go to port, consequently we wished the tow to pull the stern in the opposite direction." (46)
>
> "I expected that he would turn to port, keep turning our stern." (36) (also, 57, 73)

After he was out some distance the mate signalled the master of the "Edith" to stop, as the line had been cast off, and within three or four seconds he stopped his engine. From the moment that the tug had cast off the line the master of the "Edith" naturally expected the tug to complete whatever maneuver it thus undertook. From that moment the "Edith" depended on the towboat. The master realized that the matter had been taken out of his charge (Dep. McDonald, 68).

It was the tugboat captain that told the man on the "Edith" to haul in the line (137-8). It was the tugboat captain who ordered his men to take the line off the bitts of the tug (174).

Not even when he dropped the stern line did he advise the "Edith" what he proposed to do (327), nor did he ask for a tow line from the "Edith" until they were both drifting together (328).

He undertook this ticklish maneuver without ascertaining what lines he could get. In response to the court he said:

> "Q. You didn't know what you were going to do and you did not know what he was going to do?
> A. No" (331); and in his final answer, that "it was confusion." (339)

But for the confusion and its resulting consequences, he was to blame.

The tug is bound to give proper instructions for the management of the towing.

Winslow v. Thompson, 134 Fed. 546;

38 Cyc., 565 (Note 81).

Here the master of the "Fearless" guessed at the "Edith's" intent—and guessed wrong. On his own admission he should have towed the "Edith" further into the stream, possibly a thousand feet further (339). He dropped the line at a point where his own maneuver could not have been properly performed, when there was no reason for not holding the line, and when by dropping it he rendered the movement intended by the master of the "Edith" impossible.

The prime, and, we submit, the sole, fault in the matter lay with the tug for placing the "Edith" in an emergency, and the gist of the case is, we submit, summed up in the testimony of the master:

> "Q. What do you think was the cause of this disaster?
> A. Getting the line in the wheel.
> Q. And what was that caused by?
> A. Caused by the towboat letting it go without any orders of any kind or even tooting his whistle."
> (Dep. Capt. McDonald, 78)

There is no dispute that the captain of the tug let go the tow line without orders so to do. He so admitted (308).

The mate of the "Edith" stated positively that the line was cast off without a signal from or to the

"Edith" (83-85) (Dep., Sivert Hansen) and that the line was dropped before anyone on the "Edith" knew any thing about it and while its whole length was in the water (98). The captain of the "Edith" testified that he gave no signal to cast off (36), but on the contrary expected the tug to hang on until the customary signal had been given to cease towing (45-6).

Notice of intention to case off must always be given by the tug.

> *The O. L. Halenbeck,* 110 Fed. 556;
> *Frost v. Ball,* 43 Fed. 170;
> *The J. P. Donaldson,* 21 Fed. 671.

III.

THE TUG'S MANEUVER INEVITABLY INVOLVED THE "EDITH" IN DANGER.. AFTER THE LINE WAS CAST OFF, IT WAS NECESSARY FOR THE "EDITH" TO HAUL IT IN BEFORE SHE COULD USE HER ENGINES—AND WHILE HER ENGINES WERE STOPPED SHE WAS BOUND TO DRIFT TOWARD OR AGAINST THE PIERS.

This is clear from the testimony of claimant's witnesses. Thus the tug witness Driver testified:

> "Q. When you towed him out of Slip 44, you expected to bring him out here and drop the line and come around and catch him on the bow, didn't you? A. Yes, sir.
>
> Q. And you knew that while you were doing that he was going to drift?
>
> A. We would have the time to do it up there in that position, we would have time to get a hawser up.

Q. You knew he would drift, didn't you?

A. Not to such an extent. (142)

* * * * * * *

Q. *You knew he would have to stop his engines to pull in to that line?*

A. *Most assuredly.* (143)

Q. And while he was hauling it in, his engine would be stopped? A. Yes.

Q. And he would drift?

A. To a certain extent.

Q. He would drift for all the time it took to haul in that rope? A. Yes.

Q. That is correct, is it? A. Yes.

Q. And then you expected to go around on his bow and give him another line? Is that right? A. Yes.

Q. And you didn't have a line ready?

A. We had a hawser ready.

Q. Didn't you say you couldn't pass that to him?

A. I was speaking of the emergency that we were in at that time." (143-144)

The witness Kraatz, the second tug witness called by claimant, testified to the same effect:

"Q. You have performed that maneuver before, have you? A. Yes.

Q. You expected the engines of the vessel to stop, didn't you, while they are taking in the line when you cast it off? A. Yes.

Q. Otherwise it is likely to foul the wheel?

A. Otherwise it is likely to foul the wheel. (186)

* * * * * * *

Q. You would expect the 'Edith to drift?

A. She would drift a little, I suppose.

Q. She would be bound to drift some distance?

A. She would be bound to drift some distance." (186)

It took the tug four minutes to get around amidship of the "Edith" (337), and the tug captain testified that he knew that after the line had been dropped she would inevitably drift toward the piers.

"Q. When you cast off that stern line, you knew how much wind and tide there was, didn't you?
A. Yes, I knew.
Q. You knew that a ship drifting with that wind and tide would gather headway, didn't you?
A. Yes.
Q. And would keep drifting faster, and faster, and faster? A. Yes.
Q. And your idea, nevertheless, was to drop that line off the stern, run around and get one off the bow, and head her upstream?
A. *My idea was to tow the ship further out; I would have towed her further out in the stream.*
Q. *How far would you have towed her out?*
A. *Possibly a thousand feet further; but when the captain stopped backing I came to the conclusion that he wanted me to let go; otherwise, he had no reason to stop backing; I could have kept on backing out into the stream.*
Q. *That was your judgment?*
A. *That was my idea of it.*
Q. *That was your idea of his conclusion?*
A. *Yes.*
Q. *Now if, in point of fact, his idea was that you should hang on to his stern, as he has testified, then your idea as to what he wanted was a mistaken idea: Was it not?*
A. *It was confusion.*" (339)

The expert Gray, manager of the claimant, likewise said that the wheel should not be turning while the stern line was being hauled in.

"Q. Would you have the wheel turning astern while it was being hauled in? A. No, sir.
Q. It would foul, wouldn't it?
A. It might foul. (254)

* * * * * * *

A. *I say no. I would stop the propeller while I was getting that line in.*" (255)

And yet the same witness said that when the line was cast off by the tug, the "Edith" should have backed while the tug came around to her bow! (250).

And, finally, the tug captain admitted that after the line was cast off proper seamanship required that the captain of the "Edith" should stop his wheel.

> "Q. You would not approve starting an engine if there was a 20 or 25-fathom line over the stern of the ship hanging in the water?
>
> A. In what direction do you mean? Either direction?
>
> Q. Yes.
>
> A. Well, if the line was tight, it would not make any difference.
>
> Q. If it was hanging in the water?
>
> A. No, I would not approve of it.
>
> Q. As a matter of fact, every seaman always has in mind keeping his wheel clear of a line that has been cast off, hasn't he? A. Correct.
>
> Q. And always aims so to operate that his wheel won't become foul when a line is cast off?
>
> A. Correct.
>
> Q. *If, then, there is danger of the line fouling, he stops his engine, does he not, until it is in?*
>
> A. *Yes.*
>
> Q. *That is good seamanship?*
>
> A. *That is seamanship, yes."* (324-325)

And subsequently Captain Sandstrom testified that if he backs it is apt to catch on either side if it hangs in the water and he said that if the "Edith" had been backing "the suction of the water will pull the line in there" (326).

At the time the tow line was dropped the "Edith" was about 700 feet from the piers and had out one hundred and fifty feet of line, and according to the master of the tug it would take five minutes to haul this in (330); according to witness Kraatz, six minutes (176). During this time the "Edith's" wheel would be stopped. It took the "Fearless" four to eight minutes to get to the bow of the "Edith" (claimant's witness Capt. Sandstrom, 330, 337). The "Edith" in any aspect of the case, would be drifting practically until the "Fearless" took a tow line (330). The tug, we submit, had no right to undertake the operation so close to the piers and on so close a margin of time.

A three knot tide means that the tide is running at the rate of 18,240 feet an hour, or 304 feet a minute (315). Added to this was a wind blowing not less than eighteen miles an hour (the captain of the "Edith" estimated it at more). The "Edith", while drifting, would gather headway rapidly (Capt. Sandstrom, 339), and drift 1800 feet while the "Fearless" got around to her starboard bow (ib. 330, 338-9).

In other words, the operation the captain of the tug undertook involved placing the "Edith" in a position of danger and he himself admitted that she should have been towed further out into the stream (339).

The emergency thus created would not have arisen, *first*, if the tug which took the tow line on the order of the master had held on to it until the "Edith" directed that it should be released; *second*, if the tug, intending to perform the maneuver which it undertook, had towed the "Edith" further out from the piers, so that she would not have drifted too close to the piers to save her during the time which would necessarily elapse while she was hauling in the stern tow line.

The master of the "Edith" was justified in not expecting the tug to drop the stern line without a signal of any kind, or even "the customary tooting of the whistle"; and the captain of the "Fearless" was grossly at fault in attempting to convert an "assist" into a towage operation at a point where the maneuver which the tug undertook could not have been safely performed.

Since the casting off of the "Edith's" stern line required the master of the "Edith" to stop his engine it made little difference in the subsequent events whether (a) the master stopped his engine because he thought the line was already in the wheel, or (b) whether in point of fact it had already fouled the wheel, or (c) whether he stopped his engine in order to haul in the line, so that it would not foul the wheel. *The essential point is that under all the rules of seamanship his engine had to be stopped; and while his engine was stopped, his vessel was helpless and was bound to drift.* For this condition the "Fearless", which cast off the stern line, was responsible.

<hr />

IV.

THE TUG WAS CLEARLY AT FAULT FOR CASTING OFF THE STERN TOWING LINE AT A TIME WHEN THE "EDITH'S" ENGINES WERE TURNING, THUS CAUSING HER WHEEL TO FOUL BEFORE IT COULD BE STOPPED.

The answer admits that the line was cast off after the "Edith's" engines were started ahead (answer 22).

Captain Gray, general manager of the claimant, who verified the answer (25), said this was incorrect (265). It is likely that Captain Gray's statements in the answer, made shortly after his investigation of the facts of the case, are more reliable than his recollection on the witness stand more than a year after the event. The mate of the "Edith" testified that the vessel's engines were moving ahead when the tow line was cast off (97). The line was in the water and the wheel fouled before the master of the "Edith" could stop his engines, the mate meanwhile hauling it in (78).

It is asserted by the claimant that the loop of the line being around the wheel shows that most of it was hauled in. But it appears that two pieces of line were wrapped around the wheel. How much the mate of the "Edith" could get in while the captain was stopping his engines, how quickly they could be stopped completely, which parts of the line were cut, how much was hauled in after the engines were stopped, whether the loop fouled at the time or later when the vessel left Pier 32 and proceeded to the drydock, are all matters of conjecture, which, we submit, can not prevail against positive and direct testimony.

In any event immediately after the tow line was cast off

> "a signal was *at once* given to the master of the steamship 'Edith' by the mate of the said steamship who was standing on the poop deck that the tow line had been cast off by the master of the tug 'Fearless'." (Claimant's answer, 15; Test. Hansen, 85)

More, the mate of the "Edith" could not do.

With respect to the casting off of the line, the claimant called four witnesses, the crew of the tug, including the men who actually hauled the line on the tug. They testified before the trial judge. From their more or less confused statements on the subject the trial court reached the conclusion:

"He", the master of the tug, "was also at fault in casting off the line without warning and while the 'Edith's' wheels were turning" (355).

That conclusion, supported by oral testimony and conforming to the averments of the claimant's answer, should not, we submit, be here reversed (infra p. 60).

Some point was made on the trial in respect to the distinction between taking the line off the bitts on the tug and casting it overboard. But it appears quite clearly that when the line was removed from the bitts, the men could not long hold it against the tide and wind.

The witness Kraatz, who held the line on the tug, said he had to let it go because of the weight; he could not hold it up any longer (187-8), and his companion Taylor said the line was taken off the bitts while the "Edith's" engines were turning, and pulled out of the deckhands' hands by the tide (192, 197).

Kraatz said:

"I took it (i. e., the line) off the bitts and held onto the line as long as I could and then I let go" (162);

and obviously a 30 fathom tow line could not be held long in a strong tide and wind, with the other end fastened to a 2700 ton steamer. When the line was taken off the bitts it was equivalent to casting the line off the tug.

It is argued that the tug captain correctly interpreted the "Edith's" intention by casting off the line after her engines were stopped. The difficulty with this assumption is that the captain of the tug as the event showed *incorrectly* interpreted the "Edith's" intentions. In any case if we are to believe the claimant's witnesses who testified that the "Edith" was backing at the time the line was cast off, the tug captain was at fault for taking the line off his bitts with the "Edith's" propeller going astern; if the testimony that the "Edith's" propeller was moving forward is to be believed, the captain of the tug was at fault for casting off while the vessel's propeller was moving; and if the testimony of the captain of the "Fearless" is to be believed, that the "Edith's" engines were stopped when he cast off, the answer is that there was no occasion and no emergency which compelled him to drop the line without instructions. In any aspect of the case, therefore, the captain of the "Fearless" was at fault for dropping the line without a signal to or from the "Edith".

V.

THE TUG WAS AT FAULT FOR NOT PASSING A LINE TO THE "EDITH" AFTER PLACING THE "EDITH" IN PERIL.

The learned District Judge found that

"The 'Fearless' should have passed to the 'Edith' after letting go of her and while she was drifting a line of sufficient strength to hold her and should

have been prepared to do so. This was not done.''
(298)

The tug had a number of six inch and seven inch
lines on board, besides a twelve inch hawser. No
attempt was made to pass any of these to aid the
''Edith'' after she was set adrift. The reasons assigned
by the witnesses for the claimant are extraordinarily
conflicting.

The ''Fearless'' was at fault for not passing up its twelve inch hawser.

In the stern of the tug ''Fearless'' lay a twelve inch
hawser which the ''Edith' wanted and failed to get in
her distress. It was afterward used to tow her into
drydock (297).

In the libel it is alleged that the master of the tug
was not prepared with a line, and was unable to pass
one to the ''Edith'' after going around her, though
requested to do so by the first officer of the ''Edith'' (7).

The failure to pass the hawser was, we submit, a
gross fault. It is explained in so great a variety of
ways by the tug's witnesses that we submit no credence
can be given to any of the numerous theories advanced
by claimant, except that the hawser had not been
engaged for.

The tug captain testified with great positiveness that
no one on the ''Edith'' asked for a line, that there
was no argument under the bow of the steamer on the
subject, and that there were no words spoken about it.

"Q. You did not-hear the mate ask for the
12-inch hawser when you were somewhere near
this position? A. No.

Q. Just before you got here? A. No.

Q. You did not hear anyone on your tug refuse to pass that hawser? A. No.

Q. You personally did not refuse to pass it?

A. I did not refuse to pass it because I was not asked for it there.

Q. I am asking only about the time before you got into this position here.

A. *In fact, I think if they had asked me for the hawser in that position I would have been compelled to give it to them.*

Q. You did not hear the mate say, 'That is a bum tugboat, it has no lines'?

A. No, I did not hear that.

* * * * * * *

Q. You heard no discussion of any kind there?
A. No.

Q. You say now positively that you were not asked for that hawser while you were out there in the stream? A. No, I was not, positively.

* * * * * * *

Q. It is alleged in the answer here that the first officer of the steamship 'Edith' asked the tug to pass a large 12-inch hawser. Do you know of whom that was asked?

A. No, I don't know anything about that."
(321-2)

This' strenuous denial by the tug captain that he refused to pass a 12-inch hawser, *which he admits he would have passed if it had been asked for* (and which we believe was not passed up merely because it had not been engaged for the sum of five dollars) (see testimony of claimant's manager, Captain Gray, 269-270), is contrary to the admissions of the answer, which are that the claimant

"*does admit that the first officer of said steamship asked said tug to pass a large 12-inch hawser lying on the stern of said tug, but that said hawser was so heavy that the men on the forecastle head of said 'Edith' would not have been able to have taken said hawser aboard, and it would not have been practicable to have passed said large hawser at the time."* (16)

The tug captain is further impeached on this subject by the testimony of the other witnesses for the tug. The witness Driver, the first witness called, testified:

"Q. Did you hear the officer of the 'Edith' ask you for a line? A. Yes." (141)

The next witness for the claimant, Kraatz, testified:

"Q. What transpired when you reached the bow of the 'Edith'?

A. There was an argument started as to who was going to pass a line.

Q. What was the argument?

A. The mate hollered from the forecastle-head, 'The bum towboat hasn't got lines'. The skipper sung out to the mate, 'You couldn't pull up that line if I gave it to you'. That lasted for about three minutes." (164)

*   *   *

"Q. You said that when you went around to the starboard bow of the 'Edith' there was an argument there about the line? A. Yes.

Q. The officer on the 'Edith' wanted the tug to pass his hawser? A. Yes.

Q. And the tug wanted the officer to pass a line to the tug? A. Yes.

Q. The tug was directly under the bow of the 'Edith'? A. Yes.

Q. If you were going to pass a line from the tug to the 'Edith' you could not have been in any better position to do it, could you, if you were out in the stream?

A. That was as near as we could get." (177-8)

We submit it may fairly be assumed that Captain Sandstrom's recollection on this matter as given on the trial is in error. He himself testified that he reported the occurrences in question immediately after the event at the office of the claimant (303), that he had not discussed it much since (303), and was therefore giving his recollection as of the date of the occurrence in March, 1916. His recollection more than a year after the occurrence is not as valuable as his knowledge of the occurrence on the day of the happening, and the answer obviously was prepared on the report made to the claimant's officers. The admission in the answer, therefore, and the testimony of three witnesses that the "Edith's" mate asked for the line, is obviously correct. Some of the witnesses for the claimant said that the hawser was too heavy to pass to the "Edith". But according to the captain of the tug, no opportunity was given to the "Edith" to take it aboard. The answer averred that it was not suitable for the purpose of performing the towage operation in question. Some of the claimant's witnesses said that the hawser was suitable for the purpose, but would require more men than were on the forecastle deck of the "Edith" (145).

The captain of the tug thought six men could have hauled it aboard (334). Captain Randall thought three to four men could have handled it (243). But as the tug captain says that the "Edith' did not ask for the hawser, and Gray says that if she had he would not have passed it up, it matters not how many men were required to haul it up.

One of the witnesses said it would have been passed to the "Edith" but it had not been engaged for. It seems that the price for the use of the tug's hawser would have been five dollars (247-8), and the closing question and answer put to Captain Gray, the manager of the claimant, indicate that it was the failure to have an agreement for the payment of this sum which resulted in allowing the "Edith" to drift on to pier 32.

> "Q. Now, captain, if the 'Edith' had engaged for the tug's lines, or if she had an understanding with you that in case she wanted them she was to have them, would that 12 inch hawser have been passed up to the 'Edith'? A. Yes, sir." (269-270)

And, again:

> "The only reason it was not passed out is that it was not engaged for." (259)

On the testimony of those witnesses of the claimant who said that the hawser was suitable for the towage operation in question, given sufficient time or sufficient men, it would, of course, have been possible to have passed it to the "Edith". It nowhere appears that the captain of the tug or anyone else on the tug asked for more men on the forecastle head of the "Edith" to haul up the hawser.

Furthermore, the deck of the "Edith" was only twenty-four feet above the deck of the "Fearless" (324). The wire pennant which was attached to the hawser weighed three and one-half pounds to the foot (242). Twenty-four feet would have taken the pennant on board the "Edith" and would have weighed eighty-four pounds. It is not apparent that in spite of the friction three men could not have pulled a one and one-half inch pennant, weighing eighty-four pounds, through the chock of the "Edith", which must have been large enough to accommodate a twelve inch hawser. Nor is it apparent why more men would not have been prepared on the "Edith" to take the wire pennant in question, if more men were required. It must be concluded, we submit, from the testimony of the captain of the tug, as well as from the testimony of the general manager of the claimant, that neither the hawser nor any other line was passed to the "Edith" because the tug declined to do so.

The "Fearless" was at fault for not being prepared with and passing one of her seven inch lines.

Equally inexcusable is the conduct of the "Fearless" in not having on board or in failing to pass one of her 7-inch lines to the "Edith". While the claimant made much in the court below of the rotten condition of the line which was passed by the "Edith" in the emergency in which she had been placed by the "Fearless" (see answer to libel 22, 24, also, test. tug captain 293) *the tug's witness Kraatz testified that there was no line other than the 12-inch hawser on board the "Fearless" which was as good as the line which was passed by the "Edith"* (184-185). After he had been questioned about all the lines on the tug he testified: .

> "Q. None of these lines were as good, as I understand you, as the line which you got from the 'Edith'? A. No." (185)

Captain Gray, claimant's manager, indignantly denied this (263), and said the lines were all good but suitable only for short jobs. The captain of the tug, the principal witness for claimant, said the six inch lines were bad (316), but the seven inch lines were good. But he testified:

> "Q. Why couldn't you have passed the 'Edith' one of your good 7-inch lines with the 6-fathom wire when you were under the bow there?
> A. I didn't see any men while I was waiting under the bow there." (318)

Later he changed this:

> "Q. And you say that the reason you did not pass up one of your own 7-inch lines was that you did not see any men on the forecastle deck?
> A. That is not the reason; *because I was not asked for any of these 7-inch lines.*
> Q. The reason you did not pass up a 7-inch line is because there were——
> A. They did not ask me for it." (322)

The statement in the claimant's answer that the first officer of the "Edith" asked the tug to pass its hawser, was then called to the attension of the witness and he took the ground that the seven inch lines were too short for the service (322). But the seven inch lines with pennant were twenty-six fathoms long and the full amount of line taken when the vessels left the slip was twenty to twenty-five fathoms. The captain of the tug admitted that in an emergency a twenty-six fathom line could have been used to hold the "Edith" (323).

Was the tug justified in attempting this maneuver without either proper lines on board or ascertaining what lines the "Edith" had for use in this strong tide and wind?

If the twelve inch hawser in question and the seven inch lines were not suitable for the towage operation which the tug undertook was it not the duty of the tug to have on board some equipment that would be suitable? When the master of the "Edith" engaged the tug he asked "to have a boat ready to help me to the dry-dock" (Dep. Henry McDonald, 30). Was the "Fearless' ready? Was such equipment aboard as she should have had?

The tug's equipment must be sufficient for the undertaking, otherwise the tug is at fault.

In *Gilchrist Trans. Co. v. Great Lakes Towing Co.,* 237 Fed. 432, it is said:

> "If an accident can be * * * attributed to the inadequacy of the tow to perform the service she has undertaken, then she has not fulfilled her full measure of duty to the tow."

The tug is bound to furnish safe and sound appliances.

38 Cyc. 564.

A tug which is insufficiently equipped with hawsers is at fault for any resulting accident.

> *Baker-Whitely Coal Co. v. Neptune Navigation Co.,* 120 Fed. 247.

In the case last mentioned a tug made fast a hawser to the port quarter of the "Wilhelmina". The Wilhelmina" was then asked for another rope which was also made fast. When the hawser taken from the "Wilhelmina" was tightened it parted and the propeller of the steamship struck the pier out of which she was being towed. It was held that the "Wilhelmina" was

not even partially liable for the injury, the court
saying tugs

> "should be duly equipped for such services. Such
> equipment includes sufficient hawsers. There was
> no special danger in the work required of the tug-
> boat 'Britannia'. * * * The port was the home
> port of the tug, where the required equipment
> could have been obtained. * * * The testimony
> shows that the tug was not properly equipped with
> hawsers and that it was compelled to borrow one
> from the steamship."

It was pointed out in that case that the action of the
tug rendered the steamer helpless, though it had employed her only for the purpose of assisting her with
the tug's ropes. The "Wilhelmina", it was pointed
out, might have backed out with her own steam had
she not relied on the tug.

It is, of course, apparent from the record that the
captain of the "Edith" had no idea that the "Fearless"
would attempt the maneuver which it undertook. He
could not be expected to be prepared with a line at
the "Edith's" forecastle head.

The answer alleges that the line which the "Edith"
passed when she was *in extremis* was rotten and insufficient (22). No blame can attach to the "Edith" for
not being prepared with a line at her bow when she
expected no towing service except from her stern.
There was no time to bring up a good line when she
was as close to the piers as the tug's maneuver and
failure to care for her, left her.

And, finally, Captain Sandstrom, who said that his
7-inch lines were in good condition, testified that even a

good line would probably not have prevented the "Edith" from striking (316, 317, 323). In other words, by the time she had drifted to her point of danger, if the line which she passed from her bow to the tug had held, she nevertheless would have struck the dock. *This testimony from the master of the "Fearless" himself condemns the maneuver which he undertook, and which he admits could not have been performed even with a sound line.*

The testimony on this subject in this case was that of the captain of the "Fearless", members of her crew, and of the manager of claimant. These witnesses testified in open court before the trial judge. His conclusion from their evidence that the tug was at fault in not being prepared with proper lines and in failing to pass one to the "Edith" should not, we submit, be disturbed unless clearly against the weight of evidence (infra pp. 60-63).

The tug, we submit, was grossly at fault in refusing to pass the line asked for; the excuse offered by the general manager of the claimant, that the line had not been engaged for, was insufficient and the tug should not have attempted the maneuver which it did without full and adequate equipment to perform it.

VI.

THE TUG CANNOT JUSTIFY ITS FAILURE TO PERFORM ITS ATTEMPTED MANEUVER BY A CLAIM THAT THE "EDITH'S" PROPOSED MANEUVER WAS NOT FEASIBLE.

When the tow line was taken off the tug's bitts, which was equivalent to casting it off, without signal or order

from or to the "Edith", the tug took the operation into
its own hands. The maneuver contemplated by the
master of the "Edith" then became impossible of performance. Unless the tug turned the stern of the
"Edith" to starboard, the bow could not be turned to
port. On the other hand the tug captain admitted that
at the time he cast off, his tug's position was such
that he could have turned the vessel's stern to starboard
as well as he could have from any other position (312).
It was his view that this could not be done against the
wind (311) although the master of the "Edith" thought
otherwise (Dep. Henry McDonald). The "Edith's"
helm was starboard, her propeller moving ahead, all of
which the tug's captain saw and knew. He could "readily" see the wheel (324). There was only one maneuver possible with these two factors, that was to pivot
the ship by turning her bow to port while her stern went
to starboard, but the captain of the tug did not think
it the proper maneuver. As he himself said, he used
his own judgment and let go, and from that moment,
having made the captain's plan of turning into the
wind and tide impossible of performance, the "Fearless" took the responsibility of turning the vessel
around.

The tug cannot escape responsibility on the ground
that because the captain of the tug was not aboard the
"Edith" he was not in charge of the operation. One of
claimant's witnesses, Captain Boster, admitted that at
times when in charge of a tow the tugboat captain is
on his tug, and on the tow only when the tug is lashed
alongside (219-220). Claimant's witness Captain W. M.

Randall also knew of cases where the tugboat captain took charge of undocking steamers without being on the bridge (236).

As these were claimant's own representatives their testimony should be conclusive on the point.

The captain of the "Edith" testified that he wanted to turn his vessel to port on a starboard helm, and to have the "Fearless" hang onto his stern, pulling the stern to starboard, thus pivoting his ship in the direction of Hunter's Point.

"Q. What procedure did you expect the tow to follow in towing you out?

A. I expected that he would turn to port, keep turning our stern.

*   *   *   *   *   *   *

Q. Did you give any signal to the tugboat to cast off her line?

A. No, I did not." (Dep. McDonald, p. 36)

"Q. Is it customary for the ship to assist in turning by the use of her own engine. A. Yes.

Q. How does she generally do that?

A. By going ahead either starboarding or porting her wheel as the case might require.

Q. And the tugboat, during this maneuver, does what?

A. Does the pulling around and down to the ship's head in the same direction.

*   *   *   *   *   *   *

Q. In this case when the 'Fearless' was taking you out?

A. We wished our head to go to port, consequently we wished the tow to pull the stern in the opposite direction." (Dep. McDonald, 45-46)

"Q. And you say that you had anticipated that he would swing your stern to his port, and to your own starboard?

A   No, swing my bow to port and swing the stern around to starboard.

Q.   He was made fast to your stern?   A.   Yes.

Q.   And you anticipated that he would swing your stern to your starboard, did you not?

A.   Yes.''   (ib. 57)

The experts summoned by the claimant—all of them officers or employees of the claimant—testified that the maneuver proposed by the master of the ''Edith'' was not feasible.

Both the first and the second experts called by the claimant, Captains Boster and Randall, thought that the captain's proposed maneuver was not the proper method of turning the vessel because of the wind and tide.

''Q.   Then the principal reason, really—isn't that a fact—that the principal reason why you think that the captain's way of trying to do this thing on that day was not possible, was because there was a strong ebb tide and strong southeast wind; isn't that so?   A.   Yes.'' (Captain Boster, 218)

Captain Randall thought that it was the proximity of the dock which was the principal objection to the manner in which the captain of the ''Edith'' intended to turn the vessel.

''Q.   Which leads me to ask you if it is not a fact that the objection to that maneuver is one based largely on conditions; there are conditions when it · can be done and conditions when it cannot be done?

A.   Close to the dock is the principal condition you have to consider.

Q.   And the tide and the wind?

A.   Tide and wind would be the second condition.''   (240)

And he thought the maneuver which the ''Edith'' wanted to perform could possibly have been done a half a mile away from the dock (235). And Captain C. Randall, the fourth expert summoned by the claimant, thought that Captain McDonald's proposed maneuver could have been performed in the absence of wind or tide (275).

The gist of the claimant's testimony is that the "Edith" was too near the docks to turn the vessel in the manner in which the captain of the "Edith" proposed to turn it. In point of fact, as the event developed, she was not out far enough for the performance of the maneuver which the "Fearless" undertook; and as the "Fearless" dropped the tow line, she must be responsible for the fact that the "Edith" was too close to the dock to be turned with safety by either maneuver.

The captain of the "Edith" was certain that he could have turned his ship as he planned. Does it lie in the mouth of claimant whose tug rendered the "Edith's" maneuver impossible, to claim that it could not have been safely performed?

VII.

THE MASTER OF THE "EDITH" WAS NOT AT FAULT FOR NOT DROPPING HIS ANCHORS.

The tug's maneuver contemplated that the "Edith" should stop her engines, drifting while hauling in the stern line. *As the tug intended to take a bow line and tow the "Edith" against tide and wind, dropping the anchors of the "Edith" would have prevented the tug's maneuver.* The master of the "Edith", after the tug cast off the line, expected the tug to take charge (Dep. Henry McDonald, 67-68).

Had the tug been prepared with proper lines, or attempted the maneuver at a greater distance from the piers, the captain's failure to drop his anchors could not be urged. The "Edith" most assuredly would have assumed the responsibility of rendering the tug's proposed maneuver impossible by dropping her anchors at any time between the casting off of the stern line and the tug's taking of a bow line. But this was the only period of time during which, from the testimony of all of the witnesses, she could have safely dropped her anchors, if at all. After the tug reached the "Edith's" bow she could not have dropped her anchors without running the risk of swinging the vessel on to the pier, stern first, and smashing the wheel and doing other damage even more serious than that which was done.

The tug captain was asked to mark on a chart the place where he started to pull on the bow line, and testified:

"Q. Put it the way you were when you started to pull, captain.
A. When I started to pull?
Q. Is that about correct?
A. That is about correct.
Q. When you pinned that model there just now did you have in mind how close you were putting it to pier 34? Is that where you want it?
A. About one hundred and fifty feet from the wharf.
Q. *About one hundred and fifty feet from pier 34. You think the 'Edith' could have dropped her anchor in that position in safety?*
A. *Not there."* (314)

Captain Boster testified that the place for the "Edith" to have anchored would have been before she got to pier 36 (214), which was before the tug took the bow line (214). Nor could the "Edith" have anchored with safety after the bow line parted.

Thus the tug captain testified:

> "Q. So that after the line was parted she could not have dropped her anchor without damaging herself?
>
> A. No, she was too close there." (314)

Thus on the tug's own theory the "Edith" could not have properly dropped her anchors before she gave the bow line to the tug. The only time at which she could under any circumstances have anchored without the danger of swinging on to the piers was before she had drifted into danger.

But to do this would have obviously interfered with such maneuvers as the tug might be undertaking. Surely it was not within the province of the tug captain to deliberately cast off the line at a place where, in his judgment, the "Edith" should have anchored to save herself. *The tug captain certainly cannot claim that when he cast off the tow preparatory to running around for a bow line, he expected the "Edith" to drop her anchors.* Would not claimant, if the "Edith" had attempted to anchor, claim that by doing so she had frustrated the operations attempted by the tug? And is there any claim that the tug thought or suggested that the "Edith" should anchor seven hundred feet from the piers? And was not the "Edith", when the tug took the operation into its own hands, justified in relying on the tug to complete it without interference?

In this connection we call attention to the testimony of the witness Boster, one of claimant's captains who testified as an expert. He was particular to say, *not* that the captain of the "Edith" *should* have dropped his anchor, but that he *could* have dropped it.

"Q. Your idea is that she should have dropped the anchor before she ever got to Pier 38?

A. I didn't say she *should* have dropped it; I say she *could* have dropped it." (188)

Finally, the tug here can not escape liability either in whole or in part on the claim that after the emergency had arisen that the master of the "Edith" did not take every possible step to prevent the disaster. The failure to drop anchor in an emergency, if it is an error, was, as was said in the case of the "Oceanica", "An error *in extremis* and not an act of negligence".

The Oceanica, 144 Fed. 301, citing *The Steamer Webb*, 14 Wall. 406.

To the same effect is the

A. M. Ball, 43 Fed. 170.

The hypercritical scrutiny of what could or could not have been done after the event has taken place is not the test of reasonable diligence or care.

The Wilhelm, 47 Fed. 89.

In *The Kalkaska*, 107 Fed. 959, it was claimed the vessels which had been placed in peril by a tug could have saved themselves, but the court said:

"We cannot think the maneuver of these two vessels, in extremis, and in the presence of impending peril, can be allowed to excuse the fault of the Kalkaska, even if different action might possibly have avoided or lessened the extent of the disaster.

When a vessel is placed in a perilous position from the fault of another vessel she is not to be held to strict rules of navigation; in such case a mistake made in the agony of almost certain collision is regarded as an error for which the vessel which caused the peril should alone be held responsible.''

Citing

> *The Columbia,* 109 Fed. 660;
> *The Nichols,* 7 Wall. 656.

In the latter case it was said:

"Mistakes committed in such moments of peril and excitement, when produced by the mismanagement of those in charge of the other vessel, are not of a character to relieve the vessel causing the collision from the payment of full damages to the injured vessel."

See also numerous authorities cited in *The Columbia,* supra.

"Where a vessel has been brought into imminent danger by the negligence of another, she mav not ordinarily be condemned for any error of her master while she is in extremis, and he is endeavoring to extricate her (The Ludwig Holberg, 157 U. S. 67, 15 Sup. Ct. 477, 39 L. Ed. 620).''

> *The Gilchrist Trans. Co. v. Sicken,* 147 Fed. 470.

The trial court made the finding that

"the 'Edith' was not at fault for not dropping her anchor as she was entitled to believe that the 'Fearless' would care for her properly". (355)

On this point the expert and eye witnesses summoned by the claimant testified before the trial judge, to wit: Captains Boster, Randall, Gray and the tug captain. Their evidence clearly supports the finding, and the finding, we submit, should not be disturbed (infra p. 60).

VIII.

THE CAPTAIN OF THE "EDITH" WAS NOT AT FAULT FOR NOT BACKING HIS ENGINES.

Counsel argue that the master should have gone astern on the "Edith's" engines. But the testimony of all the witnesses called by the claimant who were questioned on the subject shows that it was the duty of the master to stop his engine after his stern line had been cast off, and until he had hauled that line in (supra p. 14). By the time he had his line in he had drifted into a position where he was in danger. He was then helpless, and his efforts to back his engine did not save him from striking the piers.

The captain of the "Fearless" himself testified that the tug could not have expected the master of the "Edith" to go astern on his engines after the tug cast off the tow line. He said:

"Q. You would not approve starting an engine if there was a 20 or 25-fathom line over the stern of the ship hanging in the water?

A. In what direction do you mean? Either direction? Q. Yes.

A. Well, if the line was tight, it would not make any difference.

Q. If it was hanging in the water?

A. *No, I would not approve of it.*" (324)

"Q. And if this (line) were cast off, it would naturally hang under the counter of the ship, would it not. A. Hang across the rudder of the ship.

Q. With a right-hand screw turning to the right, if the line were hanging in that position and the screw turning, it would be pretty apt to foul, would it not?

A. If he *didn't back* it would not foul, but if he backed *it is apt to catch on either side* if it hangs in the water." (325)

And the experts summoned by the claimant all agreed that when the line was cast adrift it was proper seamanship for the captain to stop his engine (supra p. 13).

IX.

THERE WAS A SAFE WAY OF TURNING THE VESSEL AROUND WITH THE WIND AND TIDE WITHOUT LETTING GO OF THE STERN LINE.

The claimant's witnesses admitted that the stern of the vessel could have been turned into the tide and wind so that her bow would point with the tide and wind, and she could then have proceeded on a port helm, making a complete half circle, and going up to Hunter's Point Drydock. This would not have involved the taking of any further line from the "Edith", nor would it have involved the risky maneuver of the tug dropping the stern tow line, then running around the "Edith's" bow and catching her bow line while she was drifting. It would have been, as Captain Gray, the claimant's manager, testified, a safe maneuver, although it would have taken more time (255-6). It would have involved the tug's hanging on to the stern of the "Edith" and until it was turned by the tide and wind in the opposite direction, it is true, from that in which the captain of the "Edith" intended it to be turned. But if the "Fearless" had hung on to the stern until the captain's intentions had been ascertained, or the maneuver described by Captain Gray agreed upon with the captain, the accident would not have happened. *The trouble was caused when the tug cast off the line and put the captain in the position where he could not pivot.* The tug did this in order to perform a maneuver which proved perilous and which failed, whereas by holding the stern line it could either have aided the captain of the "Edith" in carrying out his attempted maneuver or could have led the captain into a maneuver which, as claimant's witness, Captain Gray said, would have been safe.

X.

THE TUG DID NOT USE REASONABLE CARE AND SKILL SUCH AS THE LAW REQUIRES.

"The master of a tug is bound to use reasonable care and skill in the management of a tow and to exercise them in everything relating to the work until accomplished. The want of either in such cases is a gross fault and the offender is liable to the extent of the full measure of the consequences."

The Margaret, 94 U. S. 494.

Gilchrist Trans. Co. v. Great Lakes Towing Co., 237 Fed. 432.

In the last named case the rule with reference to the duties and liabilities of tugs is fully set forth and amongst other matters the tug is charged with the knowledge of the ordinary currents and tides and impliedly warrants that she has sufficient power and ability to perform the service which is to be undertaken and the conditions which are to be reasonably anticipated. She must "Know whether under the condition then prevailing or reasonably to be expected, it is safe to make the proposed venture."

The Margaret, 94 U. S. 494, and other cases.

The tug must know all the conditions which are essential to the safe performance of her undertaking.

The Harry M. Wall, 187 Fed. 278.

In the case last above referred to the tug attempted to tow a vessel through a draw, the narrowness of which compelled the tug to cast off with the intention of taking a line again as soon as the vessel was clear. The vessel failed to respond, largely, if not wholly, because of the ebb tide setting against her starboard bow. The fundamental fault was that the master of the tug miscalculated the tide. The tug was held responsible.

In the *M. A. Lennox* case No. 8987, 16 Fed. Cases 540, the facts were peculiarly analogous to the case at bar.

There the "M. A. Lennox" towed the steamer "Corsica" out into the East River, stern foremost, then stopped, cast off the hawser, and attempted to get alongside the ship to take a second hawser from her starboard bow in order to tow her upon a hawser to her place of destination. There was evidence that the hands on the ship failed to promptly catch the heaving lines which were thrown from the tug, after the stern hawser was dropped, by means of which the second hawser was to be taken on board the tug, and this "prevented getting hold of the ship by the bow hawser in time to keep her off the piers." The tug, however, was held responsible. Judge Benedict said:

"The maneuver, which this tug undertook to perform, was to start the ship out by a stern line and then drop it and make fast to a bow line and get headway on the ship before she would run across the river. It was a maneuver not unattended with risk, but which could have been accomplished by the exercise of care and skill. * * * It was the duty of the master of the tug to determine the distance he would require for his maneuver, that is, to stop, drop his stern hawser and make fast to the bow line.''

The court held that the maneuver put the ''Corsica'' in danger, and said:

''A ship cannot be considered as otherwise than in danger when she is drifting towards piers, and so near as to require not only great diligence, but good fortune to prevent her from striking.''

And the court concluded:

''In arriving at this conclusion, I have not overlooked the defense which has been sought to be rested upon evidence tending to show that the ship was being transported under the direction of her own master, and that in point of fact the master of the tug acted under direction of the master of the ship in determining the distance out to which the ship was taken. A careful consideration of the testimony given by the various witnesses has convinced me that there was nothing in the action of the master of the ship on this occasion which can absolve the master of the tug from the responsibility of a negligent performance of the maneuver which he undertook.''

The tug was held responsible although it appeared that the master of the ship gave some orders in regard to the handling of the ship as she was coming out of the dock.

It is apparent that the operation attempted by the tug in this case was a usual method of undocking near the piers in the prevailing tide and wind. Captain

Gray said that by immediately going astern the "Edith" could have helped the tug to get into a position for a bow line and kept herself off the piers. But as the "Edith's" wheel had to be stopped until the line was in she was certain to drift close to the piers before the tug circled to her bow. It was plainly negligence for the "Fearless" to attempt the movement under the existing conditions of tide and wind.

XI.

THE VARIOUS MANEUVERS OPEN TO THE "EDITH". THE TUG'S MANEUVER CONDEMNED AS PERILOUS.

This court, we submit, will not consider the various possibilities open to the "Edith," ingeniously devised for her by counsel for appellant, and which "after the event" he "may think would have been best" (*The James P. Donaldson,* 19 Fed. 264, Appt's Br. 33). Not a syllable of testimony was tendered in respect to the various maneuvers suggested by counsel for appellant. To argue them in these briefs is to try the case on the expert opinion of counsel for the litigants, assuming a technical knowledge of navigation in which we frankly confess ourselves wanting. Three possible maneuvers were discussed at the trial, and testimony offered regarding them:

First. The maneuver intended by the captain of the "Edith", to wit, to back his ship out of the slip, to pivot it with a port helm while the tug pulled his stern to starboard, and then to proceed on his way. This maneuver, as we know, was not completed because the tug, without warning or notice, dropped the tow line.

Second. The maneuver intended by the tug, and which failed and resulted in the accident, namely, to drop the tow line and, while the ''Edith'' was hauling in the line and drifting, to run around to her bow and pull her into tide and wind. This maneuver failed because undertaken without notice, and too near the docks (Tug Captain's test. 339), and because no line was passed to the ''Edith''.

Third. The maneuver described by Captain Gray, claimant's manager (256), by which the ''Edith'' could have proceeded northwesterly on a port helm, making a complete turn with the tide and wind. The witness said this would have been a safe maneuver. It would not have involved dropping the tow line until the ''Edith's'' bow was turned into tide and wind, and she was on her way. But it was not a maneuver intended or attempted by either vessel or tug. That the ''Edith'' did not propose to turn the vessel in this manner is admitted; that neither the tug captain nor any of his crew proposed to assist the ''Edith'' in the maneuver last described is equally undisputed and clear from the testimony. It therefore is of little aid to the tug that a third maneuver was open to the ''Edith'' which the tug had no intention to aid her to perform, and which was not a customary maneuver under these circumstances with claimant's tug captains.

It is very clear from the evidence of the tug's captain and his crew that what the tug undertook is claimant's usual method of assisting a vessel out of the slips and up the bay. And, furthermore, it is very clear that what was here attempted to be done was exactly what

the tug proposed to do when she went to assist the
"Edith" (test. tug captain, Capt. Sandstrom (330-339)
and crew, Driver (142-4), Kraatz (185), supra p. 11).
The libellant contended at the trial and has always
maintained that it was a perilous maneuver, undertaken
at the tug's risk.

The counsel for the tug themselves characterized the
tug's proposed maneuver as "difficult" and claimed that
that court erred

> "in not holding, deciding and decreeing that the
> accident and the resulting injury and damage to
> the 'Edith' were due to *the negligence and fault of
> the 'Edith' herself in compelling the 'Fearless' to
> undertake said difficult maneuver.*" (Assignment
> of Errors, 19, Rec. 309)

In other words, counsel claimed that the 'Edith' was
guilty of negligence in compelling the tug to undertake a
maneuver which the tug intended to perform before the
"Edith" left her slip!

As we have seen, if the tug had held on to the
"Edith's" tow line, the operation attempted would
never have been put under way. But can the tug escape
responsibility for the results of a "difficult" maneuver
which the tug assumed to perform pursuant to her captain's plans merely because the "Edith" did not block
the performance? By charging the "Edith" with negligence for forcing the tug into this maneuver, claimant
convicts the tug, which as the record amply shows, *at no*
stage of the operation intended or attempted any other
maneuver.

XII.

THE "EDITH" IS NOT ESTOPPED; THE TUG'S MANEUVER WAS NOT ADOPTED BY THE "EDITH".

Appellant's brief is predicated on the theory that the captain of the "Edith" assumed responsibility for the tug's maneuver because he did not object to it. The entirely new theory is now advanced in the case that after the tow line was cast off from the tug into a tide running three miles, with an eighteen mile gale blowing, the "Edith", instead of hauling in the line as rapidly as possible, should have stopped her engines (she could not turn them without danger of fouling her wheel while the line was in the water (supra p. 38) and while thus drifting, signal to the tug, which dropped her tow a few hundred feet from the piers, to fish for the line—"with its boat hook from its tow stern" (Appt's Br. 14), suggests counsel for appellant.

The statement that the line "lay in the water without slack" (Appt's Br. 14-15) is contrary to the evidence. The line was taken off the bitts, and the bight in it was so great and wind and tide so strong that the deckhands could not hold on to it (supra p. 18, tug crew Kraatz (162), Driver (147), Taylor (192)).

The claim that the "Edith" should have directed the tug to again pick up the line (after the tug cast it off without notice), or be held responsible for the outcome of the tug's perilous maneuver, is, we submit, as inadmissible as it is new in the case. Not an intimation of such a defense is offered in the answer to the libel; not an insinuation of the kind is found in the assignments of error; not a syllable of testimony was offered that such a thing could have been done under the weather conditions at the time, or that it should have been attempted. The captain of the "Edith", his own maneuver having been rendered impossible by the action of the tug, naturally and properly left the next step in the operation to the action of the tug. He is not to be blamed, we submit, for not instructing the tug to attempt to recover the line which it had just cast off. The trial court, we submit, properly found that the master of the "Edith", after the tug took matters out of his hands, and without his orders, was entitled to rely on the tug's completing what it had undertaken.

We take it that had the master of the "Edith" ordered the tug to attempt to pick up the cast off line, and had disaster ensued in the attempt, he would have been justly blamed. He can not be said to have adopted a maneuver which he could not prevent or stop; the line was cast off without warning, and his engines had to be stopped at once. No court has yet held, we take it, that a vessel which is placed in *extremis* by a tug that drops its tow without notice, acquiesces in the tug's maneuvers because it does not attempt to frustrate them.

The cases cited by counsel in support of the claim of "estoppel" on the part of the "Edith" all involved an expressed adoption by the complaining vessel of a maneuver resulting in the accident. This appears from an examination of the authorities cited.

The Santa Maria, 227 Fed. 149 (Appt's Br. 38), In this case two tugs, the "Sweepstakes" and the "Mehrer", were held jointly responsible for negligence in navigation. The "Sweepstakes" signaled her proposed course for passing the "Mehrer", and the "Mehrer" answered the signal and agreed to the maneuver. It was held that the "Mehrer" having agreed to the maneuver and attempted to execute it, could not complain of the "Sweepstakes'" conduct.

The Luther C. Ward, 149 Fed. 787 (Appt's Br. 38). In this case two tugs attempted to pass each other by going to starboard, with the result that the tow of one collided with a dredge. The first tug, the "Tice", signalled her proposed course with two blasts, and the "Ward" responded with two blasts, indicating that she agreed to the proposed maneuver. It was held that the "Ward" could not then throw sole responsibility on the "Tice" for proposing the operation.

In *The Luckenback,* 124 Fed. 947 (Appt's Br. 38), the facts were similar to those in the last cited case, except that here the "Luckenback", after answering the signals of another tug, the "Flint," failed to complete the agreement thus reached between them. It was held that the "Luckenback" was not entitled to claim that the "Flint" was negligent, but that having adopted the course proposed for both tugs by the "Flint", should have been vigilant in completing it.

In the case of *The Albemarle,* 1 Fed. Cas. 299, 9 Blatchford 200 (Appt's Br. 39), there was a collision between the "Albemarle" and the "Brady", approaching each other from opposite directions. The "Brady" blew one whistle to signify her intention to pass to the right. The "Albemarle" responded with one whistle, indicating her assent. Thereupon the "Brady" ported.

There was a dispute as to whether the "Albemarle" ported or starboarded. The court held that both vessels should have ported at an earlier stage. In the course of the opinion, the court said:

> "I do not say that the Albemarle, by assenting to the signal of the Brady to port the helm and go to starboard, is estopped to allege that it was wrong in the Brady to do so, or that, in a sudden exigency, caused by the fault of another vessel, she is to be held accountable for an erroneous judgment formed on the instant. But here the Brady gave the signal and waited a reply. That reply assured her that the approaching vessel concurred with her in her opinion as to what was required of both. Then, and not until then, she ported her helm, and the Albemarle did the same."

The distinction between the cases relied upon by counsel and the case at bar is well marked in this decision. The mere assent to an erroneous or perilous maneuver given on the spur of the moment, or in the exigencies of a situation, should not create an estoppel against the vessel so assenting. In all the cases relied upon by counsel for appellant the vessel assenting to a maneuver which resulted in a disaster was held to be estopped by its assent *only* where the assenting vessel had been notified of the proposed maneuver, and had expressed her concurrence in it and willingness to undertake it.

The court in the case of the "Albemarle" was particular to point out that the "Brady", before swinging to port, not only gave a signal, "but waited a reply", and, as the court says, "then, and not until then, she ported her helm." The "Albemarle" was held estopped because her assent was given "in no sudden exigency, for the 'Brady' did not change until the assent of the 'Albemarle' thereto (to port) was given.'' And this is precisely the distinction which we here urge upon the court. The tow rope in this case was cast off by the tug without warning. It would have been easy, as counsel for appellant points out, for the master of the tug to have inquired of the mate of the "Edith" whether the rope was to be cast off. After it was cast off, if it is conceivable that the master of the "Edith" should have directed the tug to recover the rope in the tide and the wind then prevailing, the most that could be said is that such a determination could have been reached by the master in the exigency of the case, and his failure to give the order would not constitute an assent to the tug's maneuver. It is because the tug failed to do in this case what the "Brady" did in the "Albemarle" case, namely, to signal her intention and wait for the "Edith's" reply, that we conceive that no question of estoppel can arise against the "Edith".

So in *The Arthur L. Palmer,* 115 Fed. 417 (Appt's Br. 39), it was held that where a vessel *assents by signal* that another shall cross her bows, she cannot urge the attempted maneuver as a fault.

In *The San Rafael,* 141 Fed. 270 (Appt's Br. 39), it was similarly decided that after the "Sausalito" had answered the signal of the "San Rafael to pass to port, the "San Rafael" having blown two whistles and the "Sausalito" having answered, neither vessel could escape responsibility for the maneuver which was a negligent undertaking.

In *The Electra,* 139 Fed. 158 (Appt's Br. 39), a steamer and lighter collided after exchanging signals to pass to the right, and each was held at fault for waiting too long in carrying out the maneuver.

The Transfer No. 9, 170 Fed. 944, and *The Columbia,* 195 Fed. 1000 (Appt's Br. p. 40). In both of these cases vessels which exchanged signals and thus agreed to the maneuver signalled, were held to have assented to the maneuver.

We have examined and here commented on all of the cases cited by counsel in support of the alleged "estoppel" in this case. We submit that none of them sustains the extraordinary proposition that the master of a steamship is estopped from charging a tug with negligence or that he must be held to adopt the tug's action because he fails to direct the tug to recover a tow line, which the tug has cast off without signal or notice in a gale of wind and a swiftly running tide.

Counsel argue with some elaboration that the "Edith" left the tug in ignorance of the fact that she could not turn her wheel—that the vessel was converted to a "hulk," etc., etc. But the tug's crew, as counsel for appellant points out, were within easy speaking and seeing distance of the "Edith's" stern. Furthermore, the tug *expected* the "Edith's" wheel to remain still, during the time the line was hauled in (supra p. 12), a sufficient time for the "Edith" to drift into danger (supra p. 15).

To the suggestion that the tug acted in an emergency and is not chargeable with gross negligence (Appt's Br.

33), we answer that the maneuver the tug attempted was not undertaken in an emergency, but was the precise operation she intended to perform when she left the slip. Her captain and crew so testified (supra, pp. 11 et seq.).

XIII.

THE ALLEGED FAILURE TO PRODUCE TESTIMONY.

Counsel direct much of their argument to the alleged "failure" to produce the logs of the "Edith", and to the fact that more of the "Edith's" crew were not called as witnesses.

The only references to the log books of the "Edith" contained in the apostles on appeal are a half dozen questions and answers concluding with the following:

> "Q. The log books remained on the vessel?
> A. I imagine they did.
> Mr. McGRANN. I called for a production of the log books bearing on this occurrence." (48)

The call was at the time of the taking of the deposition of the witness Henry McDonald in New York City on the 28th day of March, 1917, being approximately three months prior to the trial of the action. It does not appear that appellant's counsel ever thereafter considered the question of the production of the log books and *non constat* from the record the books were in fact produced and examined by appellant's counsel.

Admiralty Rules 35 and 36 of the United States Supreme Court provide for demand and notice for the production of writings and for orders with respect thereto.

There was no order of court ever made for the production of these books, and even if libellant had failed to produce the logs, there was no duty resting upon libellant to produce them in the absence of an order of court or a written notice as required by these rules.

> *The Washtenaw,* 163 Fed. 372;
>
> *Havemeyer, etc. v. Compania Transatlantic, etc.,* 43 Fed. 90.

But in any event the point raised is highly specious. It is quite apparent that the log books could have had no bearing on the issues of fact tried before the court. The facts in regard to the movements of the "Edith" are entirely undisputed, except perhaps as to the single circumstance that some of the tug's witnesses thought the "Edith's" propeller was turning when the stern tow was cast off—others thought the wheel was not moving.

The maneuver contemplated by the captain of the "Edith" is not in issue; that the tug dropped the tow rope is admitted; that the tug intended to run around the "Edith's" bow and take a tow line while she was drifting, is testified to by the tug-captain himself and his crew, and is not disputed; that the tug failed to pass up a line while the "Edith" was drifting is not denied; that the line passed out in the emergency by the "Edith" from her bow failed to hold and was not a good line, is not disputed; that the tug had lines which it could have passed is not denied; that it failed to pass them because they were not specially contracted for is testified to by the manager of the claimant; that the "Edith" asked the tug for a line is denied by

the tug captain, but testified to by two members of the
tug's crew, who heard the request, and is expressly
averred in the claimant's answer; that the wind and tide
were strong and caused the "Edith" to drift rapidly is
alleged in the answer of claimant and not denied; that
the "Edith" failed to anchor, fearing thereby to em-
barrass the tug's maneuver, is not disputed; that the
"Edith' was right in not turning her engines while the
line was in the water is admitted and characterized as
good seamanship by the tug's witnesses; that while thus
compelled to stop her engines she drifted into danger
is admitted by various of claimant's witnesses; that the
tug captain failed to consult the "Edith's' master is not
denied; that he took the stern line in an operation in
which he was to "assist" the "Edith" and cast it off
without an order from or notice to the "Edith" is not
denied.

What possible light or relevancy could the ship's logs
have on these circumstances, or on the facts of the case
on which it was tried? And why should either counsel
have wished to use the logs?

Is not counsel plainly grasping at a circumstance in
this case of no significance, undoubtedly contrary to the
fact, and endeavoring to draw from it the sinister inference attached to the suppression and mutilation of
evidence in the cases cited by him? *Is it not entirely
probable that so astute and experienced a practitioner
as the counsel who tried the case below would have
brought the demand for the logs, if these had been with-
held from inspection, to the attention of the trial court,
or would have had the record show a refusal to produce*

them? Is it not equally probable that he would have offered them in evidence or excepted to the refusal (if there was a refusal) to produce them, if they could have had any bearing on the case? And not having done so, should the failure to respond to a demand for evidence which claimant thought it unnecessary to press, be seized upon and urged upon this court? Would it be fair to counsel or the trial court to even consider an alleged failure to produce evidence for which no request was made at the trial, which was never asked for except on the taking of a sealed deposition, taken months before the trial and which deposition was offered in the case without reading? Are such objections considered as grounds for reversal on appeals to this court in admiralty? We submit they are not.

Similarly, what possible light could other witnesses from the "Edith" have thrown on this case? The movements of the "Edith" are not in dispute, although the facts as to the turning of her wheel, which was in plain view of the crew of the tug, were the subject of various theories advanced by claimant, whether in the answer, or that proven by some of the tug witnesses, or that proven by others, or that now taken on the appeal. The difficulty of producing the other witnesses from the "Edith" was obvious from the master's deposition (48); and while this in a proper case might be no excuse, the uselessness of doing so here, is apparent from the fact that no single fact to which they could have testified would have aided in fixing the responsibility for this accident.

While the record here contains nothing to sustain the contention that the logs were not offered, it is apparent from the authorities that even if there had been a failure to produce the logs, or to call further witnesses from the "Edith", these circumstances would be considered by the court only if it appeared that the logs or other witnesses could throw light on material facts in the case. Such is the effect of the decisions cited by counsel.

They are the following:

The Sicilian Prince, 128 Fed. 133 (Appt's Br. 40). Here the trial court found that log books which had been produced by the vessel were intentionally made in meager fashion. A page falling between two relevant dates in the case *had been cut from one of the log books,* and no explanation for the mutilation offered. Obviously the court was justified in drawing an unfavorable conclusion.

The Prudence. 191 Fed. 993 (Appt's Br. 41). The mate in the pilot house at the time of the collision was not summoned as a witness—which the court said was matter for observation.

The Santa Rosa, 249 Fed. 160 (Appt's Br. 41). The proceeding was to limit the liability which arose out of the wreck of the steamer at Point Arguello on the Pacific Coast. The opinion shows that:

"During the trial the production of these logs (that is, the logs of the vessel) was demanded by claimants and petitioner promised to produce them. This was not done, so that it may at least be assumed that their production would not have helped petitioner's case."

One issue in that case was whether or not the "Santa Rosa" was navigating at the time of the disaster with the course and speed of the vessels of the fleet of which she was one, usual upon the run in question. The fog and weather conditions prevailing would have rendered her conduct in proceeding in the usual manner, negligent. The trial court observed that the failure to produce the vessel's logs, "requested and promised", would indicate that her course and speed were the usual ones. The logs, therefore, would go to the very gist of the case, and the failure to produce them after they were promised would obviously be a circumstance against the vessel. The opinion cited by counsel for appellant in the "Santa Rosa" case was rendered by the learned Judge who tried the case at bar. The report shows that his opinion was delivered on February 20, 1918. The memorandum opinion of the trial court in this case was filed February 8, 1918 (299), twelve days before the opinion filed in the case of the "Santa Rosa". *Is it conceivable that the judge of the court below would have drawn so strong an inference against the "Santa Rosa" from the failure to produce her logs, and yet have completely overlooked the fact that the logs of the "Edith" in the case at bar were not produced, if their production had in point of fact been refused, or if the logs themselves were of any moment in the case?*

The New York, 175 U. S. 187 (Appt's Br. 41). Signals and lights were overlooked by the "New York". There was a charge that there was a defective lookout. None of the officers or crew of the "New York" were put on

the stand to explain why the blasts were not answered
or lights observed, and the failure to explain this negligence was the proper subject of an unfavorable deduc-
tion by the court.

The Alpin, 23 Fed. 815 (Appt's Br. 42). The vessel
had stranded. None of the officers or crew, twenty-nine
in number, nor the two passengers, many of these eye-
witnesses to the stranding, were called to the stand.
Naturally the court drew an unfavorable inference.

Clifton v. United States, 4 How. 242 (Appt's Br. 42).
The case involved liability for fraudulent importations.
The importer failing to produce his account books,
although they were frequently demanded. This was
properly held to militate against him.

The Fred M. Laurence, 15 Fed. 635 (Appt's Br. ib.).
It was admitted there was perjury on one side or the
other, and the failure to call the single witness who
could have cleared up the essential fact in the case, was
held to create an adverse suspicion.

The Bombay, 46 Fed. 665 (Appt's Br. ib.). The proceeding was one to charge the vessel with a fine for
dumping ashes into the Bay of New York. It was noted
by the court that the firemen who did the dumpiing
were not produced.

The Georgetown, 135 Fed. 854 (Appt's Br. ib.). It
was said that the failure to produce witnesses likely to
know of the circumstances of a collision weakens the
case of a vessel where there is a direct conflict amongst
the witnesses.

The Sandringham, 10 Fed. 556 (Appt's Br. ib.) The action was a salvage case. The court observed that three witnesses for the ship

> "discredit their own testimony by statements sin-gularly untrue, and I have no choice but to reject it when it is in conflict with the evidence of the wrecking officers; and their testimony is the more open to distrust from the fact that the first mate of the ship was not examined *on the principal points in dispute".* (Italics ours.)

The Gladys, 135 Fed. 601 (Appt's Br. ib.) A collision case. One of the vessels called no witnesses, and the court observed that the failure to take the testimony of those navigating a tug in a suit for collision tends against her *in the absence of equivalent testimony.*

The Freddie L. Porter, 8 Fed. 170 (Appt's Br. ib.). The vessel failed to call the lookout and wheelman on duty at the time of the collision, and this was held to be open to remark, the only witnesses produced being the mate, whose story the court found could not be accurate.

These are all of the authorities cited by counsel. In none of them (nor, indeed, in any others that we have been able to find) is it indicated:

First: That there is a presumption that the demand for the log books of a vessel was refused, because the record does not affirmatively show that the logs were produced. Indeed it may well be that in this case the logs, or copies thereof, were exhibited by counsel for claimant during the progress of the trial, and that he

.considered them of as little consequence on the issues involved in this case as did counsel for the libellant.

Second: That any significance is to be attached to, or unfavorable inference be drawn from, the fact that some members of the crew of a vessel were not produced as witnesses, unless it appears in some manner that their testimony would have thrown some light on the issues in the case, or that they could have shown some relevant, if not important, fact.

XIV.

DESPITE ANY CONFLICT OF EXPERT OR OTHER TESTIMONY, THERE IS AMPLE EVIDENCE IN THE RECORD TO SUPPORT THE FINDINGS OF THE DISTRICT COURT, AND THE WELL ESTABLISHED RULE OF THIS COURT, THAT FINDINGS OF FACT WILL NOT BE REVERSED WHERE THE TRIAL COURT HEARD THE EVIDENCE, SHOULD OBTAIN.

The decision of a trial court in admiralty, on questions of fact, based upon conflicting testimony or the credibility of witnesses examined before the judge, is entitled to great respect and will not be reversed unless manifestly contrary to the evidence.

1 C. J., Par. 314, p. 1351.

On appeal in admiralty an appellate court will not reverse the decision of a district judge upon conflicting testimony, where all or a major part of the evidence was presented in open court, as under such circumstances the district judge, having the opportunity to see the witnesses and observe their appearance and manner, is in a better position than is the appellate court to weigh their evidence and determine the credibility which should be given to the testimony of the respective witnesses.

This rule was applied by the Circuit Court of the Ninth Circuit in *The Hardy,* 229 Fed. 985, opinion by Gilbert and Ross, Circuit Judges, Rudkin, District Judge, concurring. The court said:

> "The court below found upon testimony, the most of which was taken in open court, that the steamer was not responsible for the parting of the hawser * * * ;While there are many features of the evidence which tend to discredit the testimony of the officers and men of The Hardy * * * we are not convinced that the record is such as to take the case out of the well settled rule which has been followed by this and other courts, that in cases on appeal in admiralty when questions of fact are dependent upon conflicting testimony, the decision of the District Judge who had the opportunity to see the witnesses and judge of their appearance, manner and credibility, will not be reversed unless it clearly appears to be against the weight of the evidence."

Citing: *The Alejandro,* 56 Fed. 62, 71; *Perriam v. Pacific Coast Co.,* 153 Fed. 140; *Peterson v. Larson,* 127 Fed. 617.

This rule is particularly applicable to the instant case, where all the *appellant's witnesses* were heard in open court.

In *The Dolvadarm Castle,* 222 Fed. 838, Circuit Judge Gilbert, speaking for the court, said:

> "It is contended that the evidence failed to show that the damage was caused by perils of the sea. In considering this contention it is to be observed

that all of the testimony of the *appellant's* witnesses was heard in open court, and that the only testimony offered on depositions was that of the officers of the barge. The well settled rule is applicable, that the findings of fact of the trial court will not be disturbed in this court, unless it clearly appears that there was error."

Citing: *Whitney v. Olsen,* 108 Fed. 292; *Perriam v. Pacific Coast Co.,* supra; *The Bailey Gatzert,* 179 Fed. 44.

"Whether negligence imputed is a proximate cause, or merely collateral or immaterial, is a question of fact, and where the conclusion of the District Court is not against the preponderance of the evidence it cannot be disturbed."

The Curtin, 217 Fed. 245, 247. Citing: *The Oregon,* 158 U. S. 186; *The City of Macon,* 92 Fed. 207; *The Lord O'Neil,* 66 Fed. 77; *Marsden on Collisions at Sea,* 6th Edition, 14. See, also, *The Sampson,* 217 Fed. 344, 347; *The Elenore,* 217 Fed. 753. See, also, *The Belgenland,* 114 U. S. 355, 357; *The Tornado,* 119 U. S. 110, 115; *Irvine v. The Hesper,* 122 U. S. 256, 266.

The burden is on the appellant to show that the decree of the subordinate court is erroneous.

The Lady Pike, 88 U. S. 1, 8.

The case would be otherwise were the appeal by the libellant, whose witnesses have been heard upon depositions.

The Santa Rita, 176 Fed. 890, 893.

Appellant cannot complain that its case was not supported by the testimony of its own witnesses, when they were heard in open court. There is therefore nothing in this appeal to take the case out of the ordinary rule, that the decision of the district judge in admiralty upon questions of fact will be accepted by the appellate court, unless the evidence clearly preponderates against it.

> *Geary etc. v. Dunseith,* 239 Fed. 814, 816.

In the case at bar the trial court received the depositions of the "Edith's" officers and heard the testimony of the crew of the tug, of the superintendent, manager and other employees of the claimant, who testified as experts.

The court decided the disputed issues, such as whether the line was cast off by the tug while the "Edith's" wheels were turning, whether the tug was prepared with a sufficient line, whether the "Edith" was at fault for not dropping her anchor, whether the "Edith" was entitled to rely on the tug, against the claimant.

Similarly, the trial court listened to much testimony on the issue whether the "Edith's" captain properly "planned the maneuver", the point which is so conspicuously and elaborately considered in appellant's brief and much expert testimony on this subject was offered. In brief the case was tried as to all essential defenses by the tug *viva voce.*

We submit the court's findings should stand, and that the judgment should be affirmed.

Dated, San Francisco,
> October 24, 1918.

> > Respectfully submitted,

> > > E. S. PILLSBURY,
> > > F. D. MADISON,
> > > ALFRED SUTRO,
> > > OSCAR SUTRO,
> > > *Proctors for Appellee.*

SHIPOWNERS AND MERCHANTS TUGBOAT COMPANY
(a corporation), claimant of the American
Steam Tug "Fearless", her boilers, engines,
tackle, apparel and furniture,

Appellant,

VS.

A. H. BULL & COMPANY, INC. (a corporation),

Appellee.

REPLY BRIEF FOR APPELLANT.

WILLIAM DENMAN,
McCUTCHEN, OLNEY & WILLARD,
Proctors for Appellant.

PERNAU-WALSH PRINTING CO.

Index.

Table of Cases Cited.

No. 3199

United States Circuit Court of Appeals

For the Ninth Circuit

SHIPOWNERS AND MERCHANTS TUGBOAT COMPANY (a corporation), claimant of the American Steam Tug "Fearless", her boilers, engines, tackle, apparel and furniture,

Appellant,

vs.

A. H. BULL & COMPANY, INC. (a corporation),

Appellee.

REPLY BRIEF FOR APPELLANT.

I.

The "Edith's" Captain Let Her Drift From Off Pier 42 Almost to Pier 32 in Plain View of Her Danger Without Dropping His Anchors or Attempting to Use His Engines—and Herein of the Relevancy of the Non=Production of Witnesses and Logs.

The striking fact in this case, however one approaches its consideration, is that the "Edith" in broad daylight and clear weather, with her captain on the bridge, her engines uninjured and in full command and her heavy anchors ready for instant dropping, collided with the end of a pier after drifting for eighteen hundred feet towards this obvious danger, without attempting to turn over her engines or drop her anchors.

The captain of the "Edith" explains this apparently unpardonable neglect by asserting (a) that he did not use his engines till at the very last moment, because he erroneously believed (and without consulting his chief engineer) that the end of a hawser dropped by the tug had caught in his propeller and disabled it; and (b) that he did not drop his anchors because, although he did not advise the tug of his erroneous belief that his propeller would not turn, he left it "up to the tug" (but without telling her) to save the vessel by some other method than dropping his anchors.

The above facts clearly appear from the depositions of the captain and mate of the "Edith", the only witnesses offered by the libelant, from the dozen persons on the "Edith" who had knowledge which bore on the mishap.

Obviously, the paramount question then is what was the interval of time and the distance drifted between the fouling of the hawser in the propeller when the "Edith's" engine stopped and the collision with the pier-head. If we could tell the minute when the "Edith's" engine stopped and the minute when they started up again just before the vessel crashed into the pier, we can determine the most important element in fixing the "Edith's" captain's causal responsibility, that is, his responsibility for not dropping his anchors and for not trying his engines to see if, in fact, the fouled hawser end had done any hurt to them, and for not telling the tug's captain, if he intended to give up the control to him, that he believed the propeller unworkable.

If the "Edith's" captain did not have a reasonable time *after* the hawser caught in the propeller to determine whether she was disabled and to shift the command and give the information to the tug's captain, then he may find some excuse. If he did have abundant time after he was told of the fouling of the hawser to do these things, he is clearly at fault. On this, the "Edith" had the burden of proof, for it must show the causal chain leading to her injury.

The analysis of the evidence (and the absence of it) on this essential point is not difficult. It was the easiest circumstance to prove in the libelant's case. The captain and the mate agree and it is uncontradicted that the line was fouled and the "Edith's" captain knew it before her propeller, which was then going ahead, was stopped. The captain testifies:

"Q. When you started slow ahead on your engines what happened?
A. Shortly afterward the mate sang out and said the line was cast off the boat, and before the engine stopped it was in the wheel.
Q. That is, it fouled the propeller?
A. Fouled the propeller.
Q. Did you give any signal to the tugboat to cast off her line? A. No, I did not.
(Mr. McGRANN). Q. May I understand that answer—you say the mate said this?
A. The second.
Q. Is that what the mate said or is that the statement of the captain, is the last part what the mate said or is that what you said?
A. That is what I got about it from him.

(Mr. FARWELL). Q. What report did the mate make to you?

A. That the line was in the wheel.

* * * * * * *

Q. At that time your engines were going ahead?

A. Had been going ahead, they were stopped when the line got into the wheel.''

(Apostles pp. 36, 37.)

Q. Did you say that the mate had hauled in the line?

A. Not then, when the engines were stopped, *but before we took time to stop them* the mate was hauling the line in, and it was afoul of the wheel.''

(Apostles p. 60.)

The second mate says:

"Q. What did you do when you saw the 'Fearless' had let go the stern-line?

A. Gave the signal to the captain to stop the engines.

Q. Did the captain stop the engines?

A. Yes, sir.

Q. Was it necessary to stop the engines?

A. Yes, because the line was foul.''

(Apostles p. 84.)

Now the "Edith's" mate and tug's captain agree that the tug dropped the tow line when the "Edith" was off pier 44, and the captain tells us that he stopped his engines off pier 42.

"Q. Do you know what pier the ship was off when the tug cast off the tow-line?

(HANSEN). A. She was off 44 then.''

(Apostles p. 101.)

"Q. In which direction did you pull her?

(SANDSTROM). A. Well, right out of the slip.

Q. Straight out into the bay? A. Yes.

Q. Did you receive any assistance from the steamer by her engines?

A. The steamer was backing at the same time.

Q. Now, you subsequently let go from the steamer's hawser, did you, afterwards?

A. I let go after the steamer stopped.

Q. Now, about how far off the end of pier 44 were you at the time that the hawser was finally let go?

A. Well, in the neighborhood of 700 feet; it might have been a little less or it might have been a little more.

Q. What pier were you about opposite at the time that you let go?

A. Well, just about opposite 44.

Q. Opposite 44? A. Yes."

(Apostles pp, 287, 288.)

"Q. Had you drifted down along the piers? (McDONALD). A. Yes.

Q. Opposite what pier were you when you stopped your engines?

(McDONALD). A. Off pier 42 I believe."

(Apostles p. 38.)

He did not start them till within 150 to 200 feet from pier 32 (Apostles p. 67).

In the absence of all other testimony, we would be compelled to accept this testimony of the "Edith's" captain as controlling on the question as to when he knew the line had fouled his propeller. It was his ship, and he would not be too liberal against his own interest, in his opinion as to the amount of time and distance he was to travel, in which he could have taken measures to protect his vessel from suffering injury. On later cross-examination he stuck to this statement, although all the piers passed between 42 and 32 were specifically enumerated as measuring his drift after stopping his propeller, because he thought it fouled by the line (Apostles 68).

But the absence of the other testimony from the "Edith" is most significant. If the stopping of the engines subsequent to the fouling of the propeller had not occurred this long time before their starting again at 150 feet from pier 32,—too late to save her from colliding,—the engineer's testimony, refreshed from the engine room logs, would have shown the exact truth.

Every person who has any knowledge of steamship operation knows that the engineer sets down in his log the times of the stoppings, startings and changings of speed and direction of his engines, and he did so in this case (48). He would also note the time of the crashing into the dock.

Captain McGrann, one of the best of the maritime lawyers at the New York bar, cross-examined the "Edith's" captain. On his direct examination the captain had testified to the above facts as to his knowledge of the supposed fouling before the engines had stopped and his long drift after this before he tried to see whether they were in fact fouled. Mr. McGrann's cross-examination was at once directed to this point and he located the assistant engineer and the vessel's engine room logs as still on the "Edith" which was to arrive in New York ten days from that date, March 20. The cross-examination and demand for the logs was as follows:

"Q. How about in the engine-room, don't they keep a record in the engine-room?

A. They keep a record in the engine-room.

Q. Do you know whether they kept any on this occasion? A. I think so.

Q. Where is the 'Edith' now? A. Porto Rico.

Q. Do you trade between Porto Rico and the east coast?

A. And New York, yes, at present.

Q. When is she due here again, do you know? A. In about two weeks.

Q. Is the chief engineer still on board the 'Edith'? A. No, he is not there.

Q. Are any of the officers, to your knowledge, on the 'Edith' that were on her then?

A. Not any, to my knowledge. Yes—I think the first assistant.

Q. The log-books remained on the vessel, didn't they? A. I imagine they did.

Mr. McGRANN. I call for the production of the log-books bearing on this occurrence.''

(Apostles 47-48.)

The "Edith" did arrive in New York in April (80). Neither the logs were produced nor the depositions nor testimony offered of the chief or assistant engineers. The deposition of the second mate was taken in New York on May 15th. The same reluctance regarding the logs was shown by New York proctors as in San Francisco. The appellee's San Francisco proctor now admits that wherever the original logs were he took nothing but copies to the court.

Appelle says of the non-production of the logs *inter alios* (brief 53) that

"It is quite apparent that the log books could have had no bearing on the issues of fact tried before the court."*

---

*This concession of the appellee's brief came in reply to a brief in which (pp 15, 18) we had made the above point.

Mr. McGrann made it perfectly clear that he was seeking the log and engineer's testimony on the fact as to how long the supposedly damaged engine had been stopped before the disaster. We must therefore assume that the engine room logs would have shown that they were stopped long enough to have drifted from pier 42 to pier 32.

The failure to produce the engineer who would have refreshed his memory from the engineer's logs is as significant as the non-production of the log books. The adverse inference from his non-production is not dependent on any demand.

Now as to the bridge log and official log which were asked for during the cross-examination of the master. The master is required "immediately after the occurrence (collision) to cause a statement thereof and of the circumstances under which the same occurred," to be entered in the official log. A penalty is prescribed for not doing so (R. S. 4290, 4292). The universal practice of the sea calls for a full statement in the logs of every occurrence on the ship affecting her navigation or concerning any disaster to which she may be subject.

The captain said in his deposition that in his opinion the cause of the disaster was "getting the line in the wheel" (78). What did he say *in his log* as to the time when he knew the line got in the wheel? Under the theory of appellee's brief (53) that this log would not have conflicted with the captain, we are entitled to assume that he knew it was in the wheel when he was off pier 42, and that he drifted past piers 42, 40, 38, 36 and

34 to within 150 feet of pier 32 without dropping his anchors and before he even tried his engines to see if he could save his ship from the obvious danger.

II.

The "Edith's" Captain Could Have Saved Her During a Long Period After Passing Pier 42 When He Knew the Hawser Was Fouled, by Dropping His Anchors, and Herein of the Further Relevancy of the Logs and the Apparently Purposeful Agreement In an Admitted Untruth, by the "Edith's" Master and Second Mate.

In our last section we have shown that the "Edith's" captain knew off pier 42 that the hawser was caught in the propeller. He also knew that in such a contingency he was in danger and should have dropped his anchors. We now show that if he had done so his vessel would have not been injured.

An illuminating case on the effect on proximate causation of the failure to drop anchors to avoid damage after a proven fault by the tug is

The M. E. Luckenbach, 200 Fed 630.

In that case, the tug, through its fault, collided with a sailing vessel and was compelled to cast off the tow line of a barge. Like the "Edith" (with the captain's delusion as to his engines) the barge was without power and it was her duty to anchor. She failed to do so and grounded and was lost. The tug's fault was held not the proximate cause of the loss of the barge. The court says at p. 637.

"The situation, then, appears to have been this: There was a collision between the schooner and the barge 'Ropes', in which, however, the contact was so slight that no damage was done to either vessel. Nevertheless the captain of the 'Ropes', in the exercise of what is conceded to have been a wise precaution under the circumstances, cast off the hawser connecting the two following barges. It was the obvious duty of the captain of the 'Conner' to anchor at once, even if he had not been signaled by the tug to do so. Eventually he did so, dropping his 3,500-pound port anchor. The evidence shows that the bottom was good for anchorage; and that the anchor put over should have sufficed to hold such a barge, if sufficient chain were put out. Nevertheless, about 15 minutes later the barge was carried by the tide and cast aground on a shoal spot nearly three-quarters of a mile distant, with the 3,200-pound starboard anchor on board. The necessary conclusion is, either that the captain of the barge neglected to anchor until just before grounding, or that, although he did put over one anchor shortly after being cast off, the barge dragged on the anchor and he neglected to give out sufficient chain, or, at all events, to put over his second anchor. In view of the irreconcilable conflict in the testimony, it is very difficult to determine just what happened. Evidently Capt. Printz did not get his anchor down as quickly as he claims. But I believe that the barge dragged her anchor for a considerable part of the distance traversed, due to the action of the tide and swell on a short anchor chain. In either event the neglect on the part of the captain of the barge to take the simple precautions which the situation required constitutes the proximate cause of the stranding. It is not a case of concurrent fault on the part of the tug and the barge. The fault of the barge was not a contributing cause of the damages claimed. The evidence shows that Capt. Printz had ample opportunity, after learning that his barge was adrift, to anchor her. There was nothing in the surrounding circumstances to cause any particular excitement on the part of an experienced mariner in the fact that his barge was cast adrift, and he was ordered to anchor. It was a simple, obvious precaution, and called for the exercise of merely ordinary care. If Capt. Printz had exercised ordinary care, the barge would not have grounded.

The libel and petition are dismissed, without costs.''

The "Edith's" captain's and mate's excuse for not dropping his anchors was that his vessel was *only 40 feet* off pier 42 when the propeller fouled and that if he had dropped his anchors when so close to the docks she would have been swung against them by wind and tide and been injured.*

Our diagram in our opening brief showed that the "Edith's" drift, in the onsetting wind and tide, must have started from about seven hundred feet off pier 42 to have ended inside pier 32, as described by her captain. *The "Edith's" reply brief admits the correctness of this statement and names 700 feet as the distance the "Edith" backed from the dock's end* (appellee's brief p. 14). It is agreeable to be thus at one with our opponents on a point which we frankly disclosed in our opening brief as logically a necessity in our case.

The significant thing here is that the "Edith's" captain and mate swear circumstantially that the "Edith" reached but 40 feet from pier 44 when her moving out

---

*Appellee's suggestion that the "Edith's" captain refrained from dropping his anchors in the face of the common danger of the wind, tide and (undisclosed) disabling of the engine, because it would interfere with the *tug's* mareuvers (in ignorance of this danger) is dismissed with the comment that it was the best it could do for the "Edith's" captain.

from the wharves stopped and every force to which she
was subject, including her own engines (Apostles p. 36)
was thereafter setting her on the wharves. Their testimony is as follows:

"Q. Some projections on the side of the ship
were scraping along the dock?

A. Yes, sir, scraping along the dock.

Q. How long did you keep your engines slow
ahead at that time?

A. I should say three or four seconds.

Q. Was it what you could characterize as just
getting her under way? A. That is all."

"A. Then he kept on towing her until I should
judge she was 30 or 40 feet outside of the dock.

Q. Your bow was 30 or 40 feet beyond the end
of the dock? A. Yes, sir."*

(Capt. McDonald, p. 35.)

"Q. What happened when your bow was about
30 or 40 feet off the end of the pier?

A. I started slow ahead again, slow ahead, thinking the towboat was going to turn the ship around
by the stern."

(pp. 35-36).

"Q. How far was the bow of the 'Edith' distant
from the end of the piers then?

A. Somewhere about 30 feet I should judge.

Q. Of the pier ends? A. Yes.

Q. Had you drifted down along the piers?

A. Yes.

Q. Opposite what pier were you when you
stopped your engines?

A. Off pier 42 I believe."

(p. 38.)

---

*It will be noted that it was from pier 44, along which the "Edith"
had been scraping, that the 30 or 40 feet are to be measured. Not
pier 46 as appellee tries to explain it.

"Q. In the answer it is alleged in the last three lines of page 8 and the beginning of page 9 'that the steamship had been backed out of the slip and into the bay approximately 700 feet when the hawser had been cast off'; is that a correct statement?

A. No, I consider not.

Q. Did any part of your ship ever get 700 feet out into the stream? A. No, I don't think so.

Q. How far did you say your bow was when the second hawser was cast off?

A. About 30 or 40 feet from the end of the dock.''

(Captain McDonald, p. 44.)

"Q. Do you know what pier the ship was off when the tug cast off the tow-line?

A. She was off 44 then.''

(Second mate Hansen, p. 101.)

"Q. How far were you out at the time the 'Fearess' let go the stern-line?

A. About 30 or 40 feet.

Q. From what? A. From the dock.

Q. What end of the vessel was 30 or 40 feet from the dock. A. The bow.

Q. What did you do when you saw the 'Fearless' had let go the stern-line?

A. Gave the signal to the captain to stop the engines.

Q. Did the captain stop the engines?

A. Yes, sir.

Q. Was it necessary to stop the engines?

A. Yes, because the line was foul.''

(Second mate Hansen, pp. 83-84.)

"Q. The claimant's answer states that at the time the line was cast off by the 'Fearless' you were 700 feet away from the pier, is that so?

A. No, sir.

Q. Are you sure of it? A. Yes, sir.''

(Second mate Hansen, p. 85.)

These men were 200 feet apart from one another, looking at the dock end from different elevations on the ship, and from different angles and both state the *same exact figure* of distance from the dock which turns out to be untrue and absurdly and impossibly untrue.

We have no difficulty in determining why this extraordinary and untrue concurrence was attained by these two officers. The captain goes on to testify, despite the on setting wind and tide, that he drifted down parallel to the pier head lines and but 30 feet from them and closing in on them (62). He was asked the obvious question why if danger was imminent he did not drop his anchors and he says that he did not do so because the wind and tide would have swung him onto the docks because there was not clear room. He says:

"Q. Don't you think it would have retarded the ship if you had two anchors down under the forefoot?

A. It would have stopped her if you had got room.

Q. Aside from the room proposition would not two anchors underneath the forefoot have stopped the ship?

A. That seems to be a very material question because——

Q. What is your judgment about it?

A. When we anchor in the stream the anchor is supposed to hold the ship.

Q. What I want to know is, aside from what you have in mind about the swinging of the ship, would not the dropping of both anchors under the forefoot have brought her up in some position?

A. Yes, it would have turned her around.

Q. Now, then, if she had swung you think she would have swung onto the pier do you?

A. Onto the pier, yes, I do.

Q. Would she not have taken the course of the tide?

A. She would probably, after she got clear of the pier.

* * * * * * *

Q. Assuming that you were 30 or 40 feet out from the end of the piers and you have said that your ship would have stopped with two anchors down, and that she would have swung on the tide, and that the tide was parallel to the ends of the piers, don't you see that you would have had clearance off the pier then?

A. No, you are not giving us any allowance for the chain, the chain I would have to give the ship to pick her up."

(pp. 63-64.)

All this danger from swinging at anchor, rested on the theory that the "Edith's" line of drift was but 40 feet off the pier-head lines. With the drift commencing 700 feet off, the distance now agreed on by both parties, absolutely no excuse remains for not dropping the "Edith's" anchors as soon as the captain knew the line had fouled in the propeller. As we show in the diagram in our opening brief, he could have anchored his ship safely long before he reached pier head 32 against which he finally brought up.

Did the captain say *in his log* that the vessel was 700 feet from the dock when she began to drift and is this the reason why appellee's proctor admits the captain's and mate's figures are wrong by the difference between an exactly untrue 40 feet for each and the real 700 feet? Without any suggestions that this is the reason for its non-production, it may well be that the "Edith's" proctor, having invoked a high standard, admits the 700 feet rather than gainsay advantage from the failure of Eastern counsel to refresh the captain's memory from the log or offer it in evidence.

However this may be, the purposeful choice of 40 feet as the distance from the dock because it excused the failure of the "Edith's" captain to drop the anchors is very persuasive evidence that at the true distance of seven hundred feet the failure to drop them was entirely inexcusable.

We submit that it is clearly proven that for a considerable time after the tug dropped its hawser off pier 44 and until it had been hauled in so that the end fouled in the propeller, the ship's engines continued to turn ahead. That the captain was told the line had fouled and thereafter stopped his engines. That he was then off pier 42 and fully realized his danger. That his anchors were ready for dropping and would have saved his ship from any injury if dropped anywhere over a large part of his drift. That he did not drop them and that he assigned an admittedly untruthful reason for not doing so, and therefore that the "Edith" is responsible for the injury to her.

We submit further that the "Edith's" captain erred in not telling the tug's captain that he had resigned control to him so he could have ordered the anchors dropped as he undoubtedly would have if he had been told, at the same time, of the supposed condition of the "Edith's" engines.

III.

The "Edith" Could Have Reversed Her Engines From Pier 42 on and Have Saved Herself—and Herein of the Further Relevancy of the Logs.

The "Edith's" mate and the tug's captain agree that the tow line was dropped when the "Edith" was off pier 44 (101, 288). The "Edith's" captain says that his engines continued to go *ahead* for some time till the line fouled in his propeller, and that he thereafter stopped his engines, and began to drift. This drifting, after the known fouling of the line, began at pier 42. In view of the evidence grouped in the first chapter of this brief we must assume these facts to be true. We here show that if he had tried his engines at any point up to 300 feet of pier 32 he would have cleared that dock.

The significant thing in this connection is that both the "Edith's" captain and mate agree that during this period after the line was dropped the "Edith's" engines were *going ahead* (60, 98) and hence throwing the water behind the vessel from which the tow line stretched at full length on the water. That is to say, that as long as any considerable part of the line lay in the water, it would be driven *away from* the ship by the backward moving waters. It is hence not surprising that we find that it was the *eye on the end* of the hawser that fouled. Had the propeller been reversing and sucking the waters of the bay toward the ship, the result would probably have been different.

Proctors in argument suggest that the line may have fouled at some other point than the end. The answer to this is that the second mate who stood over it as it was hauled in, and must have known if it had fouled before then, says that it was the end (Hansen, 86, 100).

Since all this occurred before the ship had drifted past pier 42, it becomes immaterial how long anybody thought it would take to haul in the tow line. The "Edith's" second mate had three or four men to help him (89), and the tug's captain says it would take 5 minutes for two men to haul it in. Somebody else gives a guess of six minutes. Somebody else says there was a tide of from two to three miles. These are guesses as to time and rate and have little value against the statement of the captain that the process was finished and his engines stopped at a certain and definite place, viz: pier 42.

We submit that it was inexcusable error, causing the injury to the vessel, not to have at least tried his engines out somewhere between pier head 42 and pier head say 34, and determined whether they were, in fact, incapacitated. His failure even to ask the chief engineer whether he found any trouble with his engines (68) is a minor but important element in this negligence. That had the captain tried to use his engines at any place up to 300 feet of pier 32 he would have cleared her is apparent from the fact that starting them at 200 feet from the pier he cleared about two-thirds of her 327 foot length and he had little over 100 feet more to go. The testimony on this is as follows:

"Q. When this last hawser parted how far were you from pier 32?

A. We were probably 150 or 200 feet.

Q. At the time that the third hawser parted how was your stern with reference to the end of pier 32, was it inside of it, with reference to a line tending to cross the end of pier 32?

A. It would be pretty nearly square with it.

Q. So that the entire ship would be inside the end of pier 32?

A. Inside the dock, yes, inside of pier 32.

* * * * * * *

Q. There was no line between you and the tug?

A. No.

Q. What did you do when you got that report?

A. I went full speed astern, fragments of the seven-inch line was fast to the wheel.

Q. What happened then?

A. The ship went astern but not sufficient to clear the dock, pier 32.

Q. And you came into collision?

A. With the end of the dock.

Q. What part of the dock hit her?

A. The corner of the dock.

Q. Whereabouts did it hit on the 'Edith'?

A. Probably about one-third from the bow.

Q. One-third of the length aft? A. Yes."

(Apostles pp. 39, 40, 41.)

Did the captain in his account in the log of the circumstances leading to the collision with the dock confess his error in not trying out his engines? It may well have appeared there, though his testimony to the admittedly false 40 feet distance makes us doubt it. But should we have been denied the right, universally conceded in admiralty cases, of examining *for ourselves* the official log and the mate on the bridge who made the bridge log entries or else to see the bridge log and determine from one or another source what the records of the ship had to say about this disputed point.

IV.

The Line of the Tug Was Unloosened When the "Edith's" Engines Were Stopped—and Herein of the Further Relevancy of the Testimony of the Missing First Mate and Engineer and of Their Logs.

The captain of the tug says that the "Edith's" engines reversed and helped back her till she was 700 feet from pier 44, when he saw her propeller stop, and assumed that she was going no further astern (312, 313) and desired his presence at her bow. He unloosened his line (under the eye and control of the "Edith's" mate) and finally it was dropped in the water.

This assumption of the tug's captain is, in part, justified or not justified by a consideration of the point where the "Edith's" backing stopped and the length of time the engines were stopped between their going astern and turning ahead which both the "Edith's" captain and mate admit they were doing when the end fouled.

The "Edith's" captain says that he started to back slowly and then seeing the vessel was going astern too fast sent his engines ahead to stop her and then stopped his engines *before his vessel left the wharf, and that the tug then pulled her 40 feet beyond the dock,* without assistance from the "Edith" (58, 59) where the tug stopped towing and dropped the line. The two captains differ in two points (1) as to the "Edith's" distance from the docks when the towing stopped, and (2) as to whether the "Edith" continued reversing till she was 700 feet from the dock.

In view of the admission of the "Edith's" captain's untruthfulness about the 40 feet distance, we may be entitled to assume the same regarding his story as to the engines. However, is it not potent that the "Edith's" engineer could have told us whether he started reversing, after the first order to go ahead on his engines to check the backing, and that he could have refreshed his memory from his log? We submit that we are entitled to assume that the failure to produce either the engineer or his log is a confession that the allegation of our answer (Apostles 21) and the statement of the tug's captain is true, namely, that the "Edith" did continue to reverse till she was 700 feet out into the stream, and that her stopping indicated that this was as far as she intended to go.

The mate on the bridge, his bridge log, the official log, the engineer and the engine room log each had or should have had something to offer on these disputed questions. The "Edith" with the burden of proof on her, produces none of them and offers no explanation.

It will be remembered that the "Edith's" captain, who, it is undisputed, had command of the maneuver at any rate till the line was dropped, had provided no code of signals between the vessels and hence left to the discretion of the tug the interpretation of the "Edith's" intended maneuvers (appellant's opening brief, pp. 9, 10). It was not necessary for the tug to indicate by whistle that it had cast off its line when it did so under the eye of the mate only 30 fathoms away. The "Edith's" captain tells us that he expected to receive and give his information through the mate and not by whistle communication (56).

It is submitted that the libellant has not sustained its burden of proof, either that the "Fearless" was negligent in casting off its line when it saw the propeller stop 2100 feet from the place of collision, or that this act was the proximate cause of the loss where in the intervening two-fifths of a mile the "Edith" neither dropped her anchors nor reversed her engines, nor gave to any one else the knowledge of a necessity to do either of these things, or the power to compel her to do them.

V.

Appellee's "Out of the Record" Statements and Subsequent Admission That the Log Books Were Not in Fact Produced at the Trial Below. Its Failure to Introduce Them in the Trial de Novo in This Court.

At the hearing of the appeal, proctor for appellee interrupted appellant's argument to suggest that although it did not appear in the record, he had, in fact, in the lower court at the trial shown *the logs* or copies of them to the opposing counsel and that opposing counsel had indicated to him he had no interest in them. Appellee's brief (p. 52) says that the court may infer from the absence of any comment in the record that "the *books* were in fact produced and examined by appellant's counsel."

Appellee, in a letter to the court, now modifies this statement, and says that it did not have the log books at the trial in the lower court at all, but that at most it had copies of them which it *thinks* it showed to opposing counsel who tried the case in the lower court, but that it is willing to accept his statement as to whether or not he saw the log books or copies.

In response to appellee's out of the record statements at the hearing on the appeal and in the correspondence which this method of procedure necessitated, two telegrams were sent to Mr. Campbell, who tried the case in the court below. The telegrams and their replies are as follows:

"San Francisco, October 26, 1918.
Ira A. Campbell,
   Washington, D. C.
   Greetings: In Bull Fearless Case Griffiths and I made strong point logs not produced though demanded in New York depositions. Sutro intimates you declined examination of log which was in court room. This inconceivable to us. Gray and Griffiths both state did not see logs of 'Edith'. Please wire me statement which I can use in answer to Sutro if he makes oral statement at argument. I will not use it unless he intimates in court that his logs were in fact inspected or inspection was declined.
                 William Denman."

"Washington DC 1247P 29   1918 Oct 29 AM 10 04
William Denman
   Merchants Exchange San Francisco Calif.
   I have never seen log book of steamer Edith whose owner is suing shipowners Merchants Tugboat Company owner of tug Fearless for damages arising out of collision with pier in San Francisco harbor stop if log was in possession of counsel for Edith at time of trial before Judge Dooling it was never disclosed to me and I knew nothing of it notwithstanding previous demand had been made for its presentation.
                 Ira C. Campbell."

"San Francisco, November 20, 1918.
Ira A. Campbell,
　　Washington, D. C.
　　Bull Fearless Case. Referring Mr. Denman's wire to you and your reply regarding logs Mr. Sutro now says his recollection is that he showed you not the original logs but copies of the logs at the trial, but that you evidenced no interest in them. Neither Captain Gray nor myself recall having seen either logs or copies or having heard from the other side of either at the trial. Please wire me your recollection immediately.
　　　　　　　　Farnum P. Griffiths."

"1918 Nov 21 AM 8 48
AH Washington DC 101 5A 21
Farnham P. Griffiths
　　1107 Merchants Exchange Bldg San Francisco
　　Calif
What I said in my former wire to Denman about not having seen Ediths logs also applies to alleged copies thereof for I have never seen originals nor copies stop Mr. Sutro is mistaken in his recollection that he showed me copies of logs
　　　　　　　　Ira A. Campbell."

We may therefore assume it as a fact that the original logs were neither in the court room for production, nor their production waived. That is to say, the court is now relieved of the difficult task of inferring non-production, from the failure of the record to show production.

It is hard to see how an admiralty lawyer could for a moment consider a want of interest in *copies* as a waiver of production of the original log books. The entries in the bridge logs are made by different persons in the different watches appearing on each page and the different handwritings are identified by the signatures at the bottom of the page. If, for instance, the entries of the bridge log regarding the dropping of the hawser and the vessel's distance from pier 44 were made by the captain they would have a different evidentiary value from those of some other officer's. The failure to note an important matter in these entries by the captain would have a different value from absence of comment by the third mate who had no responsibility for the maneuver.

This is presuming the entries were true. But will anyone contend that the two officers, who testified so insistently and untruly that their vessel never proceeded more than 40 feet beyond pier 44, when their proctor admits that she was towed 700 feet, would hesitate to alter a log entry from 700 feet to 40 feet?

Would they hesitate to erase an entry to the effect that they knew beforehand that the tow line was to be cast off in time to tell the tug captain it did not fit into their plans and prevent the casting off,—such an entry as, that the second mate saw the deck hand start to unloosen the end?

Would they hesitate to alter an engine room log entry showing that the "Edith", in fact, did back out from the dock for a long distance and then did stop her engines for an appreciable time during which the tug may have dropped its lines in proper belief that it was as far as the "Edith" desired to go?

None of this would be shown in the copies, though quite likely discoverable in the originals.

The appeal is a trial *de novo*. Appellee was willing to go outside the record as to matters it thought had transpired at the trial below. *Why did it not produce the original log books at the hearing in the upper court or ask time within which to do so?* This it could have done without any discussion as to its propriety.

Appellee argumentatively suggests that the books would have thrown no light on the situation, but may it not be as mistaken in this inference it suggests the court should make, as it was regarding the inference that the books themselves were in the courtroom at the trial? Both are, of course, proper argumentative points on the record, but is the first inference any more warranted by the real facts than the second now turns out to be?

We submit that the log books, as well as the testimony of those who made the entries in them, are shown by the preceding chapters of this brief to be necessary for a full disclosure of the acts and intentions of the ''Edith''.

––––––

VI.

Appellee Has Not Explained the Failure to Produce the First Mate, His Bridge Log, the Official Log, the Man at the Wheel, the Engineer, the Assistant Engineer, the Engine Room Log and Scratch Logs, and Any of Her Seven or Eight Sailors Handling the Tow Lines, All of Whom Were Eye=Witnesses to Disputed Facts.

To sustain her burden of proof, the ''Edith'' attempted to show amongst other things (1) that she was but 40 feet from the dock when the tow line was dropped; (2) that she had not been reversing after leaving the dock and up to the time she was 700 feet off, and therefore that there was no stopping of her propeller as an indication to the tug that she was far enough off the docks; (3) that the propeller was going ahead when the line was dropped; (4) but stopped as soon as it was dropped; (5) that a very short time elapsed from the time the tow line was hauled in till she collided with the dock during which anything could have been done; (6) that his line of drift 40 feet off the docks was too close to permit him to anchor; (7) that her captain was warranted in not trying to use his engine to save himself in face of a known danger.

On all these points there was a disagreement which we believe on the evidence actually offered should be resolved against the libelant. It is apparent, however, that the first mate who was on the bow of the vessel, the man at the wheel, the sailors who handled the lines, the engineer, the assistant engineer and the four logs each had some evidence to give in one or another of the disputed points. They were not produced and their non-production is not explained.

It was not necessary to demand the logs to give us the inference from their non-production. The men who made the entries were not produced, and the adverse inference from their non-production is not dependent on any demand that they be put on the stand. They would have used the logs to refresh their memories and the demand for examination of the entries would be made on cross-examination as in the case of the captain.

But the logs were in fact properly demanded. A deposition is a part of the trial or becomes one as soon as introduced in evidence. The logs of a ship which are kept under the control of a vessel's captain and signed by him are properly demanded on his cross-examination.

The libelant, by its own act placed in the record the demand of opposing counsel for the log's production. It was as much a demand *at the trial* as the preceding questions and answers of the cross-examination properly leading up to the demand were evidence *at the trial.*

Counsel speaks of the depositions as having been "sealed" when sent to the court. We are not able to see the relevancy of this suggestion. Libelant's proctor who examined the captain in the deposition heard the demand, and the proctor at the hearing presumably read the depositions before he offered them in evidence and made the demand a part of the trial.

The cases cited by counsel are not relevant nor are the rules referred to. Both concern the right to an *inspection* of documents *prior to* the trial, analogous to the right of discovery in equity. They have nothing to do with the demand to produce a log *at the trial.*

Admiralty Rules 35 and 36 of the Supreme Court do not refer in any way to the production of documents. Proctor must have had in mind rules 35 and 36 of the District Court. These are as follows:

35. "Discovery of documents before trial.
After joinder of issue, and before trial, any party may apply to the court for an order directing any other party, his agent or representative, to make discovery, on oath, of any documents which are, or have been, in his possession or power, relating to any matter or question in issue. And the court may

order the production, by any party, his agent or
representative, on oath, of such of the documents
in his possession or power relating to any matter
in question in the cause as the court shall think
right, and the court may deal with such documents,
when produced, in such manner as shall appear
just.''

36. "Notice of production, before trial, of docum-
ments referred to in pleadings or affidavits.

Any party shall be entitled at any time, by notice
in writing, to require any other party in whose
pleadings or affidavits reference is made to any
document, to produce such document for the inspection of the party giving such notice, or of his
proctor, and to permit copies thereof to be taken;
and any party not complying with such notice within
five days, or such further time as may be allowed
by consent or by order of the court, shall not be at
liberty afterwards to put such document in evidence on his behalf, unless he shall satisfy the court
that he had some reason which the court shall deem
sufficient for not complying with such notice, in
which case the court may allow the document to be
put in evidence on such terms as it shall think fit.''

By their very title, these rules apply to the production or inspection *before* trial.

In *The Washtenaw*, 163 Fed. 372, the court merely
considers its power to give the equitable relief of discovery *before* trial, and the same is true of *Havemeyers
etc. Co. v. Compania Transatlantic Espanola*, 43 Fed. 90.

VII.

Summary of Tug's Answers to Various Arguments of Appellee.

Not "up to" tug to assume control. We have before
shown that the "Edith's" captain could not claim he

had transferred the dominion of the maneuver because he did not convey the information as to his delusion that his engines could not be used to assist, and give the tug the option to insist that the anchors be dropped, or to take another stern line and pull the "Edith" further out, or to try out the engines and see whether the "Edith" could not herself back out of danger as she in fact could.

Tug blameless in negotiations for the new tow line from the "Edith's" bow. However we may interpret the conflict of testimony as to the negotiations for the third tow line, we have shown that every act of the tug's captain was done in ignorance of the fact that the "Edith's" captain did not intend to assist with his engines which at any time, till the very end, could have backed her into safety. This is apparent from the fact that they did back her *two-thirds her length after the last line had been made fast* (which took considerable time) *and had parted* and that she cleared all but one remaining one hundred odd feet of her length and proceeded alone and unaided to Hunter's Point.

Can it be thought possible that the tug captain would not have instructed the "Edith's" captain to have tried to back his engines long before the "Edith" was within 200 feet of pier 32 if he had known that the command of the "Edith" had in fact been transferred to him? And yet if the attempt to back the "Edith" had been made at any time before she was within 300 feet of the pier, she would have gone clear. In any event if the tug's captain was to be made responsible for any delay or misunderstanding in the negotiations for the third line, he should have had intelligent freedom of choice.

The five dollars additional charge did not prevent the passing up of the hawser. The office manager of the tow boat company who was not an eye witness said:

> "Q. Now, captain, if the 'Edith' had engaged for the tug's lines, or if she had an understanding with you that in case she wanted them she was to have them, would that 12-inch hawser have been passed up to the 'Edith'? A. Yes, sir." (269-270.)

And, again:

> "The only reason it was not passed out is that it was not engaged for." (259.)

This at best is mere after-opinion of an absent party, but it clearly means that if the contract had been definitely made, the tug's captain might have carried it out on the demand of the "Edith's" captain even if he did not believe it was the best thing to do.

Can it be supposed that the mere question of $5.00 would have influenced the tug's captain if he had been told that the "Edith's" engines were dead, and that she was a mere helpless barge? In viewing this case it must be always borne in mind that the "Edith" knew she would not use her engines and that the tug's captain did not.

The "Edith's" captain acquiesced in the tug's going to the "Edith's" bow and taking a line there. After the tow line was dropped the tug was at all times within hailing distance of the "Edith". Her captain, knowing he did not intend to use her engines, permitted the tug to steam along her starboard side to her bow, negotiate there for a time, gave out the line, and *motioned to the tug to pull the "Edith's" head to starboard* (66). He knew that the tug was entitled to believe his engines were in good condition because he had not told the tug's captain to the contrary. If the engines had been working the distaster would not have happened. If the "Edith's" captain had ordered the tug to take a tow line at the stern he would have easily hauled her back *lengthwise* and the disaster would not have occurred. Instead, he acquiesced in the tug attempting a maneuver dangerous because of the unknown crippling of the engines,—the maneuver which compelled the tug to travel the greatest distance and to exert the greatest strain on the hawser, i. ρ., at right angles to her length, while it would move the "Edith" the minimum distance from pier 32.

The tug's willingness to attempt to tow from the bow of the steamer after dropping the line is no excuse for not dropping anchors. The "Edith" should have dropped her anchors or should have told the tug captain that her propeller was disabled (or conclusively thought to be) and left it to the tug to determine whether the anchors should be dropped. As she did neither, her acquiescence in the tug's movement to the bow and giving the tug a tow line is an acceptance of any result which might have been prevented if the anchors had been dropped or if the tug, knowing the real danger, had been permitted to use that or some other method of extricating the "Edith" from her position.

Absurd to say that "Edith's" captain should have refrained from dropping her anchors because it would interfere with tug's proposed maneuver. The tug did not know of the prime necessity for dropping anchors, i. e., the concealed delusion as to the engines. The "Edith" is estopped to say that she yielded her right to drop anchors to the tug's maneuver, unless she told the tug of the new and dangerous condition affecting the probability of success.

VIII.

The "Edith's" Faults Are Clearly Shown and This Court Should Decide the Case on Its Merits.

Appellee's brief cites certain cases where the court had refused to disturb the decree of the court below, but they none of them present the following features distinguishing this case:

(1) In none has the captain when under oath said that the proximate cause was a particular act as her "getting the line in the wheel" (78) while not a word concerning fouled propeller or caught tow line appears in the libel (4 to 12).

(2) In no one of them did the successful party's own depositions clearly prove that his vessel was in the wrong as is shown by those of the "Edith's" captain and second mate in this case. As it stands, it clearly appears that if everything in the oral testimony be taken as true, nevertheless the appellee's depositions show the "Edith" in unexcusable fault and that her fault is the proximate cause of the collision.

(3) In no one of them has the successful vessel failed to produce the ship's official log, her first mate,

who was on the forecastle head, the log he kept, the man at the wheel, the engineer and assistant, the engine room logs and any of the eight or nine sailors handling the lines, and rested its case on but two depositions in which appears such a purposeful coincidence of testimony as the two statements of a 40 foot distance from the dock when their own proctor admits it to have been 700 feet.

(4) In no one of them did the vessel drift for 1800 feet in plain sight of her danger and then collide with the dock in broad daylight with her anchors at the bow and her engines, though in good condition, not used till the last 200 feet of the drift.

(5) In no one of them did the captain of the successful vessel in the suit confess to a delusion as to his engines which converted his vessel from a powered steamer into a barge, which fact he concealed from the tug he claims was in control and which he was to assist.

(6) In no one of them did the lower court fail to follow this court's requirement to render an opinion to show what the line of reasoning was by which it reached the conclusion which this court is asked to accept.

Taking up the lower court's findings, one by one:

"1. The master of the 'Fearless' was at fault in not consulting with the master of the 'Edith' as to the maneuvers intended by him before he undertook to execute them."

We say that the deposition of the "Edith's" captain and mate show that her captain was in command at the start of the maneuver; that he established no method of communication with the tug, and that he is responsible if faulty planning was the cause of its failure.

"2. He was also at fault in casting off the line without warning and while the 'Edith's' wheels were turning."

We say that the depositions of the "Edith's" captain shows he contemplated that the second mate at the hawser end should be the eye of the ship and that the unloosening of the hawser under the mate's eye without protest was an acquiescence in subsequently dropping it, and that permitting the tug to come to the bow and giving it a line there was further acquiescence; and that the failure to tell the tug that the propeller was fouled and that the "Edith's" captain would not attempt to start it estops the "Edith" from claiming that the fault, if any, in dropping the line transferred the dominion from the steamer to the tug.

"3. To these faults the accident was due."*

We say that the depositions of the captain and mate show conclusively (corroborated by the failure to produce logs or other witnesses) that the so-called faults were not the proximate cause of the loss but that the cause of the loss was the failure to drop anchors off pier 42 (1800 feet from pier 32) when the captain thought his propeller fouled and concluded not to use it, but concealed that fact from the tug; or, that the cause of the loss was the "Edith's" failure to try her engines and back out of the danger, as she could have done up to within 300 feet of pier 32; that the

---

*We have fully discussed contributory negligence and division of damages in our opening brief at page 43.

"Edith" is estopped to say the tug caused the loss as she did not advise the tug that she had passed the responsibility up to the tug with full information that she was no longer a powered boat but was converted into a barge.

> "4· The 'Fearless' should have passed to the 'Edith', after letting go of her and while she was drifting, a line of sufficient strength to hold her and should have been prepared to do so. This was not done."

We say that this court must examine the testimony on this point as the District Court did not find that the discussions and delay (if any) over the third hawser was causative of the loss. The tug is not to blame for not passing up the heavy line if it did not think it practicable at the time it was requested. All her acts must be viewed with reference to her ignorance of the (mental) disability of the steamer's engines and her belief that the steamer could back herself into safety.

> "5· The 'Edith' was not at fault for not dropping her anchor, as she was entitled to believe that the 'Fearless' would care for her properly."

We have shown the error in this finding in the answers to the other four. All the testimony we have from the "Edith" shows that the "Edith" is estopped to say that command had been passed "up to the tug", because she did not tell the tug she could not use her engines and also because she acquiesced in the tug's coming to tow her round from the bow, a maneuver possible of success only if the "Edith's" engines helped. In the absence of notice of the fouled propeller, the tug must be exonerated, for it is clear that its conduct would have been entirely different had it known the facts, or that its function had been converted from an "assist" into a "command".

Prayer.

WHEREFORE, we pray that the decree of the District Court be reversed and that the "Edith" be declared solely in fault and the libel dismissed.

Dated, San Francisco,
    November 27, 1918.

Respectfully submitted,

WILLIAM DENMAN,

McCUTCHEN, OLNEY & WILLARD,

Proctors for Appellant.

No. 3199

IN THE

United States Circuit Court of Appeals

For the Ninth Circuit

SHIPOWNERS AND MERCHANTS TUGBOAT COMPANY (a corporation), claimant of the American Steam Tug "Fearless", her boilers, engines, tackle, apparel and furniture,

Appellant,

vs.

A. H. BULL & COMPANY, INC. (a corporation),

Appellee.

REPLY BRIEF FOR APPELLEE.

Upon Appeal from the Southern Division of the United States District Court for the Northern District of California, First Division.

DEC 6 -

E. S. PILLSBURY,
F. D. MADISON,
ALFRED SUTRO,
OSCAR SUTRO,
Proctors for Appellee.

(a corp
Steam T
tackle, a

vs.

A. H. Bru

———

Upon App

Appella
the argun
court in
"Edith's
the same
page 52
p. 22)

We sta
that we h

SHIPOWNERS AND MERCHANTS TUGBOAT COMPANY
(a corporation), claimant of the American
Steam Tug "Fearless", her boilers, engines,
tackle, apparel and furniture,

Appellant,

vs.

A. H. BULL & COMPANY, INC. (a corporation),

Appellee.

No. 3199

REPLY BRIEF FOR APPELLEE.

Upon Appeal from the Southern Division of the United States District Court for the Northern District of California, First Division.

Appellant's counsel now makes the suggestion that on the argument in this court we attempted to mislead the court in respect to the possible presence of the "Edith's" log books at the trial in the court below. At the same time counsel incorrectly states what we said at page 52 of our opening brief. (Appellant's Reply, p. 22.)

We stated at the argument that it was our impression that we had exhibited copies of the log books to opposing counsel; that our recollection was not sufficiently clear on the subject to justify a positive statement in that respect. No demand of any kind having been made after the case was set for trial before Judge Dooling, nor during the trial, for the production of the log books, there was obviously no occasion to bring them to court, and our recollection is clear, of course, that the books were not in court. We made no statement to this court to the contrary.

Claiming that he thought the court had been misled by our remarks on this subject, Mr. Denman, of appellant's counsel, requested that we address a letter to this court stating the facts. This we did by letter dated November 19, 1918, as follows:

"To the Honorable, the Judges of the United States Circuit Court of Appeals, Ninth Circuit.

Dear Sirs:

Mr. Denman, counsel for appellant in the above case, has requested that I state to the court the facts in regard to the logs of the steamship 'Edith.' I therefore take the liberty of addressing this letter to the court.

Mr. Denman observes that the trial has 'wandered * * * far out of the record,' and refers to our remarks at page 59 of our brief. We there say that none of the cases cited by him hold that

'there is a presumption that the demand for the log books of a vessel was refused because the record does not affirmatively show that the logs were produced. Indeed it may well be that in this case the logs, or copies thereof, were exhibited *by* (should be *to*) counsel for claimant during the progress of the trial, and that he considered them of as little consequence on the issues involved in this case as did counsel for the libelant.'

Mr. Denman is apprehensive that the quoted matter may mislead the court as 'an out of record statement of fact.' It is argument pure and simple, and the court no doubt will so consider it.

In point of fact, the depositions taken in New York contain the only demand·in the record for the logs. The depositions were filed but were not read at the trial. Whether or not the logs were produced in New York when the demand was made does not appear; the record is silent in this regard. The fact, however, is that from the time the depositions were taken in New York in March, 1917, until the filing of appellant's brief in this court in October, 1918, neither the court nor counsel on either side made mention of either the original log books or their presence or absence. There was, therefore, no occasion to have had them in court. I was under the impression that at the trial before Judge Dooling I showed Mr. Campbell copies of the logs, but that he evinced no interest in them. If his recollection differs from mine on this point, I am willing to abide by his.

I am sending a copy of this letter to Mr. Denman.

Very respectfully,

Oscar Sutro."

In the face of the concluding statement in the foregoing letter, appellant's counsel telegraphed to Mr. Campbell, giving his own recollection, the recollection of Captain Gray, and reply from Mr. Campbell followed that we are mistaken in our recollection.

Therefore, says counsel, the court now knows that the logs were not produced, "nor their production waived". (Appellant's Reply, p. 24.)

This method of supplementing the record is new in the practice as we know it. It would appear that counsel's request to us to clear up what he deemed an ambiguity in our argument to the court was to lay the foundation for correspondence which might be injected into a reply brief, and which is found at page 24 of appellant's reply. Mr. Denman's apparent purpose is, by the use of correspondence between various counsel for appellant, framed to supplement an otherwise silent record, to bolster up a position which on the record is untenable.

The further suggestion is now made by counsel in a brief served on us one month after the argument, that the log books should have been produced at the hearing in this court. Counsel's complaint at the argument was that these books were not produced in the court below, and until the filing of his reply on November 27, 1918, not the slightest intimation or suggestion was made by counsel for appellant that he either desired to see the log books, or that their inspection would be helpful to him in the preparation of his appeal.

THE LOGS WERE NOT USED IN EVIDENCE BY EITHER SIDE BECAUSE THE MATERIAL FACTS ARE UNDISPUTED.

We suggested in our brief that the logs were not used in evidence by counsel on either side, because they could throw no light on the salient facts of the case. An examination of the grounds on which appellant thinks the logs were material confirms our argument.

I. Appellant suggests the log books were important to determine:

the captain of the "Edith's" "causal responsibility" as related to the stoppage of the engines. (Appellant's Reply, pp. 1-9.)

But every witness in the case agreed that when the tug cast off the line it was the captain's duty to stop his engines. (Appellant's Brief, pp. 11-14.) It is admitted that the "Edith's" mate signalled the captain to stop his engines immediately after the line was cast off (Claimant's Answer, p. 15), and not disputed that the captain stopped his engines immediately upon the signal.

Nor was the element of time between the dropping of the line and the collision in serious dispute. The tug witnesses swore that it was five to seven minutes. (Apostles, pp. 330, 176, 337.) The tug's captain knew, as an expert, that when the line was dropped it was necessary to stop the engines, and he required no information from the "Edith's" master on the subject. (Apostles, p. 324; Appellee's Brief, pp. 13-14.)

The logs could clear up nothing here.

II. Appellant argues that:—

the "Edith" could have saved herself by dropping her anchors. (Appellant's Reply, pp. 9-16.)

The captain did not drop them: at first, because it would have blocked the tug's maneuver; later, because it would have been dangerous, as is admitted by the tug's witnesses. (Appellee's Brief, pp. 33-36.) In any event, *it is an undisputed fact in the case that the anchors were not dropped.* The logs could add nothing to the admitted fact.

The case of *The M. E. Luckenbach,* 200 Fed. 630, cited by counsel in this connection, is clearly distinguishable, for there, one of three barges was cast adrift and failed to anchor after the tug, which had charge of the operation, ordered it to anchor.

III. Appellant argues that

the "Edith" could have reversed her engines and have saved herself. (Appellant's Reply, pp. 17-20.)

She did not reverse: at first, because until the line which the tug had cast off was hauled in, her engines had to be stopped to prevent further or any fouling. All of the witnesses agreed on this (Appellee's Brief, p. 13, pp. 38-39); later, when she did reverse, she was *in extremis.*

In any case it is an undisputed fact that the "Edith's" engines were either stopped or remained stopped after the tow line was cast off, and that they were not reversed until the line had been hauled in and the vessel *in extremis.* Again the logs could show no more than the undisputed facts.

IV. Finally counsel makes the point that

the line of the tug "was unloosened" when the "Edith's" engines were stopped. (Appellant's Brief, pp. 20-22.)

We referred in our brief to the admission in the answer that the tug cast off the line while the "Edith's" engines were turning (Appellee's Brief, p. 16), and while some of the witnesses testified that the "Edith's" engines were stopped when the tow line was dropped (ib. p. 6, Apostles, p. 313), others said the engines were turning at the time. (Apostles, pp. 97, 192, 197.) But, as pointed out in our brief (p. 16), the casting off of the tow line required the engines to be stopped, and the "Edith" was bound to drift while the line was being hauled in.

The logs could add nothing to the facts for whether they showed the engines turning or not, when the tow line was dropped, the fact that it was dropped without notice rendered the "Edith" equally helpless until it was hauled in and justified the captain's reliance on the tug to complete the operation.

Finally, we note the argument that the logs might have shown that the "Edith" reversed her engines "till she was 700 feet out into the stream, and that her stopping indicated that this was as far as she intended to go." (Appellant's Brief, p. 21.) This is not disputed by either side in the case.

The logs, therefore, would add nothing on this point.

The difficulty with the tug's case is that it dropped the tow line at a distance of 700 feet from the docks without notice to the "Edith" and thus rendered impossible the movement contemplated by the captain of the "Edith," namely, to pivot his vessel while the tug held fast to the stern of the ship. As counsel now admits the "Edith's" captain "had command of the maneuver at any rate till the line was dropped." (Appellant's Reply, p. 21.) After that the tug was responsible, the tug's captain having assumed to act on his own judgment.

These, then, are the four points advanced by counsel as subject to illumination by the production of the logs. In each the facts are admitted.

Is it not obvious from counsel's argument that there was no issue in the case on which the logs could be material, and no facts to be proved by the logs? And is that not plainly the reason why so careful an attorney as Mr. Campbell neither demanded the log books, nor noted their absence, and that they have no importance except such as Mr. Denman now seeks to attribute to the failure to use them as evidence?

We except to the suggestion made by appellant at page 7 of the reply that counsel for libellant in New York or here were "reluctant" regarding the production of evidence. It is a gratuitous statement unfounded in fact and unwarranted by the record.

There is one point concerning the merits of the case which the appellant for the first time emphasizes in its last brief. It seems to be assumed by appellant that sinister purposes underlay the error of the captain as to the distance at which he found himself from pier No. 42 at the moment that the tug dropped her tow without warning to him. Considering the "Edith's" captain's unfamiliarity with San Francisco harbor, the varying lengths of the piers opposite which he was cast adrift, the rapid succession of events, and the excitement of the occasion, it is not remarkable that twelve months later, in giving his deposition in New York, he should have erroneously estimated his distance from the piers when the tug dropped her tow. In any event, the further out he was, the easier it was for the tug to perform the maneuver contemplated by her, and the less excuse there was for the tug's letting go of the tow.

The argument of appellant that the accident was caused by the "Edith's" failure to drop her anchors is already answered in our brief, but it may be appropriate to point out that at best dropping anchors in such a case is a recourse *in extremis* which may *prevent* an accident; but that the failure to drop them does not, therefore, *cause* the accident.

The gist of appellant's reply is based on the suggestion of non-production of testimony, the possible relevancy of which to the issues in this case is not apparent. The *tug* is the vessel whose conduct is under investigation. It is useless to attempt to shift the issue. If the tug was not justified in her conduct, the decree should be affirmed. Whether or not she was justified was at least the principal issue under investigation by the trial court, and on which the determination of this controversy rested. No conduct on the part of the "Edith" could have rendered her solely liable, for at best any maneuver which she might have undertaken would have been defensive and to save herself *in extremis* from the actions of the tug. The case was so viewed and tried by the court and by all counsel until the advent of Mr. Denman in the case. On those issues the non-production of the evidence of which he now complains could have thrown no light. We submit that it is too late now to urge this court to reverse a decree because testimony was not adduced which counsel on neither side asked for, and which counsel on neither side apparently wanted, and the absence of which was not even called to the attention of or noted by the trial court.

We submit that the decree should be affirmed.

Dated, San Francisco,
    December 2, 1918.

                    Respectfully submitted,
                            E. S. PILLSBURY,
                            F. D. MADISON,
                            ALFRED SUTRO,
                            OSCAR SUTRO,
                            Proctors for Appellee.

Index

No. 3199

United States Circuit Court of Appeals

For the Ninth Circuit

SHIPOWNERS AND MERCHANTS TUGBOAT COMPANY (a corporation), claimant of the American Steam Tug "Fearless", her boilers, engines, tackle, apparel and furniture,

Appellant,

vs.

A. H. BULL & COMPANY, INC. (a corporation),

Appellee.

APPELLANT'S REPLY TO APPELLEE'S SECOND GROUP OF "OUT OF THE RECORD" STATEMENTS.

I.

Appellee's Erroneous "Out of the Record" Statement That Appellant Has Shifted Its Ground on Appeal.

It is with great discomfort that we are again called upon by the reply brief of the appellee to consider and refute new and further "out of the record" statements of too serious import to the interest of our client to warrant our ignoring them. This last brief of the appellee suggests a shifting of the tug's theory of the case on the appeal, when a new proctor for the tug was added.

The court will recall that, in our briefs heretofore filed, it has been our contention that the proximate cause of the damage to the "Edith" was (1) either the failure to drop her anchors or to try out her engines when her captain knew, off pier 42, that a piece of tow line had caught in her propeller; or (2) the failure to tell the captain of the tug of this mishap and transfer the command of the maneuver to him, with full knowledge, so that *he* could have the choice of ordering the dropping of the anchors, or the trying out of the propeller, or of towing from the stern directly away from the docks, instead of attempting to tow from the port bow of the "Edith", under the erroneous belief that he was to receive the assistance of her reversing engines. We contended that this was the proximate cause of the loss, because, despite previous mishaps, there was abundant time and distance between pier 42 and pier 32 to have brought her to a place of safety. This was made clear beyond the question of a doubt by the showing that her reversing in the last two hundred feet of the sixteen hundred feet between pier 42 and pier 32 brought the "Edith" within one hundred and ten feet of safety; that is, within one hundred and ten feet of clearing pier 32, and backing far out into the bay to a point of complete safety.

Our contention here involved the fault of the "Edith" and her captain as the proximate cause of the injury and as rendering the tug entirely free from liability.

The appellee, in its last brief, makes, at page 9, the following statement to the effect that this was not the position taken by the tug in the lower court:

> "The gist of appellant's reply is based on the suggestion of non-production of testimony, the possible relevancy of which to the issues in this case is not apparent. The tug is the vessel whose conduct is under investigation. It is useless to attempt to shift the issue. If the tug was not justified in her conduct, the decree should be affirmed. Whether or not she was justified was at least the principal issue under investigation by the trial court, and on which the determination of this controversy rested. *No conduct on the part of the 'Edith' could have rendered her solely liable, for at best any maneuver which she might have undertaken would have been defensive and to save herself in extremis from the actions of the tug. The case was so viewed and tried by the court and by all counsel until the advent of Mr. Denman in the case.*"

This statement involves the consideration of the brief of the proctors for the tug in the District Court, for in that brief necessarily are embodied the tug's views of the issue under which the case was there tried. This brief is not a part of the Apostles. The appellee does not offer it now, but asks the court to proceed on its statement of this "out of the record" evidence.

Mr. Denman's advent in the case came in the summer of 1918, when he was associated with Mr. Farnham P. Griffiths of the firm of McCutchen, Olney & Willard in the preparation of the briefs in this court.

The arguments in the tug's brief in the District Court on the question of proximate causation are summarized in the following captions of different chapters of the brief:

"THE CONTRACT WAS FOR AN 'ASSIST', NOT A TOWAGE. The tug was an attendant on the steamer, not chargeable with responsibility of a tug in control of the operation, for the steamer was under her own power and in command of her master."
(Tug's brief District Court, page 2.)

"The collision was *solely* caused by the negligent handling of the 'Edith'."
(Tug's brief District Court, page 15.)

"The getting of the line in the wheel was *solely* the 'Edith's' fault in working her engines while hauling in the line."
(Tug's brief District Court, page 26.)

"The letting go of the line by the 'Fearless' was not negligence, and she did not thereby become responsible for the failure of the 'Edith' to avoid collision with pier 32."
(Tug's brief District Court, page 37.)

"The 'Edith' failed in her duty to furnish a good line to the 'Fearless'."
(Tug's brief District Court, page 41.)

"The failure of the 'Edith' to anchor caused the collision."
(Tug's brief District Court, page 49.)

"The failure of the master to go astern on the 'Edith's' engines caused the collision."
(Tug's brief District Court, page 52.)

It is submitted that Mr. Denman's advent in the case has not in the slightest way changed the tug's attitude towards the collision, which has been from the beginning that the "Edith" was solely at fault. We are not aware of a word of the tug's proctors in the record in the lower court which indicated, in the slightest way, that the tug, at any time, had any other position, than that the "Edith's" negligence was the *sole* proximate cause of the collision.

We submit that the charge of shifting the theory of the case on the addition of a new proctor on appeal is not borne out by a consideration of the "out of the record" evidence on which the charge necessarily rests.

II.

Appellee's Erroneous "Out of the Record" Statements Concerning a Failure to Call the Lower Court's Attention to Absence of Testimony.

We regret to note a further "out of the record" statement of the appellee which is not borne out by the facts. The appellee's reply brief says, at page 9:

> "The gist of appellant's reply is based on the suggestion of non-production of *testimony*, the possible relevancy of which to the issues in this case is not apparent. * * * ' We submit that it is too late now to urge this court to reverse a decree because the *testimony* was not adduced which counsel on neither side asked for and which counsel on neither side apparently wanted, *and the absence of which was not even called to the attention of or noted by the trial court.*"

In our briefs in this court, we have called to the attention of the court the absence of the testimony of the various witnesses on the "Edith", which would have had a vital bearing on the case. We have pointed out that even if we had not demanded the logs, the testimony of these witnesses, or, at any rate a portion of them, would, undoubtedly, have been refreshed from the logs, or would have caused, on cross-examination, the production of the logs.

We have summarized our contention in this court on this question in the following headings of our reply brief:

> "I. The 'Edith's' captain let her drift from off pier 42 almost to pier 32 in plain view of her danger without dropping his anchors or attempting to use his engines—*and herein of the relevancy of the non-production of witnesses* and logs."

> "IV. The line of the tug was unloosened when the 'Edith's' engines were stopped—and herein of *the further relevancy of the testimony of the missing first mate and engineer* and of their logs."

> "VI. Appellee has not explained the failure to produce the first mate, his bridge log, the official log, the man at the wheel, the engineer, the assistant engineer, the engine room log and scratch logs, and any of her seven or eight sailors handling the tow lines, all of whom were eyewitnesses to disputed facts."

The testimony in the case shows that the first mate and the engineer were primarily responsible for the keeping of the bridge and engine room logs.

At page 52 of the tug's brief *in the lower court,* the failure to produce the testimony of these two officers

and other officers and members of the crew is called
to the attention of the District Court in the following
language:

> "What did the master do to prevent the col-
> lision? Not a single solitary thing. It did occur
> to him that he ought to do something (Dep. 36), but
> he didn't do it until too late. He could readily
> see that they were in a position of danger from
> drifting down, and knew that they surely must
> bring up against something (Dep. 42). After the
> line was in the wheel, did he have any communica-
> tion with the engine room? No. Did he send any
> word to the engineers about it? *No* (Dep. 42).
> Yet he drifted from off pier 42 to between piers
> 34 and 32 (Dep. 42-3). He really thought he did
> go aft, but could not remember even that—'I swear
> I think I did—no, I could not say that I did (Dep.
> 35). Apparently, he remained on the bridge, did
> not examine the line, did not have any communica-
> tion whatever with the engineers—in fact, did
> nothing! Splendid seamanship, wasn't it? *Is it
> any wonder that the first mate, or the chief en-
> gineer, or any of the other officers or members of
> the crew were not called as witnesses to inform us
> as to what was done aboard ship?"*

Since appellee has invoked this "out of the record"
method in the trial of the case, we will have to beg the
court to assume that, unless appellee contradicts our
assertion as to the contents of the brief in the lower
court, our excerpts from it are to be deemed correct.

We submit that counsel's remarks about the failure
to call the absence of testimony to the attention of the
District Court are not borne out by the brief of the tug
in that court.

III.

Inaccuracies in Appellee's Reply Brief on the Question of the Time it Took the "Edith" to Drift From Pier 42 to Pier 32 in Its Attempt to Excuse the Non=Production of the Testimony of the Engineer or the Evidence of His Log.

One of the vital questions in this case has been the time occupied by the "Edith" in drifting from pier 42, where the captain discovered that the line was in his propeller, to pier 32 on which the "Edith", who had been backing at the last instant, was impaled somewhere around one-third of the distance from her bow.

Concerning this, appellee's reply brief at p. 5 says:

> "Nor was the element of time between the dropping of the line and the collision in serious dispute. The tug's witnesses swore that it was five to seven minutes (Apos. pp. 330, 176, 337.)"

The Apostles at the pages indicated say nothing of the kind. At page 176 nothing is said about the length of time the "Edith" drifted, nor is there anything from which that time could be inferred. The only testimony on that page is that of the tug's deckhand as to the length of time it would have taken the "Edith" to haul in a tow line.

At page 330 the tug's captain says:

> "A. *As soon as I got under the bow I laid there all the time while he was drifting.*
> Q. You *drifted together* from that position to where you say you got the line?
> A. To where I got the line.
> Q. How long did it take you to go that distance?

A. It was a long time, I imagined—possibly 8 minutes—6 or 7 minutes, somewhere around there.''

The most that can be said for this testimony is that it took somewhere between 6 and 8 minutes, after the tug had dropped its line from the stern of the ''Edith'' and had gone to her bow, where she lay all the time they were drifting together, to drift to the point where the tug took the ''Edith's'' third tow line. The period of time *before* this, i. e., from the dropping of the line to the arrival of the tug, which had to turn clean around, at the bow of the vessel, is not included. The period of time *after* the tug took the third line, which included the movement of the tug from the port bow of the ''Edith'' to the end of the line, the starting of the tug's engines in towing, and up to the time of the breaking of the line and thereafter, the period during which the ''Edith'' backed herself from dead in the water to over 200 feet astern, is also not included.

More than this, the tug's captain testified, in supplement to his estimate of six to eight minutes of the drift together, that it took three or four minutes for him to move from the point where he dropped his line *to admidships* on the ''Edith's'' starboard side. This testimony is as follows:

''Q. How long did it take you, captain, to go around after the line had been cast off, to this position amidships of the 'Edith'?
A. Possibly four minutes.
Q. Four minutes? A. Three or four minutes.
Q. Three to four minutes? A. Yes.
Q. It took you three or four minutes to come from the stern of the 'Edith' around on the starboard side until you were about amidships?

A. About that.

Q. Three or four minutes? A. Yes.

Q. In those three or four minutes she drifted from the position opposite pier 44 to a position amidships between 44 and 42? A. Yes."

(Apos. pp. 337-8.)

How long it took for the "Edith" to drift from the point where the tow boat took the third line, to the collision—covering the transactions in running to the end of the line, applying power, breaking the lines and backing the "Edith" over 200 feet from a standstill —is not estimated; but it is fair to presume that it took not less than four minutes.

This would make it a fair inference from the captain's testimony, that not less than *fifteen* minutes were consumed in drifting from off pier 42, where the "Edith's" captain learned that the line was in his propeller, to the point of collision.

Appellee, in his last brief, clearly disputes this, and says that it was between 5 and 7 minutes.

We ask again, how can the appellee, in view of this conflict, excuse the non-production of its engineer? In the ordinary course of his duties, he would enter in his engineer's log (1) the time off pier 42, when the captain, believing the line in the wheel, ordered him to stop his engines; and (2) the time he started his engines again to go astern just before she struck pier 32, and (3) the time when the "Edith" crashed into the pier. The engineer in making these entries glances at the clock and puts the time down to the very minute. The testimony shows that the entries presumably were made (Apos. p. 48.) Did the appellee fear that if the engineer were produced his cross-examination, based upon his log, would show that the tug's captain's estimate was correct; namely, that there was a period of nearly 15 minutes during which the ''Edith'' could have dropped her anchors, or at least have made the attempt to find out whether the imagined disablement of her propeller, in fact, existed?

Conclusion.

In conclusion, we desire to beg counsel and the court to believe us when we say that it will take a third wandering from the record to convince us that any of these errors of statement were intentional. We regret that they were not of such slight bearing on the issues that, without damaging our client's interest, we could have ignored them.

Dated, San Francisco,
December 21, 1918.

Respectfully submitted,

WILLIAM DENMAN,

McCUTCHEN, OLNEY & WILLARD,
Proctors for Appellant.

No. 3199

United States Circuit Court of Appeals

For the Ninth Circuit

SHIPOWNERS AND MERCHANTS TUGBOAT COMPANY
(a corporation), claimant of the American
Steam Tug "Fearless", her boilers, engines,
tackle, apparel and furniture,

Appellant,

vs.

A. H. BULL & COMPANY, INC. (a corporation),

Appellee.

APPELLANT'S PETITION FOR A REHEARING.

*To the Honorable William B. Gilbert, Presiding Judge,
and the Associate Judges of the United States
Circuit Court of Appeals for the Ninth Circuit:*

With all deference, we beg to point out that the opinion in this case does not touch on the five principal points raised in our briefs and at the argument. It is written as if the brief had never been filed, or the argument heard. Also, we beg to show a decision of the Circuit Court of Appeals of the Second Circuit reported since the decision here, which seems in direct conflict on the question of the failure to drop anchors.

The opinion finds that it was negligence for the tug to have dropped its tow line when it did; and that it was not negligence for the steamer not to have dropped her anchors during the period in which she drifted over 1800 feet towards the obvious point of danger.

The court also finds that the fouling of the tow line required the *stopping* of the engines. It makes no finding on the uncontradicted fact that the engines never were in fact out of commission by reason of the fouling, and could have been *started again* at any time after the fouling was reported to the captain off pier 42.

The five principal points made by brief and argument and ignored by the opinion, were:

I.

FIRST POINT IGNORED BY OPINION.

The uncontradicted testimony was that the fouling did not *in fact* in any way affect the engines and propeller. Without any communication with the engine room, the Captain wrongly assumed it had stopped them and wrongly failed to use them till he had drifted nearly 1800 feet and then coming to his senses tried them out and found that they worked perfectly. Even after this long delay, he backed his ship so that all but about 100 feet of his vessel cleared the projecting dock.

His failure to try his engines during his long drift, and his stupid reliance on a wrong assumption during all the period of danger, we urged was negligence. On its face, this is a clear defense if, as is demonstrable, he would have backed the additional 100 feet by a reasonably diligent use of his engines. This evidence is summarized in our briefs, but we here repeat it.

Our opponent's master says in his deposition:

"Q. You didn't have any difficulty in operating the engines, did you?

A. Not after we started, no.

Q. Was that the first effort that you had made from the time that the line was cast off, as you say, up to the time that the bow-line parted?

A. Yes.

Q. Why was it that you did not make an effort to start your engines before?

A. I was *rather afraid* when the seven-inch line fouled the wheel, thinking the towboat would have it performed or we would get out without that.

Q. Didn't you think that there was a position of *danger* there?

A. *I could readily see it.*

Q. When did you first see that?

A. The danger of the line being around the wheel?

Q. No, I mean did you think there was a position of danger from your drifting down, as you have described?

A. Yes, I did.

Q. You knew that eventually you must bring up against something, did you not?

A. I surely did.

Q. How was it, I want to know why it was that you did not start your engines before you did?

A. Because I didn't want to, I was afraid to attempt that, I was depending on the towboat.

Q. Had you had any communication with the engine room from the time that the second line was cast off up to the time that the third line was cast from your bow to the tug?

A. No.

Q. Had not sent any word down to the engineers about this?

A. No.

Q. *And yet in that time you had drifted down from off pier 42 to this position between pier 34 and pier 32, is that true?*

A. *Yes.*

Q. Do you know how long that distance is?

A. No.

Q. Didn't you think that the situation there demanded that you take some risk to save your vessel from collision with the pier?

A. I was expecting the towboat to do something, depending on the towboat.

Q. You were relying on the towboat?

A. Depending on the towboat.

Q. You did not anticipate that this towboat could handle your steamer in that wind and tide without some assistance from the steamer, did you?

A. No, but it could easily swing us around, though. (Apostles pp. 67, 68, 69.)

* * * * * * *

Q. As to the fouling of the propeller, you now know, of course, that the propeller, if it was fouled at all, at the time you thought it was, was not fouled sufficiently to have prevented moving the engines, was it?

A. We found that out afterwards.

Q. So that you were acting under a misapprehension of the situation, were you?

A. Apparently, yes. (Apostles p. 76.)

Q. You concede now that your engines could have been moved?

A. That has the same effect on your mind as if it was not.

Q. Won't you concede that your engines could have been moved?

A. Anyone would have to concede that because it was done, but the effect on your mind is just the same, I should judge.'' (Apostles p. 78.)

Here is a clear confession of his error and fault. It is a demonstration that if the ''Edith's'' captain had tried out his engines long prior to the last 200 feet of his drift he would have cleared the dock and no injury could have occurred. In the face of the known danger it is obvious that he should have done so.

We submit that we should be permitted a rehearing where demonstrable evidence and argument of this character is not given a word of consideration in the court's opinion.

II.

SECOND POINT IGNORED IN OPINION.

The opinion finds that the duty of the tug was merely that of an "assist" to the steamer. The supreme command was with the steamer's captain at the start of the maneuver. If, because of the dropping of the tow line, her captain desired the *control* of the maneuver to be transferred to the tug, the tug was entitled to know of any changed conditions on the steamer. Here a steamer, apparently of full power, without knowledge of the tug had become, in effect, a mere barge.

The tug, if it became the dominant and the steamer the mere assistant, should have been told of the steamer's captain's intent not to use his engines, based on the erroneous belief that they were disabled. As the steamer's captain says, she was as much disabled, as long as he indulged his erroneous belief, as if the engines were out of her (Apostles p. 78).

The evidence is uncontradicted that this information as to the error of the "Edith's" captain was not communicated to the tug at any time.

We argued that if the tug was the dominant she should have been told of the captain's belief so that she, the tug, could have assumed the responsibility of ordering the "Edith's" engines to be tried. It is plain that if the tug had known of this belief of the "Edith's" captain, she probably would have ordered him to try out the engines in ample time to have backed her the 100 feet further, necessary to clear the dock on which she struck. At any rate, she was entitled to have the chance to give this order.

This is a defense rational on its face. It merits, at least, the court's consideration. The opinion did not consider it. We respectfully submit that we should be heard upon it.

III.

THIRD POINT IGNORED BY THE OPINION.

We have pointed out that the tug should have been advised of the error in the "Edith's" captain's mind causing the supposed disablement of her engines.

If the tug had known this, she would not have relied on the "Edith's" engines to assist in turning into the wind by a tow line from the bow. She would have taken a line from the stern and pulled her directly backwards—lengthwise through the water. Certainly she would have covered much more than 100 feet necessary to clear the dock.

This argument we pressed on the court. It is rational on its face. It was not considered. A rational disposition of the case requires its consideration. We respectfully submit we should be reheard.

IV.

FOURTH POINT IGNORED IN OPINION.

The fourth point is that if the tug, when she became the dominant had been properly informed of the "Edith's" delusion as to her engines *she could have ordered* the "Edith" to drop her anchors. It is demonstrable that the "Edith" would have sustained no injury in this event. The tug, if she had cast on her the whole responsibility, should have been given the chance to give this order.

This is a rational defense. It was pressed in brief and argument. It is not considered in the opinion. We respectfully submit we should be given the chance to reargue it.

V.

FIFTH POINT IGNORED BY THE OPINION.

The opinion finds that it was negligent for the tug to have started out on the "assist" without learning from the steamer, the dominant, what the dominant's plans were. But, the dominant when it passed its line to the tug knew and assented to a plan of operation based on signals. She acquiesced in the dropping of the line by hauling it in. Her captain and mate's testimony squarely shows that the "Edith" was in fault for a misunderstanding as to how her captain was to communicate to the tug. As we said in our opening brief:

It is vitally important that the "Edith's" master, who was in command of the maneuver, not only failed to communicate to the tug which of the four possible maneuvers he contemplated (Dep. pp. 50, 51, 58), but failed to give the tug any code of whistle signals to guide the tug from time to time as the maneuver he chose developed.

He, therefore, must be charged with leaving to the discretion of the master of the tug the determination from the obvious actions of the ship what the next act of the tug was to be and the reasonable expectancy that if the tug started on a maneuver which was not helpful to his plan the "Edith's" captain would advise him *viva voce* through the particular mate who guarded the end of the tow line fastened to the ship, the point to which the eye of the tug master would naturally turn.

The master of the "Edith" being the dominant mind, was therefore solely responsible if this less certain method was productive of any confusion which might possibly arise.

However, not only did the "Edith's" master fail to communicate his plan or arrange for whistle signals, but he also failed to notify the second mate in charge of the after tow line that he was to act as the agent through whom commands would be given to direct the activities of the tug or stop her if she was not acting in coordination.

Captain McDonald's deposition says (56):

"Q. At any rate you didn't arrange any signals?
A. No.
Q. You depended on passing word by the second officer?
A. By the second officer.
Q. What was the second officer's name?
A. Hanson."

Hanson's deposition is as follows:

"Q. You said you expected the tug to get orders from the master?
A. Yes.
Q. How were you expecting the master of your ship—he was on the bridge, isn't that right?
A. Yes.
Q. How did you expect the master on the bridge of your ship to give an order to the tug to go ahead?
A. By the whistle.
Q. What whistle would he make?
A. That depends on which way they make it out between them.
Q. What?
A. They make that out between them what kind of a whistle they are going to use.
Q. They usually agree on what the signal shall be?
A. Yes." (Apostles pp. 90, 91.)

"Q. Your duty on the stern is to keep an eye on the towing line?
A. But we are not supposed to watch the tug too; he is supposed to give us a signal what to do.
Q. Who is?

·A.   The tug captain.

Q.   What signal did you expect the tug to give?

A.   I expected the tug captain to blow a short blast the same as the rest of them do.

Q.   Had you ever been towed by that tug before?

A.   No.

Q.   Did you ever have any conversation with her master before starting out as to what signals he would give you?

A.   No, sir.'' (Apostles p. 99.)

The "Edith's" captain expected the communication to be through the second mate; the second mate knew nothing about this, but expected the communication to pass between the two captains by whistles. He neither looked at the tug's captain nor his own but busied himself with other matters about the ship at important moments (99, 98).

In this basic disorganization from which the subsequent confusion and damage arose, the master of the tug had no part. It was not his duty to inform the "Edith's" second mate that his own captain had not advised the tug of the intended maneuver and that he had arranged no code of whistle signals with the tug, and that he, the "Edith's" mate, was the person to whom he was to look for any correction of any action on his part which did not fit into the "Edith's" undisclosed plans. When the second mate gave him the "Edith's" hawser and told him to go ahead, he was entitled to rely on the scheme of communication in both his and Captain McDonald's minds, i. e., through the second mate.

(Opening Brief, pp. 9, 10, 11.)

This is a rational statement of a fault on the "Edith's" part. If there was fault on the tug's part in planning for the "assist", it was equally shared by the steamer by her failure to make arrangements. The court's opinion nowhere considers this rational defense. We respectfully submit that we are entitled to a rehearing on this point.

VI.

THE "EDITH'S" CAPTAIN'S ADMISSION THAT HE FELL INTO HIS ERROR REGARDING THE DISABLEMENT OF THE "EDITH'S" ENGINES AT PIER 42—THAT IS AT THE BEGINNING OF HIS 1800 FOOT DRIFT.

This evidence, which was not ours but in the Edith's depositions, is set forth in the first chapter of our reply brief. It is our opponent's case, not ours. It shows abundant time to have saved the "Edith" if the tug had been put in possession of the essential fact of her captain's delusion as to his engines.

VII.

A CONFLICTING CIRCUIT COURT OF APPEALS DECISION REPORTED SINCE THE DECISION OF THIS CASE.

Since the decision of this case, there has appeared in the Federal Reporter, the case of *"The Westchester"* (Circuit Court of Appeals, Second Circuit), 254 Fed. Rep. 576, advance sheet No. 4. In this case, the Circuit Court of Appeals, Second Circuit, seems to be in complete opposition to the opinion in this case, regarding the obligation of the tow to use her anchors, where the tug, though found negligent, has left her in a position of danger.

That case was a weaker case on causation against the tow than the one here under consideration. In that case, the tow had no anchor on board, and the court found : :

"But if an anchor had been on board, and had been used, it cannot be said with reasonable certainty that stranding would have been avoided.

The tide must have been of considerable strength, for the tug's cable parted; anchors are habitually carried at the bow, and the Sinclair was being towed stern first; instant action was necessary, the available time short, and whether under such circumstances the maneuver could have been successfully performed is doubtful.

To sustain the result, if not the reasoning, below, The M. E. Luckenbach (D. C.), 200 Fed. 630, affirmed 214 Fed. 571; 131 C. C. A. 177, is pressed upon us. It is true in one sense that here, as there, 'concurrent faults'—i. e., negligent acts contemporaneously operating to produce injury— do not exist. But the word relied upon, 'concurrent', must be taken as synonymous with 'contributing', and in both The Luckenbach and The Sunnyside, supra, it was found as matter of fact that, despite a fault which put a tow adrift, there would have been no resulting injury, had it not been for a new and independent piece of negligence; therefore the wrongdoer first in point of time was held not responsible, although not innocent.

Here we infer negligence (i. e., unseaworthiness) in the tug from the unexplained breaking of her shaft, and find negligence admitted by the barge's admission of no anchor. When faults are thus shown, all the guilty, if their fault could have caused the injury, must, to escape liability, affirmatively show that they did not, in point of fact, cause the same. The Madison, 250 Fed. 852;

_____ C. C. A. .. .... Neither party has borne that burden, in this case; therefore the damages and costs below should be divided."

The Westchester, 254 Fed. Rep. 576, at 578.

In the case at bar, it is obvious that with the "Edith's" engines out of commission, whether through delusion, or otherwise—she was like the barge in *The Westchester* case. The burden was therefore *upon the "Edith's" captain* to show why he did not drop his anchors.

The captain endeavored to discharge this burden by saying that he relied on the tug; but the evidence is uncontradicted that he never, at any time, communicated to the tug his delusion that his engines were out of commission. It is no excuse for not dropping the anchors to say, "I can stand by idly and do nothing, and rely on the tug and permit my ship to drift as a helpless hulk against the pier", an obvious fate in sight for over 1800 feet, when, in fact, she was not a hulk at all, but in full possession of her power, and when, in fact, the tug believed, and properly believed, that she was in full possession of her power and could back the necessary additional 100 feet to safety at any moment.

We submit that in view of the clear difference of reasoning between the case at bar and *The Westchester* case, since reported, that we should be granted a rehearing.

CONCLUSION.

The "Edith" "cannot have her cake and eat it too". If she wishes to cast the responsibility on the tug after the tow line was dropped, she must show that she gave to the tug the information upon which primarily rested the successful discharge of that responsibility.

We argued four points resting on this hypothesis. We have failed to obtain their consideration. Justice would seem to require, that, even if this be due to a failure of advocacy, the court, on recognizing that they have not been considered, should rehear the case.

The recent case of *The Westchester* would seem to give additional warrant for the rehearing.

Dated, San Francisco,
    March 15, 1919.

WILLIAM DENMAN,
McCUTCHEN, OLNEY & WILLARD,
Proctors for Appellant
and Petitioner.

CERTIFICATE OF COUNSEL.

I hereby certify that I am of counsel for appellant and petitioner in the above entitled cause and that in my judgment the foregoing petition for a rehearing is well founded in point of law as well as in fact and that said petition is not interposed for delay.

Dated, San Francisco,
    March 15, 1919.

WILLIAM DENMAN,
Of Counsel for Appellant
and Petitioner.

No. 3199

7

United States Circuit Court of Appeals

For the Ninth Circuit

SHIPOWNERS AND MERCHANTS TUGBOAT COMPANY
(a corporation), claimant of the American
Steam Tug "Fearless", her boilers, engines,
tackle, apparel and furniture,

Appellant,

vs.

A. H. BULL & COMPANY, INC. (a corporation),
Appellee.

APPELLEE'S REPLY TO
APPELLANT'S PETITION FOR A REHEARING.

E. S. PILLSBURY,
F. D. MADISON,
ALFRED SUTRO,
OSCAR SUTRO,
Proctors for Appellee.

FILE

MAR 20 19

F. D. MONCKT
c

PERNAU-WALSH PRINTING CO.

No. 3199

United States Circuit Court of Appeals

For the Ninth Circuit

SHIPOWNERS AND MERCHANTS TUGBOAT COMPANY
(a corporation), claimant of the American
Steam Tug "Fearless", her boilers, engines,
tackle, apparel and furniture,

Appellant,

vs.

A. H. BULL & COMPANY, INC. (a corporation),

Appellee.

APPELLEE'S REPLY TO
APPELLANT'S PETITION FOR A REHEARING.

Appellant asks for a rehearing and complains that
the opinion in this case "is written as if the brief had
never been filed or the argument heard".

It is also urged that the opinion "does not touch on
the five principal points" raised in appellant's briefs
and argument. The petition for rehearing specifies the
five points "ignored by the opinion".

I.

The first point appears to be that the captain of the
"Edith" failed to use his engines after the tug had

dropped the tow line. But the testimony of all of the witnesses on both sides of the case was that it was the duty of the captain of the "Edith" to forthwith stop his engines when the tow line was cast off, so as to prevent the fouling of the line in the wheel. Such was the testimony of the tug witness Driver (Apostles 143-144), the tug witness Kratz (Apostles 186), the tug captain himself (Apostles 339), and the manager of the claimant (Apostles 255. See Appellee's Brief, pp. 14-16, p. 38.).

Despite this state of the record, appellant now appears to claim that the captain of the "Edith" should have turned his engines forthwith upon the tug's dropping the tow. Until this contention was made, and up to the time of the filing of the petition for rehearing, we understood that it was practically a conceded point in the case, based upon the unanimous testimony of all of the witnesses, that it was the duty of the captain of the "Edith" to stop his engines and to haul in the cast off line with his engines at rest. The record shows that while he was hauling in the line with his engines still, he was bound to drift towards the piers (Appellee's Brief, pp. 11-16). The record clearly supports the conduct of the captain in not performing the unseamanlike act of turning his propeller with a tow line hanging from the stern of the ship, and this whether he feared the line was already fouled in the wheel or whether he hoped to haul in the line before it fouled the wheel.

That the point was not overlooked in this honorable court's opinion is apparent from the statement by Judge Ross that the tug's captain

"without giving any notice whatever of his intention so to do, let go the tow line, which soon got into the wheel, thus fouling the ship's propeller *and making necessary the stopping of her engines."*

The finding that the action of the tug's captain made it necessary to stop the engines of the "Edith" is the only possible conclusion on the record in this case, and is in conformity with the testimony of the witnesses for the tug itself (Appellee's Brief, pp. 11-16, 38-39).

II.

Appellee's second point "ignored by the opinion" is that the master of the "Edith" was at fault for not communicating to the captain of the tug the fact that the "Edith" intended to stop her engines after the tug cast off the tow. But it appears from the testimony of the captain of the tug that he would expect the master of the "Edith" to stop his engines after the tow line was cast off (Apostles 324, 325), and the other witnesses, members of the crew of the tug, testified that after the tow line was cast off the captain of the "Edith" "would have to stop his engines to pull in that line" (Apostles 143, 186). The action of the captain of the "Edith" in stopping his engines was directly called for by the action of the tug in casting off the line. The tug could not expect the "Edith" to turn her engines with the tow line in the water. If it was good seamanship for the captain of the "Edith" to stop his engines (see testimony of tug captain, Apostles 324), the tug captain should have known that such a course would be, as it was, followed.

III.

The third point "ignored by the opinion", and urged as a ground for rehearing, seems to be substantially a repetition of the second point. Appellant urges that "if the tug had known" that the "Edith's" engines would be stopped after the line was cast off, the tug would have taken a stern line and pulled the "Edith" "directly backwards". So far as we are aware this position is new. Nowhere in the record have we found the suggestion that when the tug ceased pulling on the "Edith's" stern and dropped the tow line, compelling the "Edith" to stop her engines until the line was hauled in, the tug should have been given an opportunity to take another line, or pick up the same line, and continue doing what it had ceased to do without notice to the "Edith" and again pull the "Edith's" stern backwards through the water. Just what the purpose of such a maneuver would be is not clear. Certainly it was not testified to by any witness, nor, so far as we know, heretofore urged. In fact we submit the suggestion is wholly inadmissible.

IV.

The fourth point 'ignored by the opinion" is that if the tug had been advised that the maneuver was in its hands, it could have ordered the "Edith" to drop her anchors. This point was expressly commented upon in the closing paragraph of the opinion of Judge Ross, in which he said that the court is not "able to agree with the proctors for the appellant that the master of the ship should be held in fault in failing to drop her anchors, the condition of the wind and water, and the location of the ship with respect to the various piers being duly considered."

Appellant now advances the theory that if the captain of the tug had known that the "Edith's" engines were to be stopped, he "could have ordered the 'Edith' to drop her anchors". But, as we have already observed, the captain of the tug should have known and must have intended when the tow line was cast off that the engines of the "Edith" should be stopped until it was hauled in, and by the time it was hauled in she was in a position of danger where her anchors could not be dropped (see Apostles 314). And certainly the captain of the tug, who expected, after dropping the stern line, to run around and take a bow line from the "Edith", could not have expected the "Edith" to drop her anchors while his maneuver, which involved pulling her into the wind and tide by her bow, was in process of performance (Appellee's Brief, pp. 34-36). It is equally certain that the tug would have claimed immunity from responsibility for any damage which might have resulted if the "Edith" had dropped her anchors and thus blocked the tug's maneuver.

V.

The fifth point "ignored by the opinion" relates to the failure of the tug to arrange with the captain of the "Edith" in regard to the method of performance of the maneuver. Judge Ross not only announced the conclusions of the court on this subject, but did so with considerable detail. Not only is the point not ignored by the opinion, but it is the subject-matter of pages 2 to 5 of the opinion, which concludes:

> "Such a movement on the part of the tug was not only not directed by the master of the ship, but was directly contrary to the latter's own movement and plan, and was commenced without the slightest notice to the ship of the tug's action."

The point is discussed in appellee's brief, pages 5 to 11, and we think the record is very clear that the tug, contrary to the claimant's rule on the subject, proceeded in this case to conduct an independent maneuver without advising the captain of that fact. Its duty as an assistant tug was to follow the ship's maneuvers and orders. The tug had no right, without notice to the "Edith", to cast off a tow line which no emergency required it to drop, and which it could have held on to with perfect safety, and which the maneuver planned by the "Edith's" captain required it to hold.

VI.

To the sixth point of the petition for rehearing, we reply that it was the "Edith's" duty to forthwith stop her engines when the tow line was cast off and until it was hauled in; and by the time it was hauled in she had drifted into a position of danger where her anchors could not be safely dropped (Appellee's Brief, p. 34).

The case of *The Westchester*, 254 Fed. 576, which counsel says he considers opposed to the decision in this case, is not in the remotest degree in conflict with anything in the opinion of this court.

In that case a tug in tow of a barge became disabled by the breaking of her propeller shaft. The tug immediately anchored. The barge had no anchor and the hawser parted. The Circuit Court of Appeals for the Second Circuit held that the barge was negligent for not having an anchor. Her failure to drop an anchor contributed to the accident. After the tug anchored there was only one possible maneuver for the barge, and that was to drop an anchor. She undoubtedly would have done so if she had not gone out negligently without anchors.

The case is entirely different from the case at bar. The "Edith" was equipped with anchors. The point in the present case was not that the "Edith" was not prepared to drop her anchors, but that she was not called upon by the tug's maneuver to do so (Appellee's Brief, pp. 33-37). In fact the conclusions of this court and of the trial court were that the master of the "Edith" was not to be blamed for not dropping her anchors. In this case the maneuver, after the tug dropped the "Edith's" tow line, continued in full operation and would have been interfered with by the dropping of anchors. In the case of the "Westchester" when the tug dropped her anchor it was plainly the duty of the barge to drop her anchor. The negligence of the barge in having no anchor contributed directly to the accident in that case. We submit the cases are in no way parallel.

The accident in this case was caused by the tug dropping a tow line without notice to her tow, and undertaking a perilous maneuver, which the tug failed to accomplish. The record shows that the tug was not even properly equipped with lines for the performance of the operation it had undertaken. Had the tug held on to the stern line, which it took from the "Edith", the accident would not have happened. We submit that when the tug cast off the line without notice, it did so on its own responsibility, and that it is liable for the resulting damage.

We respectfully submit that the petition for rehearing should be denied.

Dated, San Francisco,
    March 19, 1919.

E. S. PILLSBURY,

F. D. MADISON,

ALFRED SUTRO,

OSCAR SUTRO,

Proctors for Appellee.

United States

Circuit Court of Appeals

For the Ninth Circuit.

XAVIER SERVEL,

Plaintiff in Error,

vs.

G. R. JAMIESON and MATHIESON MURRAY,
Co-partners Doing Business Under the Firm
Name of JAMIESON & MURRAY,

Defendants in Error.

Transcript of Record.

Upon Writ of Error to the United States District Court of the District of Montana.

Filmer Bros. Co Print, 330 Jackson St., S. F., Cal.

No. 3200

United States
Circuit Court of Appeals
For the Ninth Circuit.

XAVIER SERVEL,

Plaintiff in Error,

vs.

G. R. JAMIESON and MATHIESON MURRAY,
Co-partners Doing Business Under the Firm
Name of JAMIESON & MURRAY,

Defendants in Error.

Transcript of Record.

Upon Writ of Error to the United States District Court of the
District of Montana.

Filmer Bros Co. Print, 330 Jackson St., S F., Cal.

United States
Circuit Court of Appeals

For the Ninth Circuit.

XAVIER SERVEL,

Plaintiff in Error,

vs.

G. R. JAMIESON and MATHIESON MURRAY,
Co-partners Doing Business Under the Firm
Name of JAMIESON & MURRAY,

Defendants in Error.

Transcript of Record.

Upon Writ of Error to the United States District Court of the
District of Montana.

Filmer Bros Co. Print, 330 Jackson St., S. F., Cal.

INDEX TO THE PRINTED TRANSCRIPT OF RECORD.

[Clerk's Note: When deemed likely to be of an important nature, errors or doubtful matters appearing in the original certified record are printed literally in italic; and, likewise, cancelled matter appearing in the original certified record is printed and cancelled herein accordingly. When possible, an omission from the text is indicated by printing in italic the two words between which the omission seems to occur.]

Index.

F. B. REYNOLDS, Esq., of Billings, Montana,
>Attorney for Plaintiff and Plaintiff in Error.

Messrs. NORRIS, HURD & McKELLAR, of Great Falls, Montana,
>Attorneys for Defendants and Defendants in Error. [1*]

In the District Court of the United States in and for the District of Montana.

No. 638.

XAVIER SERVEL,

>Plaintiff,

vs.

G. R. JAMIESON and MATHIESON MURRAY, Copartners Doing Business Under the Firm Name of JAMIESON & MURRAY,

>Defendants.

BE IT REMEMBERED that on November 24, 1917, plaintiff filed his complaint herein, in the words and figures following, to wit: [2]

---

*Page-number appearing at foot of page of original certified Transcript of Record.

In the District Court of the United States for the District of Montana, (Billings Division).

XAVIER SERVEL,

Plaintiff,

vs.

G. R. JAMIESON and MATHIESON MURRAY, Copartners Doing Business Under the Firm Name of JAMIESON & MURRAY,

Defendants.

Complaint.

Plaintiff, for cause of action, alleges:

I.

That plaintiff is, and was at all the times hereinafter mentioned, a resident and citizen of the State of Idaho, and is, and was at all the times hereinafter mentioned, engaged in the business of dealing in sheep.

II.

That defendants, G. R. Jamieson and Mathieson Murray, are, and were at all the times hereinafter mentioned, residents and citizens of the State of Montana, and copartners doing business under the firm name and style of Jamieson & Murray, with their principal place of business at Glasgow, Montana.

III.

That on or about the 14th day of March, 1917, plaintiff and defendant entered into a written contract, whereby defendants promised to sell and deliver to plaintiff all the wether sheep produced in the year 1917 by certain bands of ewes owned by defendants, described as follows, to wit: About five thousand head of ewes, known as Browning Brothers' band; about three thousand five hundred head, known as White Brothers' band; [3] about one thousand two hundred head, known as the W. S. Kirkland band; and eight thousand ewes, known as the Jamieson & Murray ewes, in all about seventeen thousand seven hundred ewes, delivery to be made of said wether lambs between the 25th day of September, 1917, and the 29th day of September, 1917, exact date to be at option of plaintiff, at Porcupine Creek, above Nashua, Montana, and at the town of Saco, Phillips County, Montana; that plaintiff was to pay for said lambs ten cents per pound, as follows: Three thousand dollars upon the execution of the contract, and the balance of the purchase price upon delivery of said lambs, a copy of which contract is hereto attached, marked Exhibit "A," and thereby made a part hereof, and that the said sum of Three Thousand Dollars was paid upon the execution of said contract, as above mentioned.

IV.

That said ewes produced five thousand three hundred thirteen wether lambs, suitable for delivery under said contract at the time and places in said contract mentioned, and were then and there of a combined weight of three hundred thirteen thousand three hundred twenty-five pounds.

V.

That plaintiff, by C. M. Stitt, his duly authorized agent and representative, was present upon the 28th and 29th days of September, 1917, at the places mentioned in said contract, for the delivery of said lambs, in company with defendants, and that he was then able, ready, and willing to receive and pay for said lambs at said times and places, and offered so to do, and that plaintiff was able, ready, and willing to perform all of his obligations under said contract, but that defendants refused to deliver said lambs to plaintiff, did not deliver them, or any part thereof, to him, and still refuse so to do.　[4]

VI.

That at the times and places mentioned in said contract for the delivery of said lambs they were of a reasonable value of fifteen cents per pound, or a total valuation of Forty-six Thousand Nine Hundred Ninety-eight and 70/100 Dollars; that the contract price for said lambs was Thirty-one Thousand Three Hundred Thirty-two and 50/100 Dollars, and that by reason of the failure of defendants to deliver the lambs as aforesaid, plaintiff was damaged in the sum of Fifteen Thousand Six Hundred Sixty-six and 20/100 Dollars, being the difference between the contract price of said lambs and the value thereof at the times and places of delivery, together with the sum of Three Thousand Dollars, being the down payment made upon said contract, making a total sum of Eighteen Thousand Six Hundred Sixty-six and 20/100 Dollars loss to plaintiff by reason of the default of defendants in fulfilling the terms of said contract, for which he claims damage.

WHEREFORE, plaintiff demands judgment against defendants for the sum of Eighteen Thousand Six Hundred Sixty-six and 20/100 Dollars damages, together with interest thereon at the rate of eight per cent per annum from and after September 29, A. D. 1917.

F. B. REYNOLDS,

Attorney for Plaintiff. [5]

State of Montana,

County of Yellowstone,—ss.

F. B. Reynolds, being first duly sworn, deposes and says, that he is the attorney for plaintiff, and that he makes this affidavit for and in behalf of said plaintiff, for the reason that plaintiff is absent from the county of Yellowstone, State of Montana, in which said county and State said attorney resides; that he has read the foregoing complaint, knows the contents thereof, and that the same is true to the best of his knowledge, information and belief.

F. B. REYNOLDS.

Subscribed and sworn to before me this 23d day of November, A. D. 1917.

[L. S.]   A. B. RENWICK,

Notary Public for the State of Montana, Residing at Billings, Montana.

My commission expires Dec. 29, 1918. [6]

Exhibit "A" to Complaint.

THIS AGREEMENT, made and entered into this fourteenth day of March, 1917, by and between G. R. Jamieson and Mathieson Murray as co-partners doing business under the firm name and style of Jamieson & Murray, of Glasgow, Montana, the parties of the first part, and Xavier Servel of the

City of Great Falls, Cascade County, Montana, the party of the second part;

WITNESSETH, that WHEREAS, the said parties of the first part are now the owners and in the possession of the following band of ewes, to wit:

(a)   That band of ewes consisting of about five thousand (5000) head known as "Browning Brothers' Band."

(b)   That band of ewes consisting of about thirty-five hundred (3500) head, known as the "White Brothers' Band,"

(c)   That band of ewes consisting of about twelve hundred (1200) head, known as the "W. S. Kirkland Band," and

(d)   Eight thousand (8000) ewes known as the "Jamieson & Murray Ewes,"

in all about seventeen thousand seven hundred (17,000) ewes, which in the season of 1917 are expected to produce Six Thousand (6000) wethers, more or less,

AND WHEREAS, the said party of the second part is desirous of purchasing of said parties of the first part all of the wether sheep produced in the year 1917 by said ewes,

NOW, THEREFORE, in consideration of the payment of the sum of Ten (10) cents per pound at the times and under the conditions hereinafter specified by said party of the second part to the said parties of the first part, the said parties of the first part hereby covenant, promise and agree to sell to the said party of the second part all of the wether sheep produced by the aforesaid ewes in the year

1917, and to accept therefor [7] the sum of Ten (10) cents per pound, which the said party of the second part agrees to pay as hereinafter specified.

And it is further agreed and stipulated in consideration of the premises that said parties of the first part will deliver said wether sheep except about five hundred (500) head, at the scales of said parties of the first part now owned by them situated on Porcupine Creek above Nashua, Montana, and that such delivery will be made between the 25th day of September, 1917, and the 29th day of September, 1917, the exact date to be at the option of said party of the second part, and that the remainder of said wethers, consisting of about five hundred (500) head, will be delivered by said parties of the first part to said party of the second part between said dates at the town of Saco, Phillips County, Montana, and said party of the second part agrees to accept delivery of said wether sheep at the times and places herein mentioned.

And it is further mutually agreed by and between the parties hereto that said party of the second part has paid at the date of the execution of this instrument the sum of Three Thousand (3000) Dollars, as a part of the purchase price therefor, receipt whereof is hereby acknowledged by said parties of the first part, and said party of the second part will pay the remainder of the purchase price of said wether sheep at the time and upon the delivery thereof to said party of the second part by said parties of the first part;

It is further mutually agreed, promised and covenanted that said party of the second part shall not be required to receive or pay for any sick or crippled wethers, but the same in said bands shall be retained by said parties of the first part.

And it is further agreed, promised and covenanted that said wether sheep shall be placed in corrals with their mothers at about sunset on the day preceding the delivery thereof and [8] shall remain with their mothers in said corral over night and shall be cut out the following morning and weighed and the weights so obtained shall be the basis of payment of the purchase price as herein above mentioned.

And it is further mutually agreed by and between the parties hereto that time is of the essence of this agreement and that upon the expiration of the time for delivery as herein provided the rights of said party of the second part hereunder shall cease and terminate, and he shall have no right, claim or interest in or to said sheep after the expiration of said period of time.

The terms and provisions of this agreement shall extend to and be binding and obligatory upon the heirs, executors, administrators and assigns of the respective parties hereto.

IN WITNESS WHEREOF, the said parties have hereunto set their hands the day and year in this agreement first above written.

JAMIESON & MURRAY,
By M. MURRAY.
XAVIER SERVEL.

Witnessed by:
JOS. FARQUHAR.

Filed Nov. 24, 1917. Geo. W. Sproule, Clerk. by C. R. Garlow, Deputy Clerk. **[9]**

––––––

Thereafter, on December 18, 1917, answer of defendants was duly filed herein, in the words and figures following, to wit: **[10]**

In the District Court of the United States for the District of Montana.

XAVIER SERVEL,

Plaintiff,

vs.

G. R. JAMIESON and MATHIESON MURRAY, as Copartners Doing Business Under the Firm Name of JAMIESON & MURRAY,

Defendants.

Answer.

For their answer to the complaint of the plaintiff herein, the defendants admit, deny and allege as follows:

I.

Deny that they or each of them has any knowledge or information, and allege that they do not have any knowledge or information sufficient to form a belief as to the matters set forth in paragraph I of said plaintiff's complaint and therefore deny the same.

II.

Admit the allegations of paragraphs II, III, IV of said plaintiff's complaint.

III.

Deny the allegations of paragraphs V and VI of plaintiff's complaint.

Wherefore, having fully answered plaintiff's complaint herein, defendants pray judgment that plaintiff take nothing by this action and that the defendants have judgment against the plaintiff for their costs and disbursements herein incurred.

NORRIS, HURD & McKELLAR,

Attorneys for Defendants.   [11]

State of Montana,
County of Cascade,—ss.

George E. Hurd, first being duly sworn, deposes and says:

That he is one of the attorneys for the above-named defendants, that he has read the foregoing answer of said defendants, knows the contents thereof, and that the same is true to the best of his knowledge, information and belief, that he makes this verification for and on behalf of said defendants for the reason that neither of said defendants at the time this verification is made are within the county of Cascade, State of Montana, which is the county wherein affiant resides.

GEORGE E. HURD.

Subscribed and sworn to before me this 11th day of December, 1917.

[Notarial Seal]   HARVEY B. HOFFMAN,
Notary Public for the State of Montana, Residing at Great Falls, Montana.

- My commission expires August 7, 1920.

. Service of the foregoing answer and receipt of a copy thereof are hereby admitted this 14 day of December, 1917.

F. B. REYNOLDS,
Attorney for Plaintiff,

Filed Dec. 18, 1917. C. R. Garlow, Clerk. **[12]**

Thereafter, on March 29, 1918, said cause came on regularly for trial and was duly tried, the journal record thereof being in the words and figures following, to wit:

In the District Court of the United States, District of Montana.

No. 638.

XAVIER SERVEL

vs.

JAMIESON & MURRAY.

Minutes of Court—March 29, 1918.

This cause came on regularly for trial this day, respective parties being present with their attorneys, F. B. Reynolds, Esq., appearing for the plaintiff and Messrs. Norris & Hurd appearing for the defendants. Thereupon the following were duly impanelled, accepted and sworn as a jury to try the cause, viz.: Oscar Prescott, C. H. McLean, F. G. Gruel, C. E. Watson, C. M. Harris, Evan Jones, Chas. E. Pullin, J. O. Frazier, A. H. Bennett, J. R. Harvey, E. I. Holland and Gus Nordquist.

Thereupon Xavier Servel, Mr. Stitt and James Rae were sworn and examined as witnesses for plaintiff and certain documentary evidence offered and admitted; whereupon the plaintiff asked leave to amend the complaint herein, to which amendment defendants objected, said objection being sustained and exception of plaintiff noted. Whereupon, the plaintiff having rested, defendants moved the Court to direct the jury to return a verdict herein in favor of the defendants, and, after due consideration, Court ordered that said motion be granted and that a verdict in favor of the defendants and against the plaintiff be, and hereby is, entered by the clerk.

Thereupon judgment ordered entered accordingly.

Thereupon, on motion of counsel for plaintiff, said plaintiff was granted a period of thirty days within which to prepare, serve and file a bill of exceptions herein.

Entered, in open court March 29, 1918.

C. R. GARLOW,
Clerk. **[13]**

Thereafter, on March 30, 1918, judgment was duly rendered and entered herein, in the words and figures following, to wit:

In the District Court of the United States, in and for the District of Montana.

XAVIER SERVEL,

Plaintiff,

vs.

G. R. JAMIESON and MATHIESON MURRAY, Copartners Doing Business Under the Firm Name of JAMIESON & MURRAY,

Defendants.

Judgment.

This cause came regularly on to be heard on the 29th day of March, 1918, having by order of said Court been continued from the 28th day of March, 1918, the date whereon it had theretofore, pursuant to order of said Court, been set for trial. F. B. Reynolds, Esq.; appeared as counsel for plaintiff and Norris & McKellar appeared as counsel for the defendants. A jury of twelve competent and qualified persons were selected, sworn and impaneled to try the issues of fact involved therein. Whereupon the plaintiff introduced documentary evidence and witnesses were sworn and testified in his behalf, and thereafter said plaintiff rested and announced that he had no further evidence to offer or submit to the jury in said cause. Whereupon the defendants moved the Court for an order directing and requiring the jury herein to return a verdict in favor of the defendants, which order was by the Court on the 29th day of March, 1918, duly granted and the Clerk of said court was ordered to enter in the records of [14] said court a verdict in favor of the defendants herein, which verdict was duly entered of record by the clerk of said court.

WHEREFORE, by reason of the law and premises and said verdict, it is ordered, adjudged and decreed that the plaintiff herein, Xavier Servel, take nothing by this action and that said defendants, G. R. Jamieson and Mathieson Murray, as copartners doing business under the firm name and style of Jamieson & Murray, do have and recover judgment in their favor and against said plaintiff, Xavier Servel, for their costs and disbursements incurred and expended herein, amounting to and taxed at the sum of $472.00 Dollars, with interest thereon at the rate of eight per cent per annum from and after the date hereof until paid.

Judgment rendered this 30th day of March, 1918.

C. R. GARLOW,

Clerk.   [15]

United States of America,

District of Montana,—ss.

I, C. R. Garlow, Clerk of the United States District Court for the District of Montana, do hereby certify that the foregoing papers hereto annexed constitute the judgment-roll in the above-entitled action.

Witness my hand and the seal of said court at

Great Falls, Montana, this 30th day of March, A. D. 1918.

[Seal]   C. R. GARLOW,

                     Clerk.

[Indorsed]: Judgment-roll. Filed March 30, 1918. C. R. Garlow, Clerk. **[16]**

Thereafter on May 6th, 1918, plaintiff's bill of exceptions was duly settled, allowed and filed herein, being in words and figures following, to wit: **[17]**

In the District Court of the United States, for the District of Montana, (Great Falls Division).

XAVIER SERVEL,

                     Plaintiff,

       vs.

G. R. JAMIESON and MATHIESON MURRAY, Copartners Doing Business Under the Firm Name of JAMIESON & MURRAY,

                     Defendants.

Bill of Exceptions.

BE IT REMEMBERED, That the above-entitled cause came on regularly for trial upon the 29th day of March, A. D. 1918, before the above-entitled court, Honorable George M. Bourquin, United States District Judge for Montana, presiding, sitting with a jury; F. B. Reynolds appearing as attorney for plaintiff, and Norris & Hurd appearing as attorneys for defendants, whereupon the following proceedings were had and evidence introduced, to wit:

Testimony of Xavier Servel, in His Own Behalf.

XAVIER SERVEL, the plaintiff herein, being duly sworn, testified as follows:

My name is Xavier Servel. I am the plaintiff in this case. I live at Robin, Idaho. Have lived there for fifteen years. I went to Montana about a year ago and bought some lambs. I made a contract with the defendants in this case at that time.

Contract in question identified, marked exhibit 1, and received in evidence, a copy of which contract is attached to the complaint filed herein. [18]

I was right here in Great Falls at the time this contract was made. Neither of the defendants were here. I first sent my contract to them, and they sent it back and sent me this new contract, and they expressed in their letter that if I had accepted the contract, to send them a check for Three Thousand Dollars, and the deal was made, and I signed the contract, and sent them the check. The contract was signed when I received it from Jamieson & Murray. I made my first payment by check.

Check in question is identified, marked exhibit 2, and received in evidence. (Said exhibit 2 is check, dated March 14, 1917, drawn by Xavier Servel upon bank in Ogden, Utah, in the sum of Three Thousand Dollars, payable to Jamieson & Murray.)

I afterward sent Mr. Stitt to receive the sheep. I was not here at the time of the delivery of the sheep. I did not at any time receive any advice, directly or

(Testimony of Xavier Servel.)

indirectly, from the defendants that they would not accept check in final settlement.

Mr. HURD.—That is objected to as incompetent, irrelevant and immaterial, and no foundation laid for it.

The COURT.—Sustained.

Mr. REYNOLDS.—Exception.

Testimony of C. M. Stitt, for Plaintiff.

C. M. STITT, a witness called and sworn in behalf of plaintiff, testified as follows:

My name is C. M. Stitt. I live at Fort Morgan, Colorado. I am the gentleman referred to by Mr. Servel as the one authorized to receive these sheep. I came to Montana for that purpose. I had an interest in the sheep. I had purchased them from another party—Hatcher & Snyder, of Denver, Colorado.

I arrived at Glasgow the 25th of September, 1917. At about one or one thirty. I met Mr. Jamieson. I met him on the street in Glasgow. I had a conversation with him at that time. He was in his automobile, and I was walking along the street, and [19] I guess he suspicioned that I was the man that had come to receive the sheep, and I told him that I was.

I told him that I had come to receive the sheep, and that if he would take me out where they was, that I was ready to receive them. He said that he was going back out to where they were weighed, and he would take me in his automobile to the place. I

(Testimony of C. M. Stitt.)

waited until he got ready to go, and I got in the automobile and we went, first to Nashua and then from there to Porcupine Creek, which is about five miles north of Nashua, I believe. We reached there late in the evening, possibly six o'clock.

There was nothing done toward receiving the sheep that evening. Before I had got there, part of the sheep had been weighed, and there was a bunch of sheep in the corrals to be divided out and weighed in the morning. They were separated, the ewe lambs and the wether lambs, and the wether lambs were weighed, at first, and I took the weight down, and then the ewe lambs were weighed. I think we were through weighing them about eight o'clock, or possibly a little later.

The White Brothers' lambs were also weighed there. That was a part of these lambs that were out on the range, and as they wanted to get the ewe lambs weighed, they were brought in by mutual consent, and were weighed without standing over night, which the contract called for. They were weighed while we had our dinner, and I think it was possibly after twelve o'clock before we commenced weighing them. That was the last bunch weighed there.

We did not do anything in particular for awhile after weighing them. We talked in regard to the bunch that was to be weighed at Saco, and how we were to get over there. They were to be weighed the next morning—the morning of the 29th. I did not go direct to Saco. I went in an automobile with Mr. Browning of Nashua, and I rode in an automo-

(Testimony of C. M. Stitt.)

bile from there to   [20]   Glasgow that evening, and from Glasgow I took the night train, which was two or three hours late, and went to Saco, and got there about three o'clock in the morning and went to bed at a hotel at Saco, and got up about six o'clock. A man by the name of Johnson went with me to Saco. I never saw him only once before that time, but when Mr. Browning was taking me to Nashua the night of the 28th we met him being taken out to the camp with another man, and they said his name was Johnson.

We went to bed after reaching Saco. This man Johnson and me slept together, and in the morning we had our breakfast together and hired an automobile and went to the weighing where this small bunch of lambs were being weighed. We reached there at seven o'clock, or possibly a little later. It was the morning of the 29th of September. Saturday.

After reaching there, we proceeded with the weighing of the lambs after they were separated. There were two hundred seventy-nine wether lambs and a few ewe lambs, but I couldn't tell you the number of ewe lambs. We finished weighing there at Saco at possibly eight o'clock, or a little later.

After the lambs were finished weighing, I offered to pay for that car of lambs or what was there, the wether lambs, and Mr. Jamieson was there and he said he would not settle for any of the lambs until they were all settled for, and that was all that was

(Testimony of C. M. Stitt.)

said in regard to settling. Mr. Murray was not there.

After they were all weighed, Mr. Jamieson had his automobile there, and Mr. Jamieson and Mr. David Rae and Mr. Johnson and myself got into the automobile and we went first to Saco and from Saco to Glasgow in the automobile. We reached Glasgow right about one o'clock. I did not have any conversation with Mr. Jamieson on the road in regard to settlement.

I mentioned at Glasgow that we would go on down to Nashua, and if he would come down after dinner we would settle for the lambs after dinner. Mr. Murray was down there. I **[21]** mentioned it and also he did. He said he would come down as soon as he had dinner and we would settle down there. I understood him to say that Mr. Murray was at Nashua. Mr. David Rea and myself then took the train, that I guess is the regular train, about one o'clock or such a matter, to Nashua. I think we reached Nashua a little after two o'clock, possibly two or half past two.

When we reached Nashau we hadn't any dinner, but the first thing we did was to go to the stock yards, and I found out that Mr. Murray wasn't there then, and so went and got our dinner after that. I did not find him at Nashua at all that afternoon. I rode in an automobile back to Glasgow. Reached Glasgow at four or four-thirty, Saturday afternoon.

After reaching Glasgow, I met Mr. Jamieson first. I met him right close to the bank, if it wasn't in the

(Testimony of C. M. Stitt.)

bank, the Farmers' and Stockgrowers' Bank. I am not sure, it was either right in the bank or on the street right at the bank. I told Mr. Jamieson I was ready to settle for the lambs. He said I could settle with Mr. Murray. That was all the conversation I had with Mr. Jamieson. After that we found Mr. Murray. Just down the street a little ways. That was not more than ten minutes after my meeting with Mr. Jamieson.

I then had a conversation with Mr. Murray in regard to settlement. I told Mr. Murray that I was ready to settle for the lambs. He asked me how I wanted to pay for the lambs, and I told him I would have to give him a check, and he said, "If you haven't got the currency, you cannot have the lambs, and if you have you can, but we won't accept a check." And I told him I didn't have thirty thousand dollars in my pocket, but I could get it if it was necessary. I told him I always had bought lambs by check, and had never given the currency before.

I told him I had always paid by check and my check was [22] good, and I could prove my check was good, and if he would give me a little time I would wire to the bank and have them guarantee the check, and also could have it guaranteed by Hatcher & Snyder, and would also leave the sheep there until they got the money, and would also pay for any damage or expense they might incur while they held the lambs until I would get the currency there. I told him I could draw a draft on Hatcher & Snyder, and that they would pay it.

(Testimony of C. M. Stitt.)

I remember the only thing that I said in regard to currency was that I would get the currency just as soon as it was possible to get it. The banks were closed and it was Saturday, and the only way I could get it would be by wire. They said the time was up and that they would not accept a check, and that I could not have the lambs. At that time I had made arrangements with a bank for the payment of my check.

Mr. NORRIS.—Just a moment. Any arrangement he had for the payment of this check is not in compliance with the terms of the contract.

The COURT.—The objection will be sustained. The contract calls for payment and delivery consecutively at a particular time. Time was made the essence of the contract, and under such circumstances, the law and the contract calls for money and it permits the seller to demand money, and he did demand it and it was not forthcoming. Now, the fact that you might have it at some other bank, whether a mile away or half way around the world, I cannot see that that would be material. Objection sustained.

Mr. REYNOLDS.—Plaintiff offers to prove by witness Stitt, upon the stand, that he had made arrangements with bank at Ft. Morgan, Colorado, for payment of any check that he might draw on it in payment of the lambs in question.

Mr. HURD.—To which offer the defendants object, for the reason that the matter offered to be proved by this witness is irrelevant [23] and im-

(Testimony of C. M. Stitt.)

material and does not tend to show any compliance with the terms of the contract, and there is no foundation laid for any such testimony.

The COURT.—The objection to the offer will be sustained.

Mr. REYNOLDS.—Exception.

Q. Mr. Stitt, were you able at that time to produce the currency just as soon as it could be wired from the bank?

Mr. NORRIS.—We object to his ability to produce it later.

The COURT.—Sustained.

Q. Mr. Stitt, if the defendants had acquiesced in that offer of the currency and had not refused to accept it, would you have produced the currency for the payment of the lambs by wire?

Mr. NORRIS.—We object to that on the ground that the evidence sought to be brought out by this witness is irrelevant, incompetent and immaterial and there is no foundation laid, and therefore it is not responsive nor illustrative of any issues in this case, and instead of showing a compliance with the contract, it is practically opposed to the terms of the contract.

The COURT.—Sustain the objection.

Mr. REYNOLDS.—Plaintiff offers to prove by the witness Stitt, upon the stand, that he could have produced the currency or legal tender for payment of lambs in question just as soon as it could have been procured by telegram from his bank at Ft. Morgan, Colorado, and would have done so if defendants had

(Testimony of C. M. Stitt.)

not told him that it would be useless.

Mr. NORRIS.—We object to the offer of the testimony because of the fact that it is incompetent, irrelevant and immaterial and has no pertinent value in the case and is not responsive to the issues set forth in the pleadings, nor is it justified by any evidence heretofore produced, and there is no foundation laid for it, and it is indefinite as to the time when this money could have been produced and by reason of the further fact that on [24] account of the indefinite character of the proposed offer of testimony, it cannot be determined whether or not the witness could or would have produced that money on that date, or at some subsequent time.

The COURT.—Objection sustained.

Mr. REYNOLDS.—Exception.

I did have a conversation upon Sunday, the 30th of September, with one of the defendants, relative to having received a message from my bank at Ft. Morgan.

Q. And what was that conversation?

Mr. NORRIS.—To which we object, your Honor, as incompetent, irrelevant and immaterial. This is introduced evidently for the purpose of showing that on the day succeeding the date the contract expired, this conversation was had, and showing no attempt to comply with the terms of the contract.

The COURT.—The objection will be sustained.

Mr. REYNOLDS.—Exception.

Mr. REYNOLDS.—Plaintiff offers to prove by witness Stitt, on the stand, that his bank at Ft. Mor-

(Testimony of C. M. Stitt.)

gan, Colorado, telegraphed to defendants, guaranteeing to pay his check for the lambs in question, and that defendants admitted to him that they had received said telegram.

Mr. NORRIS.—To which offer the defendants object, for the reason that the same is incompetent, irrelevant and immaterial, and does not show a compliance with the terms of the contract, and in fact shows that the terms of the contract were not and had not been complied with, and the evidence sought to be introduced would detail facts and circumstances occurring after the expiration of the date on the contract was to have been performed and does not tend to show an attempt to perform under the conditions of the contract on the date that the contract required [25] it to be performed.

The COURT.—Sustained.

Mr. REYNOLDS.—Exception.

Q. Did you, on the 30th of September, have a talk with the defendants or either of them relative to the reception of a message by them, from the Bank of Montana, relative to the payment of any draft you might draw on Hatch & Snyder?

Mr. NORRIS.—To which we object, your Honor.

The COURT.—Sustained.

Mr. REYNOLDS.—Exception.

Mr. REYNOLDS.—Plaintiff offers to prove by witness Stitt upon the stand that defendants admitted to him on Sunday, September 30th, that they had received telegram from Montana National Bank of Billings, guaranteeing any draft that he

(Testimony of C. M. Stitt.)

might draw on Hatcher & Snyder, in payment of the sheep in question.

Mr. NORRIS.—To which we object.

The COURT.—Sustained.

Mr. REYNOLDS.—Exception.

Document marked Exhibit 3.

This is the notice I gave Mr. Murray. The 30th of September.

Mr. REYNOLDS.—We offer this in evidence.

Mr. NORRIS.—To which offer of the plaintiff, proposed Exhibit No. 3 in evidence, the defendants object, for the reason that the same is incompetent, irrelevant and immaterial, and no foundation has been laid for it, and it does not tend to prove or disprove any facts material to this case, nor is it supported by any testimony herein, and on its face shows that the notice was given on September 30th, the day following the date on which   [26]   the contract was to have been performed and the contract had expired.

The COURT.—The objection will be sustained.

Mr. REYNOLDS.—Exception.

A copy of Plaintiff's Exhibit 3 offered in evidence, but refused, is as follows:

Plaintiff's Exhibit No. 3.

Jamison & Murray,

    Glasgow, Montana.

I, C. M. Stitt, acting as representative for Xavier Servel and Hatcher & Snyder, do hereby offer to procure legal tender money with which to pay for your lambs on Monday, October 1st, or as soon as the same can be procured from Banks at Glasgow or Great Falls, which will be within a couple of days, providing you will deliver lambs to me upon such payment. We also offer to indemnify you for all damage involved in the delay.

C. M. STITT.

For XAVIER SERVEL.

HATCHER & SNYDER.

Witnessed:

Mr. REYNOLDS.—I have here a deposition from the cashier of the Ft. Morgan bank which I offer in evidence, but assume that there will be an objection to it.

Mr. NORRIS.—The deposition and the fact that it is a deposition and the manner of its taking, or the irregularity of its taking, will not be objected to, but the deposition is objected to on the ground that it is incompetent, irrelevant and immaterial, and not tending to show anything in compliance with the terms of the contract, and the same objections that have heretofore been made.

The COURT.—Objection sustained.

Mr. REYNOLDS.—Exception.

Deposition above referred to and offered in evidence is deposition of L. M. Meeker, and is as follows:

Deposition of L. M. Meeker, for Plaintiff.

I am cashier of First National Bank of Fort Morgan, and occupied that position throughout the entire

(Deposition of L. M. Meeker.)
month of September, 1917. I am acquainted with Mr. Stitt. He is a customer of the bank.

I knew of his going to Glasgow, Montana, in the latter part of September, 1917, for the purpose of receiving some lambs under the Hatcher & Snyder contract. I heard Mr. Stitt's testimony to-day, and it was for the purpose of receiving the [27] lambs, testified to by him, that he was going to Montana. Before he went to Montana, he made arrangements with me relative to taking care of any check that he might draw, in payment of said lambs. The firm of Stitt & Patterson made arrangements with me, as cashier of the bank, for credit of $100,000, and C. M. Stitt for credit of $75,000. Mr. Stitt had our permission to check upon our bank. If any check had come to us in payment of the lambs at that time, in the amount of $40,000, we would have had to honor it; we had made arrangements. Our resources at that time were about $1,075,000. Cash on hand at that time, $175,000.

We received Plaintiff's Exhibit 1 from Mr. Stitt while he was in Montana. (Referring to exhibit 1 attached to deposition of C. M. Stitt, and being telegram from C. M. Stitt, asking bank to guarantee payment of his check.) We received that at about seven o'clock in the evening, September 29, 1917. We replied immediately upon receipt of the message by telegram to the Farmers & Stockholders Bank of Glasgow, Montana.

Plaintiff's Exhibit 5 is the message sent by the First National Bank of Fort Morgan to the Farmers

(Deposition of L. M. Meeker.)

& Stockgrowers Bank of Glasgow, Montana, on September 29, 1917. (Referring to exhibit 5 attached to deposition, asking Farmers & Stockgrowers Bank to advise Jamieson & Murray that it would guarantee payment of check drawn upon it in payment of lambs in question.) It is a carbon copy and is identically the same. I sent the message myself, at about seven thirty P. M.

Testimony of James Rea, for Plaintiff.

JAMES REA, a witness called and sworn in behalf of plaintiff, testified as follows:

My name is James Rea. I live in Billings, Montana, and am a livestock dealer. I have been in that business all my life; I have never been in anything else. I handle sheep.

I was representing Story & Work. Story & Work bought the ewe lambs out of the Jamieson & Murray lamb crop, to be delivered last September. I went to Glasgow to receive these lambs, and reached there the 24th or 25th.

The parties that bought the wether lambs didn't show up at the time I was there and when we started weighing the ewe [28] lambs we weighed the wether lambs at the same time, and I sort of supervised the weighing of the wether lambs for the party that bought them. Mr. Murray asked me to keep track of the figures, so that there wouldn't be any controversy over it afterwards.

I had a conversation with Mr. Jamieson relative to the delivery of these wether lambs to Mr. Stitt

(Testimony of James Rea.)

on a certain contract. When we was riding out from Glasgow to Nashua—they were to be weighed near Nashua, and he told me when we were riding out alone in the car that he didn't care whether the fellow that bought the wether lambs showed up or not, because the lambs were higher then and he didn't care whether he delivered them or not. While we were weighing the lambs, Mr. Murray said the same thing. He said he didn't care whether he delivered the wether lambs to the party that bought them or not. I was familiar at that time with the value of lambs of this character, between Nashua and Saco.

Q. What was the market value at such time, of such lambs, per pound?

Mr. HURD.—Just a moment. There isn't any foundation so far for any such evidence.

Mr. REYNOLDS.—May it please the Court, I would ask the Court for leave to amend the complaint by adding at the end of paragraph 5 of the complaint the following:

"That the above-mentioned offer was made by valid check and draft after the banks had closed on the 29th day of September, 1917; that said check and draft were refused; that the plaintiff thereupon offered to secure the legal tender money for such payment as soon as it could be telegraphed to Glasgow, Montana, from his home at Fort Morgan, Colorado, and that the defendant refused said offer and thereupon sold said lambs to one Johnson." [29]

Mr. NORRIS.—May it please the Court, we object for the reason that it doesn't change the issues in the

'(Testimony of James Rea.)

case and is not material under the issues of the case and it would not admit evidence that would be competent and that it contradicts the preceding part of said paragraph 5 and other portions of the complaint and contradicts the contract itself.

The COURT.—The proposed amendment does not benefit the plaintiff's case any, and the objection will be sustained.

Mr. REYNOLDS.—Exception.

JAMES REA is recalled to the stand for further examination.

Mr. REYNOLDS.—Plaintiff offers to show by the witness, James E. Rea, on the stand, that the market value of lambs in question at weighing points, near Nashua and Saco on the 29th day of September, 1917, was fifteen cents to fifteen and one-half cents per pound.

Mr. HURD.—The offer is objected to on the ground that the evidence proposed to be offered is irrelevant and immaterial, and there is no foundation laid for it, in that there has not at this time been shown any violation of the terms and provisions of the contract.

The COURT.—Yes, this offer to show the value of the lambs is immaterial, as the plaintiff did not comply with the terms of the contract and the matter of the value is entirely irrelevant. The objection will be sustained.

Mr. REYNOLDS.—Exception.

Q. Is there, or is there not, a custom relative to the method of payment of the purchase price for sheep,

(Testimony of James Rea.)

and if so, was there such a custom in force in September, 1917? [30]

Mr. NORRIS.—To that we object, on the ground that it is incompetent, irrelevant and immaterial and no foundation has been laid for it, and on the ground that it calls for the conclusion of this witness.

The COURT.—Objection sustained.

Mr. REYNOLDS.—Exception.

Mr. REYNOLDS.—Plaintiff offers to show by witness James E. Rea, on the stand, that it is and has been for many years the custom in all parts of Montana and in the northwestern States generally among sheep men to pay for sheep purchased by means of a check or draft, and that such is true regardless of the amount of money involved, and that it is the custom of vendor to notify the vendee that the payment of the check or draft be guaranteed by bank upon which it is drawn if he has objection to the check, and in time that such guarantee can be procured by the time fixed for delivery, and that such custom applies to the payment by check or draft drawn on bank or person in a sister State, the same as though drawn on a bank of the State of Montana.

The COURT.—Do you renew the objection?

Mr. NORRIS.—Yes.

The COURT.—It will be sustained.

Mr. REYNOLDS.—Exception.

Testimony of Xavier Servel, in His Own Behalf (Recalled).

XAVIER SERVEL is recalled for further examination.

Mr. REYNOLDS.—Your Honor, I asked Mr. Serval as to whether he had notice, but I did not make any offer of proof.

The COURT.—Very well.

Mr. REYNOLDS.—Plaintiff offers to prove by plaintiff, Xavier Servel, on the stand, that he never had any notice from defendants, either directly or indirectly, that they would require currency for final payment on the contract in question.

Mr. NORRIS.—To the offer we object, on the ground stated in our [31] objections to that line of testimony.

The COURT.—Objection sustained.

Mr. REYNOLDS.—Exception.

Testimony of C. M. Stitt, for Plaintiff (Recalled).

C. M. STITT is recalled for further examination.

I was at Glasgow during the summer—in July. I saw Mr. Murray at that time in Glasgow. I had a conversation with him at that time relative to the delivery of these sheep. I informed him that I had bought these sheep from Hatcher & Snyder. I informed him that I expected to receive the sheep at the time of delivery on the Servel contract.

Neither of the defendants at any time gave me any notice, either directly or indirectly, before about 4:30 P. M. of the 29th of September, 1917, that they

(Testimony of C. M. Stitt.)

would require legal tender money for final payment on the contract in question.

Mr. HURD.—We ask that the answer be stricken out and we object on the ground that it is incompetent, irrelevant and immaterial.

The COURT.—Just as the Court stated heretofore, no notice was necessary under the law. Objection sustained.

Mr. REYNOLDS.—Exception.

Mr. REYNOLDS.—Plaintiff offers to prove by C. M. Stitt, witness on the stand, that he did not receive any notice of any kind from defendants before 4:30 P. M. of the 29th day of September, 1917, that they would require legal tender money for final payment on the contract in question.

Mr. HURD.—The offer of proof is objected to on the ground stated in the former objection.

The COURT.—Sustained.

Mr. REYNOLDS.—Exception. Plaintiff rests.

(And thereupon the plaintiff rested his case.)
[32]

Mr. HURD.—At this time, may it please the Court, we ask for a directed verdict in favor of the defendants.

The COURT.—This motion for directed verdict will be granted. It is only a question of law, gentlemen of the jury, and the clerk will enter such a verdict of record.

Mr. REYNOLDS.—Exception.

The COURT.—The exception will be noted.

Mr. REYNOLDS.—May it please the Court, may

we have thirty days in which to prepare a bill of exceptions?

The COURT.—The thirty days will be granted. :

L. B. REYNOLDS,

Attorney for Plaintiff.

Order Settling Bill of Exceptions, etc.

United States of America,

District of Montana,—ss.

I, George M. Bourquin, Judge of the District Court for the District of Montana, do hereby certify that the foregoing is a full, true and correct bill of exceptions in said action, and that the recitals therein regarding the testimony introduced are true and correct, and that the same contains a full, true and correct copy and statement of all the evidence and proceedings upon the trial of said action; and I do further order as well as certify that this bill of exceptions is now by me hereby settled, allowed and approved as a true and correct bill of exceptions in said action.

Dated in open court this 6th day of May, A. D. 1918.

BOURQUIN,

Judge.

Filed May 6, 1918. C. R. Garlow, Clerk. **[33]**

Thereafter on August 9th, 1918, plaintiff's Assignment of Errors was duly filed herein, in the words and figures following, to wit: **[34]**

In the District Court of the United States, for the District of Montana (Great Falls Division.)

XAVIER SERVEL,

Plaintiff,

  vs.

G. R. JAMIESON and MATHIESON MURRAY,
 Copartners Doing Business Under the Firm
 Name of JAMIESON & MURRAY,

Defendants.

Assignment of Errors.

Comes now the above-named plaintiff, Xavier Servel, and presents and files with his petition for a writ of error herein, his assignment of errors, as follows, to wit:

I.

The Court erred in sustaining objection of defendants to testimony of plaintiff, which testimony, objection, and ruling were as follows, to wit:

> "I did not at any time receive any advice, directly or indirectly, from the defendants that they would not accept check in final settlement."
>
> Mr. HURD.—That is objected to as incompetent, irrelevant and immaterial, and no foundation laid for it.
>
> The COURT.—Sustained.
>
> Mr. REYNOLDS.—Exception.

II.

The Court erred in sustaining objection of defendants to testimony of C. M. Stitt, which testimony, objection, and ruling were as follows, to wit:

"At that time I had made arrangements with a bank for the payment of my check." [35]

Mr. NORRIS.—Just a moment. Any arrangement he had for the payment of the check is not in compliance with the terms of the contract.

The COURT.—The objection will be sustained.

III.

The Court erred in sustaining objection of defendants to plaintiff's offer of proof by his witness Stitt, which offer, objection, and ruling were as follows, to wit:

Mr. REYNOLDS.—Plaintiff offers to prove by Witness Stitt upon the stand, that he had made arrangements with bank at Fort Morgan, Colorado, for payment of any check that he might draw on it in payment of the lambs in question.

Mr. HURD.—To which offer the defendants object, for the reason that the matter offered to be proved by this witness is irrelevant and immaterial, and does not tend to show any compliance with the terms of the contract, and there is no foundation laid for any such testimony.

The COURT.—The objection to the offer will be sustained.

Mr. REYNOLDS.—Exception.

IV.

The Court erred in sustaining objection of defendants to question of plaintiff's attorney to witness C. M. Stitt, which question, objection, and ruling, were as follows, to wit:

Q. Mr. Stitt, were you able at that time to produce the currency just as soon as it could be wired from the bank?

Mr. NORRIS.—We object to his ability to produce it later.

The COURT.—Sustained.

V.

The Court erred in sustaining objection of defendants to question of plaintiff's attorney to witness C. M. Stitt, which question, objection, and ruling were as follows, to wit: [36]

Q. Mr. Stitt, if the defendants had acquiesced in that offer of the currency and had not refused to accept it, would you have produced the currency for the payment of the lambs by wire?

Mr. NORRIS.—We object to that on the ground that the evidence sought to be brought out by this witness is irrelevant, incompetent, and immaterial and there is no foundation laid, and therefore it is not responsive nor illustrative of any issue in this case, and instead of showing a compliance with the contract, it is practically opposed by the terms of the contract.

The COURT.—Sustain the objection.

VI.

The Court erred in sustaining objection of defendants to plaintiff's offer of proof, which offer, objection, ruling, and exception were as follows, to wit:

Mr. REYNOLDS.—Plaintiff offers to prove by the witness Stitt upon the stand, that he could have produced the currency or legal tender for the payment of lambs in question just as soon as it could have been procured by telegram from his bank at Fort Morgan, Colorado, and would have done so if defendants had not told him that it would be useless.

Mr. NORRIS.—We object to the offer of the testimony because of the fact that it is incompetent, irrelevant and immaterial and has no pertinent value in the case and is not responsive to the issues set forth in the pleadings, nor is it justified by any evidence heretofore produced, and there is no foundation laid for it, and it is indefinite as to the time when this money could have been produced, and by reason of the further fact that on account of the indefinite character of the proposed offer of testimony, it cannot be determined whether or not the witness could or would have produced that money on that date, or at some subsequent time.   [37]

The COURT.—Objection sustained.

Mr. REYNOLDS.—Exception.

VII.

The Court erred in sustaining objection of defendants to question of plaintiff's attorney to witness C. M. Stitt, which question, objection, ruling, and exception were as follows, to wit:

"I did have a conversation upon Sunday, the
30th of September, with one of the defendants,
relative to having received a message from my
Bank at Fort Morgan."

Q. And what was that conversation?

Mr. NORRIS.—To which we object, your
Honor, as incompetent, irrelevant, and immaterial. This is introduced evidently for the purpose of showing that on the day succeeding the
date the contract expired, this conversation
was had, and showing no attempt to comply
with the terms of the contract.

The COURT.—The objection will be sustained.

Mr. REYNOLDS.—Exception.

VIII.

The Court erred in sustaining objection of defendants to plaintiff's offer of proof by witness
C. M. Stitt, which offer, objection, ruling, and exception were as follows, to wit:

Mr. REYNOLDS.—Plaintiff offers to prove
by witness Stitt on the stand, that his Bank at
Fort Morgan, Colorado, telegraphed to defendants, guaranteeing to pay his check for the
lambs in question, and that defendants admitted
to him that they had received said telegram.

Mr. NORRIS.—To which offer the defendants object, for the reason that the same is incompetent, irrelevant, and immaterial, and does
not show a compliance with the terms of the
contract, and in fact shows that the terms of the
contract were not and had not been complied

with, as the evidence sought to be [38] introduced would detail facts and circumstances occurring after the expiration of the date on
which the contract was to have been performed,
and does not tend to show an attempt to perform under the conditions of the contract on
the date that the contract required it to be performed.

The COURT.—Sustained.

Mr. REYNOLDS.—Exception.

IX.

The Court erred in sustaining objection of defendants to question of plaintiff's attorney to witness
C. M. Stitt, which question, objection, ruling, and exception were as follows, to wit:

"Q. Did you, on the 30th of September, have a
talk with the defendants, or either of them, relative to the reception of a message by them, from
the Bank of Montana, relative to the payment
of any draft you might draw on Hatch &
Snyder?

Mr. NORRIS.—To which we object, your
Honor.

The COURT.—Sustained.

Mr. REYNOLDS.—Exception.

X.

The Court erred in sustaining objection of defendants to plaintiff's offer of proof by witness
Stitt, which offer, objection, ruling, and exception
were as follows, to wit:

Mr. REYNOLDS.—Plaintiff offers to prove
by witness Stitt upon the stand, that defendants

admitted to him on Sunday, September 30th, that they had received telegram from Montana National Bank of Billings, guaranteeing any draft that he might draw on Hatcher & Snyder, in payment of the sheep in question.

Mr. NORRIS.—To which we object.

The COURT.—Sustained. [39]

Mr. REYNOLDS.—Exception.

XI.

The Court erred in sustaining objection of defendants to plaintiff's offer of exhibit 3, which offer, objection, ruling, and exception were as follows, to wit:

Document marked exhibit 3.

"This is the notice I gave Mr. Murray the 30th of September."

Mr. REYNOLDS.—We offer this in evidence.

Mr. NORRIS.—To which offer of the plaintiff, proposed exhibit 3 in evidence, the defendants object, for the reason that the same is incompetent, irrelevant, and immaterial, and no foundation has been laid for it, and it does not tend to prove or disprove any facts material to this case, nor is it supported by any testimony herein, and on its face shows that the notice was given on September 30th, the day following the date on which the contract was to have been performed, and the contract had expired.

The COURT.—The objection will be sustained.

Mr. REYNOLDS.—Exception.

XII.

The Court erred in sustaining objection of defendants to the offered evidence of the deposition of L. M. Meeker, Cashier of the First National Bank of Fort Morgan, Colorado, which offer, objection, ruling, and exception were as follows, to wit:

Mr. REYNOLDS.—I have here a deposition from the Cashier of the Fort Morgan Bank which I offer in evidence, but assume that there will be an objection to it.

Mr. NORRIS.—The deposition and the fact that it is a deposition and the manner of its taking, or the irregularity of [40] its taking, will not be objected to, but the deposition is objected to on the ground that it is incompetent, irrelevant, and immaterial, and not tending to show anything in compliance with the terms of the contract, and the same objections that have heretofore been made.

The COURT.—Objection sustained.

Mr. REYNOLDS.—Exception.

XIII.

The Court erred in sustaining objection to plaintiff's application for leave to amend his complaint, which proposed amendment, objection, ruling, and exception were as follows, to wit:

Mr. REYNOLDS.—May it please the Court, I would ask the Court for leave to amend the complaint by adding at the end of paragraph 5 of the complaint the following:

"That the above-mentioned offer was made by valid check **and draft** after the banks had

closed on the 29th day of September, 1917; that
said check and draft were refused; that the
plaintiff thereupon offered to secure the legal
tender money for such payment as soon as it
could be telegraphed to Glasgow, Montana,
from his home at Fort Morgan, Colorado, and
that the defendant refused said offer, and thereupon sold said lambs to one Johnson.''

Mr. NORRIS.—May it please the Court, we
object for the reason that it doesn't change the
issues in the case and is not material under the
issues of the case, and it would not admit evidence that would be competent, and that it contradicts the preceding part of said paragraph 5
and other portions of the complaint, and contradicts the contract itself.

The COURT.—The proposed amendment
does not benefit the plaintiff's case any, and the
objection will be sustained.

Mr. REYNOLDS.—Exception.   [41]

XIV.

The Court erred in sustaining objection of defendants to offer of proof of plaintiff by witness James
E. Rea, which offer, objection, ruling, and exception
were as follows, to wit:

Mr. REYNOLDS.—Plaintiff offers to show
by the witness James E. Rea on the stand, that
the market value of lambs in question at
weighing points, near Nashua and Saco on the
29th day of September, 1917, was fifteen cents
to fifteen and one-half cents per pound.

Mr. HURD.—The offer is objected to on the

ground that the evidence proposed to be offered is irrelevant and immaterial, and there is no foundation laid for it, in that there has not at this time been shown any violation of the terms and provisions of the contract.

The COURT.—Yes, this offer to show the value of the lambs is immaterial, as the plaintiff did not comply with the contract, and the matter of the value is entirely irrelevant. The objection will be sustained.

Mr. REYNOLDS.—Exception.

XV.

The Court erred in sustaining objection of defendants to question of plaintiff's attorney to witness James E. Rea, which question, objection, ruling, and exception were as follows, to wit:

Q. Is there, or is there not, a custom relative to the method of payment of the purchase price of sheep, and if so, was there such a custom in force in September, 1917?

Mr. NORRIS.—To that we object, on the ground that it is incompetent, irrelevant, and immaterial, and no foundation has been laid for it, and on the ground that it calls for this conclusion of this witness.

The COURT.—Objection sustained.

Mr. REYNOLDS.—Exception. [42]

XVI.

The Court erred in sustaining objection of defendants to plaintiff's offer of proof by witness James E. Rea, which offer, objection, ruling, and exception were as follows, to wit:

Mr. REYNOLDS.—Plaintiff offers to show, by witness James E. Rea on the stand, that it is, and has been for many years, the custom in all parts of Montana and in the northwestern states generally among sheep men to pay for sheep purchased by means of a check or draft, and that such is true regardless of the amount of money involved, and that it is the custom of vendor to notify the vendee that the payment of the check or draft be guaranteed by bank upon which it is drawn if he has any objection to the check, and in time that such guarantee can be procured by the time fixed for delivery, and that such custom applies to the payment by check or draft drawn on bank or person in a sister State, the same as though drawn on a bank of the State of Montana.

The COURT.—Do you renew the objection?

Mr. NORRIS.—Yes.

The COURT.—It will be sustained.

Mr. REYNOLDS.—Exception.

XVII.

The Court erred in sustaining objection of defendants to plaintiff's offer of proof by himself, a witness on the stand, which offer, objection, ruling, and exception were as follows, to wit:

Mr. REYNOLDS.—Plaintiff offers to prove by plaintiff Xavier Servel on the stand, that he never had any notice from defendants, either directly or indirectly, that they would require currency for final payment on the contract in question.

Mr. NORRIS.—To the offer we object, on the ground stated in our objections to that line of testimony. [43]

The COURT.—Objection sustained.

Mr. REYNOLDS.—Exception.

XVIII.

The Court erred in sustaining objection and motion to strike out testimony made by defendants as to testimony of C. M. Stitt, which testimony, objection, ruling, and exception were as follows, to wit:

"Neither of the defendants at any time gave me any notice, either directly or indirectly, before about 4:30 P. M. of the 29th of September, 1917, that they would require legal tender money for final payment on the contract in question."

Mr. HURD.—We ask that the answer be stricken out, and we object on the ground that it is incompetent, irrelevant, and immaterial.

The COURT.—Just as the Court stated before, no notice was necessary under the law. Objection sustained.

Mr. REYNOLDS.—Exception."

XIX.

The Court erred in sustaining objection of defendants to offer of proof of plaintiff by witness C. M. Stitt, which offer, objection, ruling, and exception were as follows, to wit:

Mr. REYNOLDS.—Plaintiff offers to prove by C. M. Stitt, witness on the stand, that he did not receive any notice of any kind from defendants before 4:30 P. M. of the 29th day of September, 1917, that they would require legal tender money for final payment on the contract in question.

Mr. HURD.—The offer of proof is objected to on the ground stated in the former objection.

The COURT.—Sustained.

Mr. REYNOLDS.—Exception.

XX.

The Court erred in sustaining motion of defendants for [44] directed verdict, which motion, ruling, and exception were as follows, to wit:

Mr. HURD.—At this time, may it please the Court, we ask for a directed verdict in favor of the defendants.

The COURT.—This motion for directed verdict will be granted. It is only a question of law, gentlemen of the jury, and the Clerk will enter such a verdict of record.

Mr. REYNOLDS.—Exception.

The COURT.—The exception will be noted.

XXI.

The Court erred in rendering judgment in favor of the defendants herein.

WHEREFORE, said plaintiff prays that said judgment may be reversed.

F. B. REYNOLDS,

Attorney for Plaintiff, Xavier Servel.

Filed Aug. 9, 1918. C. R. Garlow, Clerk. [45]

Thereafter on August 9th, 1918, petition for Writ of Error was duly filed herein in the words and figures following, to wit: [46]

In the District Court of the United States for the District of Montana, (Great Falls Division).

XAVIER SERVEL,

Plaintiff,

vs.

G. R. JAMIESON and MATHIESON MURRAY, Copartners Doing Business Under the Firm Name of JAMIESON & MURRAY,

Defendants.

Petition of Plaintiff, Xavier Servel, for Writ of Error.

Xavier Servel, plaintiff in the above-entitled cause of action, feeling himself aggrieved by the proceedings had in said cause and by the action of the Court and the judgment entered in said cause on the 30th day of March, A. D. 1918, for the sum of Four Hundred Seventy-two Dollars costs, in favor of defendants and against plaintiff, and holding that plaintiff shall not recover from defendant upon the cause of action set forth in his complaint filed herein, comes now F. B. Reynolds, his attorney, and petitions said Court for order allowing said plaintiff to prosecute a writ of error, to the Honorable, the United States Circuit of Appeals, for the Ninth Circuit, under and according to the laws of the United States in that behalf made and provided; and also that an order be made, fixing the amount of security which the said plaintiff shall give upon said writ of error, and that upon the giving of said security all proceedings in this court be suspended and stayed until the determination of said writ of error by the United States Circuit Court of Appeals for the Ninth Circuit.

And the said plaintiff herewith presents his assignments of error in accordance with the rules of the said United States [47] Circuit Court of Appeals and the course and practice of this Honorable Court, and your petitioner, the plaintiff, will ever pray, etc.

F. B. REYNOLDS,

Attorney for Xavier Servel, Plaintiff.

Filed Aug. 9, 1918.   C. R. Garlow, Clerk.   [48]

Thereafter on August 10th, 1918, order granting Writ of Error and Fixing Bond was duly filed and entered herein, being in words and figures following, to wit: [49]

In the District Court of the United States for the District of Montana, (Great Falls Division).

XAVIER SERVEL,

Plaintiff,

vs.

G. R. JAMIESON and MATHIESON MURRAY, Copartners Doing Business Under the Firm Name of JAMIESON & MURRAY,

Defendants.

Order Granting Writ of Error and Fixing Amount of Supersedeas Bond.

On motion of F. B. Reynolds, attorney for plaintiff in the above-entitled cause of action, the foregoing petition for writ of error is hereby granted, and it is ordered that a writ of error to have reviewed in the United States Circuit Court of Appeals for the Ninth Circuit, the judgment described in said petition, be, and hereby is, allowed, and that the amount of the bond on said writ of error be, and hereby is, fixed at the sum of One Thousand Dollars, and it is further ordered that the same shall operate as a supersedeas until the determination of said writ of error by the United States Circuit Court of Appeals for the Ninth Circuit.

GEO. M. BOURQUIN,
United States District Judge.

Filed Aug. 10, 1918.   C. R. Garlow, Clerk.   **[50]**

Thereafter on August 10th, 1918, Bond on Writ of Error was duly approved and filed herein, being in words and figures following, to wit: **[51]**

In the District Court of the United States for the District of Montana, (Great Falls Division).

XAVIER SERVEL,

Plaintiff,

vs.

G. R. JAMIESON and MATHIESON MURRAY, Copartners Doing Business Under the Firm Name of JAMIESON & MURRAY,

Defendants.

Bond on Writ of Error.

KNOW ALL MEN BY THESE PRESENTS, That we, Xavier Servel, as principal, and C. L. Wilcox, and O. B. Parham, both of Billings, Yellowstone County, Montana, as sureties, are held and firmly bound unto G. R. Jamieson and Mathieson Murray, copartners doing business under the firm name of Jamieson & Murray, defendants in the above-entitled cause of action, in the full and just sum of One Thousand Dollars, to be paid to said defendants, for which payment well and truly to be made, we bind ourselves, our heirs, executors, and administrators jointly and severally firmly by these presents.

Sealed with our seals and dated this 8th day of August, A. D. 1918.

WHEREAS, lately at a session of the District Court of the United States, in and for the District of Montana, in an action pending in said court between Xavier Servel, as plaintiff, and G. R. Jamieson and Mathieson Murray, copartners doing business under the firm name of Jamieson & Murray, defendants, a final judgment was rendered against said plaintiff and in favor of said defendants, and the said plaintiff, Xavier [52] Servel having obtained from said Court a writ of error to reverse the judgment in said action, and a citation directed to said G. R. Jamieson and Mathieson Murray, defendants as aforesaid, is about to be issued, citing and admonishing said defendants to be and appear at the United States Circuit Court of Appeals for the Ninth Circuit, to be holden at San Francisco, California:

NOW, THEREFORE, the condition of the above obligation is such that if the said Xavier Servel shall prosecute his writ of error to effect and shall answer all damages and costs that may be awarded against him, if he fails to make his plea good, then the above obligation to be void, otherwise to remain in full force and virtue.

OWEN B. PARHAM.
C. L. WILCOX.
XAVIER SERVEL.

Witness:
D. R. PRAGUE.

State of Montana,
County of Yellowstone,—ss.

C. L. Wilcox and O. B. Parham, the sureties who executed the within undertaking, being by me duly sworn, depose and say each for himself and not one for the other that he is a resident and freeholder within the County of Yellowstone, and that he is worth the sum mentioned in the foregoing undertaking, over and above all his debts and liabilities which he owes or has incurred and exclusive of property exempt by law from execution.

OWEN B. PARHAM,
C. L. WILCOX. [53]

Sworn to and subscribed before me this 8th day of August, A. D. 1918.

[Seal]   F. B. REYNOLDS,
Notary Public for the State of Montana, Residing at Billings, Montana.

My commission expires April 21, 1919.

The foregoing bond is hereby approved this 10 day of Aug., A. D. 1918.

GEO. M. BOURQUIN,
United States District Judge.

Filed Aug. 10, 1918.   C. R. Garlow, Clerk.   [54]

———

Thereafter on August 10th, 1918, a Citation was duly issued herein, which original citation is hereto annexed, and is in words and figures following, to wit: [55]

In the District Court of the United States for the District of Montana, (Great Falls Division).

XAVIER SERVEL,

Plaintiff,

vs.

G. R. JAMIESON and MATHIESON MURRAY, Copartners Doing Business Under the Firm Name of JAMIESON & MURRAY,

Defendants.

Citation on Writ of Error.

The President of the United States, to G. R. Jamieson and Mathieson Murray, Copartners Doing Business Under the Firm Name of Jamieson & Murray, GREETING:

You are hereby cited and admonished to be and appear at the United States Circuit Court of Appeals, for the Ninth Circuit, to be held at the City of San

Francisco, in the State of California, within thirty days from the date hereof, pursuant to writ of error filed in the clerk's office of the District Court of the United States, in and for the District of Montana, wherein Xavier Servel is plaintiff in error, and you are defendants in error, to show cause, if any there be, why the judgment in said writ of error mentioned should not be corrected and speedy justice should be done to the parties in that behalf.

GEO. M. BOURQUIN,

United States District Judge.

Service of the foregoing citation acknowledged and copy thereof received this —— day of ————, A. D. 19—.

————————————,

Attorneys for Defendants in Error.   [56]

[Endorsed]: No. 638. District Court United States, District of Montana. Xavier Servel, Plaintiff, vs. G. R. Jamieson, et al., Defendants. Citation on Writ of Error.   [57]

———

Thereafter on August 10th, 1918, a Writ of Error was duly issued herein, which original Writ of Error is hereto annexed and is in words and figures following, to wit: [58]

*In the District Court of the United States for the
District of Montana, (Great Falls Division).*

XAVIER SERVEL,

                                    Plaintiff,

        vs.

G. R. JAMIESON and MATHIESON MURRAY,
    Copartners Doing Business Under the Firm
    Name of JAMIESON & MURRAY,

                                    Defendants.

Writ of Error.

United States of America,—ss.

The President of the United States, to the Honor-
    able, the Judge of the District Court of the
    United States, for the District of Montana,
    GREETING:

Because, in the record and proceedings as also in
the rendition of the judgment of a plea which is in
said District Court, and between Xavier Servel,
plaintiff in error, and G. R. Jamieson and Mathieson
Murray, defendant in error, a manifest error hath
happened, to the great damage of the said Xavier
Servel, the plaintiff in error, as by his complaint
appears:

We, being willing that error, if any hath happened, should be duly corrected and full and speedy
justice done to the parties aforesaid in this behalf,
do command you, distinctly and openly, to send the
record and proceedings aforesaid, with all things concerning the same, to the United States Circuit Court
of Appeals, for the Ninth Circuit, together with this

writ, so that you have the same at the city of San Francisco, in the State of California, on the 9th day of September, A. D. 1918, next, in the said Circuit Court of Appeals, to be then **[59]** and there held, that the record and proceedings aforesaid being inspected, the said Circuit Court of Appeals may cause further to be done therein to correct that error what of right and according to the laws and customs of the United States should be done.

WITNESS, the Honorable EDWARD D. WHITE, Chief Justice of the United States the 10th day of August, in the year one thousand nine hundred eighteen.

[Seal]   C. R. GARLOW,
Clerk of the District Court of the United States, in
    and for the District of Montana.

Service of the within and foregoing writ of error and receipt of copy thereof is hereby acknowledged this —— day of ———, 19—.

———————————,
        Attorneys for Defendants in Error.

Answer of Court to Writ of Error.

The answer of the Honorable, the District Judge of the United States for the District of Montana, to the foregoing writ:

The record and proceedings whereof mention is within made, with all things touching the same, I hereby certify, under the seal of said District Court of the United States, to the Honorable, the United States Circuit Court of Appeals for the Ninth Circuit, within mentioned, at the day and place within contained, in a certain schedule to this writ annexed, as within I am commanded.

By the Court.

[Seal]   C. R. GARLOW,
                                              Clerk.   **[60]**

[Endorsed]: No. 638. District Court United States, District of Montana. Xavier Servel, Plaintiff, vs. G. R. Jamieson, et al., Defendants. Writ of Error. **[61]**

In the District Court of the United States for the District of Montana, (Great Falls Division).

XAVIER SERVEL,

                                              Plaintiff,

                    vs.

G. R. JAMIESON and MATHIESON MURRAY,
      Copartners Doing Business Under the Firm
      Name of JAMIESON & MURRAY,
                                    Defendants.

Acknowledgment of Service of Papers on Appeal.

We hereby acknowledge due service of order granting writ of error and fixing amount of supersedeas bond, citation on writ of error and writ of error in the above-entitled cause of action, and receipt of copies of them respectively.

Dated August 16, 1918.

                    NORRIS, HURD & McKELLAR,
                    Attorneys for Defendants.   **[62]**

' Thereafter on August 10th, 1918, Praecipe for Transcript was duly filed herein, in words and figures following, to wit: **[63]**

In the District Court of the United States for the District of Montana, (Great Falls Division).

XAVIER SERVEL,

Plaintiff,

vs.

G. R. JAMIESON and MATHIESON MURRAY, Copartners Doing Business Under the Firm Name of JAMIESON & MURRAY,

Defendants.

Praecipe for Transcript of Record.

To the Clerk of the Above-entitled Court:

You are hereby requested to make a transcript of record to be filed in the United States Circuit Court of Appeals for the Ninth Circuit, pursuant to writ of error allowed in the above-entitled cause, and to incorporate into such transcript of record the following papers, to wit:

1. Judgment-roll.
2. Bill of exceptions of plaintiff, Xavier Servel.
3. Assignments of errors of plaintiff, Xavier Servel.
4. Petition of plaintiff, Xavier Servel, for writ of error and supersedeas, and allowance of same.
5. Bond on appeal.
6. Writ of error.
7. Citation on writ of error.

Request is further made that the same be duly
certified by you as required by law and the rules of
Court.

F. B. REYNOLDS,

Attorney for Plaintiff, Xavier Servel.

Filed Aug. 10, 1918.   C. R. Garlow, Clerk.   **[64]**

Certificate of Clerk U. S. District Court to Transcript of Record.

United States of America,

District of Montana,—ss.

I, C. R. Garlow, Clerk of the United States District Court for the District of Montana, do hereby
certify and return to the Honorable, the United
States Circuit Court of Appeals for the Ninth Circuit, that the foregoing volume, consisting of 64
pages, numbered consecutively from 1 to 64, inclusive, is a full, true and correct transcript of pleadings, orders, verdict and judgment, and all proceedings had in said cause, and of the whole thereof, required to be incorporated in said transcript by plaintiff's praecipe, as appears from the original records
and files of said court in my custody as such clerk;
and I do further certify and return that I have annexed to said transcript and included within said
pages the original citation and writ of error issued
in said cause.

I further certify that the costs of transcript of record amount to the sum of Twenty-four & 50/100 Dollars ($24.50), and have been paid by plaintiff in
error.

WITNESS my hand and the seal of said court at Helena, Montana, August 20, 1918.

[Seal] C. R. GARLOW,
Clerk. [65]

[Endorsed]: No. 3200. United States Circuit Court of Appeals for the Ninth Circuit. Xavier Servel, Plaintiff in Error, vs. G. R. Jamieson and Mathieson Murray, Copartners Doing Business Under the Firm Name of Jamieson & Murray, Defendants in Error. Transcript of Record. Upon Writ of Error to the United States District Court of the District of Montana.

Filed August 23, 1918.

F. D. MONCKTON,
Clerk of the United States Circuit Court of Appeals for the Ninth Circuit.

By Paul P. O'Brien,
Deputy Clerk.

United States
Circuit Court of Appeals
For the Ninth Circuit

XAVIER SERVEL,

Plaintiff in Error,

vs.

G. R. JAMIESON AND MATHIESON MURRAY,
A Co-partnership Doing Business Under the Firm
Name of Jamieson & Murray,

Defendants in Error.

Brief of Plaintiff in Error

STATEMENT OF FACTS.

This action was brought by plaintiff in error against defendants in error to recover damages for failure to deliver sheep in accordance with the terms of a contract, made and entered into by and between the parties herein.

The contract in question was made on or about the 14th day of March, 1917, in the State of Montana, and provided that defendant should sell and deliver to plaintiff all the wether lambs produced in the year, 1917, by certain bands of ewes owned by defendants, and therein described, delivery to be made between the 25th day of September, 1917, and the 29th of September, 1917, exact date to be at option of plaintiff, at Porcupine Creek, above Nashua, Montana, and at the Town of Saco, Phillips County, Montana.

Plaintiff as party of the second part promised to pay for said lambs, "the sum of ten cents per pound."

It was further agreed, "that said party of the second part has paid at the date of the execution of this instrument the sum of Three Thousand Dollars as a part of the purchase price therefor, receipt whereof is hereby acknowledged by the said parties of the first part, and said party of the second part will pay the remainder of the purchase price of said wether sheep at the time and upon the delivery thereof to said party of the second part by said parties of the first part."

The contract further provided that the wether lambs should remain with their mothers in the corrals over night, and should be cut out the following morning and weighed, and the weights so obtained should be the basis of payment of the purchase price, as hereinabove mentioned.

The contract further provided, "and it is further mutually agreed by and between the parties hereto that time is of the essence of this agreement, and that upon the expiration of the time for delivery, as herein provided, the rights of said party of the second part hereunder shall cease and terminate, and he shall have no right, claim, or interest in and to said sheep after the expiration of said period of time."

Thereafter plaintiff by separate contract made a sale of said wether lambs to Hatcher & Snyder, a stock firm of Denver, Colorado. Thereafter Hatcher & Snyder by separate contract made a sale of said lambs to Patterson & Stitt, of Fort Morgan, Colorado, sheep dealers of that place. Inasmuch as Patterson & Stitt were ultimately to receive these lambs, the plaintiff, instead of going to Montana to receive them personally, authorized C. M. Stitt, of the firm of Patterson & Stitt, to receive said lambs for him.

Mr. Stitt, for the purpose of receiving these lambs, went to Glasgow, Montana, the home of the defendants upon the 25th day of September, 1917, arriving there at about one thirty o'clock in the afternoon. Shortly after arrival he met defendant Jamieson upon the street in Glasgow, and had a conversation with him at that time relative to the delivery of the sheep. He told Mr. Jamieson that he had come to receive the sheep, and that if he would take him out where they were, that he was ready to receive them, to which defendant replied that he was going out to where they were, and would take him out there in his automobile. Thereupon Mr. Stitt went with Mr. Jamieson, first to Nashua, and then from there to Porcupine Creek, which is about five miles north of Nashua, at which place a portion of the lambs were to be delivered, reaching there late in the evening. The next forenoon they started in weighing the lambs. The weighing of the lambs at this point was completed shortly after noon of the 28th inst. Thereupon Mr. Stitt went to Saco to receive the lambs at that point, reaching Saco late at night of the 28th inst. Upon the morning of the 29th inst. they weighed the lambs at Saco, finishing weighing at about eight o'clock in the morning, or a little later. After the weighing was completed, Mr. Jamieson took Mr. Stitt to Glasgow in his automobile, reaching there at about one o'clock in the afternoon. Mr. Jamieson said that Mr. Murray was at Nashua, and that they should go to Nashua for settlement. Mr. Stitt went by train, understanding that Mr. Jamieson was to come by automobile after he had had his dinner. Mr. Stitt reached Nashua at about two o'clock, and searched for Mr. Murray, but he was not there, so Mr. Stitt secured an automobile and went back to Glasgow, reaching there at about four o'clock of that afternoon. This was on Saturday, September 29th.

After reaching Glasgow he met defendants upon the street, and told them that he was ready to settle for the lambs. Defendant Murray asked him how he wanted to pay for them, and he told them that he would give them a check, to which Mr. Murray replied, "If you haven't got the currency, you cannot have the lambs, and if you have, you can, but we won't accept a check." Mr. Stitt told him that he did not have thirty thousand dollars in his pocket, but he could get it if it was necessary. He told him that he always had bought lambs by check, and had never given the currency before. He also told them that his check was good, and that he could prove that his check was good, and would wire his bank and have them guarantee it. He also offered to leave the sheep with them until he got the money, and to pay them for whatever expense or damage might be incurred by their so keeping them until he would get the money. He also offered to draw a draft upon Hatcher & Snyder, and stated that they would pay it. He also said, in regard to the currency, that he would get it just as soon as it could be transmitted by wire. The banks were closed and it was Saturday. They said that the time was up, and that he could not have the lambs.

Mr. Stitt testified that at the time he had made arrangements with his bank for payment of his check. This testimony, however, was stricken out upon motion of defendant, over objection of plaintiff. Plaintiff then offered to prove by Mr. Stitt that he had made arrangements with the bank at Fort Morgan, Colorado, for payment of any check that he might draw on it, which offer was refused.

Plaintiff offered to show by Mr. Stitt that he could have produced the currency or legal tender for payment of the lambs in question just as soon as it could be procured by telegram from his bank at Fort Morgan, Colorado, and would have done so if defendants had not told him that it would be useless, which offer was refused.

Plaintiff also offered to prove by C. M. Stitt that his bank at Fort Morgan, Colorado, telegraphed to defendants, guaranteeing to pay his check for the lambs in question, and that defendants admitted to him that they had received said telegram, which offer was refused.

Plaintiff also offered to prove by Mr. Stitt that defendants admitted on Sunday, September 30th, that they had received a telegram from the Montana National Bank at Billings, guaranteeing the payment of any draft that he might draw on Hatcher & Snyder in payment of the lambs in question, which offer was refused.

Plaintiff also offered to prove by Mr. Stitt the service upon defendants, upon the 30th day of September, 1917, of a written offer to procure the legal tender money as soon as the banks would open upon Monday morning in payment of the sheep in question, and also to compensate defendants for any damage that they might suffer by reason of holding the sheep until that time, being document marked in the case as Exhibit No. 3, which offer was refused.

Plaintiff also offered in evidence deposition of L. M. Meeker, cashier of the First National Bank of Fort Morgan, Colorado, showing that the firm of Patterson & Stitt had made arrangements for a credit of One Hundred Thousand Dollars, and C. M. Stitt for a credit of Seventy-five Thousand Dollars with said bank, and that before Mr. Stitt left for Montana he had made arrangements with said bank to take care of any check that he might draw in payment of said lambs; that said bank would have honored his check for any amount up to at least Forty Thousand Dollars; that its resources at that time were over One Million Dollars; that its cash on hand was One Hundred Seventy-five Thousand Dollars, and that he, as Cashier, had sent a telegram guaranteeing the payment of any check that would be drawn upon said bank, which offer was refused.

Plaintiff also offered to show, by plaintiff and by said C. M. Stitt, that neither one of them had received any notice whatever that defendants' would require legal tender money in payment of the lambs in question until the demand was made upon Mr. Stitt about four o'clock the afternoon of Saturday, the 29th inst., which offers were refused.

Plaintiff also offered to show, by witness James E. Rea, who had qualified on the stand as an expert sheep man, that it is, and has been for many years, the custom in all parts of Montana, and in the northwestern states generally among sheep men, to pay for their purchase of sheep by means of a check or draft, and that such is true regardless of the amount of money involved, and that it is the custom of the vendor to notify the vendee that the payment of a check or draft must be guaranteed by bank upon which it is drawn if he has any objections to the check, and in time that such guaranty can be procured by the time fixed for delivery, and that custom applies to the payment by check or draft drawn upon bank in a sister state, the same as though drawn on a bank in the State of Montana, which offer was refused.

Plaintiff took exception to each of the rulings of the Court in sustaining objection to the several offers.

After plaintiff, by his representative, Mr. Stitt, had made all of the offers to defendants, and they were refused by them, they, the next morning, sold and delivered said sheep to one Johnson. The contract price of the lambs in question was ten cents per pound, while, at the time of delivery, they were fifteen cents per pound, as appears from the offer of proof by witness, James E. Rea, this making a difference between the contract price of the lambs and the value thereof at the time fixed for delivery of the sum of Fifteen Thousand Six Hundred Sixty-six and 21-100 Dollars. This action was, therefore, brought to recover the down payment of Three Thousand Dollars, together with damages in the amount of difference, as above set forth.

The down payment of Three Thousand Dollars was made upon this contract by plaintiff's personal check, drawn upon a Utah Bank, to which no objection was made.

At the conclusion of plaintiff's evidence, upon motion

of defendants, the Court directed a verdict in favor of defendants, upon the ground that plaintiff had failed to perform his obligation under the contract to make payment for the lambs in question.

The vital question is, whether or not, under the circumstances of this case, plaintiff forfeited his right to a delivery of the lambs in question under said contract, or, in default thereof, his right of action on the contract for damages.

SPECIFICATIONS OF ERROR.

I.

The Court erred in sustaining objection of defendants to testimony of plaintiff,, which testimony, objection, and ruling were as follows, to-wit:—

"I did not at any time receive any advice, directly or indirectly, from the defendants that they would not accept check in final settlement."

MR. HURD: That is objected to as incompetent, irrelevant and immaterial, and no foundation laid for it.

THE COURT: Sustained.

MR. REYNOLDS: Exception. (Record ——)

II.

The Court erred in sustaining objection of defendants to testimony of C. M. Stitt, which testimony, objection, and ruling were as follows, to-wit:—

"At the time I had made arrangements with a bank for the payment of my check."

MR. NORRIS: Just a moment. Any arrangement he had for the payment of the check is not in compliance with the terms of the contract.

THE COURT: The objection will be sustained. (Record ——)

III.

The Court erred in sustaining objection of defendants to plaintiff's offer of proof by his witness Stitt, which offer, objection, and ruling were as follows, to-wit:—

MR. REYNOLDS: Plaintiff offers to prove by witness Stitt upon the stand, that he had made arrangements with bank at Fort Morgan, Colorado, for payment of any check that he might draw on it in payment of the lambs in question.

MR. HURD: To which offer the defendants object, for the reason that the matter offered to be proved by this witness is irrelevant and immaterial, and does not tend to show any compliance with the terms of the contract, and there is no foundation laid for any such testimony.

THE COURT: The objection to the offer will be sustained.

MR. REYNOLDS: Exception. (Record ——)

IV.

The Court erred in sustaining objection of defendants to question of plaintiff's attorney to witness C. M. Stitt, which question, objection, and ruling were as follows, to-wit:—

Q. Mr. Stitt, were you able at that time to produce the currency just as soon as it could be wired from the Bank?

MR. NORRIS: We object to his ability to produce it later.

THE COURT: Sustained. (Record ——)

V.

The Court erred in sustaining objection of defendants to question of plaintiff's attorney to witness C. M. Stitt, which question, objection, and ruling were as follows, to-wit:—

Q. Mr. Stitt, if the defendants had acquiesced in that offer of the currency and had not refused to accept it, would you have produced the currency for the payment of the lambs by wire?

MR. NORRIS: We object to that on the ground that the evidence sought to be brought out by this witness is irrelevant, incompetent, and immaterial, and there is no foundation laid, and therefore, it is not responsive nor illustrative of any issue in this case, and instead of showing a compliance with the contract, it is practically opposed by the terms of the contract.

THE COURT: Sustain the objection. (Record ——)

VI.

The Court erred in sustaining objection of defendants to plaintiff's offer of proof, which offer, objection, ruling, and exception were as follows, to-wit:—

MR. REYNOLDS: Plaintiff offers to prove by the witness Stitt upon the stand, that he could have procured the currency or legal tender for payment of lambs in question just as soon as it could have been procured by telegram from his Bank at Fort Morgan, Colorado, and would have done so if defendants had not told him that it would be useless.

MR. NORRIS: We object to the offer of the testimony because of the fact that it is incompetent, irrelevant and immaterial and has no pertinent value in the case and is not responsive to the issues set forth in the pleadings, nor is it justified by any evidence heretofore produced, and there is no foundation laid for it, and it is indefinite as to the time when this money could have been produced, and by reason of the further fact that on account of the indefinite character of the proposed offer of testimony, it cannot be determined whether or not the witness could or would have produced that money on that date, or at some subsequent time.

THE COURT: . Objection sustained.

MR. REYNOLDS: . Exception. (Record ——)

VII.

The Court erred in sustaining objection of defendants to question of plaintiff's attorney to Witness C. M. Stitt, which question, objection, ruling, and exception were as follows, to-wit:—

"I did have a conversation upon Sunday, the 30th of September, with one of the defendants, relative to having received a message from my Bank at Fort Morgan."

Q. And what was that conversation?

MR. NORRIS: . To which we object, your Honor, as incompetent, irrelevant, and immaterial. This is introduced evidently for the purpose of showing that on the day succeeding the date the contract expired, this conversation was had, and showing no attempt to comply with the terms of the contract.

THE COURT: . The objection will be sustained.

MR. REYNOLDS: Exception. (Record ——),

VIII.

The Court erred in sustaining objection of defendants to plaintiff's offer of proof by witness C. M. Stitt, which offer, objection, ruling, and exception were as follows, to-wit:—

MR. REYNOLDS: Plaintiff offers to prove by witness Stitt on the stand, that his Bank at Fort Morgan, Colorado, telegraphed to defendants, guaranteeing to pay his check for the lambs in question, and that defendants admitted to him that they had received said telegram.

MR. NORRIS: To which offer the defendants object, for the reason that the same is incompetent, irrelevant, and immaterial, and does not show a compliance with the terms of the contract, and in fact shows that the terms of the contract were not and had not been complied with, as the evidence sought to be introduced would detail facts and circumstances occurring after the expiration of the date on which the contract was to have been performed, and does not tend to show an attempt to perform under the conditions of the contract on the date that the contract required it to be peformed.

THE COURT: Sustained.

MR. REYNOLDS: Exception. (Record ——)

IX.

The Court erred in sustaining objection of defendants to question of plaintiff's attorney to witness C. M. Stitt, which question, objection, ruling, and exception were as follows, to-wit:—

Q. Did you, on the 30th day of September, have a talk with the defendants, or either of them, relative to the reception of a message by them, from the Bank of Montana, relative to the payment of any draft you might drawn on Hatch & Snyder?

MR. NORRIS: To which we object, your Honor.

THE COURT: Sustained.

MR. REYNOLDS: Exception. (Record ——)

X.

The Court erred in sustaining objection of defendants to plaintiff's offer of proof by witness Stitt, which offer, objection, ruling, and exception were as follows, to-wit:—

MR. REYNOLDS: Plaintiff offers to prove by witness Stitt upon the stand, that defendants admitted to him on Sunday, September 30th, that they had received a telegram from Montana National Bank of Billings, guaranteeing any draft that he might draw on Hatcher & Snyder, in payment of the sheep in question.

MR. NORRIS: To which we object.

THE COURT: Sustained.

MR. REYNOLDS: Exception. (Record ——)

XI.

The Court erred in sustaining objection of defendants to plaintiff's offer of Exhibit 3, which offer, objection, ruling, and exception were as follows, to-wit:—

Document marked Exhibit 3.

"This is the notice I gave Mr. Murray the 30th of September."

MR. REYNOLDS: We offer this in evidence.

MR. NORRIS: To which offer of the plaintiff, proposed Exhibit 3 in evidence, the defendants object, for the reason that the same is incompetent, irrelevant, and immaterial, and no foundation has been laid for it, and it does not tend to prove or disprove any facts material to this case, nor is it supported by any testimony herein, and on its face shows that the notice was given on September 30th, the day following the date on which contract was to have been performed, and the contract had expired.

THE COURT: The objection will be sustained)

MR. REYNOLDS: Exception. (Record ——)

XII.

The Court erred in sustaining objection of defendants to the offered evidence of the deposition of L. M. Meeker, Cashier of the First National Bank of Fort Morgan, Colorado, which offer, objection, ruling, and exception were as follows, to-wit:—

MR. RENOLDS: I have here a deposition from the Cashier of the Fort Morgan Bank which I offer in evidence, but assume that there will be an objection to it.

MR. NORRIS: The deposition and the fact that it is a deposition and the manner of its taking, or the irregularity of its taking, will not be objected to, but the deposition is objected to on the ground that it is incompetent, irrelevant, and immaterial, and not tending to show anything in compliance with the terms of the contract, and the same objections that have heretofore been made.

THE COURT: Objection sustained.

MR. REYNOLDS: Exception. (Record ——)

XIII.

The Court erred in sustaining objection to plaintiff's application for leave to amend his complaint, which proposed amendment, objection, ruling, and exception were as follows, to-wit:—

MR. REYNOLDS: May it please the Court. I would ask the Court for leave to amend the complaint by adding at the end of paragraph 5 of the complaint the following:

"That the above mentioned offer was made by valid check and draft after the banks had closed on the 29th day of September, 1917; that said check and draft were refused; that the plaintiff thereupon offered to secure the legal tender money for such payment as soon as it could be telegraphed to Glasgow, Montana, from his home at Fort Morgan, Colorado, and that the defendant refused said offer, and thereupon sold said lambs to one Johnson."

MR. NORRIS: May it please the Court, we object for the reason that it doesn't change the issue in the case and is not material under the issues of the case, and it would not admit evidence that would be competent, and that it contradicts the preceding part of said paragraph 5 and other portions of the complaint, and that contradicts the complaint itself.

THE COURT: The proposed amendment does not benefit the plaintiff's case any, and the objection will be sustained.

MR. REYNOLDS: Exception. (Record ——)

XIV.

The Court erred in sustaining objection of defendants to offer of plaintiff by witness James E. Rea, which offer, objection, ruling, and exception were as follows, to-wit:—

. MR. REYNOLDS: Plaintiff offers to show by witness James E. Rea on the stand, that the market value of lambs in question at weighing points, near Nashau and Saco on the 29th day of September, 1917, was fifteen cents to fifteen and one-half cents per pound.

MR. HURD: The offer is objected to on the ground that the evidence proposed to be offered is irrelevant and immaterial, and there is no foundation laid for it, and that there has not at this time been shown any violation of the terms and provisions of the contract.

THE COURT: Yes, this offer to show the value of the lambs is immaterial, as the plaintiff did not comply with the contract, and the matter of the value is entirely irrelevant. The objection will be sustained.

MR. REYNOLDS: Exception. (Record ——)

XV.

The Court erred in sustaining objection of defendants to question of plaintiff's attorney to witness James E. Rea, which question, objection, ruling, and exception were as follows, to-wit:

Q. Is there, or is there not, a custom relative to the method of payment of the purchase price of sheep, and if so, was there such a custom in force in September, 1917?

MR. NORRIS: To that we object, on the ground that it is incompetent, irrelevant, and immaterial, and no foundation has been laid for it, and on the ground that it calls for the conclusion of the witness.

THE COURT: Objection sustained.

MR. REYNOLDS: Exception. (Record ——)

XVI.

The Court erred in sustaining objection of defendants to plaintiff's offer of proof by the witness James E. Rea, which offer, objection, ruling, and exception were as follows, to-wit:—

MR. REYNOLDS: Plaintiff offers to show, by witness James E. Rea on the stand, that it is, and has been for many years, the custom in all parts of Montana and in the northwestern states generally among sheep men to pay for sheep purchased by means of a check or draft, and that such is true regardless of the amount of money involved, and that it is the custom of the vendor to notify the vendee that the payment of the check or draft must be guaranteed by bank upon which it is drawn if he has any objection to the check, and in time that such guarantee can be procured by the time fixed for delivery, and that such custom applies to the payment by check or draft drawn on bank or person in a sister state, the same as though drawn on a bank in the State of Montana.

THE COURT: Do you renew the objection?

MR. NORRIS.: Yes.

THE COURT: It will be sustained.

MR. REYNOLDS: Exception. (Record ——)

XVII.

The Court erred in sustaining objection of defendants to plaintiff's offer of proof by himself, a witness on the stand, which offer, objection, ruling, and exception were as follows, to-wit:—

MR. REYNOLDS: Plaintiff offers to prove by plaintiff Xavier Servel on the stand, that he never had any notice from defendants, either directly or indirectly, that they would require currency for final payment on the contract in question.

MR. NORRIS: To the offer we object, on the ground stated in our objections to that line of testimony.

THE COURT: Objection sustained.

MR. REYNOLDS: Exception. (Record ——)

XVIII.

The Court erred in sustaining objection and motion to strike out testimony made by defendants as to the testimony of C. M. Stitt, which testimony, objection, ruling, and exception were as follows, to-wit:—

"Neither of the defendants at any time gave me any notice, either directly of indirectly, before about 4:30 P. M. of the 29th of September, 1917, that they would require legal tender money for final payment on the contract in question."

MR. HURD: We ask that the answer be stricken out, and we object on the ground that it is incompetent, irrelevant, and immaterial.

THE COURT: Just as the Court stated before, no notice was necessary under the law. Objection sustained.

MR. REYNOLDS: Exception. (Record ——)

XIX.

The Court erred in sustaining objection of defendants to offer of proof of plaintiff by witness C. M. Stitt, which offer, objection, ruling, and exception were as follows, to-wit:—

MR. REYNOLDS. Plaintiff offers to prove by C. M. Stitt, witness on the stand, that he did not receive any notice of any kind from defendants before 4:30 P. M. of the 29th day of September, 1917, that they would require legal tender money for final payment on the contract in question.

MR. HURD: The offer of proof is objected to on the ground stated in the former objection.

THE COURT: Sustained.

MR. REYNOLDS: Exception. (Record ——)

XX.

The Court erred in sustaining motion of defendant's for directed verdict. which motion, ruling, and exception were as follows, to-wit:—

MR. HURD: At this time, may it please the Court,

we ask for a directed verdict in favor of the defendants.

THE COURT: This motion for directed verdict will be granted. It is only a question of law, gentlemen of the jury, and the Clerk will enter such a verdict of record.

MR. REYNOLDS: Exception.

THE COURT: The exception will be noted. (Record ——)

XXI.

The Court erred in rendering judgment in favor of the defendants herein.

ARGUMENT.

A.

Specifications of error numbered 1, 2, 3, 4, 5, 6, 7, 8, 9, 10, 11, 12, 15, 16, 17, 18, 19, 20, and 21 involve the general proposition that under the circumstances of this case, defendants had no right to declare the contract forfeited and refuse to make delivery of the sheep in question to plaintiff, and therefore will be considered together upon this general proposition.

The rule is well established that in ordinary contracts for sale of sheep, time is never deemed of the essence of the contract unless expressly so provided.

Curtis & Freeman vs. Parham, 49 Mont., 140.

Rev. Codes of Mont., 1907, 5047.

When time is not of the essence of the contract, neither party can rescind or claim a violation of the contract after performance becomes due, without giving the other party an opportunity to make tender of performance, and, on the other hand, the duty is imposed on the other party to the contract, to make, within a reasonable time after the performance is due, a tender of performance, unless excused therefrom by the attitude of the first party.

Curtis & Freeman vs. Parham, supra.

Rev. Codes of Mont., Sec. 4963.

It is, therefore, clear that if it was not for the fact that the contract in question in this case contains a clause whereby time is made of its essence, defendants, under the circumstances of this case, would not have had any right whatever to declare the contract forfeited on the part of plaintiff.

The only question, then, is whether or not, under the circumstances of this particular case, with such a clause as above mentioned in the contract, defendants were justified in declaring the contract forfeited. It is the contention of plaintiff that defendants were not justified in so doing.

In support of plaintiff's contention, he will set forth three different propositions, which separately and collectively sustain such contention, and which will be discussed in their order.

1.—The conduct of defendants constituted an attempted forfeiture of plaintiff's interest in the contract in question, and, under the circumstances of this case, it will be unconscionable for the Court to permit defendants to enforce such forfeiture.

2.—Plaintiff's offered performance was sufficiently substantial to entitle him to sustain an action upon the contract.

3.—Plaintiff having made tender of payment within the time limited by the contract, in accordance with the custom of the country and commercial usage, the obligation rested upon defendants: upon their demand for legal tender money, to give to plaintiff reasonable time within which to procure such legal tender money, before they could treat the contract as forfeited by plaintiff.

I.

Any forfeiture of the contract in question, as sought to be made by defendants under the circumstances of this case would be manifestly unfair and unconscionable, and should not be permitted.

Plaintiff, in good faith, sent his representative, C. M. Stitt, to the places at which delivery was to be made, in ample time to receive the sheep within the time limited by the contract. He was met by one of the defendants, and together they went to the several places in the country where the sheep were being kept, counted and weighed them. As the lambs were kept in different places, it required substantially a day and a half for such work of counting and weighing, the same being completed the forenoon of Saturday, September 29th, the last day upon which delivery was to be made. He offered settlement to defendant Jamieson, who referred him to defendant Murray. It was agreed between them that Mr. Stitt should go to Nashua, where a portion of the lambs were to be shipped, and at which point defendant Jamieson told plaintiff Mr. Murray was. It was understood that defendant Jamieson after lunch should follow by automobile, Mr. Stitt going by train. Mr. Stitt went to Nashua, failed to find defendant Muarry, and thereupon returned to Glasgow, where he met both of them about four o'clock in the afternoon, the banks being closed at that time. He offered payment by check, which was refused He offered to have his check guaranteed by the bank upon which it was to be drawn, which offer was refused. He offered to draw a draft upon Hatcher & Snyder, stating that it would be honored, and offered to secure assurance from Hatcher & Snyder that such draft would be honored, but such offer was refused. He then stated that he was not carrying thirty thousand dollars in cash upon his person, but that he would procure the legal tender money just as soon as it could be wired from Fort Morgan, Colorado, which would necessarily involve a delay until the banks should open the next Monday morning, and also offered to allow defendants to keep the lambs until such money was received, and to pay them all damage and expense incurred by so doing. This offer was also refused.

Regardless of the refusals of defendants, Mr. Stitt wired and secured that day a message from his bank at Fort Morgan, Colorado, to defendants, guaranteeing payment of any check that would be drawn in payment of the sheep in question. The responsibility of the bank was ample to protect the payment of such check. He also wired Hatcher & Snyder, and telegrams were received the next morning from both Hatcher & Snyder and the Montana National Bank, a live bank of Billings, guaranteeing the payment of any draft that should be drawn by him upon Hatcher & Snyder.

The Court will doubtless take judicial notice of the fact that comparatively few obligations are met by the payment of legal tender, practically all the business of the country being conducted upon a credit basis by means of checks and drafts. Plaintiff was ready, able, and willing to perform all his obligations under the contract, and offered so to do within the time limited by the contract, and in accordance with the universal method of performance in commercial dealings, and, as plaintiff offered to show upon trial, particularly in accordance with the custom prevailing in the matter of making payment upon sheep contracts.

Upon being advised that such manner of performance would not be acceptable, he then offered to procure the legal tender just as soon as a telegram could bring it from Fort Morgan, Colorado, to Glasgow, Montana, and payment thereof could be had through the bank. This was all that any person could reasonably expect under the circumstances.

Forfeiture has been defined by the Court as follows:

> "A forfeiture is where a person loses some right, property, privilege, or benefit in consequence of having done or omitted to do a certain act."

Vol. 2, Words & Phrases, 611. 2nd Ed.

> "Forfeiture usually signifies loss of property by way of compensation for injury to the person to whom the property is forfeited, as well as punishment."

Idem.

> "Forfeiture is a penalty for doing or omitting to do a certain required act."

Idem.

It is evident, then, that if under the circumstances of this case, defendants are to be deemed justified in refusing delivery of the lambs in question, plaintiff will suffer a forfeiture by losing a substantial right or interest in the contract and in the sheep to be delivered thereunder, merely because he did not have nearly Thirty Thousand Dollars in legal tender money on his person.

It is elementary that forfeitures are not favored, and that they will not be enforced where they will work an injustice. The Montana Supreme Court has been especially emphatic in denouncing forfeiture in such cases.

Courts will not enforce forfeitures when enforcement thereof would be unconscionable.

> *Fratt vs. Daniels-Jones Co.,* 133 Pac., 700. See 702
> 2nd column. (Mont.)
>
> *Cook-Reynolds vs. Thipman,* 47 Mont., 298. See 300.
> 6th line from bottom. 133 Pac., 694.
>
> *Suburban Homes Co. vs. North,* 50 Mont., 108. See
> 118, middle of page. 145 Pac., 2.

Forfeiture will not be enforced when "the party for whose benefit it was inserted had waived the provision or is estopped to insist upon its enforcement, or performance has been prevented by some intervening circumstances sufficient to relieve the party from the performance of any other provision of the contract."

> *Fratt vs. Daniels-Jones Co., supra.*

A party will be relieved from forfeiture, "if his breach of duty was not grossly negligent, wilfull or fraudulent."

> *Cook-Reynolds Co. vs. Thipman,* supra.

While the foregoing cases involve forfeitures of land contract, and the facts are not similar, yet the principle is the same. No forfeiture should, therefore, be permitted when the "breach of duty was not grossly negligent, wilfull, or fraudulent." Plaintiff does not concede that he was guilty of any breach of duty, but even though he was, it was not grossly negligent, wilfull, or fraudulent.

The offered performance by plaintiff was made in good faith, and was designed to secure to defendants all the benefits reserved to them by the contract, would have done so if accepted, and when it was refused, plaintiff offered to make payment by legal tender money just as soon as the telegraph wires could transmit it, all of which offers were refused.

Such refusals on the part of defendants evidently were not made in good faith, but in avoidance of the contract, for if defendants merely desired what was coming to them, they could not consistently have rejected all these offers. By reason of the advance price of lambs between the date of the contract and the time of maturity, their value at time of delivery was approximately Fifteen Thousand Dollars more than the contract price, making a very strong inducement to make an excuse, no matter how slight, for repudiation of the agreement.

Furthermore, such suspicion is emphasized by the fact that not one word was said by either of the defendants to plaintiff or Mr. Stitt about legal tender until after the banks were closed upon Saturday, the 29th day of September, and they knew that it was then impossible to secure it. When plaintiff offered settlement to defendant Jamieson at about noon of that day, there was then probably time within which legal tender money could have been procured upon that day, but in furtherance of their design, defendant Jamieson sent Mr. Stitt upon a fruitless chase to Nashua, whereby the time between noon and the closing of the banks was consumed.

Under ordinary circumstances, and particularly in case the price of lambs hade gone down instead of having become higher, if plaintiff had tendered defendants legal tender money, they doubtless would have objected to it, and would have insisted upon his giving a check or draft, perhaps, with a guaranty of its payment. In this case, however, they waited until they knew it was physically impossible for him to produce the legal tender until the following Monday morning, and then made the demand, not because they wanted it, but because they perceived a chance to use that pretext as a means of escaping their obligation to deliver to plaintiff the sheep in question.

The courts are constituted to insure honest and fair dealing between men, and to punish fraud and deceit. If defendants are permitted to escape their obligations under this contract in the manner in which they have attempted to do, then the result is punishment for him who has, in good faith, attempted to fulfill his agreement, and reward for him who, by fraud and trickery, seeks to avoid his obligations.

II.

Plaintiff contends that his offer of performance was substantial and such as was contemplated by the parties at the time of making the contract, and was, therefore, sufficient upon which to base an action to recover thereon.

Where one has offered to make payment by medium which is recognized as a customary and usual method of payment, the contract itself not requiring payment by any particular kind of money or currency, and as soon as he is informed that legal tender money will be required, offers to procure such legal tender money just as soon as it can be transmitted by telegram, and such offer has been refused by the promisee, then he has made such substantial performance as will sustain an action upon the contract.

The general rule is nicely stated in R. C. L. as follows:

> "By the common law, a party to a contract was compelled to show a literal performance of the stipulations of it before he could claim damages for a non-

performance against the other. Expressions in some of the more recent cases seem to indicate a tendency to relax the rigor of this rule. Thus, it is said that the law looks to the spirit of a contract and not the letter of it, and that the question therefore is not whether a party has literally complied with it, but whether he has substantially done so. Other courts have said that substantial, and not exact, performance, accompanied by good faith, is all the law requires in case of any contract to entitle a party to recover on it. Although a plaintiff is not absolutely free from fault or omission in every particular, the court will not turn him away if he has in good faith made substantial performance, but will enforce his rights on the one hand, and preserve the rights of the defendant on the other, by permitting a recoupment."

6 R. C. L., Contracts, Sec. 342.

While the foregoing statement of the law is especially applicable to performance of contracts whereby work and materials are to be furnished, nevertheless, the same principle is applicable to any kind of performance.

"It has been frequently held that acts, insufficient in themselves to make a complete tender, may operate as proof of readiness to perform, so as to protect the rights of a party under a contract, where a proper tender is made impossible by reason of circumstances not due to fault of the tenderer."

Shaeffer vs. Coldren, 85 Atl. 98.

Hault vs. Unger, 71 Atl., 843. (See 844, 2nd col.)

29 Am. and Eng. Enc'y of Law (2nd Ed.) 697.

In the case of Shaeffer vs. Coldren, supra, action was brought upon option contract, of which time was necessarily of its essence The plaintiff tried to make tender to defendant on the evening of Saturday, the last day in which the contract could be complied with, but he could not do so because of being unable to find defendant. He renewed the offer the next Monday morning. It was held that he had not forfeited his contract.

"In the absence of any provision in the contract, or of any circumstances excluding it, contracts for the payment of money refer to the ordinary and usual currency in which business is transacted."

30 Cyc., 1210.

Fabbri vs. Kalbfleisch, 52 N. Y., 28.

" 'Money' covers anything representing property, and passing as such in current business transactions."

Hendry vs. Benlisa, 20 So., 800.

"The time, place, and mode or manner of payment are usually fixed by contract, though when not so fixed the law or even custom, or the course of dealing between the parties, and like circumstances, may determine it."

3 Elliott on Contracts, Sec. 1930.

U. B. Blalock & Co., vs. W. D. Clark & Bros., 49 S. E., 88. (N. C.)

"The eleventh prayer was, 'that, before the plaintiff would be entitled to recover, he must satisfy the jury by a preponderance of the evidence that at the time he demanded the cotton he had then and there the money to pay for the cotton,' which the Court gave, but added, 'or was able, ready and willing to pay for the cotton according to the custom of the community in buying and paying for cotton in large lots, of 160 bales or more, by giving valid checks for the same, or by shipping with bill of lading attached to sight draft, if the jury shall find by a preponderance of the evidence that there was a well known and established custom in that community to pay for cotton in such lots in that way, and if the jury shall further find by a preponderance of the evidence that there was nothing said in the contract, or at the time of making it, about how the cotton should be paid for.' "

U. B. Blalock & Co. vs. W. D. Clark, 49 S. E., 88. (N. C.)

"Stipulations which are necessary to make a contract reasonable, *or conformable to usage,* are implied, in respect to matters concerning which the contract manifests no contrary intention." (Italics ours.)

Rev. Codes of Mont., 1917, Sec. 5044.

The contract in this case contained nothing whatever as to manner or medium of payment, it merely providing that plaintiff should pay "the sum of ten cents per pound." As suggested in the approved instruction in the last above cited case, and in the quoted statute, when plaintiff made tender of payment, in accordance with the established custom for the payment of sheep, he did all that was contemplated by the parties at the time of the making of the contract, and as was implied therein. When he signed the contract, he in effect said, "I will receive these sheep not later than the 29th of September, 1917, and will pay for them by the usual medium of exchange," and, in compliance therewith, he was at points of delivery promptly on time to receive them and to pay for them as promised.

The fact that defendants accepted a check upon a Utah bank for first payment upon the contract sustains such an interpretation. The Courts will construe a contract as the parties themselves have construed it.

National Bank of Gallatin Valley vs. Ingle, 53 Mont., 415.

The fact that afterward the legal tender money was not actually produced is immaterial, inasmuch as defendants advised plaintiff that even though it should be produced, it would not be accepted. The law does not require any party to do an idle and useless thing.

An offer to perform is equivalent to performance for the purpose of sustaining an action for damages.

Rev. Codes of Mont., 1907, Sec. 4929. 8036.

6 R. C. L., Sec. 330.

Lehrkind vs. McDonnell, 51 Mont., 343. See 350.

The thing to be delivered, if any, need not in any case be actually produced upon an offer of performance, unless the offer is accepted.

Rev. Codes of Mont., 1907, Sec. 4940.

Lehrkind vs. McDonnell, 51 Mont., 343.

If a debtor is ready, able, and willing to pay, the actual production of it may be waived by the absolute refusal of the creditor to accept it.

3 Elliott on Contracts, Sec. 1970.

Sonia Cotton Oil Co. vs. Steamer "Red River," 30 So., 303.

McPherson vs. Fargo, 74 N. W., 1057.

3 Elliott on Contracts, Sec. 1972.

Woods vs. Bangs, 48 Atl., 189. (Pa.)

Blair vs. Hamilton, 48 Ind., 32.

Hazard vs. Loring, 10 Cush., 267. (Mass.)

Jones vs. Preferred Bankers, etc., Assur. Co., 79 N. W., 204. (Mich.)

Stephenson vs. Kilpatrick, 65 S. W., 773. (Mo.)

Rogers vs. Tindall, 42 S. W., 86. (Tenn.)

Tender is not necessary where it would be a useless ceremony or the vendor has repudiated the contract.

39 Cyc, 2089.

Thus, plaintiff acted with the usual business caution, and in accordance with business principles, and, having tendered such performance, he substantially, at least, performed his obligations under the contract, and is entitled to sustain his action thereon for damages.

III.

When plaintiff tendered his valid check in payment on the contract, and defendants refused to accept the same and demanded currency or legal tender, then the obligation rested upon them to give to plaintiff a reasonable time within which to procure such legal tender.

Plaintiff tendered payment within the time and in the manner contemplated by the contract, and in accordance with the usage and custom covering such transactions. Payment by legal tender would be an unusual method of payment, and one for which it could not be expected that he would be prepared. Often times it is necessary, in receiving sheep in the State of Montana, to go long distances in the country to weigh and receive them, far from the protection that society affords in the city. The contract frequently involves considerable money, and it would be deemed foolhardy and unbusinesslike for any person to carry with him large sums of money, such as approximately Thirty Thousand Dollars, as was involved in this transaction, in cash for payment upon such contract. This is especially true when the exact amount involved cannot be ascertained until after the sheep have been weighed, and the amount due upon the contract must be estimated beforehand in order surely to be prepared for the payment.

Thus, when a party goes to receive sheep, and is prepared to make payment by valid check or draft, and, as in the case in question, is prepared to give a guaranty that would satisfy any ordinary man that such check or draft would be paid, he certainly has done all that can be expected of him under the usual method of business transactions, especially when the contract does not mention the medium of payment required, and no notice is given that legal tender will be demanded, thereby putting the purchaser on his guard.

When, therefore, the defendants, upon tender of a valid check and draft, refsued to accept the same, and demanded legal tender money or the currency, a delay was necessarily involved to enable plaintiff to procure such legal tender money or currency. The delay, then, was due to the act of the defendants in asking and demanding of plaintiff that he do something which had not been anticipated by plaintiff, and, which under the usual methods of transacting business, would not be expected.

Although time is made of the essence of the contract, "if the party prevents performance by the other, he cannot insist on the stipulation."

C. J., 689.

> "The grantor of an option who prevents its exercise during the time limited must give a reasonable time for its exercise after any obstruction that he has interposed is removed."

13 C. J., 689.

3 Elliott on Contracts, Sec. 1912.

Other cases sustaining the general proposition that the party preventing performance within the time limited, cannot insist upon the stipulation as to time being of the essence of the contract, are as follows:

King Iron Bridge & Mfg. Co. vs. St. Louis, 43 Fed., 768. 10 L. R. A., 826.

Ward vs. Matthews, 14 Pac., 604.

District of Columbia vs. Camden Iron Works, 21 Sup. Crt. Rep., 680.

Hollister Bros. vs. Bruthenthal & Bickert, et al., 70 S. E., 970. (Ga.)

Stimpson Computing Scales Co. vs. Taylor, 61 S. E., 1131. (Ga.)

Ritchie vs. Topeka, 138 Pac., 618. (Kan.)

Rees vs. Logsdon, 11 Atl., 708. (Md.)

Dannat vs. Fuller, 24 N. E., 815. (N. Y.)

Spina vs. Arcadia Orchards Co., 131 Pac., 218. (Wash.)

McDonald vs. Cole, 32 S. E., 1033. (W. Va.)

Case vs. Beyer, et al., 125 N. W., 947. (Wis.)

First Nat. Bank of Portland vs. Carroll, 35 Mont., 302.

"Where a stipulation for performance at a particular time has been waived, the party in whose favor the waiver operates is thereafter bound only to perform within a reasonable time."

13 C. J., 690.

Inasmuch as respondents interposed a condition of performance on the part of appellant which involved a delay beyond the time limited by the contract, then necessarily the stipulation as to time was waived, and appellant had a reasonable time within which to comply with such condition.

A payment or tender of payment by check is sufficient unless objection is made to the tender on the ground that it is not cash.

Milwaukee Land Co. vs. Ruesink, et al., 50 Mont., 489. See 506.

In this case, then, the tender by appellant of a valid check and draft was sufficient up to the time of defendants' refusal to accept the same. If sufficient until defendants made objection, then surely opportunity must be given appellant to meet the objection so made.

If party makes tender of check, without notice that legal tender money will be required, and such check is refused, party should have opportunity of securing the money and making a good and valid tender.

McGrath vs. Gegnor, 26 Atl., 502.

Shaeffer vs. Coldren, 85 Atl., 98.

Sharp vs. Todd, 38 N. J., Eq., 324.

> "We take it to be well settled that, where a tender is made, whether it be by ordinary bank notes or by check on a bank, and the tender is refused, not because of the character or quality or the tender itself, but on other grounds, the tender thus made and refused will be considered in law lawful tender; and for the reason that all objections to the character of the tender will be considered as having been waived: *and for the further reason that, if objection had been made on the ground that the tender was not made in lawful money, the party would have had the opportunity of getting the money and making good and valid tender."* (Italics ours.)

McGrath vs. Gegnor, 26 Atl., 502.

Thus, under the reasoning and law above set forth, plaintiff contends that upon defendants' making objection to his valid check and draft, offered by him, and upon his offer to satisfy such objection by procuring the legal tender money, and they having refused to give him a chance to get it, he was not in default, and they had no right to repudiate the contract.

B.

Specifications of error No. 2, 3, 4, 7, 8, 9, 10, and 12, involve the admissibility of evidence on the part of plaintiff, showing the arrangements that he had made for the payment of check or draft that might be drawn in payment of the sheep in question.

Such evidence is admissible for the purpose of showing the plaintiff's ability and readiness to perform his part of the contract.

Ives vs. Atlantic, etc., R. Co., 55 S. E., 74.

Plaintiff offered, in support of the check which he tendered in payment, the testimony of the Cashier of the Bank at Fort Morgan, Colorado, upon which the check was to be drawn, setting forth the responsibility of the bank, and also the fact that arrangements had been made to honor any check that should be drawn upon it in payment of the sheep purchased under the contract in question.

The plaintiff also offered guaranty by Montana National Bank of the draft which was tendered in payment, said bank being an active bank of Billings, Montana, and also the guaranty by Hatcher & Snyder of said draft, and their responsibility, which was ample to take care of it.

C.

Specification of error No. 11 involves the offer of plain· tiff to introduce in evidence Exhibit No. 3, which was a written offer to produce the legal tender money in payment for the sheep in question, and an offer of compensation for any delay that might result to the defendants.

While this offer of compensation and to procure the
legal tender was made the day after the last day mentioned
in the contract for its fulfillment, yet it was upon Sunday,
and before any opportunity had been given to secure the
legal tender and make the payment, and in confirmation of
the verbal offer of the day before.

> "An offer in writing to pay a particular sum of
> money, or to deliver a written instrument or specific
> personal property, is, if not accepted, equivalent to
> the actual production and tender of the money, in-
> strument, or property."

Rev. Codes of Mont., 1907, Sec. 8036.

D.

Specification of error No. 13 involves the refusal of the
Court to allow the amendment to the complaint asked for by
the plaintiff.

The proposed amendment was as follows:

> "That the above mentioned offer was made by
> valid check and draft after the banks had closed on the
> 29th day of September, 1917; that said check and
> draft were refused; that the plaintiff thereupon offered
> to secure the legal tender money for such payment as
> soon as it could be telegraphed to Glasgow, Montana,
> from his home at Fort Morgan, Colorado, and that
> the defendants refused said offer, and thereupon sold
> said lambs to one Johnson."

Plaintiff asked for this amendment, not because he
deemed his complaint insufficient, but to save any question
in regard thereto. Plaintiff contends that the complaint sets
forth performance upon the part of plaintiff, which is sufficient to constitute a good cause of action, and that his acts
did constitute a full performance of all the obligations rest-

ing upon him insofar as to entitle him to base his action to recover upon the contract.

If, however, such should not be deemed by this Court to be the law, and it was necessary for the plaintiff to set forth the facts whereby the time for payment of the purchase was necessarily extended, then the Court should have allowed the amendment, in the interest of justice between the parties.

E.

Assignment of error No. 14 relates to the offer of plaintiff to show by the witness, James E. Rea, the market value of lambs in question at the weighing point.

This testimony was excluded as immaterial, inasmuch as under the theory of the case adopted by the lower Court, plaintiff was unable to establish any case by reason of its failure to show sufficient performance or offer of performance on his part.

If plaintiff's contention as to the sufficiency of his performance should be sustained, then, of course, the Court erred in rejecting this testimony. ⏤

Under all the circumstances of this case, plaintiff submits that the District Court erred in excluding the offered evidence, and in directing verdict for defendants.

Respectfully submitted,

F. B. REYNOLDS,

Attorney for Appellant.

UNITED STATES
CIRCUIT COURT OF APPEALS
FOR THE NINTH CIRCUIT

XAVIER SERVEL,

Plaintiff in Error.

vs.

G. R. JAMIESON AND MATTHIESON MURRAY,
A Co-partnership Doing Business Under the Firm
Name of Jamieson & Murray,

Defendants in Error.

BRIEF OF DEFENDANTS IN ERROR

F. B. REYNOLDS,
Attorney for Plaintiff in Error.
NORRIS, HURD & McKELLAR and
EDWIN L. NORRIS,
Attorneys for Defendants in Error.

Filed, October ...., 1918.

....Clerk.

UNITED STATES
CIRCUIT COURT OF APPEALS
FOR THE NINTH CIRCUIT

XAVIER SERVEL,
Plaintiff in Error.

vs.

G. R. JAMIESON AND MATTHIESON MURRAY,
A Co-partnership Doing Business Under the Firm
Name of Jamieson & Murray,
Defendants in Error.

BRIEF OF DEFENDANTS IN ERROR

ARGUMENT

A.

The argument of defendants in error will follow
generally the sequence of the argument of plaintiff in
error as found in his brief. It is insisted that defendants did have the right to declare the contract forfeited
and refuse to make delivery of the sheep in question

to plaintiff after the day fixed in the contract therefor, under the circumstances of this case.

It is admitted that in ordinary contracts for sale of sheep time is never deemed of the essence of a contract unless expressly so provided. The contract in the instant case, however, provides:

> "And it is further mutually agreed by and between the parties hereto that time is of the essence of this agreement and that upon the expiration of the time for delivery as herein provided the rights of said party of the second part hereunder shall cease and determine, and he shall have no right, claim or interest in or to said sheep after the expiration of said period of time."

Under the foregoing provision of the contract, time having deliberately been made of the essence of the contract, the parties thereto must, in the absence of waiver or estoppel, expect that the provision will be given full force and effect

> *Fratt vs. Daniels-Jones Co.,* 47 Mont. 487, 133 Pac. 700.

It seems, therefore, that the defendants were justified in treating the plaintiff's rights as terminated upon his failure to tender the purchase price within the time limited.

Our attention will be next directed to the three propositions upon which plaintiff in error relies to sustain his contention that defendants were not justified in treating the plaintiff as in substantial breach, and therefore justified in regarding the plaintiff's rights under the contract as forfeited.

I. Plaintiff contends that any forfeiture of the contract in question as sought to be made by defendants under the circumstances of this case would be manifestly unfair and unconscionable and should not be permitted.

Argument of plaintiff opens with the statement that he sent his representative, C. M. Sitt, to the place at which delivery was to be made. Attention of the court is called to the fact that, while defendants at no time required further credentials as to the rights of Mr. Stitt to demand the delivery of these sheep, nevertheless the record discloses that the plaintiff testified that he sent Mr. Stitt for the sheep purchased and that when Mr. Stitt appeared he claimed these sheep as the purchaser from a third party, Hatcher & Snyder of Denver, Colorado. If defendants on the record of this case may be regarded as having accepted Mr. Stitt as one authorized to receive these sheep, it is respectfully submitted that defendants had an equal right to insist that upon the delivery of these sheep payment therefor should be had and made in legal tender. A stranger to the contract from a sister state ought in the exercise of reasonable care to be dealt with fairly but at arm's length. Representations that the money is at some place in a sister state is placing the money at too great a distance from the place where the sheep were to be delivered and payment was to be made to require defendants in equity and good conscience to have accepted the personal check or draft of Mr. Stitt. Neither do we see that a guaranty by a bank of a sister state that payment of such check would be made entitled plaintiff to require defendants to accept such check in lieu of legal tender.

It is immaterial that many or most private business obligations are conducted upon a credit basis by means of checks and drafts because the law entitles obligees for the payment of certain sums to demand that payment be made in legal tender and the fact that they frequently waive such right in no way affects their legal right in reference thereto, particularly when the transaction is had with a stranger from a sister state and third and fourth parties are introduced who were strangers to the original transaction. It might be observed at this time that on motion by defendants for a nonsuit on such a record as is before this tribunal the plaintiff has had every opportunity to put his best foot forward and a careful scrutiny of this record will disclose that this plaintiff has availed himself of every such opportunity.

By the terms of the contract, delivery of the sheep in question was to be made "between the 25th day of September, 1917, and the 29th day of September, 1917, the exact date to be at the option of said party of the second part, * * * and said party of the second part will pay the remainder of the purchase price of said wether sheep at the time and upon the delivery thereof to said party of the second part by said parties of the first part." No tender of payment was made by Mr. Stitt before the afternoon of Saturday, September 29, 1917, and the court gave notice to plaintiff in the course of the trial that it would take judicial notice of the fact that you cannot get money from Fort Morgan, Colorado, over Saturday noon. It was upon a bank at Fort Morgan, Colorado, that Stitt offered defendants his check.

The record discloses that neither plaintiff nor Mr. Stitt had taken the care or trouble to have this money within reasonable proximity at the time and place of payment. Neither does it appear that defendants had any notice that they would be expected to accept Mr. Stitt's personal check upon a bank located at Fort Morgan, Colorado, on the last day of performance when the sheep were about to be loaded in cars. We do not see that it is material that defendants accepted, at the time of entering into the contract, a check in earnest to bind the bargain inasmuch as they did at that time and were intended to have for a reasonable time thereafter the possession of the sheep contracted for as security.

It is admitted that forfeitures are generally not favored but it can hardly be said that they will not be enforced where by the breach of the contract a party thereto is by the express terms of the contract

entitled to claim a forfeiture. In this connection plaintiff has directed us to the following authorities:

> *Fratt vs. Daniels-Jones Co.,* 47 Mont. 487, 133
>   Pac. 700;
> *Cook-Reynolds Co. v. Chipman,* 47 Mont. 289,
> 133 Pac. 694;
> *Suburban Homes Co. v. North,* 50 Mont. 108,
>   145 Pac. 2.

It will be noted that these cases revolve about
section 6039, Revised Codes, Montana (section 3275,
C. C. Cal.), which is as follows:

> "Whenever, by the terms of an obligation, a
> party thereto incurs a forfeiture, or a loss in
> the nature of a forfeiture, by reason of his
> failure to comply with its provisions, he may
> be relieved therefrom upon making full com-
> pensation to the other party except in case of
> a grossly negligent, wilfull, or fraudulent breach
> of duty."

Fratt vs. Daniels-Jones Co., supra, certainly es-
tablishes the principle in the courts of Montana that
neither the provision "time is of the essence of this
contract" nor the contract containing such a provision
is invalid as against positive law or public policy and
that when this provision is inserted in contracts, "it
is the duty of courts to carry out the intention of the
parties by giving effect to that provision," citing

> *Cheeney v. Libby,* 134 U. S. 68, 33 L. Ed. 818,
>   and quoting from the latter case the follow-
>   ing:

"However harsh or exacting its terms may be, as to the appellee, they do not contravene public policy; and, therefore, a refusal of the court to give effect to them, according to the real intention of the parties, is to make a contract for them which they have not chosen to make for themselves."

The court in the Fratt case further says of section 6039, R. C., supra:

"Whatever may be the correct interpretation of the language of that section, this much is apparent; the very minimum requirement is that the party invoking the protection afforded by that section must set forth facts which will appeal to the conscience of a court of equity."

The court proceeds and cites with approval the case of Cook-Reynolds Co. vs. Chipman, supra. In Suburban Homes Co. v. North, supra, the court also cites both the Cook-Reynolds and the Fratt cases and says:

"In order to avoid the consequences of his default, we can see no reason why the defendant should not be required to bring himself within the equity of the statute as interpreted in Cook-Reynolds vs. Chipman,—Fratt vs. Daniels-Jones Co., supra, and other cases cited supra."

In Cook-Reynolds vs. Chipman, supra, the court says, where the court was considering a loss by the purchaser in the nature of a forfeiture authorized by the terms of the contract:

"From such a loss he may be relieved upon showing that he is equitably entitled to such relief, if his breach of duty was not grossly negligent, wilful or fraudulent."

Plaintiff apparently overlooked the important decision of

Clifton vs. Willson, 47 Mont. 305, 132 Pac. 424,

in reference to his contention which he seeks to sustain by the authority of the above cases.

In the Willson case the plaintiff was suing to recover damages for a breach of a contract to deliver sheep. It was conceded that plaintiff refused to accept the sheep because they were not of the character specified in the contract. The defendant counterclaimed that he offered to deliver the ewes which were not accepted. The court carefully analyzes the seller's right both at common law and under the Code provisions of this state insofar as they may modify or declare common law principles. After an analysis of the common law principle which seeks to compel parties to live up to their agreements and not encourage them in the violation thereof, in consequence of which principle it is generally held that one who is guilty of a breach of his contract by stopping short of full performance cannot recover payments made prior to the breach, the court concludes by saying in reference to section 6039, R. C., supra:

> "The statute has no application to a case where, as in this case, the plaintiff seeks to recover damages for a breach by the defendant. While he is sueing to recover his advance payments as a part of the compensation to him, the plaintiff assumes to stand strictly upon his legal rights—risking his chance of ultimate recovery exclusively upon his alleged ability to

show that his loss has been due to defendant's failure to deliver the ewes according to his agreement.'

The plaintiff in the instant case stands squarely within the construction of the statute by the Montana Supreme Court, he obviously standing upon a cause of action for an alleged breach of contract and is seeking to recover his advance payment as a part of the compensation to him for the alleged breach.

Concerning the charge of fraud and trickery at the conclusion of plaintiff's argument of this part of his brief, we wish merely to direct the court's attention to the record itself and respectfully submit that the record does not bear out the charge that is made in plaintiff's brief nor does it contain any evidence whatsoever that defendants perpetrated fraud or trickery or proposed to send Mr. Stitt upon any fruitless chase whereby the time between noon and the closing of the banks was consumed. Mr. Stitt arrived at Nashua between two and two-thirty, Saturday afternoon, September 29th, took dinner and returned to Glasgow between four and four-thirty the-same afternoon. Not only does the evidence fail to disclose fraud, but it appears therefrom that the whole time consumed by Mr. Stitt on this "fruitless chase" was no more than two hours and that during this time he procured his dinner. Concerning the suspicion of plaintiff arising from the fact that "not one word was said by either of the defendants to plaintiff or Mr. Stitt about legal tender until after the banks were closed upon Saturday, the 29th day of September," plaintiff was either under a legal obligation to tender defendants money or he was not under such an obligation. If it be admitted that plaintiff was under a legal obligation to tender money, then plaintiff is reduced to the contention that it is obligatory upon defendants to notify plaintiff of a legal obligation which he has bound himself to perform and of which he must therefore have notice. If plaintiff was not under a legal obligation to tender money, notice by defendants to tender money would avail nothing. We confess our inability to see anything in this point raised by plaintiff and presume, in the absence of any citation of authority by him that he was unable to find authority supporting his contention.

II. As to plaintiff's contention that his offer of performance was substantial and such as was contemplated by the parties at the time of making the contract, and was, therefore, sufficient upon which to base an action to recover thereon, the defendants take issue.

Neither can defendants admit that where one has offered to make payment of an obligation to pay a determinable amount upon a fixed time that a tender of a check is a substantial performance of the obligation even though it is recognized as a customary and usual method of payment, where the obligor is informed at the time of tender that the check will not be accepted and that money is demanded and where time is of the essence of the contract and an offer to procure legal tender money just as soon as it can be transmitted from a point distant in a sister state, does not cure the obligor's breach in failure to tender current money within the time fixed. The whole trouble with plaintiff's case is that he has not in good faith substantially performed his obligation to pay that medium which the law requires of him for the payment of these sheep.

Plaintiff quotes and relies upon the case of

Shaeffer v. Coldren (Pa.) 85 Atl. 98.

While the quotation from this case in plaintiff's brief has no bearing whatever on the material issues of the instant case, the court's attention is invited to the following facts in that case: (1) Coldren was to come to Bellefront on Saturday to close the transaction; (2) the parties had agreed that the obligor should tender a certified check for the cash payment on that day; (3) Coldren did not appear in Bellefront on the day appointed; (4) When Coldren failed to appear on the day agreed upon the obligor drove out into the country, a distance of several miles, to tender the performance of his part of the contract in order to exercise his option. Coldren, the seller, had agreed to accept the certified check and did not at any time insist upon a tender in money. Upon a tender by the obligor no objection was made to the tender of a check. That case, therefore, has no bearing on the issues involved herein. We agree with plaintiff that "in the absence of any provision in the contract, or of any circumstances excluding it, contracts for the payment of money refer to the ordinary and usual currency in which business is transacted." Currency, when applied to the medium of trade means coin, bank notes or notes issued by the government.

2 Words & Phrases, 1789.

Fabbri vs. Kalbfelisch, 52 N. Y. 28, is cited and quoted by plaintiff and is an authority directly against the position he cited it for.

Hendry v. Benlisa (Fla.) 20 So. 800, involved the question whether a judgment obtained during the Civil War which has been paid in confederate money and accepted must be regarded as settled. The complete sentence from which plaintiff has detached a part, is as follows:

> "No court, since the war, has held, so far as we know, that confederate treasury notes were issued by lawful authority; but 'money' has been recognized generally by the courts as a generic term, covering anything that by consent is made to represent property, and pass as such in current business transactions, and that when a judgment or debt has been paid in confederate money, and accepted, the transaction must be regarded as settled and cannot be opened."

Curiously enough, in considering U. B. Blalock & Co. vs. W. D. Clark & Bros. (N. C.) 49 S. E. 88, plaintiff quotes from an instruction to the jury to which there was no exception. The instruction excepted to was in the following words:

> "If the contract was made, and the plaintiff

came within a reasonable time, and was then
ready and able to pay the cash, or, if not ready
to pay the cash, and if the jury find by a preponderance of the evidence that there was a
well known and established custom among persons in that section, embracing Troy, who
bought and sold cotton in large lots, to pay in
valid checks, or to ship with bill of lading attached to sight draft, and the plaintiff was
ready to comply with this custom, and the defendant did not demand the cash, but refused
to deliver the cotton because the price had advanced and because of delay, then he would be
entitled to damages, if the demand for the cotton was made within a reasonable time after
8th February."

Plaintiff cites and quotes section 5044, R. C. Montana. This section is identical with section 1655, California C. C.

In Burns v. Sennett, 33 Pac. 916, page 919, the
Supreme Court of California, citing section 1655 supra,
says -

"A usage, of course, cannot be given in evidence to relieve a party from his express stipulation, or to vary a contract certain in its terms;
but it has a legitimate office in aiding to interpret the intentions of parties to a contract,
the real character of which is to be ascertained,
not from express stipulations, but from general
implications and presumptions."

Section 7887, R. C. Montana, provides that evidence may be given upon a trial of the

"Usage, to explain the true character of an
act, contract or instrument, where such true

character is not otherwise plain; but usage is never admissible, except as an instrument of interpretation."

Section 8060, R. C. Montana, provides:

"In this state there is no common law in any case where the law is declared by the Code or the statute; but where not so declared, if the same is applicable and of a general nature, and not in conflict with the Code or other statutes, the common law shall be the law and rule of decision." (See also Sec. 3552 R. C. Mont.)

Evidence of usage or custom is inadmissible, in

"That it was an attempt, under the guise of explaining language used in the contract, to ingraft upon it a new provision upon which to base a substantial defense; and that, of course, is not permissible, certainly when the usage or custom is not relied on in the pleadings."
Charles Syer & Co. v. Lester (Va.) 82 S. E. 122.

As we shall subsequently show, where the contract does not provide the character of money or currency in which payment is to be made, payment must be made in any currency which constitutes a legal tender at the time of payment. This is a substantive rule of law. There is no express provision in the contract as to the medium of payment. Therefore the common law rule is applicable.

"A usage in conflict with plain, well established rules of law, is inadmissible in evidence in any case, and must be disregarded. We may be permitted to add the remark that were the courts, by their decisions, to encourage the growth of these local usages, originating generally in lax business practice, or mistaken ideas of law, they might become as great an evil and source of as much want of uniformity in the law as was the local legislation of the past—an evil supposed to be eradicated from our political system by the new constitution."

Cox v. O'Riley, 4 Ind. 368, 58 Am. Dec. 663.

"The rule admitting evidence of the usage is always subject to this limitation, however, that proof will never be allowed to establish a usage which is repugnant to, or which controls, displaces, or alters the legal effect of any of the express terms of a contract. A usage cannot be appealed to for the purpose of eliminating terms from a contract, and in grafting upon it others different from or inconsistent with those displaced; nor will proof be heard of a usage that is contrary to public policy or good morals or to the common or statute law."

Van Camp Packing Co. v. Hartman (Ind.) 25 N. E. 901.

"A custom cannot contradict the plain and unambiguous terms of a contract, or control its legal effect. It follows, therefore, that proof of a custom will not be received when in conflict with well settled rules of law."

High Wheel Auto Parts Co. v. Journal Co. (Ind. App.) 98 N. E. 442.

These principles announced and followed by the courts of Indiana are in accord with the universal holdings of our courts, and are sustained by the following authorities:

> Barnard v. Kellogg, 177 U. S. (10 Wallace) 383, 19 L. Ed. 987;
>
> Vermilye v. Adams Express Co., 88 U. S. (21 Wallace) 138, 22 L. Ed. 609;
>
> Clark v. Allaman (Kan.) 80 Pac. 571;
>
> Homer v. Door, 10 Mass. 26;
>
> Pickering v. Well (Mass.) 34 N. E. 1081;
>
> Thomas v. Guaranty Title & Trust Co. (Ohio) 91 N. E. 183, 26 L. R. A. (n. s.) 1210.

In Barnard v. Kellogg, supra, the Supreme Court of the United States said:

> "But if it be inconsistent with the contract, or expressly or by necessary implication contradicts it, it cannot be received in evidence to affect it. See notes to
> Wigglesworth v. Dallison, 1 Smith's L. Cas.
> 670, (Doug. 200);
> 2 Pars., Cont., sec. 9, p. 535;
> Taylor, Ev., p. 943, and following.
> 'Usage,' says Lord Lyndhurst, 'may be admissible to explain what is doubtful; it is never admissible to contradict what is plain.'
> Brackett v. Royal Exch. Ass. Co., 2 Cromp.
> & J., 249.
>
> And it is well settled that usage cannot be allowed to subvert the settled rules of law. See note to Smith's L. Cases, supra. Whatever tends to unsettle the law and make it different in the different communities into which the State is

divided, leads to mischievous consequences, embarrasses trade, and is against public policy. If, therefore, on a given state of facts, the rights and liabilities of the parties to a contract are fixed by the general principles of the common law, they cannot be changed by any local custom of the place where the contract was made."

We entertain no doubt of the correctness of the court's ruling in the Blalock case cited by plaintiff and we do not see wherein that case in any wise aids the plaintiff's appeal.

The fact that defendants accepted a check upon a Utah bank given by the plaintiff upon the execution of the contract has no bearing whatever upon defendant's refusal to accept the personal check of Mr. Stitt upon parting with the sheep for the remainder of the purchase price in a sum approximately ten times the amount of the original check, particularly in view of the fact that defendants retained possession of the sheep and for considerable time after receipt of the check given in earnest to bind the bargain. As a general principle, we agree with the plaintiff that courts will construe a contract as the parties thereto have construed it and Mr. Stitt, though the record discloses that he claims the right to the sheep by virtue of a purchase from strangers to the contract, Hatcher & Snyder, may nevertheless probably be entitled to whatever benefit the plaintiff sees in this principle. We agree also that the law does not require a party to do an idle and useless thing and therefore insist that it is immaterial whether defendants advised plaintiff that they would not accept legal tender after the time fixed for payment had expired, except to negative any waiver on their part.

Plaintiff cites a long list of authorities to sustain the proposition that if a debtor is ready, able and willing to pay, the actual production of it may be waived by the absolute refusal of the creditor to accept it. No one would doubt this general proposition.

We cannot agree with plaintiff that "an offer to perform is equivalent to performance for the purpose of sustaining an action for damages." It is precisely on this proposition that plaintiff has failed in understanding the law applicable to this case. What the court held in the case of

Lehrkind v. McDonnell, 51 Mont. 343, 153 Pac. 1012, was:

> "An unconditional offer in good faith to perform, by the party upon whom the obligation rests, coupled with the ability to perform if rejected by the other party, is equivalent to full performance and extinguishes the obligation as to the party making offer
>
> (Rev. Codes, sections 49229, 4937, 4938, 4939.)"

III. Plaintiff did not tender payment within the time and in the manner contemplated by the contract.

Delivery of these sheep was to be made on Porcupine Creek, above Nashua, Montana, and at the town of Saco, Montana, and upon the delivery of the sheep payment was, by the terms of the contract, to be made. In regard to the contention by plaintiff that payment by legal tender would be an unusual method of payment and that it would be deemed foolhardy and un-businesslike for any person to carry with him approximately $30,000, as was involved in this transaction, it is submitted that representations by the plaintiff or Mr. Stitt or any other person that Mr. Stitt's personal check in the sum of approximately $30,000 would be paid by the bank upon which it was drawn located at Fort Morgan, Colorado, are not in themselves sufficient to bind these defendants to accept the check so tendered. It does not appear that a bank at Saco or Nashua or at Glasgow, where tender of the check of Mr. Stitt was made, had sufficient funds on hand to have paid this check. At least Mr. Stitt should have advanced this money and deposited it in a bank immediately available when the time for payment arrived. He did not even offer a certified check to defendants. It is immaterial that delay in making legal tender "was due to the act of defendants in asking and demanding of plaintiff that he do something which had not been anticipated by plaintiff" if plaintiff was legally bound to do that something. And it makes no difference that plaintiff expected to do something different than he was legally bound to do.

We do not doubt that if a party prevents performance of a contract by the other party thereto he cannot insist on the stipulation that time is of the essence; and the grantor of an option who prevents its exercise during the time limited, must give a reasonable time for its exercise after any obstruction that he has interposed is removed. The answer to this is that defendants interposed no obstruction to the payment of the purchase price in the instant case; neither did defendants prevent performance by the plaintiff within the time limited, and therefore the long list of authorities cited by plaintiff, while they may probably sustain the foregoing proposition, do not bear on the issues of this case. Neither has there been any act of waiver on the part of these defendants. It would be difficult to conceive more direct straightforward action on the part of these defendants evincing at all times an intent on their part to stand firmly upon the contract. Neither do we doubt that a payment or tender of payment by check is sufficient unless objection is made to the tender on the ground that it is not acceptable tender. For the proposition that if party makes tender of check, without notice that legal tender money will be required, and such check is refused, party should have opportunity of securing the money and making a good and valid tender, plaintiff cites

> *McGrath v. Gegnor* (Md. App.) 26 Atl. 502;
> *Shaeffer v. Coldren,* heretofore noticed; and
> *Sharpe v. Todd,* 38 N. J. Eq. 324.

In McGrath vs. Gegnor, supra, the tender made

by check was refused because the obligee had declared the contract to be at an end and the court held,

> "The tender thus made and refused will be considered in law a lawful tender; and for the reason that all objection to the character of the tender will be considered as having been waived; and for the further reason that, if objection had been made on the ground that the tender was not made in lawful money, the party would have had the opportunity of getting the money and of making a good and valid tender."

In connection with the last reason, it will be noted that these parties had been in the habit of making payment for their weekly delivery by check, which method of payment seems to have been usually acceptable; nor was time of payment of the essence.

Sharpe v. Todd, supra, merely holds that where one is bound to pay a mortgage on demand or within a reasonable time thereafter, on a demand under the circumstances of that case the party on whom the demand is made is entitled to a reasonable time in which to get the money. We do not see that the case is in point.

The court can hardly take "judicial notice of the fact that comparative few obligations are met by the payment of legal tender, practically all of the business of the country being conducted upon a credit basis by means of checks and drafts," because the statement is not true in regard to business transactions between strangers. If the court may take judicial notice of a

considerable use of checks and drafts in business transactions, it is submitted that it ought also to take judicial notice of the further rule and practice among
reliable and substantial business men and commercial
houses to accept no check or draft from strangers upon
parting with valuable consideration therefor, and this
practice is particularly applicable to the instant case
for the reason that Stitt was a stranger to the original
contract and from the evidence of himself on the
witness stand it appears that he made claim to a delivery of these sheep by virtue of a contract with a
third party, Hatcher & Snyder, who are also strangers
to the original transaction.

The conclusion of part (A) of plaintiff's argument illustrates the underlying fallacy of his entire
reasoning, to-wit: It assumes that these defendants
obstructed and hindered this plaintiff, and "refused to
give him a chance" to perform the obligation which
the law imposed upon him. The answer to the whole
contention is simply that not only does the record fail
to sustain him, but the record discloses that these defendants acted straightforward and upright and upon
every turn when the question presented itself stood
fairly and squarely upon their contract and required
nothing more nor less on the part of plaintiff than the
performance of the obligation which was undertaken
in the contract and which the law imposed upon him.

It is insisted by defendants that time is of the
essence of this contract and as the act on the part of

plaintiff consisted in the payment of money only, it must have been performed immediately upon the thing to be done being exactly ascertained.

> Section 5046 and 5047, R. C. Mont.;
> *Snyder et al. v. Yarbrough,* 43 Mont. 203, 150 Pac. 411;
> *Fratt v. Daniels-Jones et al.,* supra.

At law time was always of the essence of the contract. True, Chancellor Lord Thurlow is said to have held that in equity time could not be made of the essence of a contract. See Gergson vs. Riddle referred to by Mr. Romlily in arguing the case of

> *Seton v. Slade,* 7 Ves. 268,

but the court refused to apply the doctrine in Seton vs. Slade and it has been overthrown in England and has never been favorably received in this country. See

> *Hudson v. Bartran,* 3 Madd. 447;
> *Note to Jones v. Robbins,* 50 Am. Dec. 597 and authorities;
> *Hollingsworth v. Frye,* 4 Dalls. 345, Fed. Case No. 6619;
> *Jennings v. Bowman* (S. C.) 91 S. E. 731.

PAYMENT OF OBLIGATION MUST BE IN MONEY.

The contract provides that payment shall be at the time and place of delivery. Where a party has not expressly agreed to accept payment in something other than money he may enforce his just claim by a money judgment unless he has in some way estopped himself or legally waived his right to demand payment in money. It needs no positive agreement to pay in money to entitle a creditor to demand money, for the law decrees that the payment shall be in money.

Elliott on Contracts, Section 1926.

> "Where the contract is silent as to the character of the money or currency in which the payment is to be made, payment may be made in any currency which constitutes a legal tender at the time of payment. On the other hand, in the absence of an express stipulation to the contrary, the creditor is not bound to receive anything but legal tender money in payment."

22 Am. & Eng. Ency. of Law, 539;

Howe v. Waide, 4 McLean 319;

Paup v. Drew, 10 Howard (U. S.), 218;

Trigg v. Drew, 10 Howard (U. S.), 224;

Bome v. Torry, 16 Ark. 83;

Moore v. Morris, 20 Ill. 255;

Galena Ins. Co. v. Kupfer, 28 Ill. 332;

81 Am. Dec. 284;

Hancock v. Yaden (Ind.), 16 Am. St. Rep. 396, 23 N. E. 253;

Vansickle v. Ferguson (Ind.), 23 N. E. 858;

Borne v. Indianapolis Bank (Ind.), 18 Am. St. Rep. 312, 24 N. E. 173;

Farmers L. & T. Co. v. Canada, etc., Ry. Co. (Ind.), 26 N. E. 784;

Martin v. Bott (Ind.), 46 N. E. 151;

Downing v. Dean, 3 J. J. Marsh (Ky.), 378;

Lord v. Burbank, 18 Me. 178;

Bull v. Harrell, 7 Howard (Miss.), 9.

In Hancock vs. Yaden, supra, the Supreme Court of Indiana said in considering the question as to the medium of payment of an employee for services rendered:

> "The case before us affords an example, for where á man, upon request, performs services for another, the law implies that he shall be paid for them, and paid in money. It needs no positive agreement to pay in money to entitle a creditor to demand money, for the law decrees that the payment shall be in money."

Fell v. H. Fell Poultry Co. (N. J.), 55 Atl. 236;

Haskins v. Derrin (Utah), 56 Pac. 953, acc.

Some more recent decisions to the same effect are the following:

Van DeVanter v. Redelsheinier (Wash.), 107 Pac. 847;

S. Joli v. Hagensen (N. D.), 122 N. W. 1008;

McCormick v. Obanion (Mo.), 153 S. W. 267;

Goodwin v. Heckler (Pa.), 97 Atl. 475;

Moore v. Kiff, 78 Pa., 96;

Smith v. Foster, 5 Ore. 441.

"Readiness and willingness to pay is not enough; there must be a tender of the money."

Moore v. Kiff, supra;

Smith v. Foster, supra;

Sections 4903, 4939, 4938, R. C. Mont., acc.

An analysis of the Code provisions last above cited with section 4904, R. C. Montana, lend themselves to the proposition that delivery of the sheep and payment therefor were concurrent conditions; that is the intent evinced in the contract. Therefore upon tender of the sheep upon the last day provided therefor defendants were entitled to the money.

Cole v. Swanston, 1 Cal. 42, 52 Am. Dec. 288;

Ziehen v. Smith, (N. Y.) 42 N. E. 1080.

"When goods are sold and nothing is said about the time of delivery or the time of payment, the seller is bound to deliver them whenever they are demanded on payment of the price, 'but the buyer,' as is observed by Mr. Justice Bayley in

Bloxan v. Sanders, 4 B. & C. 948, 7 D. & R. 405,

'Has no right to have the possession of the goods until he pays the price.'"

Wilmshurst v. Bowker, 2 Man. & G. 792, 133 Eng. Rep. 965, by Tindal, C. J.

FORFEITURE OF DEPOSIT OF EARNEST MONEY.

As hereinbefore submitted, the case of Clifton vs.

Willson (Mont.), 132 Pac. 424, supra, ought to be controlling in this case, for under this decision no right to the amount deposited in earnest to bind the bargain can be had by plaintiff. He is seeking to recover his advance payments as a part of the compensation to him and by so doing the plaintiff assumes to stand strictly on his legal rights—risking his chance of ultimate recovery exclusively upon his alleged ability to show that his loss has been due to defendants' failure to deliver the ewes according to his agreement. His cause stands or falls upon his failure to show a breach of contract on part of defendants.

It is a generally established principle that where a deposit is made by the purchaser on a contract of sale and the day of performance is set at a future time, if, when the day of performance arrives, the purchaser is in default and thereby his contract is breached, he is not in a position to take advantage of his own wrong to recover the deposit originally made on the contract and the great weight of authority in this country is to the effect that neither a court of law nor a court of equity will permit the buyer under such circumstances to recover the deposit money so paid.

A. *Federal Courts.*
Hansbrough v. Peck, 5 Wallace (72 U. S. 497);
Kane v. Jenkinson, Fed. Case No. 7607.

B. *California.*
Rayfield v. Van Meter, 52 Pac. 666;'

San Francisco Commercial Agency v. Wide-mann, 124 Pac. 1056, citing section 1439, C. C. Cal., identical with section 4903, R. C. Montana.

C. *Illinois.*

Colvin v. Weedman, 50 Ill. 311.

D. *Indiana.*

Patterson v. Coats, 8 Blackf. 500 (distinguished in that seller had elected to rescind the contract prior to date of delivery);

Harris v. Bradley, 9 Ind. 166.

E. *Iowa.*

Stevens v. Brown, 14 N. W. 735.

F. *Kansas.*

Gibbons v. Hayden, 44 Pac. 445.

G. *Nebraska.*

Walter v. Reed, 52 N. W. 682;

Scott v. Spencer, 60 N. W. 892;

H. *New York.*

Moskowitz v. Schwartz, 126 N. Y. S. 632;

Ajello v. Albrecht & Meister Co., 142 N. Y. S. 499.

In concluding, we quote from Gibbons vs. Hayden, supra:

"The fact that counsel have not cited a single authority in support of their contention is quite conclusive evidence of the fact that their position is not well taken. On the contrary, the rule seems to be well settled that the party who has advanced money in part performance of such an agreement—the other party being ready and willing to perform on his part—cannot, without just cause or excuse. refuse to proceed with the contract, and recover back what he has advanced," citing authorities.

Turning to subdivisions B, C, D, and E of plaintiff's brief, in answer thereto it may be said that however desirable it might be on behalf of plaintiff, the law does not require the obligee entitled to money to accept in lieu thereof a mere chose in action, whether this be in the form of a written obligation on the part of a third person as by his check or draft, or whether it be a guaranty on the part of a fourth person that the promise by the third person will be fulfilled. An offer of a bank check for the amount due is not a good tender.

Larson v. Breene (Colo), 21 Pac. 498;
Barber v. Hickey (D. C.), 24 L. R. A. 763;
Hardy v. Commercial Loan Co., 84 Ill. 251;
Sloan v. Petri, 16 Ill. 262;
Collier v. White (Miss.), 6 So. 618;
Te Poel v. Shutt (Neb.), 78 N. W. 288;
Matter of Collyer, 108 N. Y. S. 600;
Volk v. Olson, 104 N. Y. S. 415;
Ugland v. Bank (N. D.), 137 N. W. 572 (option waived);
Realty Co. v. Brown (Okla.), 147 Pac. 318;
Aldrach v. Light Etc. Co. (S. C.), 85 S. E. 164;
Gunby v. Ingram (Wash.), 106 Pac. 495.

The same rule extends to drafts,

Shay v. Callanan (Ia.), 100 N. W. 55.
and certificates of deposit,

Graddle v. Warner (Ill.), 29, N. E. 1118.

In regard to the proposed amendment to the complaint asked for by plaintiff (p. 36 his brief) it is respectfully submitted that "necessarily extending" the time for payment of the purchase price is exactly what neither the plaintiff nor the court can do without consent of defendants.

Section 4927, R. C., Montana, provides:

> "Performance of an obligation for the delivery of money only is called payment."

In answer to plaintiff's contention that Mr. Stitt could not reasonably be required to carry upon his person a sum approximating $30,000 in places "far from the protection that society affords in the city," (p. 31, plaintiff's brief) we wish to suggest that the legislature of this state has provided a means whereby this common law obligation which had theretofore rested upon obligors for the payment of money, namely; that an obligation to pay money could be met only by a tender and show of money at the time and place of performance, enacted section 4944, R. C. Montana (section 1500, Cal. C. C.):

> "An obligation for the payment of money is extinguished by a due offer of payment, if the amount is immediately deposited in the name of the creditor, with some bank of deposit, within

this state, of good repute and notice thereof is given to the creditor."

Not having brought himself within the provisions of section 4944, R. C. Montana, this plaintiff stands subject to the rules of the common law except as modified by the Codes of Montana.

Respectfully submitted,

NORRIS, HURD & McKELLAR,
EDWIN L. NORRIS,
Attorneys for Defendants in Error.

Service of the foregoing brief and the receipt of a copy thereof are hereby admitted this....................day of October, 1918.

....

Attorney for Plaintiff in Error.

No. 3201

United States
Circuit Court of Appeals
For the Ninth Circuit.

TOM BROWN,

Plaintiff in Error,

vs.

HARRIET S. PULLEN,

Defendant in Error.

Transcript of Record.

Upon Writ of Error to the United States District Court of the District of Alaska, Division No. 1.

Filmer Bros Co. Print, 330 Jackson St., S. F., Cal.

No. 3201

United States
Circuit Court of Appeals
For the Ninth Circuit.

TOM BROWN,

Plaintiff in Error,

vs.

HARRIET S. PULLEN,

Defendant in Error.

Transcript of Record.

Upon Writ of Error to the United States District Court of the District of Alaska, Division No. 1.

Filmer Bros. Co. Print, 330 Jackson St., S. F., Cal.

INDEX TO THE PRINTED TRANSCRIPT OF RECORD.

[Clerk's Note: When deemed likely to be of an important nature, errors or doubtful matters appearing in the original certified record are printed literally in italic; and, likewise, cancelled matter appearing in the original certified record is printed and cancelled herein accordingly. When possible, an omission from the text is indicated by printing in italic the two words between which the omission seems to occur.]

In the District Court for the First Judicial Division, Territory of Alaska, United States of America, at Skagway, Alaska.

TOM BROWN,

Plaintiff,

vs.

HARRIET S. PULLEN,

Defendant,—ss.

Complaint.

The plaintiff, for his cause of action, complains and alleges:

I.

That he is a citizen of the United States and a resident of the Territory of Alaska.

II.

That the defendant is a resident of the Territory of Alaska, residing at Skaguay, Alaska.

III.

That the plaintiff is an able-bodied man, and a farmer from birth, therefore, an all-round stockman.

IV.

That the defendant is the reputed owner of a stock ranch and general farm situated six (6) miles, or

thereabout, from Skaguay, Alaska, at a place for-
mally called Dyea, Alaska.

V.

That on the 3d day of December, 1915, the defendant engaged the plaintiff at a monthly wage of sixty
dollars- ($60.00) per month and board, to go to Dyea,
Alaska (her ranch), and take care of her stock of
about twenty head—i. e., feed and water stock; milk,
make butter, etc.; look after buildings, and make
himself generally useful thereabout.

VI.

That the plaintiff performed his duties faithfully,
to the best interest of defendant.   [1*]

VII.

That on June 4, 1916, the plaintiff, after giving
defendant one month's notice, quit this said job, returned to Skaguay, Alaska, and demanded his pay.

VIII.

That on June 5, 1916, the defendant paid plaintiff
Fifty Dollars ($50.00) in cash and honored his writ-
ten or oral order for Ten Dollars ($10.00)—in all,
Sixty Dollars ($60.00).

IX.

That on June 5, 1916, the defendant re-engaged
the plaintiff for the same job, at a monthly wage of
Sixty-five Dollars (\$65.00) and board, until the fol-
lowing March.

X.

That the plaintiff faithfully performed his duties
until June 11, 1917, when he quit.

---

*Page-number appearing at foot of page of original certified Tran-
script of Record.*

XI.

That plaintiff demanded his pay, and on June 13, 1917, received the sum of Two Hundred Dollars ($200.00) in the form of two checks—one for $150.00 and one for $50.00.

XII.

That on divers occasions between the dates of June 5, 1916, and June 11, 1917, the plaintiff received from the defendant miscellaneous articles of wearing apparel to the value of *Twenty-eigth* ($28.00) or thereabouts, for which defendant has bills of cost.

XIII.

That the plaintiff has received in cash or otherwise a total sum of Two Hundred Eighty-eight Dollars ($288.00) from the defendant.

XIV.

That the defendant is indebted to, and owes, the plaintiff [2] the sum of One Thousand One Hundred Fifty-seven Dollars ($1,157.00), less Two Hundred Eighty-eight Dollars ($288.00), or a total of Eight Hundred Sixty-nine Dollars ($869.00), which on demand the defendant refused to pay.

THEREFORE, the plaintiff prays judgment against the defendant:

(1) For the sum of Eight Hundred Sixty-nine Dollars ($869.00), with interest thereon from June 11, 1917, to date;

(2) For his costs and disbursements in this action;

(3) For a reasonable attorney's fee—Two Hun-

dred Dollars ($200.00), being such a reasonable fee.
· Respectfully submitted:

CARL LOGAN,
Plaintiff's Attorney.

VERIFICATION.

Territory of Alaska,
First Judicial Division,—ss.

Tom Brown, being first duly sworn, on oath, deposes and says:

That he is the plaintiff in the foregoing cause of action; that he has read and understands the foregoing complaint, and that the same is true of his own knowledge.

TOM BROWN.

Subscribed and sworn to before me this 8th day of August, A. D. 1917.

. [Notarial Seal]   PHIL ABRAHAMS,
Notary Public in and for the Territory of Alaska,
Residing at Skagway, Alaska.

. My commission expires January 6th, 1918.

[Endorsed]: Filed Aug. 25, 1917, District Court, Alaska.   J. W. Bell, Clerk of District Court, Dist. of Alaska, Division No. 1.   E. A. Rasmuson, Dep. [3]

In the District Court for the District of Alaska, Division No 1, at Juneau.

No. 1716-A.

TOM BROWN,

Plaintiff,

vs.

HARRIET S. PULLEN,

Defendant.

Answer.

Answering the complaint of plaintiff, defendant says:

1. She admits the allegations contained in paragraphs 1, 2, 4, 8, 11, 12 and 13 thereof.

2. She denies the allegations contained in paragraphs 3, 7, 10 and 14 of plaintiff's complaint.

3. In answer to paragraph 5, defendant says, that she engaged plaintiff on or about the said 3d day of December, 1915, to work for her at the rate of one dollar per day and board, upon the agreement that he was to watch and care for her property at Dyea, Alaska, and to take care of and feed six head of stock at that time owned by her and kept upon said property, and defendant denies each and every other allegation in said paragraph 5 of said complaint contained.

4. Defendant denies the allegations contained in paragraph 6 of plaintiff's complaint.

5. Answering paragraph 9, defendant admits that plaintiff quit her employ on or about the time alleged, but alleges that when he returned to work

he agreed to work upon the same terms upon which he had previously been employed, to wit, one dollar per day and board, and denies that there was any agreement between the parties hereto for the employment of plaintiff's services for any specific length of time, and denies each and every other allegation in said paragraph contained not herein specifically admitted or denied. [4]

6. Defendant denies that she is indebted to the plaintiff in the sum set forth in paragraph 14 of his complaint or in any sum whatsoever, and alleges that she paid plaintiff various sums of money from time to time, in accordance with his request, among which were the specific sums set forth in said plaintiff's complaint, and alleges that on said thirteenth day of June, 1917, she settled with plaintiff in full for all claims the said plaintiff made against her, and plaintiff accepted said settlement in full satisfaction of all claims against defendant, and did not then or at any time thereafter make any demand upon defendant, or make any claim to defendant, that there was any sum or sums of money due or owing from defendant to plaintiff.

7. Defendant further denies each and every allegation in said complaint not hereinbefore specifically admitted or denied.

WHEREFORE, defendant demands judgment that the complaint against her be dismissed and for her costs and disbursements herein as by law provided.

JOHN B. MARSHALL,
Attorney for Defendant.

United States of America,

Territory of Alaska,—ss.

Harriet S. Pullen, being first duly sworn, deposes and says, that she is the defendant named in the foregoing answer; that she has read the same and knows the contents thereof and that the same is true as she verily believes.

HARRIET S. PULLEN.

Subscribed and sworn to before me this 21st March, 1918.

[Notarial Seal.]   JOHN B. MARSHALL,
Notary Public for Alaska.

My com. expires Octr. 14, 1921.

Service of a copy of the foregoing is admitted this 21st March, 1918.

J. H. COBB,
Atty. for Plaintiff.

Filed in the District Court, District of Alaska, First Division. Mar. 21, 1918. J. W. Bell, Clerk. By C. Z. Denny, Deputy. [5]

In the District Court for Alaska, Division Number One, at Juneau.

No. 1716–A.

TOM BROWN,

Plaintiff,

vs.

HARRIET S. PULLEN,

Defendant.

Reply.

Comes now the plaintiff, by his attorney, and for reply to the Answer of the defendant, alleges:

I.

He denies that the consideration of wage in the contract of employment between plaintiff and defendant was $1.00 per day or any other sum than is alleged in his complaint.

II.

He denies that when he returned to work for the defendant as alleged in Paragraph Nine of his complaint, he agreed to work for $1.00 per day and board, or for any other sum than is stated in his complaint.

III.

He denies that the defendant ever paid plaintiff any other sums of money than the sums alleged in this complaint and he denies that on the 13th day of June, 1917, or at any other time the defendant paid the plaintiff in full for all claims that the plaintiff made against her; and he further denies that he accepted from defendant any settlement or purported satisfaction in full of his claim against the defendant, and denies that there was any settlement or pretended settlement; and he further denies that the plaintiff did not then or at any time thereafter make demand upon defendant or claims for the other and further sums of money **[6]** due and owing by the defendant.

WHEREFORE he prays as in his original complaint.

CARL LOGAN,
Attorneys for Plaintiff,
J. H. COBB.

United States of America,
Territory of Alaska,—ss.

Tom Brown, being first duly sworn, on oath deposes and says the above and foregoing reply is true as I verily believe.

TOM BROWN.

Subscribed and sworn to before me this 25 day of March, 1918.

[Notarial Seal]   A. H. ZIEGLER,
Notary Public for Alaska.

My commission expires July 12, 1921.

Filed in the District Court, District of Alaska, First Division. Mar. 25, 1918. J. W. Bell, Clerk. By C. Z. Denny, Deputy. [7]

In the District Court for the District of Alaska, Division No. 1, at Juneau.

No. 1716–A.

TOM BROWN,

Plaintiff,

vs.

HARRIET S. PULLEN,

Defendant.

Judgment.

The above-entitled cause having come on for trial
on Monday, March 25th, 1918, at the hour of ten
o'clock A. M., and a jury having been duly impaneled, examined and accepted by the attorneys
for the respective parties, and sworn according to
law; and testimony of witnesses and argument of
counsel having been duly heard; the Court having
duly instructed the jury upon the law, and said jury
having retired to consider of its verdict and having
thereafter duly returned into court the following
verdict, to wit:

> "We, the Jury, duly impaneled and sworn
> in the above-entitled cause, find for the defend-
> ant";

And the motion for a new trial having been duly
overruled—

It is, therefore, ORDERED, ADJUDGED AND
DECREED, that the plaintiff take nothing by his
action herein, and that the defendant have and recover her costs herein, including an attorney's fee
of Twenty dollars, to be taxed as by law provided.

Dated Juneau, Alaska, April 4, 1918, and the
plaintiff is granted an extension of time until June
15, 1918, in which to prepare and present a bill of
exceptions.

ROBT. W. JENNINGS,
Judge.

Entered Court Journal, No. O, page 143.

O. K.—COBB.

Filed in the District Court, District of Alaska, First Division. Apr. 4, 1918. J. W. Bell, Clerk. By C. Z. Denny, Deputy. **[8]**

In the District Court for Alaska, Division No. 1, at Juneau.

No. 1716–A.

TOM BROWN,

Plaintiff,

vs.

HARRIET S. PULLEN,

Defendant.

Bill of Exceptions.

Be it remembered, that on the trial of the above-entitled cause, the following proceedings were had to wit:

Approved.

JOHN B. MARSHALL,

Atty. for Deft. **[9]**

[10]

Testimony of Tom Brown, in His Own Behalf.

TOM BROWN, the plaintiff herein, called as a witness in his own behalf, being first duly sworn, testified as follows:

Direct Examination.

(By Mr. COBB.)

Q. State your name.   A. Tom Brown.

Q. Where do you live now, Mr. Brown?

A. Treadwell.

Q. Are you employed over there?   A. Yes, sir.

Q. Do you know the defendant, Mrs. Pullen?

A. Yes, sir.

Q. Were you ever employed by her?

A. Yes, sir.

Q. When were you first employed by her?

A. I went over to Dyea on the 3d of December; I did a little work for her just before, but it didn't amount to anything—just a little carpentering or something like that.

Q. On the 3d of December of what year?

A. 1915.

Q. What were you employed to do?

A. Look after the cattle what was on the ranch, haul hay, haul wood, look after the potato-house when it was cold, saw wood and keep a fire in it; and Royal and I worked under a great big building—what they call the Pacific Hotel; we were digging the foundation out—digging for the foundation; then I made gates, and put up some fences, and repaired fences, and all kinds of common farm work.

(Testimony of Tom Brown.)

Q. Just tell the jury where this place is that you went to work at.

A. Dyea is about 4 miles from Skagway—something like that. [11]

Q. Over where the old town of Dyea used to be?

A. Yes, sir; where the rush was.

Q. Was there any agreement what you were to be paid?   A. Yes.

Q. What was it?

A. I met Mrs. Pullen in Skagway, right opposite that saloon there; and she asked me then several times, she said, "The cattle are out, Tom, and it is snowing, and Mr. Clark is not looking after them, and if you will go and look after them I will give you $60.00 a month and board"; and of course I would have to cook a great deal of it myself, you see. Mr. Clark told me he had been receiving $60.00 a month, and I think she had two boys there working putting up the telephone or something like that, and she told me herself she was paying $60.00 a month.

Mr. MARSHALL.—If the Court please we object to any evidence as to what she was paying some boys for running a telephone line.

Mr. COBB.—It is what the defendant told him.

Q. Do you know the going wages in that country for an employee employed to do the work you were, general labor?

A. Yes, never less than $3.00 a day.

Q. How long did you work under that arrangement?

(Testimony of Tom Brown.)

A. I got into Skagway June 4th, 1916, and I gave her a month's notice before I came in.

The COURT.—This contract, you say, was made in December, 1915?

A. Yes, sir.

The COURT.—Now, what about June, 1916?

A. I worked until June, 1916, at that rate of wages —from December, 1915, to June, 1916, the 5th of June, at $60.00 a month.

Q. On that date did you see the defendant, Mrs. Pullen? [12]   A. Yes, sir.

Q. Where did you see her?

A. I asked her if she had a man ready to take my place, when I came in, and she said no, she had not, she had no one to take my place.

Q. Had you given her notice before that you were going to quit?   A. Yes, sir; a month's notice.

Q. Why did you do that?

A. Because I was not satisfied.

Q. I mean why did you give the notice—what was the necessity?

A. I wanted to go to work somewhere else.

Q. You did not want to leave the cattle without attention, you mean?

A. No, sir; the reason I gave her notice I wanted to go back to either Burns or Frye-Bruhn; I had been with them for quite a number of years in White Horse.

Q. And as I understand you did not want to leave the place with nobody on it?

(Testimony of Tom Brown.)

Mr. MARSHALL.—You tried to get him to say that but he wouldn't do it.

Mr. COBB.—I am asking him now.

Mr. MARSHALL.—No, you are telling him what he said, and he didn't say anything of the kind.

Q. Was there any other reason then besides your wanting to go to work somewhere else why you took pains to give her notice?

A. Yes, because I thought if I quit without any notice and come in, she wouldn't have anyone to take care of the cattle, but when I gave her a month's notice she had time to get someone to look after the cattle.

Q. When you got into Skagway did you see the defendant, Mrs. Pullen? A. Yes, sir. [13]

Q. What, if anything, occurred between you then, Mr. Brown?

A. She gave me $50.00 then, on the 5th, I think it was, and told me if I would go back and look after the cattle and do as I had been doing she would give me $65.00; and she said she had a nephew, Mr. Smith, going along, and I told her if Mr. Smith came along I would be only too glad to have him take my place. Mr. Smith came along but she did not put him in my place, and he was working around the hotel; and after he worked a little while he quit and went over to White Horse and scabbed on the longshoremen to get money, and he told me—

The COURT.—Never mind that.

Q. Did you go back to work for her?

(Testimony of Tom Brown.)

A. Yes, sir, at $65.00 a month.

Q. She paid you $50.00 in cash—did she give you any more at that time?

A. Yes, sir; Mrs. Aimes was there cooking a little while; she cooked and did a little extra work on the potatoes. Mrs. Aimes came over and she was sick, and Mrs. Pullen came over and took her back to Skagway; and Mrs. Aimes wanted to pay the doctor bill, or something, and said she was a little short of money, and she came to the phone and she said to me, "Could I borrow $10.00 from you?" And I told her that I didn't have it, that I was short, and she said, "Can't you ask Mrs. Pullen for it? She owes you money." I said, "Tell Mrs. Pullen to come to the phone." Mrs. Pullen came to the phone and I told her to let her have $10.00.

Q. That made the $60.00, then? A. Yes, sir.

Q. How long did you work there for $65.00 a month? A. Until the 11th of June.

Q. What year? A. 1917. [14]

Q. During the time—between the time that you went to work there at $65.00 a month and the time you quit, did she pay you anything more in any way?

A. You mean between June 5th and June 11th?

Q. Yes.

A. Well, I got some clothes, yes, and I got—

Q. Explain that to the jury. You have given her credit for $28.00 in your bill here—explain it to the jury.

A. When I went back on the 5th of June or 7th of

(Testimony of Tom Brown.)

June, whatever it was—well, I came in on the 13th of January and I had $3.00 to pay for a boat; and I came in for shoes—everything was getting slippery and the horses could not stand. They were not shod at all —she did not keep the horses shod in winter—they do much better without—and I came in on the 13th of January and paid $3.00 for coming in from Dyea to Skagway.

Q. That was fare on the boat?

A. Well, an Indian brought me in in a canoe. And then I told Mrs. Pullen about paying this $3.00, and she says all right, and she gave me $6.00—do you see, $6.00, and she says, "I will charge this up to you, and you charge the $3.00 up to me," and I said all right.

Q. Did she furnish you any clothes on your order, or buy you any clothes?

A. Yes, sir; I have the bill for the clothes. She never brought no bill over herself, but what she told me they cost I put that down. January 13th I received $6.00—that is when I came over, you know.

Q. (By Mr. MARSHALL.) Just a minute—is that book you have a memoranda of the entries made at the time?

A. Yes, a book that I took up to Dyea.

Q. (By Mr. MARSHALL.) Did you write that in there at the time you [15] got the clothes, or when?

A. I beg your pardon—let me explain. On January 4th, Mrs. Pullen promised if I would go up about half a mile into a big old house with 8 rooms, she

(Testimony of Tom Brown.)

would come over and cook herself, or else bring a lady cook to cook for Mrs. Pullen and I, which she never did.

Q. (By Mr. MARSHALL.) I did not ask you that. I asked you if you wrote that memoranda in the book at the time the stuff was brought to you?

A. Well, after—

Q. (By Mr. MARSHALL.) Just answer my question.

A. After the 4th of January I did; I had this old book before.

Q. (By Mr. MARSHALL.) Did you write it at the time you got the thing?

A. Let me explain what I have marked down, what I had received from her. When her house burned down the book was burned up, and everything that I had was burned up, all my clothes, shoes, underwear, and everything; and then I explained it to you that she brought—

Q. (By Mr. MARSHALL.) And then you wrote this down afterwards in that book?

A. After the fire, because my book was burned up.

Q. (By Mr. MARSHALL.) And you wrote it from memory?

A. Well, I could remember it all.

Q. (By Mr. MARSHALL.) You wrote it from memory? A. Yes, sir.

Mr. MARSHALL.—All right.

The WITNESS.—On February the 4th, the house burnt down, and then about the 7th Mr. Moseek and

(Testimony of Tom Brown.)

Mrs. Pullen came over—I sent him in to tell her the house was burned down, and Mr. Moseek and Mrs. Pullen came over, and she brought shirts and some more things that I cannot recollect, and I gave her credit for $6.00. [16]

Q. That is what she told you it cost? A. Yes.

Q. Did you make that memorandum at the time she told you? A. I think I did, yes—yes, sir.

Q. Now, what else?

A. In this fire I lost $12.00—I lost the $6.00 that Mrs. Pullen had paid me before, and I lost $6.00 more; and I lost a pin that was worth $150.00.

Q. Never mind about that, it doesn't make any difference, but what did Mrs. Pullen bring you that you credited her with, that she bought for you after the fire?

A. There is this bill, $6.00; she told me it was for shirts, and so forth. And then on March 5th I asked her for some money, for her to let me have a little money, and she gave me $5.00, on March 5th.

Q. Have you given Mrs. Pullen credit for all she paid you in wages—did you ever receive any more than $288.00 from her?

A. That is all I received.

Q. Now, Mrs. Pullen claims there were only six head of cattle there—how many cattle did you have to take care of? A. Three horses.

Q. Three head of horses?

A. Three head of horses was there, and she had seven head of cattle—that made 10.

Q. That was when you first went there?

(Testimony of Tom Brown.)

A. Yes.

Q. How many were brought in later?

A. I raised them up from this 10 until the 11th of June when I came away. I had gotten them up to 30. I advised her to buy cows and bring them over there, and I got them up to 30.

Q. What kind of cattle were these—any milk stock among them? [17]

A. Yes, milk stock and beef stock.

The COURT.—What is the object of this, Mr. Cobb?

Mr. COBB.—I want to show the jury the character of work that he did.

The COURT.—This plaintiff claims that he had a contract, that he was to be paid so much, and that he has been paid so much. That is your case in chief. It might be admissible in rebuttal, but I cannot see the object of going into those things on direct examination.

Mr. COBB.—All right; you may cross-examine.

Cross-examination.

(By Mr. MARSHALL.)

Q. Mr. Brown, how much work did you do for Mrs. Pullen, the defendant in this case, prior to going over to Dyea?

A. I did a little gardening, and she had me work in,—

Mr. COBB.—I object to that as not proper cross-examination and as irrelevant and immaterial.

The COURT.—On what theory, Mr. Marshall, do you think that is admissible? From the pleadings it

(Testimony of Tom Brown.)

seems to be simply a controversy as to whether the contract was for $60.00 a month or $30.00 a month and board.

Mr. MARSHALL.—He has made the allegation that he is an able-bodied man, and that he did certain work over there, and we have denied those allegations.

The COURT.—Absolutely immaterial allegations, unless you propose to set up in your answer that he did not do his work.

Mr. MARSHALL.—I think we will deny that he did certain work which he says that he did—

The COURT.—But, you admit that you had a contract with him for $30.00 a month and that you have paid him, so consequently it don't make any difference about his work—you [18] paid him according to the contract.

Mr. MARSHALL.—That is very true, if the Court please—we claim to have paid him in full for the services rendered.

The COURT.—Then, your contract, according to your statement was $30.00 a month, and you say you paid him. He says the contract was $60.00 a month and that he has not been paid, so the only question in issue is what the contract was.

Mr. MARSHALL.—He alleges in here that he was an able-bodied man and that he was accustomed to receiving the going wages. We want to show that he worked for Mrs. Pullen for a small sum of money and his meals, that he had no employment, and he

(Testimony of Tom Brown.)

took up this work for that reason rather than the reason he said.

The COURT.—This suit is on a contract, and your defense is that your contract was for $30.00 a month. It is true that he alleges in his complaint that he is an able-bodied man, but that does not make any difference. It is simply a question of what the contract was, and not whether or not the services were performed, because you virtually admit the services were performed by saying that you had a contract with him for $30.00 a month and that you paid him.

Mr. MARSHALL.—Very well.

Q. I will ask you then, Mr. Brown, where you made this contract with Mrs. Pullen.

A. Right opposite the Pantheon saloon—Mr. Anderson's saloon, I met Mrs. Pullen right there.

Q. I want to ask you in regard to the payments you received, whether or not you received any other sums than those set up in your complaint.   A. No, sir.

Q. Didn't you testify a few moments ago that she paid you $5.00   [19]   there on a certain occasion?

A. Yes, in March.

Q. Now, is that admitted in your complaint?

Mr. LOGAN.—If the Court please, the complaint, I think, covers that on account of the miscellaneous articles,—that is, the $28.00 received in miscellaneous articles, that is cash and so forth.

The COURT.—You are not on the witness-stand, Mr. Logan. Your complaint alleges $28.00—he is testifying to what he was paid. Mr. Marshall is cross-examining him.

(Testimony of Tom Brown.)

Mr. LOGAN.—The reason I make the remark now is that I did not consider it proper direct examination to go into that question at this time.

The COURT.—But it is proper cross-examination.

Q. Now, when did you state that the $5.00 was paid you—was it on March 6th?

A. Some time in March I got the clothes—about March 6th.

Q. And then you say there was another sum of $3.00 paid you when you went over to Skagway, when the Indians towed you over?

A. I said there was $6.00 in January—the 13th of January.

Q. $3.00, however, was to pay for taking you over there, wasn't it?

A. I paid the $3.00 to the Indian, and she gave me $6.00; and I charged Mrs. Pullen up with the $3.00, and Mrs. Pullen said she would charge me with the $6.00.

Q. That is $11.00 which you received beside that admitted in *you* complaint, is it not?

A. I don't know.

Q. Well, you have alleged in your complaint that you received $50.00 and $10.00 at one time, and at another time you received $200.00 altogether—that is all that you admit you have received, in your complaint, isn't it?   [20]

A. I am not sure about that.

Q. Then, if that is a fact, this $11.00 was in addition to the amount that you admit you received?

Mr. COBB.—I object to that line of cross-exami-

(Testimony of Tom Brown.)

nation—it is not fair. He has admitted $28.00 there in addition to the $288.00.

The COURT.—Payment is an affirmative defense. The plaintiff alleges in the complaint he has been paid so much, and the answer admits he has been paid so much. If you claim that he was paid more than that, when you come to put in your side of the case you put in proof to that effect, but it is not cross-examination of this witness.

Q. Mr. Brown, when did you receive this $50.00 and $10.00 that you speak of, when was that?

A. About the 5th of June, 1916.

Q. You received that after you had quit work?

A. I was over from Dyea and Mrs. Pullen gave me a check in Kennedy's store for $50.00.

Q. And she at that time also gave you $10.00— when did she give you that?

A. She had never given me any such thing, not before the $50.00—that was the first I received.

Q. I am asking you when you received the $10.00 which you say you received?

A. Mrs. Aimes received the $10.00 the latter part of June or the fore part of July; she came back, I think, some time in the fore part of July, but it was in June that she asked me for the $10.00.

Q. You say here, "That on June 5th, 1916, the defendant paid plaintiff $50.00 in cash and honored his written or oral order for $10.00—in all, $60.00." When was that—on June 5th, as the pleadings say it was, or when was it? [21]

A. The ten dollars, you mean?

(Testimony of Tom Brown.)

Q. The $10.00 and the $50.00.

A. The $50.00 was on June 5th, and the other $10.00 was given to Mrs. Aimes the latter part of June, as near as I can remember. I credited Mrs. Pullen with the $10.00.

Q. At the time you received the $50.00 how much was there due you?

A. 6 months at $60.00 a month.

Q. And you only received $50.00 at that time?

A. That is all.

Q. Then, when did you re-engage with Mrs. Pullen? A. After I got that check from her.

Q. On the same day?

A. Well, I think it was the same day, or the day after; I couldn't swear, but it was somewhere right about then, I think—I couldn't swear to it; I was in Skagway 4 days before I went back.

Q. Why didn't you ask then for the balance of the money due you?

A. I did, and Mrs. Pullen said she was short of money, and she was short of a horse—the horse that died—Mrs. Pullen had only one horse over on the farm, and I would plow,—

Q. I don't care about that. I want to know why you did not demand the rest of the money that was due you at that time?

A. I did; and besides, Mrs. Pullen said, "You don't want any money over in Dyea."

Q. When you received that $50.00 check did it have any endorsement on it of what it was in payment for?

(Testimony of Tom Brown.)

A. It said, "Pay Tom Brown $50.00"; and I bought a suit of clothes in the store and gave it over to Mr. Kennedy; and Mrs. Pullen made the check out in Kennedy's, in kind of a little office where he keeps his safe.

Q. Are you satisfied the check had on it nothing but the [22] statement, pay to Tom Brown $50.00?

A. I am sure of that.

Q. It had nothing on it but "pay Tom Brown, $50.00"?

Mr. COBB.—That is not cross-examination and we object.

The COURT.—I think it might be, because it might throw light on whether there was such a contract as he claims.

Q. I will show you a check, Mr. Brown, and ask you if that is the check you received from Mrs. Pullen at the time?

A. Yes; "for services up to May 1st, 1916," was never on that—it is not the same writing as the other—it is not the same handwriting as the other.

Q. And that is the reason you say it was never on there, is it?

A. Don't you think it is a different,—

Q. I don't want to tell you what I think.

A. I will swear that, "for services up to May 1st, 1916," was never on there.

Q. And is your reason for it that it is not the same writing?   A. It don't look like the same writing.

Q. Is that your reason for swearing to that?

(Testimony of Tom Brown.)

A. I will swear there was no such thing as that, "for services up to May 1st, 1916,"—it was not on there.

Q. Is that your reason for swearing that it is not the same writing?

A. I will swear that it was not on.

Q. That is not what I asked you. You can answer the question. What is your reason for saying that it wasn't on there?

A. Because I didn't see it on.

Q. You stated just now that it was not the same writing—is that your reason for it as well?

A. It don't look like the same writing to me.

Q. That is as far as you are willing to go on that?

A. Yes. [23]

Mr. MARSHALL.—If the Court please, we offer this in evidence as Defendant's Exhibit No. 1.

Mr. COBB.—We object to it as not proper cross-examination, and not material at this time.

The COURT.—It is proper cross-examination, but it is not the time to offer it, because he denies that that is the check—he denies that that is the condition the check was in when the check was delivered to him—he does not identify the check. Wait until your side of the case comes on to be heard. You can have it identified as being denied by him.

Mr. MARSHALL.—I will mark it for identification at this time.

(Whereupon said check was marked Defendant's Exhibit No. 1 for identification.)

Q. Now, Mr. Brown, when did she pay you any

(Testimony of Tom Brown.)

more money after that $50.00?

Mr. COBB.—I object to that as not cross-examination. That throws no light upon the contract at all—that is the only thing that he has testified to.

The COURT.—You mean when did she pay him any more of the money he admits he got?

Mr. MARSHALL.—I am asking when she paid him any more money.

The COURT.—I think that is cross-examination, because it might throw light on the contract—I cannot tell whether it does or not.

Q. Answer the question, Mr. Brown.

A. Well, yes, I got $6.00, as I told you, in February—is that what you want to know?

Q. February of the next year?

A. Yes, in February, 1917.

Q. Is that all?

A. Well, I got the other sums that I told you.

Q. What were they, and when?   **[24]**

A. $5.00 in cash in March.

Q. 1917?   A. Yes.

Q. Then what else?

A. $200.00 the 13th of June—I came in on the 11th and she paid me on the 13th.

Q. Where was that paid to you?

A. Mrs. Pullen took me into her private room and made the checks out.

Q. Those checks were turned over to you for that sum?   A. Yes, the $50.00 and the $150.00.

Q. At the time they were turned over—was there

(Testimony of Tom Brown.)

any discussion between you and Mrs. Pullen as to what was due you?

A. Yes, she told me, she said, "I can only give you this here $200.00, but you go down to Royal in Treadwell and Royal will give you a good job, and I will send you the balance of the money along." I said I would rather be paid up the balance of the money that was coming to me before I left Skagway.

Q. Was there any dispute between you as to what was owing you?

A. I wanted her to settle up, and I asked her—she had three carpenters working outside—she told me this—she was paying them $6.00 a day, and another man she was paying $4.00 a day, and she told me that she could not spare the money, and that she was improving her property; she told me it was going to cost her about a thousand dollars.

Q. Now, was there any agreement between you as to the amount that was due?

A. Yes, there was; she said to me—I told Mrs. Pullen, "We will right everything up," and she said, "There is no use to reckon it up now, Tom, because I cannot pay you; but you have, I guess, something about $900.00 coming"; [25] and I said, "We will reckon it up, anyhow." We did not reckon it up. She said, "I cannot give you any more than $200.00 just now," and she did not want to give me any more.

Q. Then, what did you say to her?

A. Then, she told me if I would go down to Tread-well, her son Royal down here would give me a good

(Testimony of Tom Brown.)

job and that she would send the money along. I
told her I did not want to leave Skagway until I got
my money. And then I met Mrs. Pullen about the
2d of July, and I told her, "Mrs. Pullen, I would
like you to settle up with me as I want to go away
below." She turned around to me and she said,
"You dirty skunk, you have nothing coming"; and
she turned around from me and went down the steps.

Q. That was on what date?

A. As near as I can recall the second of July—I
wouldn't swear to it, but I think it was around there.

Q. Was there anyone present at that conversation?

A. There was a few men, longshoremen and such
like around—about three, I guess.

Q. Do you know who any of them were?

A. I forget now who they were.

Q. Can you recall their names?

A. No, sir; I cannot; I could not swear to who
they were right now.

Q. On the 13th of June she had paid you this
$200.00?   A. Yes, sir.

Q. Did you have any further conversation with
her at that time than what you have now related,
that she told you to go to Treadwell and Royal
would give you a job?

Mr. COBB.—I think that has been gone far
enough into for the Court to see that it cannot possibly be cross-examination. **[26]**

The COURT.—I do not agree with you Mr. Cobb.

(Testimony of Tom Brown.)

He is asking him now whether he had any further conversation.

Mr. COBB.—After he quit work.

The COURT.—Conversations after he quit work might throw light on what their contract was—I cannot tell.

Q. Did you have any further conversation with her at that time other than the conversations you have related, that she told you to go to Royal at Treadwell and he would give you a job—answer that question?

A. No, sir, no; I cannot recall any other conversation.

Q. That covers the whole conversation between you. Now, after the conversation with Mrs. Pullen when she gave you these checks, did you have any other conversation with her, or see her at any time, until this 2d day of July that you are talking about? A. The 2d day of July?

Q. Yes.

A. No, I did not have no conversation with Mrs. Pullen at all.

Q. You never demanded of her the additional money that you claim was due you at any time between the 13th of June and the 2d day of July?

A. No, I gave her a little time to pay it in, as I promised her.

Q. And you are unable to tell me any of the men who were present when you had this conversation with her on the 2d of July?

A. Yes, I am unable to tell you; I could not swear

(Testimony of Tom Brown.)
who they were right now.

Q. Are you certain that there were any men present? A. Certain there were men present, sure.

Q. How do you know that?

A. They were standing right by Mrs. Pullen.
[27]

Q. And they were longshoremen?

A. Yes, they were longshoremen.

Q. Don't you know what longshoremen they were in Skagway?

A. Yes, but I cannot remember now who it was; I could not swear who it was.

Q. I will ask you if these are the checks that were given you on the 13th of June?

A. Yes, but I didn't see "Paid in full."

Q. And on the other one did you, "Paid for farm work at Dyea"? A. No, I did not.

Q. You don't think either of those were on there?

A. No, I just saw, "Pay to Tom Brown, $150.00"; and, "Pay to Tom Brown, $50.00."

Mr. MARSHALL.—I ask that those be marked for identification.

(Whereupon said checks were marked Defendant's Exhibits 2 and 3, respectively, for identification.)

Q. Mr. Brown, who was present when you made your original contract with Mrs. Pullen?

A. There was nobody, only Mrs. Pullen and I.

Q. Where was that made?

A. Right opposite the Pantheon saloon, on the main street.

'(Testimony of Tom Brown.)

Q. The Pantheon saloon?

A. Yes, right on the main street.

Q. That was the original contract you made with her when you went over there? A. Yes, sir.

Q. When you made the second contract was there anyone present?

A. No, it was in Mrs. Pullen's room—private room.

Q. When you originally went to Dyea was there anyone on the place besides yourself?

A. No, sir; Clark was in Skagway, and they took me over and I rounded up the cattle and put them in the barn the best I [28] could, and Clark went back to Skagway.

Q. Then you were alone?

A. I think he worked for his board for Mrs. Pullen for about two months; he worked in January, and I think he went away in the fore part of February.

Q. Was there anyone there during that time?

A. No, sir.

Mr. COBB.—I object to that as not cross-examination.

The COURT.—I cannot tell.

The WITNESS.—Mrs. Pullen came over with Royal—a few days after he brought her over—I think they brought some groceries, or something like that, and Mrs. Pullen stayed three weeks in December, and that was the longest time that Mrs. Pullen was on that ranch while I was there.

(Testimony of Tom Brown.)

Q. I didn't ask you that. I asked you whether anyone else was there.

A. Mrs. Pullen, Royal and Clark; Royal and I worked together.

(Whereupon court adjourned until 1:30 P. M.)

AFTERNOON SESSION.

March 27, 1918, 1:30 P. M.

TOM BROWN, on the witness-stand.

Cross-examination (Cont'd).

(By Mr. MARSHALL.)

Q. I wish to ask you further, Mr. Brown, what were the articles of clothing that were brought over to you that you have allowed $28.00 for?

Mr. COBB.—That is not proper cross-examination.

The COURT.—Now, Mr. Marshall, do you offer this as throwing any light on the question of whether or not there was a contract between them? [29]

Mr. MARSHALL.—No, I simply offer it on the credibility of this witness. He states the clothing was so much, of such and such value, and I want him to testify what the value of it was.

The COURT.—This witness, under the pleadings in this case, could have gotten on the stand and simply testified that there was a contract by which he was to get $60.00 a month, and then stop—that is all he would have had to testify to.

Mr. MARSHALL.—I will withdraw the question.

The COURT.—You can go into those things when you come to your side of the case.

(Testimony of Tom Brown.)

Mr. MARSHALL.—That is all the cross-examination.

Mr. COBB.—That is all.

(Witness excused).

PLAINTIFF RESTS. [30]

DEFENSE.

Testimony of Mrs. Harriet S. Pullen, in Her Own Behalf.

Mrs. HARRIET S. PULLEN, the defendant herein, upon being called as a witness on her own behalf, being first duly sworn, testified as follows:

Direct Examination.

(By Mr. MARSHALL.)

Q. Mrs. Pullen, you are the defendant in this case? A. Yes.

Q. Where do you live? A. Skayway and Dyea.

Q. Mrs. Pullen, I wish you would state briefly what agreement you made with Tom Brown in regard to employment.

A. I told him I would give him $1.00 a day until he could find something else to do.

Q. Did you ever have any different agreement with him than that? A. No.

Q. Now, during the time that this agreement was in existence, leaving out of consideration the $250.00 which he admits you paid him and the $28.00 which he admits you furnished him in clothing, and the $6.00 and the $5.00, the two items that he testified to this morning that you gave to him—in addition

(Testimony of Mrs. Harriet S. Pullen.)
to those did you ever pay him any other sum of
money?   A. Yes, often.

Q. Have you any means at this time of telling
what those sums of money were?   A. No.

Q. What is the reason that you have not?

A. The house burned down and everything was
burned.

Q. Did you have any record?   A. Yes.

Q. What became of that record, Mrs. Pullen?
[31]

A. They were burned in the house — everything
was burned.

Q. Those were the records of the payments you
made to him?   A. Yes.

Q. Now, Mrs. Pullen, I hand you three checks,
and will ask you to look those over and tell me when
and where they were given to Tom Brown.

A. This first one for $50.00, Tom came over and
wanted to get some clothes, and I said all right, and
I took my check-book and went down to Mr. Kennedy's, the clothier, and right in Mr. Kennedy's
office—Mr. Kennedy stood right behind me and saw
me write the check,—we agreed upon it that he had
$50.00 coming to the 1st of May, and we would settle
up to the 1st of May. I wrote on there, "For services up to the 1st of May," and I handed it to Tom
Brown. Mr. Kennedy saw me write that on there,
and would so testify if I could have him here. I
handed it to Tom Brown, and Tom turned around
and handed it to Mr. Kennedy, and as you will see

(Testimony of Mrs. Harriet S. Pullen.)

Mr. Kennedy indorsed it, "Will Clayson, by James Kennedy," on the back.

Q. Now, the question was when those checks were given to him. I think you have stated fully in regard to the first $50.00 check. Tell me about the others.

A. Why, I paid them in my room, and I made it in two checks.

Q. What date was it?   A. On June 13th.

Q. And those are the checks that were given, are they?

A. Yes, these are the checks that were given. I asked Tom how much he had coming to him, and I said, "You know the books were burned, Tom, and you know that is the only account I had"; and everything was burned up when his house burned down with my things in it. I did not think he had $200.00 coming to him, but he thought he had, and I said, "Very well, we won't have any dispute over it." So I made the checks [32] in two, because, I said, "You know your failing. now"; if he would get it in one he might lose it, but he would not lose it if I made it in two, and it was made in two checks; he thanked me. I said, "Now, Tom, we are all squared, aren't we?" And he said, "Yes." And we shook hands, and he left, and he never, from that day to this, has asked me for a cent.

Mr. MARSHALL.—I offer these in evidence, if the Court please.

Mr. COBB.—No objections.

(Whereupon said checks were received in evidence

(Testimony of Mrs. Harriet S. Pullen.)

and marked, respectively, Defendant's Exhibit 1, 2 and 3.)

Q. Now, Mrs. Pullen, I will ask you whether or not the words on those checks which I have read to the jury were on the checks at the time you gave them to Tom Brown?

A. Oh, certainly they were.

Q. Now, tell how you arrived at a settlement of your account with Tom Brown.

A. Well, as I told you everything was burned up. Of course, I knew about how we stood, but I asked Tom, and that was his figures, $200.00, and I paid him exactly what he said rather than have any controversy; I thought I was over paying him a little, but I thought it was better than to have any feelings, and I paid him exactly what he asked me to pay.

Q. Did he claim any additional amount due him at that time?

A. Oh, never. He shook hands and thanked me and said goodbye.

Q. Did you ever have any such conversation with him, Mrs. Pullen?

A. I was walking on the wharf, going to Haines one day, and just as I was going down the steps Tom had been drinking and he ran into me and nearly knocked me over. I went right on, and he said, "You have been slandering me and I am going to make it hot for you." Those are the only words Tom ever said to me. He did not say I was owing him anything—he said, [33] "You have been slandering me and I am going to make it hot for you"; and the

(Testimony of Mrs. Harriet S. Pullen.)

next thing I knew this man (indicating Mr. Logan) came into my house; he had been drinking, too, and he handed me these papers for $850.00.

Mr. COBB.—I object to her answering that question in that manner.

The COURT.—The objection is overruled.

Q. That was the only words that Tom Brown,—

A. Had ever spoken to me—that is the only conversation we ever had, and I did not say anything.

Q. Now, Mrs. Pullen, what is your custom in the matter of writing on checks anything further than the mere order to pay so and so?

Mr. COBB.—I object to that as irrelevant and immaterial—that is a self-serving declaration.

The COURT.—I do not think her custom makes any difference. If she swears it was on there when she gave the check, until that is disputed in some way the custom does not make any difference.

Mr. MARSHALL.—Now, if the Court please, under the pleadings, and as your Honor has defined the issues, there is only one matter I want to go into, which I understand your Honor will not permit, and that is the question of the capability of Tom Brown as a farm-hand, and the actual value of his services. The reason I offer it is simply tending to show the reasonableness of the contract that was entered into by the defendant with him. I wish to make that offer.

The COURT.—Anything that Mrs. Pullen knew as to Tom Brown's capacity or capability at the time she made the contract is admissible as showing the

(Testimony of Mrs. Harriet S. Pullen.)

probability or improbability of her making any such contract as he alleges, but anything **[34]** going to show how Tom Brown performed his services or his duties is not admissible, because that is all covered by the payment that has been made. There is not any contest in the pleadings that Tom Brown did not do what he agreed to do. The only thing is that Mrs. Pullen says, "I never agreed to pay him more than $30.00 a month." She may show, if she can, that she knew what kind of a man he was, and knew what he was to do, and that she would not pay $60.00 a month to a man to do the services which he was to do, and which she thought were only worth $30.00 a month. She can show that, but she cannot show how he did perform his services, because that would be opening up a question that is not in the case. She can show what kind of a man Tom Brown was, as throwing light on the probability or improbability of her contract being $30.00 a month or $60.00 a month. You may go into it as far as I have indicated, but you cannot go into it to show how he performed his services, because he performed them evidently, and there is no controversy on how he performed the services.

Q. Mrs. Pullen, I will ask you then if at the time you employed Tom Brown you knew anything about his capabilities as a workman generally?

A. Oh, yes, he worked for me as a chore boy around, you know.

Q. How long had he been doing that?

A. Well, he worked with me long enough to get

(Testimony of Mrs. Harriet S. Pullen.)

some money to go to Juneau and try and get work down here. I don't know just how long. He said he thought if he could only get down here he could get work, and he came down to Juneau and he could not get work, and he came back and said, "Mrs. Pullen, I could not get anything down there. It was winter time, and I could not get anything down there."

Q. What time was it that he worked for you before going to Dyea? [35]

A. In October and November, working in the house, and doing odd jobs around generally.

Q. Did you know at the time you employed him anything about his capacity as a workman?

A. Yes, but you know it was like this, I needed somebody there all the time, don't you see, and even though he could not perform the work, I hired other men to go over and do it—I hired a man to go and plant the potatoes and I hired a man to do the haying, and I hired a man to do everything like that, to go over by the day—but he was there to kind of look after things, and I expected my son home to look after the place and things went along, and then Tom wanted to get his citizenship papers, and I kept hiring other men to do the work, and I got along with Tom's services, and I agreed to pay him $1.00 a day. I never felt that he was worth that much, as far as the work was concerned, but it was worth that much to have somebody there all the time.

Mr. MARSHALL.—You may cross-examine.

(Testimony of Mrs. Harriet S. Pullen.)

Cross-examination.

(By Mr. COBB.)

Q. You say he worked for you two months before he went over in December, 1915?

A. No, I said he had worked at odd times during the months of October and November, now and then. You know he was drinking very hard at that time.

Q. You just answer my questions.

A. Oh, yes.

Q. What sort of a place did you have over there at Dyea?

A. Oh, I had just bought this little farm.

Q. What buildings did you have on it?

A. I didn't have much of anything at that time— I fixed it up, [36] you see—I worked on it afterwards?

Q. What sort of buildings did you have over there at the time it was burned?

A. Oh, I had a nine-room cottage, which had just cost me $900.00, when Tom burned it down—I had finished it up and was getting it ready for my family.

Q. You do not accuse Mr. Brown of burning it down, do you?

A. There was nobody else there—of course he burned it down—naturally, of course; I do not say that he did it purposely—nobody would do that.

Q. Did you have it furnished?

A. I had it furnished, certainly—a sewing-machine, a lot of dishes, a new range, Majestic range, and my pans and all my milk outfit, just new—just bought it.

(Testimony of Mrs. Harriet S. Pullen.)

Q. Did you have any desks, dressers, and bureaus in it?   A. I had one bureau in it.

Q. Were you living over there at that time, at the time it burned down?

A. I had my own quarters down below; I didn't have the same house that Tom had; I had my own house.

Q. You had your own house?   A. Yes.

Q. That was not burned?   A. No.

Q. Nobody stayed in this place but Tom?

A. Nobody but Tom.

Q. How came you to leave your records in it?

A. I did the cooking there, and I had a special pantry in which I kept stores, and I had this little book under the top shelf, where it was handy for me to write down anything I bought Tom.

Q. How did it happen that you did not have it in your own house?

A. I told you I cooked up there all the time—that was the living [37] house; I was building that house for my family.

Q. You always paid these sums of money you have spoken about when you were up there cooking?

A. I handed it to him at different times; sometimes it was down at the boat, when I would meet him down there, and he would say, "Bring me over $5.00," or "Bring me over $10.00." I know one time I took him $20.00 in change; I had it tied up in my hand-kerchief—it was quite a bit of change.

Q. It was always over at Dyea that you paid him?

A. Why, yes; where else could it be?

(Testimony of Mrs. Harriet S. Pullen.)

Q. And the records were kept in Tom Brown's house and not in yours? A. Yes.

Q. In a little book that was burned up?

A. Yes.

Q. Now, Mrs. Pullen, did I understand you to tell Mr. Marshall that you kept a memorandum of all the money that you paid Tom Brown except the checks that you gave him?

A. Why, of course I kept a little memorandum.

Q. And in that memorandum you put down all the money you ever paid him except what you paid him by check?

A. I will tell you—when I would see Tom I would say, "Tom, you got so and so—you have got so and so—" and I would mark it down so we would know how we stood.

Q. That is not an answer to the question. I understood you to say to Mr. Marshall that you kept a memorandum of all the money you ever paid him except these checks, which of course were memorandums themselves, is that right?

A. It was my custom when I gave him money to make a little note of it, like anybody would.

Q. And you did that always when you gave him money?

A. I don't say I did it always but I did it sufficient to know [38] where we stood all the time.

Q. And that book was burned in the fire there?

A. Yes, it was in the pantry on the top shelf.

Q. Then, outside of these checks you have not paid him any money since that fire, have you?

(Testimony of Mrs. Harriet S. Pullen.)

A. That was only a very short time ago, you know.

Q. You can answer that question. You have not paid him any money except the checks since the fire?

A. No, not that I remember—never any money— I bought clothes all the time, and I bought him one pair of shoes that cost $9.00 and over.

Q. You put down whatever you got for him, didn't you?

A. I have it on my bills. When I would get these statements from the store I would say, "They are for Tom—just write on there they are for Tom."

Q. Where are your bills?

A. I did not bring anything along with me—I did not know this case was coming up.

Q. You have not, however, paid him any money except what you put down in that little book that burned on February 4th?   A. Yes, $200.00.

Q. I mean outside of the checks, that is all?

A. I don't remember anything on that.

Q. I hand you now Defendant's Exhibit 1, being a check dated June 6, 1916, payable to Tom Brown, $50.00, and signed by you. You say at the time you wrote out that check, the words here, "For services up to May 1st, 1916"— you wrote that at the same time?   A. At the same time.

Q. Did you use two inkstands?

A. No, I did not; I never had it in my hands— Tom got it.

Q. Is that your handwriting?   [39]

A. That is in my handwriting, sir, and the man watched me write it and will so testify.

(Testimony of Mrs. Harriet S. Pullen.)

Q. You haven't got him here to testify, have you?

A. No, but he said he would come down and testify.

Q. You had an opportunity to take his deposition, didn't you?

A. These were down here, that is why.

Q. Didn't you know that I signed a stipulation with your counsel here to take any deposition you wanted there?   A. Yes, but I was not there.

Mr. MARSHALL.—I can state that I also know that deposition was sent off to Skagway, and will be back here and be additional testimony in this case, but I did not intend to delay the case, and there has not been a boat from there for a long time.

Mr. COBB.—You did not take the deposition of Mr. Kennedy, however.

Mr. MARSHALL.—No, I did not, because I never learned of it until Mrs. Pullen came down here, and then it was too late.

Q. Now, Tom quit you on June 5th, didn't he?

A. I do not know the day.

Q. Why did you admit it in your pleadings, that he did?   A. I did not.

Q. I hand you now your answer in this case and ask you if that is your signature?

A. Yes, that is my signature.

Q. You read over the answer before you signed and swore to it, didn't you?

A. Oh, it has been so long ago—of course, I suppose I did.

Q. Now, in this you say here, "Answering para-

(Testimony of Mrs. Harriet S. Pullen.)
graph 9, defendant admits that plaintiff quit her
employ on or about the time alleged,'' that was June
5th—is that correct?

A. I don't remember that he ever quit at any time.
He was **[40]** going to go and get some work with
a cattle-man, and the answer came back that they
did not need him, and he did not have any place to
go. I saw the letter where they said,—

Q. Answer my question—I am asking you about
this—you signed and swore to that, didn't you?

A. Of course I did.

Q. And he had quit work on June 5th?

A. He had not lost any time about it, you know.

Q. Did he quit work on that day, as you admit
that he did? A. He came over to Skagway.

Q. Did he quit work—that is a very simple question.

A. I don't know how you mean; he didn't lose any
time—he worked right along.

Q. He quit his job on or about that date, didn't
he? A. Yes.

Q. Then, if you were paying him on the sixth, and
were settling with him in full, why did you put down
here, "In full to May 1st"?

A. Because he was getting his clothes ready to go
back to work—he was getting his clothes over at
the store.

Q. You did not settle with him in full that day?

A. Why, no, I settled up to the 1st of May.

Q. Now, you stated in your examination in chief
that you gave him two checks so that if he lost one

(Testimony of Mrs. Harriet S. Pullen.)
of them he would have the other?

A. Well, you know Tom's failing is drinking, and if he would cash all the $200 he might lose it all at one time, you see; and I made it out in two checks so he could cash the $50 one and have the rest left, and he would not lose it all. That is what he did, he lost every bit of his money—

Q. What was there to prevent him from cashing the $150 one, too? **[41]**

A. There was nothing to prevent it, but I fixed it so he would not be so liable to lose it all—that was all. I wrote them both at the same time—right at the same time, and I said, "Tom, you know your failing, so I will make it in two checks, so when you cash one you won't have so much money." And I went to the bank afterwards and found out that he had cashed them both about the same time.

Q. When did you find out that?

A. The time that he ran into me on the wharf; and my porter was down there and saw that action and he said to me, "Mrs. Pullen, I would have that man arrested"—

Q. Never mind about that. I am asking you simply why you took the pains to find out when he cashed them.

A. That is when I did. He said that man was telling around that I owed him so I went over to the bank and asked them if they would not look at those checks so they could be a witness to them. I said, "That man is telling that I am owing him," and I said, "I want you and your assistant here to tes-

(Testimony of Mrs. Harriet S. Pullen.)

tify"; so Mr. Landsborough and his assistant said yes, and he got those checks, and he said they were cashed about the same time, and he said they would be my witnesses to the checks—

Mr. COBB.—I move that that be stricken as not responsive and hearsay.

The WITNESS.—No, no hearsay about it.

Mr. COBB.—I ask that the jury be instructed not to pay any attention to what Mr. Landsborough said.

The WITNESS.—That is the banker who witnessed them.

The COURT.—Ask another question and let us get along.

Q. You did know then as early as about July 2d, 1916, that Tom Brown was claiming that you owed him wages?   A. The last of June?

Q. The last of June.   A. Yes.

Q. I said as early as July 3d? [42]

A. Because my porter came in and told me this, and he said, "Those two men are drunk."

Q. I am not asking you what your porter said. I am asking if you knew at that time that Tom Brown was claiming that you owed him wages?

A. Yes.

Q. You say you never learned it from him?

A. No, never.

Q. You took pains then, you say, to prepare your defense?   A. Yes, of course.

Q. You were sued in August?

A. I believe something like that.

(Testimony of Mrs. Harriet S. Pullen.)

Q. This suit was filed August 25th, the record shows.   A. Yes.

Q. You have had ever since then to prepare your defense and get your witnesses to testify for you, haven't you?

A. I never dreamed it was going to come to trial. When anybody don't owe anybody anything I don't see how you can prepare to go to trial when you don't owe him anything.

Q. If you will answer my questions we will get along faster.   You have had ever since then to prepare your defense?

A. I have had many things to do besides that.

Q. You have had ever since then, haven't you, to prepare your defense and get your testimony?

A. I never thought it would come up for trial.

Q. That is not an answer to my question.   You have had ever since then to prepare for your defense.

Mr. COBB.—That is self-evident and I will drop it.   That is all.   **[43]**

Redirect Examination.
(By Mr. MARSHALL.)

Q. Did Tom Brown ever have any conversation with you about quitting work along about the time you gave him that check?   A. The $200 check?

Q. No, the earlier check, or that summer, did he have any conversation with you about quitting work?

A. Well, you see the agreement was that he was to work for a dollar a day until he could get something to do there; you see, it was not by the month—

(Testimony of Mrs. Harriet S. Pullen.)

it was by the day, and he thought he could get on with Burns.

Q. Did he have any conversation with you about quitting, or give any reason for quitting?

A. I don't remember that he did.

Q. Did you ever have a cook over there?

A. Well, that was in July and August, I had a woman over there cooking for the whole crew.

Q. Did any question come up about quitting?

A. Before I sent the woman over, yes; he said if I did not send that woman over he would quit, but that was in July, and I sent her over.

Mr. MARSHALL.—That's all.

Mr. COBB.—That's all.

(Witness excused.)   [44]

Testimony of J. R. Neville, for Defendant.

J. R. NEVILLE, called as a witness on behalf of the defendant, being first duly sworn, testified as follows:

Direct Examination.

(By Mr. MARSHALL.)

Q. Mr. Neville, were you ever over at Dyea?

A. Yes, sir.

Q. When was that about?

A. It was in July or August—I think it was the last of July—something like that; I do not remember the date.

Q. Did you at that time have any conversation with the plaintiff in this case, Tom Brown?

A. Why, yes, some.

(Testimony of J. R. Neville.)

Q. Did he express to you any dissatisfaction with his employment over there?

Mr. COBB.—I object to that as irrelevant and immaterial, whether he was dissatisfied with it or not.

The COURT.—What is the object?

Mr. MARSHALL.—The object is to show that he showed dissatisfaction with the employment, and show the reason for it; I think the reason is relevant as throwing some light on the question of his claim for wages.

The COURT.—What do you expect to develop by this witness?

Mr. MARSHALL.—That he was dissatisfied with his work over there because he said the pay was so small, and while it is not an admission that the real contract was a dollar a day, yet it is evidence that the man was working over there for what would be, perhaps, generally regarded as small wages.

The COURT.—Did he say anything about what wages he was getting?

Mr. MARSHALL.—No, simply that he was dissatisfied with the amount of wages that he was getting—that is all there is to it.   I consider it would be evidence that would be of some value   [45]   upon that subject.

The COURT.—I do not think it would—I do not think that would throw any light on the contract one way or the other.

Mr. MARSHALL.—I think that is true, if the Court please, but I do think, as I said, it would have some bearing upon the question of wages—not what

(Testimony of J. R. Neville.)

his wages were, but whether his wages were considerable wages or whether they were small wages.

The COURT.—I do not think it elucidates the proposition one way of the other—I do not think it has any bearing in this case. The objection is sustained.

Mr. MARSHALL.—That's all.

(Witness excused.)

DEFENDANT RESTS. [46]

REBUTTAL.

Testimony of Tom Brown, in His Own Behalf (In Rebuttal).

TOM BROWN, the plaintiff herein, upon being recalled as a witness in his own behalf, having been previously sworn, testified in rebuttal as follows:

Direct Examination.

(By Mr. COBB.)

Q. Mr. Brown, you have been sworn. I hand you Defendant's Exhibit 1, being a check dated June 6, 1916, payable to you, signed H. S. Pullen, and I call your attention to the words written on here, "For services up to May 1, 1916," and ask you if those words were on there at the time you received the check and cashed it?

A. No, sir, I did not see them.

Q. I now hand you a check dated June 13, 1917, being Defendant's Exhibit No. 3, being a check for $150.00, payable to you and signed by H. S. Pullen, and I call your attention to the words written on it,

(Testimony of Tom Brown.)

"For farm work at Dyea," and ask you if those words were on there at the time you received the check? A. No, sir, I didn't see them.

Q. I hand you a check dated June 13, 1917, payable to you, for $50.00, being Defendant's Exhibit No. 2, a check signed by H. S. Pullen, and I call your attention to the words written on it, "In full to date for farm work at Dyea,"—I will ask you if those were on there at the time you received the check and had it cashed? A. No, sir, I did not see them.

Q. Mr. Brown, you heard Mrs. Pullen's testimony that the latter part of June, 1917, after you quit work up there and a short time before you brought this suit you bumped into her down at the dock and that you were drunk, and that you told her she [47] was slandering you—did any such talk as that ever occur?

A. No, sir.

Q. Any such incident occur? A. No, sir.

Q. I will ask you if at that time any intoxicants could be secured in Skagway?

A. The town was dry, sir.

Q. You heard her testimony that she knew you were not worth over a dollar a day? A. Yes, sir.

Q. I will ask you if you were employed a short time before you began work for her, in 1915, at a regular job? A. Yes, sir.

Q. You were? A. Yes, sir.

Q. What did you get?

A. Well, I was shipping cattle through here for P. Burns of Vancouver, and I got $4.00 a day and board, sir.

(Testimony of Tom Brown.)

Q. Four dollars a day and expenses?

A. Yes, sir, from Vancouver to White Horse and Dawson, and from Atlin to White Horse once in awhile.

Q. When was that?   A. In 1915.

Q. What time of the year?

A. Well, from June until September—the latter part of September.

Q. Then what did you do?

A. Well, after I came down to Skagway—I was waiting for my partner to come in from,—I came from White Horse, and had my partner back in Dawson, and I came to Skagway and longshored.

Q. What were your average earnings as a longshoreman?

A. We were getting 58 cents an hour.   [48]

Q. Do you know what was the average that you earned?

A. The boats did not come in regular, you see, but when they came in we worked day and night.

Q. What were your average earnings for a week or a month?   A. About $50.00 a month.

Q. You belonged to the longshoremen's union, did you?   A. Yes, sir.

Q. I will ask you if you are an able-bodied man and able to do an average day's work?

A. Well, sir, I am down here in the Ready Bullion on the 2300, and I worked from October until last Saturday—that is the first day I have missed except every other Sunday we change shifts, you see, and there is only four hours to work—well, it is too

(Testimony of Tom Brown.)

far to go down, and the majority of the men do not work, only the pumpmen and men that are bound to go, you see.

Q. That is the only time you have missed during the period, when they changed, is it?

A. Yes, sir, except Christmas—they laid off a day or two for Christmas holidays.

Q. The mine was closed then?   A. Yes, sir.

Q. What are your wages?   A. $3.00 a day, sir.

Q. How long have you been in Alaska?

A. I have been passing through here—sometimes I would miss a couple of seasons—since 1900.

Q. Have you ever at any time worked in Alaska for less than $2.00 a day and board?

A. No, sir, I never have.

Q. Now, I want you to describe to the jury the work that you did—that you were to do over there under your arrangement— [49] the work that you were to do—what was the work that you were hired to do? Give the jury the best idea of it you can.

A. Milk and attend to the cows, plow the land and put in the crop, haul hay; in the winter time haul wood and keep a fire in the potato-house, and a majority of the time I had to cook for myself.

Mr. MARSHALL.—We object to this, if the Court please.

The COURT.—You admit in your pleadings the work that he was to do. The only thing this is admitted for is to show whether or not it is probable or reasonable to suppose that the contract was $2.00

(Testimony of Tom Brown.)

a day or $1.00 a day. There is no contest over the fact that he did not do the work he was employed to do, but the contest is about the contract—what the contract was in regard to the work he was employed to do.

Mr. MARSHALL.—It is expressly denied that he did milk any cows or make any butter—that is milk any cows for Mrs. Pullen. They allege that he did, and we deny that he did.

The COURT.—Then the question is whether he was employed to do it or not. It is not a question of how well he did the work, but it is a question of what work he was to do and what the contract was as to that work. It is a plain, simple question, it seems to me, of whether there was a contract or whether there was not a contract—that is all there is in the case.

Q. (By Mr. COBB.) What were you hired to do?

A. Well, sir, attend to the cattle, haul wood, haul hay, attend to potatoes; and when I first went there we put a foundation under this Pacific Hotel, Royal and I, Mrs. Pullen's son.

Q. How many cattle were there there?

A. Ten altogether—7 cattle and 3 horses—one died and one was only there a little time.

Q. That is when you first began?

A. Yes, sir; that is when I first began. [50]

Q. At the time you went over there you knew more were coming? A. Yes, sir.

Q. How many were there later?

Mr. MARSHALL.—If the Court please, we ob-

(Testimony of Tom Brown.)

ject to that—under the Court's ruling it is not admissible.

The COURT.—How many more did you know were coming—is that the question?

The WITNESS.—Well, this winter I had 20, and before I left there were a lot of calves, and there were 30, when I came away, on the 11th of June.

Q. How many potatoes, do you know, were put in up there?

The COURT.—You need not answer that question.

Q. How much ground were you to take care of in potatoes?　A. About 5 acres.

Mr. MARSHALL.—If there was any specific agreement I do not believe it is proper for him to testify how much ground he was to take care of, in potatoes.

The COURT.—Here is a plaintiff who says his contract was $2.00 a day, and here is a defendant who says the contract was $1.00 a day. You may show what the facts and circumstances were at the time, and what was in contemplation of the parties at the time the contract is alleged to have been entered into, for the purpose of showing which is the more probable. That is the only bearing such testimony has on the case,—which is the more probable contract to be entered into—it does not make any difference what was done under the contract, because, whatever the man was to do, there is no complaint made in the pleadings that he did not do it—only that he has been paid for it, paid what the defendant says she agreed to pay him.

(Testimony of Tom Brown.)

Q. You say there were about 5 acres of potatoes to be taken care of? [51]   A. Yes.

The COURT.—Did you know that at the time you made this contract you are talking about?

A. Well, it was in December; the potatoes were planted the next spring.

The COURT.—Did you know at the time you made this contract with Mrs. Pullen how many acres of potatoes you were to take care of?

A. She told me she wanted five acres of potatoes planted.

Q. (By the COURT.)   Did she say so?

A. Yes, sir.

Q. (By Mr. COBB.)   Now, then, in November, 1915, just before you went over there, did you have a conversation with Mrs. Pullen in which you told her that you were coming to Juneau to see if you could get work?   A. No, sir, I did not.

Q. Did you come down to Juneau?

A. I came down to Juneau to see my cousin that used to be a timekeeper at Treadwell.

Q. You did not come for the purpose of getting work?   A. No, sir; I did not ask for work.

Q. You went back to Skagway, then, in December and made this contract to go over there, for $2.00 a day?   A. Yes, sir.

Q. I believe you stated this morning that in June, 1916, some time about a month before you quit there, you gave her notice?   A. On the 4th of May, sir.

Q. What was said when you came over to quit, between you and her?

(Testimony of Tom Brown.)

A. Well, I walked into the kitchen and Mrs. Pullen happened to be in the front room, and I waited until she came in the kitchen.

The COURT.—I think that has all be gone into, Mr. Cobb.   [52]

Mr. COBB.—All right.

Q. She did ask you, then, to go back, as I understand it, for $65.00, for the balance of the time.

A. Yes, sir.

Q. And you agreed upon that?   A. Yes, sir.

Q. Now, state to the jury whether or not Mrs. Pullen ever paid you anything on your wages for the period from December, 1915, up to the end of your first contract in June, 1916, other than the $50.00 that you testified to this morning.

A. Well, there is $6.00 in January, you know, and $5.00 in—

Q. $3.00 was for you and $3.00 to be charged back to her?   A. Yes, sir.

Q. And that was all?   A. Yes, sir.

Q. State whether or not outside of this little matter of clothes you mentioned and have already testified to, she ever paid you anything on wages for the period from June 6th or 7th, 1916, up until you quit on June 11th, 1917, except the $200.00.

A. No, sir.

Q. Which is represented by these checks?

A. No, sir, never received a cent—no, sir.

Q. You heard Mrs. Pullen's testimony about having a book that she kept up in that house?

A. Yes, sir.

(Testimony of Tom Brown.)

Q. Was there any such book as that ever kept there?

A. I never saw such a book, sir; she never produced it to me; I never saw such a book. The drawer was open where she says it was, and I used to be in there more or less every day and I never saw the book.

Mr. COBB.—You may cross-examine. [53]

Cross-examination.

(By Mr. MARSHALL.)

Q. You talked about the earnings of a longshoreman up there in Skagway? A. Yes, sir.

Q. Do you know what they earn in the winter, on an average?

A. Well, in the fall they make pretty big money.

Q. In the winter?

A. Yes, in the fall up to Christmas.

Q. You consider $50.00 a month would be about the average? A. No, sir, I do not.

Q. Isn't that what you testified to?

A. $50.00 a month?

Q. Yes.

A. No, sir; not $50.00 a month. If I said $50.00 a month I made a mistake.

Q. What did you mean to say?

A. You can make lots more than $50.00 a month. I should say $50.00 a week, more or less. The first time, I think, I went longshoring in Skagway that fall, before I went to Mrs. Pullen's, I worked that day and I worked that night, and I made $9.00.

(Testimony of Tom Brown.)

Q. I wanted to ask you with respect to that work during the winter—what is the extent of it then—how much are the average earnings in the winter?

A. I never worked later than November.

Q. Don't you know as a matter of fact that in the winter there is little or nothing to be earned up there at that work?

A. There was quite a lot of ore—loading the ores, and before I went with Mrs. Pullen the boats were coming in more or less every week loading ore, and there was quite a lot of work.

Q. Loading ore from the mine in the interior? [54]   A. Yes, sir, more or less.

Q. And what is the extent of the work on boats coming in there—on freight coming in there?

A. Well, they always rush it in in the fall to send it over to Atlin and White Horse and over to Dawson before the ice breaks up.

Q. During the winter do they send in any?

A. I told you I never done any longshore work after November.

Q. I am asking you whether you know anything about the situation there.   Don't you know as a matter of fact that, the "Spokane," "Seattle" and "Jefferson," when they go up there, stay just about an hour?

A. They might right now, but they didn't when I was up there.

Q. Don't they do that all the time during the winter?

A. I couldn't say nothing after November.

(Testimony of Tom Brown.)

Q. You have never worked in Skagway in the winter time? A. Not after November; no.

Q. At any employment?

A. I worked there this last fall until November, and then after November I went around and saw a few friends, and I came down here to Treadwell and asked for a job and got one.

Q. Didn't you say you began on October 2d at Treadwell?

A. Yes, sir; but I was in Juneau a couple of weeks looking around and seeing my friends.

Q. You said you worked up there until November, didn't you? A. November, yes.

Q. And then you got here in October?

A. I think I left Skagway about the 17th of— about the 7th of October—something like that.

Q. Didn't you say just a moment ago that you worked there until November? A. Yes. [55]

Q. You said you worked there until November?
A. Yes.

Q. And then a few minutes ago you said that you began at Treadwell on the 23d of October?

A. I made a mistake—I see where I made a mistake.

Q. That is just a mistake? A. Yes, sir.

Q. Now, you testified also that you had an express understanding with Mrs. Pullen that there were to be five acres of potatoes planted? A. Yes, sir.

Q. Where did you have that understanding with her?

(Testimony of Tom Brown.)

A. Well, right opposite Jack Anderson's—Mr. Anderson's.

Q. That was all told to you at the time she engaged you there in December?

A. She told me in the spring she would want me to put in five acres of potatoes, and also a lot of grain, and I put in about 20 acres of grain.

Q. Did she tell you anything else about what she wanted planted?

A. Well, yes; she said she would want a little small crop put in.

Q. Crop of what?

A. Well, turnips, and such like, and potatoes.

Q. As a matter of fact, Mr. Brown, when you went over there, weren't you simply going over as a sort of a caretaker of property at the time?

A. No, sir, I was not.

Q. Did you go over immediately after you made the arrangement?   A. With Mrs. Pullen?

Q. Yes.   A. Yes, sir.   [56]

Q. Did she take you over there personally?

A. No, Mr. Pratt took me over; Mrs. Pullen walked down to the wharf with me to the boat; it was snowing and she came back to Skagway.

Q. How long did Mr. Pratt remain over there?

A. I am sure he came right back that day.

Q. But during the winter?

A. Oh, he was working on the boat in December and January; I think he went away the latter part of January.

(Testimony of Thomas Moseek.)

Mr. MARSHALL.—That's all.

Mr. COBB.—That's all.

(Witness excused.)   [57]

Testimony of Thomas Moseek, for Plaintiff (In Rebuttal).

THOS. MOSEEK, called as a witness on behalf of the plaintiff, being first duly sworn, testified in rebuttal as follows:

Direct Examination.

(By Mr. COBB.)

Q. State your name.   A. Thomas Moseek.

Q. Where do you reside?

A. I have lived in the Yukon Territory for the last 12 years.

Q. Where do you reside now?

A. In Thane, Alaska; my family is in Juneau.

Q. Do you know the plaintiff, Mr. Brown?

A. I do, sir.

Q. Did you know him when he was working for Mrs. Pullen on the Dyea ranch?

A. Yes, sir, I met him in Dyea.

Q. What time were you up in Dyea?

A. I think it was the 7th or 8th of February, 1917.

Q. During the time that you were there did you see the extent of the job that he had on hand taking care of that property?   A. I did, sir.

Mr. MARSHALL.—If the Court please, that is exactly opposed to the Court's ruling, the extent of the job that he had on hand over there.

The COURT.—This question is simply did you

(Testimony of Thomas Moseek.)

see it, and he said he did.   That does not help nor hurt anybody, and it is preliminary, I presume, to the next question.

Q. Just describe to the jury the job that he had there—what he was doing?

Mr. MARSHALL.—Now, if the Court please, I object to that.

The COURT.—What is the object and purpose of that, Mr. Cobb?

Mr. COBB.—It is admitted in the pleadings that he did the work   [58] that he was to do, and the only way we can get at it is, I think, for him to describe what the man was doing, the job that he had there, to show what he had to do.

The COURT.—The objection is sustained.

Mr. COBB.—To which we except.

The COURT.—The exception will be allowed.

Mr. COBB.—That's all.

Mr. MARSHALL.—No questions.

(Witness excused.)

PLAINTIFF RESTS.   [59]

SURREBUTTAL.

Testimony of Mrs. Harriet S. Pullen, in Her Own Behalf (In Surrebuttal).

Mrs. HARRIET S. PULLEN, the defendant herein, being recalled as a witness on her own behalf, having been previously duly sworn, testified in surrebuttal as follows:

(Testimony of Mrs. Harriet S. Pullen.)

Direct Examination.

(By Mr. MARSHALL.)

Q. Mrs. Pullen, I want to ask you whether or not you had any custom with respect to writing on your checks what they were for?

Mr. COBB.—We object to that as not proper surrebuttal.

The COURT.—What is that surrebuttal of?

Mr. MARSHALL.—This morning I attempted to offer it, and your Honor said if they disputed it being on there that I could prove it was put on in accordance with a custom that she has of making notations on her checks.

The COURT.—I did not mean to say I was going to admit it no matter what arose. It would not make any difference what her custom was or was not. She goes on the witness-stand and swears it was there at the time she gave him the check—what has her custom got to do with it?

Mr. MARSHALL.—She has already testified to that, so I will have no further questions to ask her.

The COURT.—If that is all there is to it, it is not surrebuttal.

Q. (By Mr. MARSHALL.) Did you have any conversation with Tom Brown before he went over there as to the quantity of potatoes that you wanted him to plant?

A. I did not expect he was going to be over there that long, you know—he just went over to stay for a while.

Mr. MARSHALL.—That is all.

Mr. COBB.—No questions.

(Witness excused.)

TESTIMONY CLOSED. [60]

Instructions of Court to Jury.

The COURT.—(Orally.) Gentlemen of the Jury: This is a suit brought by Brown on an express contract, or what he claims is an express contract, to pay him $2.00 a day or $60.00 a month. Brown is the plaintiff in the case, and the plaintiff in every case has got to prove his case. In a criminal suit, the plaintiff, which is the Government, has got to prove its case beyond a reasonable doubt. In a civil case the plaintiff has got to establish his case by a preponderance of the evidence, by a greater weight of the evidence. In other words, Brown has got to bring before you, produce before you, stronger evidence, weightier evidence, more convincing evidence, that there was a contract at $60.00 a month, or $2.00 a day, than the defendant has got to produce that there was not any such contract.

When these parties put their case on paper the scales were just evenly balanced. You could not at that time have returned a verdict for the plaintiff, for the reason that the plaintiff has got to have better evidence and stronger evidence than the defendant has got to have. Now, let us see how the evidence has changed the situation, if it has changed it at all. The plaintiff introduces some evidence, and his side of the scales drops—he has got stronger evidence; but then the defendant comes on and introduces some evidence, and her side of the scales drops. Now, when all the evidence has been introduced if the scales are just evenly balanced, then the case is just the same as it was when they started out—neither side has a preponderance, and the plaintiff would have to lose his suit, because he has got to have stronger evidence and weightier evidence than the defendant has got to have. Now, then, what is the situation here? Plaintiff gets on the stand and swears that there was a contract for $2.00 a day, or $60.00 a month. The defendant goes on the stand and swears the contract was a dollar a day and board. Now, then, **[61]** if those two people and the circumstances in evidence are just evenly balanced in your mind and you cannot say which to believe, the scales are evenly balanced, and your verdict would have to be for the defendant; but if the testimony of Mr. Brown and the circumstances in evidence have convinced you that he is more worthy of belief —if his conduct on the witness-stand has been such as to carry conviction to your mind to a greater degree than Mrs. Pullen, then the scales are not evenly balanced—he has got the weightier side of the scales. If he has not produced more evidence, stronger and weightier evidence, then he has not got the stronger side of the scales. Now, it is for you to decide whether or not Brown has produced stronger and weightier evidence that he did have a contract at $60.00 a month or $2.00 a day than Mrs. Pullen has produced that he did not have. If he has produced more evidence, stronger evidence, that he did have that kind of a contract, then your verdict should be for him in such sum as you find to be due; but if he has not produced the stronger evidence, weightier evidence and more convincing evidence, or if the scales are just evenly balanced in your mind, then you must find a verdict for the defendant.

Mr. COBB.—You have made one error in stating the issues. The last year was $65.00, after he resumed work, and not $60.00.

The COURT.—It is virtually the same—that does not alter the principle I was trying to elucidate to the jury. I believe part of the time he does claim that his contract was $65.00 a month, and Mrs. Pullen denies that with just as much vehemence as she did the $60.00 contract. It is not a case where you can say "We will give him $45.00 a month." [62] It is either $60.00 a month or it is nothing. It is the contract that he alleges, and it is the contract that she denies that he relies on, and you cannot split the difference—you cannot do anything of that kind. It is either $60.00 a month or it is not $60.00 a month. If it is not $60.00 a month then the plaintiff cannot recover.

You are the sole judges of the credibility of the witnesses and of the weight to be attached to their testimony. Take into consideration their candor or lack of candor, their demeanor upon the witness-stand, their intelligence as to knowing the things they pretend to testify about, and their inclination or disinclination, as it has appeared in the evidence, to tell the truth, the whole truth, and nothing but the truth. You consider their interest—of course they are both interested, so far as that is concerned—

take all the facts into consideration. It is not a question of whether $1.00 a day is too little, and it is not a question of whether $2.00 a day is too much. I might agree to pay you $2.00 a day for services that are worth only 50 cents a day, or I might agree to pay you 50 cents a day for services that are worth $2.00 a day—that is not the question; when the claim is on a contract, the contract must be proven, no matter what the services were worth. The only reason the evidence was admitted as to what this man got before was for the weight it might have, or might not have, just as you look at it, on the question of whether or not such a contract was probable.

You take the pleadings, and if you find for the plaintiff assess the amount of his recovery; if you find for the defendant sign the verdict which reads for the defendant.

Mr. COBB.—We except to *the* that they find for the defendant unless they think it was a contract for $2.00 a day, because under the evidence if he was working for only a dollar a day, she would owe [63] $200.00—we except to that part of the instructions.

Which said exception was taken before the jury retired from the bar of the court.

And the above and foregoing were all the instructions given.

And because the above and foregoing matters to not appear of record, I, Robert W. Jennings, the Judge before whom said cause was tried, do hereby certify that the above and foregoing is a full, true, and correct bill of exceptions, and the same is hereby approved, allowed and ordered filed, and made a part of the 'record herein. And I further certify that said bill of exceptions was presented and allowed during the time allowed by *order* orders of the Court made during the term at which said cause was tried.

Dated this the 1st day of August, 1918.

ROBERT W. JENNINGS,

Judge.

Filed in the District Court, District of Alaska, First Division. Aug. 1, 1918. J. W. Bell, Clerk. By C. Z. Denny, Deputy. [63½]

In the District Court for Alaska, Division No. 1, at Juneau.

Nò. 1716–A.

TOM BROWN,

Plaintiff,

vs.

H. S. PULLEN,

Defendant.

Assignment of Error.

Now comes the plaintiff, and assigns the following error committed by the Court during the progress of the trial and in the rendition of the judgment herein, upon which the plaintiff will rely in the Appellate Court.

The Court erred in instructing the jury as follows:

"It is either $60.00 a month or it is nothing. It is the contract which he alleges, and the contract which she denies, that he relies on, and you cannot split the difference—you cannot do any thing of that kind. It is either $60.00 a month, or it is not $60.00 a month. If it is not $60.00 a month the plaintiff cannot recover.''

And for the said error plaintiff prays that the judgment of the Court below be reversed and the cause remanded for a new trial.

J. H. COBB,

Attorney for Tom Brown, Plaintiff.

Filed in the District Court, District of Alaska, First Division. Aug. 3, 1918. J. W. Bell, Clerk. By C. Z. Denny, Deputy. [64]

In the District Court for Alaska, Division No. 1, at Juneau.

No. 1716–A.

TOM BROWN,

Plaintiff,

vs.

H. S. PULLEN,

Defendant.

Writ of Error.

United States of America,—ss.

The President of the United States to the Judges of the District Court of the United States for Alaska, Division No. 1, GREETING:

Because in the record and proceedings as also in the rendition of a judgment of a plea which is before you, wherein Tom Brown is plaintiff and H. S. Pullen is defendant, a manifest error hath happened to the great damage of the said Tom Brown as by his petition doth appear.

We being willing that error, if any hath happened, should be duly corrected, and speedy justice done to the parties in that behalf, do command you, if judgment be therein given, that then under your seal, distinctly and openly, you send the record and proceedings aforesaid, with all things pertaining thereto, to the United States Circuit Court of Appeals for the Ninth Circuit at the City of San Francisco, State of California, so that you have the same before said Court on or before thirty days from the date of this writ, so that the record and proceeding aforesaid, being inspected, the said Circuit Court of Appeals may cause further to be done therein, to correct that error, what of right, and according to the laws and customs of the United States ought to be done.

WITNESS the Honorable EDWARD DOUGLASS WHITE, Chief Justice of the United States, and the seal of the District Court for Alaska, Division No. 1, affixed at Juneau, Alaska, this the 3d day of August, 1918.

[Seal] J. W. BELL,
Clerk.

Allowed this 3d day of August, 1918.
ROBERT W. JENNINGS,
Judge.

Filed in the District Court, District of Alaska, First Division. Aug. 3, 1918. J. W. Bell, Clerk. By C. Z. Denny, Deputy. **[65]**

In the District Court for Alaska, Division No. 1, at Juneau.

No. 1716–A.

TOM BROWN,

Plaintiff,

vs.

H. S. PULLEN,

Defendant.

Bond on Writ of Error.

KNOW ALL MEN BY THESE PRESENTS, that we, Tom Brown, as principal, and Emery Valentine, as surety, hereby acknowledge ourselves to be indebted and bound to pay to H. S. Pullen the sum of Two Hundred and Fifty Dollars, good and lawful money of the United States, for the payment of which sum well and truly to be made we hereby bind ourselves, our and each of our, heirs, executors, and administrators, jointly and severally, firmly by these presents.

The condition of this obligation is such, however, that whereas the above-bound Tom Brown has sued out a writ of error in the above-entitled cause from the United States Circuit Court of Appeals for the Ninth Circuit, to reverse the judgment rendered in said cause on the 4th day of April, 1918.

Now, if the said Tom Brown shall prosecute his writ of error to effect, and pay all such costs and damages as may be awarded against him if he fail to make his plea good, then this obligation shall be null and void; otherwise to remain in full force and effect.

Witness our hands this the 2d day of August, 1918.
                    TOM BROWN,
                              By J. H. COBB,
                         His Attorney of Record.
                    EMERY VALENTINE.
Approved as to form and sufficiency of surety, this
the 3d day of August, 1918.
                    ROBERT W. JENNINGS,
                                             Judge.

[Endorsed]: No. 1716–A. Tom Brown, Plaintiff, vs. H. S. Pullen, Defendant. Bond on Writ of Error. Filed in the District Court, District of Alaska, First Division. Aug. 3, 1918. J. W. Bell, Clerk. By C. Z. Denny, Deputy. **[66]**

In the District Court for Alaska, Division No. 1, at Juneau.

No. 1716–A.

TOM BROWN,

                                   Plaintiff,

            vs.

HARRIET S. PULLEN,

                                   Defendant.

Citation in Error.

United States of America,—ss.

The President of the United States to Harriet S.
    Pullen, and John B. Marshall, Her Attorney,
    GREETING:

You are hereby cited and admonished to be and
appear at a United States Circuit Court of Appeals

for the Ninth Circuit, to be held at the City of San Francisco, in the State of California, within thirty days from the date of this writ, pursuant to a writ of Error lodged in the clerk's office of the District Court for Alaska, Division No. 1, in a cause wherein Tom Brown is plaintiff in error, and you are defendant in error, then and there to show cause if any there be, why the judgment in said writ of error mentioned should not be corrected, and speedy justice done to the parties in that behalf.

WITNESS the Honorable EDWARD DOUGLASS WHITE, Chief Justice of the United States, this the 3d day of August, 1918.

ROBERT W. JENNINGS,

Judge.

[Seal] Attest: J. W. BELL,

Clerk.

Service admitted this the 5th day of August, 1918.

JOHN B. MARSHALL,

Attorney for Defendant in Error.

Filed in the District Court, District of Alaska, First Division. Aug. 2, 1918. J. W. Bell, Clerk. By C. Z. Denny, Deputy. **[67]**

In the District Court for Alaska, Division No. 1, at Juneau.

No. 1716–A.

TOM BROWN,

Plaintiff,

vs.

H. S. PULLEN,

Defendant.

Praecipe for Transcript of Record.

To the Clerk of the District Court for Alaska, Division No. 1, Juneau, Alaska.

Sir: You will please make up the transcript of the record for the Appellate Court in the above-entitled cause, and include therein the following papers:

1. Complaint.
2. Answer.
3. Reply.
4. Judgment.
5. Bill of Exceptions.
6. Assignment of Error.
7. Writ of Error.
8. Bond.
9. Original Citation.
10. This Praecipe.

Said Transcript to be made up in accordance with the rules of the United States Circuit Court of Appeals for the Ninth Circuit, and the rules of this Court.

J. H. COBB,
Attorney for Plaintiff in Error.

Filed in the District Court, District of Alaska, First Division. Aug. 12, 1918. J. W. Bell, Clerk. By C. Z. Denny, Deputy. [68]

In the District Court for the District of Alaska, Division No. 1, at Juneau.

Certificate of Clerk U. S. District Court to Transcript of Record.

United States of America,

District of Alaska,

Division No. 1,—ss.

I, J. W. Bell, Clerk of the District Court for the District of Alaska, Division No. 1, hereby certify that the foregoing and hereto attached 68 pages of typewritten matter, numbered from 1 to 68, both inclusive, constitute a full, true, and complete copy, and the whole thereof, of the record as per the praecipe of the plaintiff in error, on file herein and made a part hereof, in the cause wherein Tom Brown is plaintiff in error, and Harriet S. Pullen is defendant in error, No. 1716–A, as the same appears of record and on file in my office, and that the said record is by virtue of the writ of error and citation issued in this cause and the return thereof in accordance therewith.

I do further certify that this transcript was prepared by me in my office, and the cost of preparation, examination, and certificate, amounting to $32.10 has been paid to me by counsel for plaintiff in error.

In witness whereof I have hereunto set my hand and the seal of the above-entitled court this 17th day of August, 1918.

[Seal]   J. W. BELL,

                 Clerk.

By ————————,

           Deputy.   [69]

[Endorsed]: No. 3201. United States Circuit Court of Appeals for the Ninth Circuit. Tom Brown, Plaintiff in Error, vs. Harriet S. Pullen, Defendant in Error. Transcript of Record. Upon Writ of Error to the United States District Court of the District of Alaska, Division No. 1.

Filed August 26, 1918.

F. D. MONCKTON,

Clerk of the United States Circuit Court of Appeals for the Ninth Circuit.

By Paul P. O'Brien,
Deputy Clerk.

NO. 3201.

United States

Circuit Court of Appeals

For the Ninth Circuit

TOM BROWN,

Plaintiff in Error,

vs.

HARRIET S. PULLEN,

Defendant in Error.

Brief for Plaintiffs in Error

Upon Writ of Error to the District Court
for Alaska,
Division No. 1

J. H. COBB,
Attorney for Plaintiff in Error.

United States

Circuit Court of Appeals

For the Ninth Circuit

TOM BROWN,

Plaintiff in Error,

vs.

HARRIET S. PULLEN,

Defendant in Error.

Brief for Plaintiffs in Error

Upon Writ of Error to the District Court for Alaska, Division No. 1

J. H. COBB,

Attorney for Plaintiff in Error.

BRIEF OF PLAINTIFF IN ERROR

STATEMENT OF THE CASE

Plaintiff and defendant in error were plaintiff and defendant respectively in the court below, and will be so designated hereinafter.

The action was upon a contract of hiring for a balance of wages claimed to be owing. Plaintiff alleged that he was employed by the defendant on December 3rd, 1915, at $60.00 per month and worked for her at said rate till June 4th., 1916; that from June 5th., 1916, to June 11th. 1917, he was employed by and worked for defendant at an agreed wage of $65.00 per month; that he had been paid $288.00 and there was a balance due and owing of $869.00 for which judgment was prayed.

The answer admitted the hiring, the services rendered, and the period of the employment, but denied that the stipulated wages were $60.00 and $65.00 per month as claimed by plaintiff, and alleged that the stipulated wage was $1.00 per day for the entire period. It was further denied that any indebtedness was owing plaintiff, and alleged "that she paid plaintiff various sums of money from time to time in accordance with his request, among which were the specified sums set forth in the said plaintiff's complaint, and alleges that on said 13th. day of June, 1917, she settled with plaintiff in full for all claims the said plaintiff made against her, and the said plaintiff accepted said settlement in full satisfaction of all claims against defendant."

This was denied by the reply.

It will thus be seen that the pleadings presented these issues:

1st. At what wages did plaintiff agree to work during the 554 days he was in defendant's employ? Was is $60.00 per month for the first six months and $65.00 per month for the next year and six days, or was it $1.00 per day for the whole period?

2nd. How much had defendant paid the plaintiff, if anything, in addition to the $288.00 admitted?

If the jury found in favor of plaintiff's contention as to the wages then he had earned, in all, $1153.00 and there was due him a balance of $865.00, unless the jury further found that defendant had paid him in addition to the $288.00 the further sum of $276.00, the most she claimed, in which case there would still be due plaintiff $599.00 If the rate was $1.00 per day, and defendant had only paid plaintiff $288.00 then the verdict should have been for plaintiff for $276.00. The verdict could only have been legally rendered for the defendant by a finding that the rate was $1.00 per day, and that the defendant had paid the plaintiff $554.00.

The evidence for the plaintiff tended to show that he was employed Dec. 3rd., 1915, at $60.00 per month and worked at that rate for six months; that his wages were then agreed to be $65.00 per month, and he worked at this agreed rate for one year and six days; and that he had only been paid the sum of $288.00.

The evidence for the defendant tended to show that the agreed rate of wages for the entire period was $1.00 per day. Defendant testified that in addition to the $288.00 admitted to have been paid she had paid other sums, but the dates and amounts of these payments were not stated nor the aggregate amounts thereof. She further testified that on June 13th. 1917, plaintiff only claimed a balance due of $200.00, which was admittedly paid, and she produced a check for $150.00 given plaintiff on that date marked in full settlement of wages to date. Plaintiff testified that the memorandum was not on the check at the time he received it, and that at that time defendant promised at a later date to pay him the balance of his wages.

It will thus be seen that the issues made by the evidence followed very closely the issues made by the pleadings. Instead of submitting these issues to the jury, however, the Court withdrew them all in effect except the first, by instructing the jury that unless they found that the rate of wages agreed on was $60.00 per month they could not find anything for plaintiff; and this instruction was excepted to and is assigned as error. 'The jury returned a verdict for defendant, upon which judgment was entered.

ASSIGNMENT OF ERROR

The Court erred in instructing the jury as follows: "It is either $60.00 a month or it is nothing. It is the contract which he alleges, and the contract which she denies, that he relies on, and you cannot split the difference—you cannot do anything of that kind. It is $60.00 a month, or it is not $60.00 a month. If it is not $60.00 a month the Plaintiff cannot recover."

ARGUMENT

This instruction it seems to us, was obvious error. If defendant had denied the contract entirely in her answer, and the jury had found that there was no contract such as was alleged in the complaint, it might be that under the rule in an action on contract plaintiff must prove the contract as alleged, in all its terms, or fail entirely, the instruction of the Court could be sustained. But no such question is presented here. *Defendant did not deny the contract sued upon. She expressly admitted it.* The only issue she tendered on the contract, was as to the correctness of one of the terms, viz. the rate of compensation, and she alleges this term, as she claims, correctly, and then tenders the issue of full payment under the contract as corrected by her answer. This issue is met by plaintiff's denial. The issues thus raised are accepted by counsel for both parties, and evidence adduced for and against the issues as made. Having thus made and tried the issues between the parties as they actually existed, both counsel were equally astonished when the Court withdrew all of them except one, and made the plaintiff's right to recover anything for his year and a half work, depend, not upon what he had earned, and whether he had been paid that amount, *but whether he had correctly plead his rate of wages.* Yet if plaintiff had incorrectly stated this one term of a contract, otherwise fully admitted, the error had been corrected by the answer. Under the pleadings and evidence then, it was NOT $60.00 a month or nothing. Nor did it follow that if the contract was not $60.00 a month the plaintiff could not recover; for if the rate was $1.00 per day, and he had only been paid $288.00, he was, under the pleadings and evidence, still entitled to recover $276.00. And on the issue of payment the defendant's testimony was too vague and uncertain to have any probative force or effect whatever. The obviously correct instruction was that if the jury found that the rate of wages was $60.00 and $65.00 per month, as claimed by plaintiff, to find for the plaintiff for $1153.00 less the amount admitted or proved to have been paid him. If the jury found that the rate was $1.00 per day for the entire period, to find for the plaintiff for $554.00 less the sum admitted to have been paid, and less such further sums as they found had been paid. If they found that there was no rate of wage agreed upon to find for the plaintiff for the reasonable value of his services, less the sums admitted and proved to have been paid. *Rocco vs. Parczyk*, 9 Yeo (Tenn.) 328.

For the said error we respectfully submit that the judgment should be reversed and the cause remanded for a new trial.

J. H. COBB,

Attorney for the Plaintiff in Error.

No. 3203

United States
Circuit Court of Appeals
For the Ninth Circuit.

OREGON–WASHINGTON RAILROAD & NAVI-
GATION COMPANY, a Corporation,

Plaintiff in Error,

vs.

PRESTON ROYER,

Defendant in Error.

Transcript of Record.

Upon Writ of Error to the United States District Court of the
Eastern District of Washington, Southern Division.

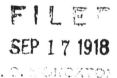
Filmer Bros Co. Print, 330 Jackson St, S. F., Cal.

United States
Circuit Court of Appeals
For the Ninth Circuit.

OREGON–WASHINGTON RAILROAD & NAVI-
GATION COMPANY, a Corporation,

Plaintiff in Error,

vs.

PRESTON ROYER,

Defendant in Error.

Transcript of Record.

Upon Writ of Error to the United States District Court of the
Eastern District of Washington, Southern Division.

Filmer Bros. Co. Print, 330 Jackson St., S. F., Cal.

INDEX TO THE PRINTED TRANSCRIPT OF RECORD.

[Clerk's Note: When deemed likely to be of an important nature, errors or doubtful matters appearing in the original certified record are printed literally in italic; and, likewise, cancelled matter appearing in the original certified record is printed and cancelled herein accordingly. When possible, an omission from the text is indicated by printing in italic the two words between which the omission seems to occur.]

Index.   Page

Names and Addresses of Attorneys of Record.

HAYDAN, LANGHORNE & METZGER, 617 Tacoma Building, Tacoma, Washington,

LINN & BOYLE, Prosser, Washington,

> Attorneys for Plaintiff and Defendant in Error,

and

A. C. SPENCER and C. E. COCHRAN, 510 Wells-Fargo, Building, Portland, Oregon,

RICHARDS & FONTAINE, Yakima, Washington,

> Attorneys for Defendants and Plaintiff in Error, [2*]

In the Superior Court of the State of Washington for Benton County.

No. 2403.

PRESTON ROYER,

Plaintiff,

vs.

OREGON-WASHINGTON RAILROAD & NAVIGATION COMPANY, a Corporation,

Defendant.

Complaint.

Comes now the above-named plaintiff, by Hayden, Langhorne & Metzger, and Linn & Boyle, his attorneys, and states to the Court:

---

*Page-number appearing at foot of page of original certified Transcript of Record.

1.

That the plaintiff now is, and at all the times hereinafter stated was, the owner in his separate and
individual right, of the following described real
property situate in Benton County, Washington, to
wit: The west one-half of the southeast quarter of
the northwest quarter (W. ½ of S. E. ¼ of N. W.
¼) of Section Twenty-eight (28) in township nine
(9) north, range twenty-five (25) east, W. M., less
the right-of-way of the Northern Pacific Railway
Company, a corporation, over and across such tract;
and comprising, less such right of way, nineteen
(19) acres, more or less, according to the Government Survey thereof.

2.

That now, and during all of the times hereinafter
specified, the Oregon-Washington Railroad & Navigation Company was a corporation organized and existing under and in virtue of the Laws of the State
of Oregon, at all of such times doing and authorized
to do business in the state of Washington, to wit:
railway business and was running and operating a
line of railway between the   **[3]**   City of Yakima
County, Washington, and Walla Walla, Walla Walla
County, Washington; and its said line of railway extending between the points above mentioned, running through Benton County, Washington, and over
and across the south one-half of the north one-half
of the northwest quarter (S. ½ of N. ½ of N. W. ¼)
of Section twenty-eight (28), and the east one-half of
the northeast quarter (E. ½ of N. E. ¼) of Section
twenty-nine (29), both of said Sections being in

township nine (9) north, range twenty-five (25) E. W. M.; the right of way of said company over and across the above described lands being one hundred feet in width.

3.

That a certain creek or water course known as "Spring Creek" has its source at the top of the Rattlesnake Hills in Benton County, Washington, and running in a general southeasterly direction for a distance of some eighteen or twenty miles, drains an area of land comprising more than twenty thousand acres, and the valley or channel through which said creek runs and has its course averages from one to ten miles in width and discharges its waters in the Yakima River. That during certain seasons of the year, caused by the melting of snow, a large volume of water flows down, and is carried off by, the channel of said Spring Creek. That the channel of Spring Creek enters Section Twenty-nine (29) in township nine (9) north, range twenty-five (25) east W. M., on the north line of said Section and near the west line of the east half of the northeast quarter of said Section twenty-nine (29), continuing in a general southeasterly direction across said east half of the northeast quarter of such Section, and the southwest quarter of the northwest quarter of Section twenty-eight (28) in township nine (9) north, range twenty-five (25) E. W. M., to a point near the southeast corner of said southwest quarter of the northwest quarter, and continues thence easterly across, and near the south line of the west half of the southeast quarter of the northwest quarter of **[4]** said

Section 28, township and range aforesaid.

4.

Some years prior to the commencement of this action the defendant, Oregon-Washington Railroad & Navigation Company, laid out and constructed a line of railway extending between the points and places specified in paragraph numbered 2 hereof, such line of railway running over and across the lands and premises also specified in paragraph numbered 2 of this complaint; and the line so constructed crossing the bed or channel of Spring Creek at a point in or near the east half of the northeast quarter of Section twenty-nine (29), township nine (9) north, range twenty-five east W. M., and the west line thereof.

5.

That when said defendant railroad company laid out and constructed its line of railroad over and across the lands of the said Section twenty-nine (29), as well as across other lands directly adjacent thereto, it was compelled to either bridge or fill the natural channel of Spring Creek at the point where said line or railway and the channel of Spring Creek intersected; that at such point defendant railway company made a fill or embankment on its own right of way for a distance of some seven hundred feet, establishing its grade five feet above the actual surface of the grade, which said grade gradually decreased in height as it proceeded easterly until it reached a surface grade near or about the east line of the northwest quarter of the northwest quarter of Section twenty-eight (28) as aforesaid, and at such latter point the land to the north started to raise as it proceeded eastward; that said defendant company placed in the bed or channel of Spring Creek a pipe or drain 48 inches in diameter for the purposes of carrying the waters of Spring Creek under its railway bed or fill and discharging the waters of such creek in its natural bed or channel on the south side of its fill or embankment, which said pipe or [5] drain was totally insufficient to carry off the waters that would flow down through the natural channel of Spring Creek, at certain seasons of the year, as defendant well knew; and plaintiff alleges and avers that fact to be that in the years 1912 and 1914 the waters of said Spring Creek came down in such volume and quantity, the outlet for their discharge at the point herein mentioned being so totally insufficient as to cause said waters to be impounded or dammed by the embankment or fill of said railway, with the west side of Spring Creek and the raise of ground mentioned above about the east line of the Northwest quarter of the northwest quarter of Section twenty-eight forming sides therefor, causing said waters to back up against said fill or embankment to an unusual depth, and until such a depth had been reached as to cause the waters thus impounded to break over the fill or embankment of said railway line of the defendant company and to flow down, over and across the lands of this plaintiff in great force and volume doing great damage thereto, but for which injury no recovery is sought in this action; that on each of such occasions portions of the roadbed were washed away, and reconstructed by said defendant company in the same manner as originally constructed, and no adequate provision being made by such company to permit the waters going down the natural channel of said Spring Creek, to pass in their accustomed way, or in any other way than through the 48 inch drain pipe as heretofore specified.

6.

That on the 23d day of January, 1916, and between January 23d and February 17th, 1916, the waters of said Spring Creek were flowing in great quantity and volume down their natural channel, the large volume of water therein being due to the melting of the snow, and said waters so flowing down the channel of Spring Creek again were impounded and backed up by the embankment or fill of the defendant company across said [6] Spring Creek, causing a large volume or reservoir of water extending from the west bank of said Spring Creek to a point near the east line of the northwest quarter of the northwest quarter of said Section twenty-eight (28), and no adequate outlet being provided therefor the same broke over such fill or embankment at or near the east line of said northwest quarter of the northwest quarter of said Section twenty-eight, and the waters thus released again swept down in great volume over and across the lands of this plaintiff, washing away the surface soil of said lands, washing away and filling with debris all flumes and irrigation ditches which were and had been constructed thereon, and cutting great gulleys or holes in said lands, thereby damaging and injuring the lands and premises of this plaintiff, and their appurtenances, in the sum of

Two Thousand Five Hundred Dollars ($2,500) and in addition thereto the force of said waters, in their sudden rush saturated with water, thereby heating and spoiling, about four tons of hay stacked thereon which was of the reasonable value of Twelve and 50/100 Dollars per ton; further washing away lumber piled upon said land of the reasonable value of Fifty Dollars, as also the private bridge which served plaintiff in crossing said Spring Creek as the same passed across his premises, in going to and from his home, the same being of the reasonable value of One Hundred Dollars; and said lumber, hay and bridge being wholly lost and destroyed, to his damage in the sum of Two Hundred Dollars; and in addition to the foregoing a cow belonging to plaintiff was caught in the waters and thrown upon his lands, and drowned, to his additional loss and damage in the sum of One Hundred Dollars.

7.

That during the months of January and February, 1916, and for a considerable period of time prior thereto, this plaintiff was engaged in the propagation and raising for sale as breeders [7] of registered Tamworth Hogs, of valuable stock; and being the 23d day of January and 17th day of February, 1916, had upon his premises as particularly described in paragraph numbered 1 hereof, a number of such hogs, all of the Tamworth Breed, and all being registered or subject to registry as full-blooded stock; that all of said animals were properly housed in various houses upon the premises specified in paragraph numbered 1 hereof; and 13 of the sows were due to farrow between the dates from about March 10th to April 1st, 1916; that all of said hogs and houses were flooded by the rush of said waters of Spring Creek over and across this plaintiff's lands and premises, as specified in paragraph numbered 6 of this complaint, and notwithstanding that prior thereto all of said animals were in a healthy and rugged condition, and that at all times during said flood and subsequent thereto this plaintiff practiced every precaution to prevent injury and sickness occurring by reason of the shock from and extremely cold temperature of said waters, all of said hogs developed acute colds accompanied by violent coughs. That the colds and coughs of two of said brood sows and one shoat became so acute that two died and plaintiff was compelled to kill the other, and they and each of them were a total loss to this plaintiff. That such shock and exposure caused the brood sows to farrow from ten days to two weeks earlier than the proper time for their so doing, 125 pigs being dropped by the 13 sows; that these pigs were so weak, because of their mothers' condition at the time of and prior to birth by reason of the shock and exposure as aforesaid, that 57 died shortly after birth; that this plaintiff used every effort to save the balance, and succeeded in keeping 5 alive until they were about four months of age, and 12 until about five months of age, but their weakened condition and continual coughing compelled plaintiff to kill these seventeen, and they, and each and all of them were a total loss to plaintiff. That 43 of the pigs so farrowed continued weak and subject to [8] spells of coughing, and because of such condition, being wholly unfit for breeders, plaintiff was compelled to sell the same when 7 months of age at a great loss and sacrifice. That the two registered boars kept by plaintiff with his herd, for breeding purposes, because of their weakened condition from the shock experienced and cold contracted, were materially checked in growth and efficiency; the eleven sows farrowing early and because of such shock and continued weakened condition, likewise were wholly unfit for breeding purposes for the following breeding season; and four gelts owned by plaintiff were materially checked in growth and value as breeders because of such shock and cold contracted; all of the foregoing being to plaintiff's loss and damage as particularly itemized and specified as follows:

Loss of brood sows of reasonable value of
$100.00 each. $200.00
Loss of one fall shoat.................... 25.00
Loss on 9 pigs, at $10.00 each. 90.00
Loss of 57 pigs at farrowing, of reasonable
value of $7.00 each. 399.00
Loss of 5 pigs, died from cough at about 4
months, reasonable value $15.00 each... 75.00
Loss of 17 pigs, 4 and 5mo., reasonable value
$20.00 each. 340.00
43 pigs sold for meat at about 7 months:
43 pigs for breeders at $25.00 each.$1075.
Cash received from sale as meat... 241.00
                                   _____
Loss on 43 pigs. ....$ 834.00 834.00

Injury to two boars as breeders. 50.00
Damage to eleven sows as breeders. 330.00
Damage to four gelts. 60.00

Total loss and damage on hogs. $2403.00

WHEREFORE, plaintiff prays judgment against the defendant Oregon-Washington Railroad & Navigation Company, a corporation, for the sum of Five Thousand Two Hundred and Three Dollars ($5203) together with his costs and disbursements expended herein.

(Signed)   HAYDEN, LANGHORNE & METZGER, and
LINN & BOYLE,
Attorneys for the Plaintiff.

State of Washington,
County of Benton,—ss.

Preston Royer, being first duly sworn, upon his oath **[9]** deposes and says: I am the plaintiff named in the attached and foregoing complaint; that I have read such complaint, know the facts therein stated, and the same are true, as I verily believe.

(Signed)   PRESTON ROYER.

Subscribed and sworn to before me this 1st day of September, A. D. 1917.

(Signed)   LON BOYLE,
Notary Public for Washington, Residing at Prosser, Washington.

[Endorsement]: Filed October 15, 1917.   Filed U. S. District Court, Eastern Dist. of Washington, Oct. 26, 1917.   W. H. Hare, Clerk.   By E. E. Wright, Deputy.   **[10]**

In the District Court of the United States for the Eastern District of Washington, Southern Division.

No. 641.

PRESTON ROYER,

Plaintiff,

vs.

OREGON-WASHINGTON RAILROAD & NAVIGATION COMPANY, a Corporation,

Defendant.

Answer.

Defendant, for answer to plaintiff's complaint says:

I.

Denies any knowledge or information as to whether or not the allegations of paragraph I of the complaint are true or otherwise, and therefore denies the same.

II.

Admits the allegations contained in paragraph II of the complaint.

III.

Denies the allegations contained in paragraph III of the complaint, except that the surface water caused by melting snow and falling rain upon a certain area of Rattlesnake Hills, Benton County, Washington, sometimes flows down a gully, entering and extending across the lands described in said paragraph, but defendant denies that the drain or gully whereby said surface water flows away is a creek or water course or stream of water, and defendant will further allege the facts in respect thereto in its further answer. [11]

IV.

Admits the allegations contained in paragraph IV.

V.

Denies the allegations contained in paragraph V of the Complaint, except defendant admits that in the gully or drain which entered and crossed Section 29 and other lands adjacent thereto, defendant filled the same, except there was retained therein a drain pipe forty-eight inches in diameter, passing through and under the defendant's railroad track.

VI.

Denies each and every allegation contained in paragraph VI, except as hereinafter alleged.

VII.

Denies each and every allegation contained in paragraph VII.

Defendant further answering said Complaint alleges:

I.

Defendant is a corporation organized under and by virtue of the laws of the State of Oregon, with its principal office and place of business in said state, but it has taken all the steps necessary and has been authorized to transact its business in the State of Washington. It is the owner of a line of railroad as alleged in paragraph 11 of the complaint, extending from Wallula to North Yakima, Washington, passing through Benton County and along the north side of the Yakima River.

II.

Near the station of Biggam in Section 29, Twp. 9, North Range 25, E. W. M., defendant's line of railroad passes over a gully or drain. This gully or drain originates at Rattlesnake Hills five or six miles north of said point, extends in a general southerly direction until it reaches the substantially level [12] ground in Sections 28 and 29, where same turns in an easterly direction and extends to Yakima River. By means of this gully a certain area between Rattlesnake Hills and Yakima River is drained of surface waters formed by the occasional accumulation of snow and the speedy melting thereof, and except for such drainage the gully is dry during all the year.

III.

Sunnyside Canal is located a short distance north of defendant's line of railroad and extends for several miles substantially parallel therewith. It is a large canal and so situated whereby surface water resulting from melting snow and the like between Grandview, Washington and the gully or depression referred to herein and the surface water from the territory north thereof, is empounded and run down to said gully, where there is constructed a waste-way which in the winter season is left open so that the canal operates to increase the surface water occasionally flowing in said gully and depression. This canal is owned and operated by the Government of the United States.

IV.

In Section 20, twp. 9, south, range 25, E. W. M.,
in Benton County, Washington, the gully has become somewhat well defined, and the United States
Government has constructed therein a dam, and a
portion of the gully above the dam is used as an
irrigation ditch, by which water diverted from
Sunnyside Canal is carried to another ditch extending northerly through the lands of Mr. E. E.
Starkey. Also a short distance south of the government dam Mr. Starkey had placed in said channel a dam so that the surface water, if any, should
come down said gully would overflow his premises,
which are located in the southeast quarter (SE. ¼)
of Section Twenty (20) aforesaid. [13]

V.

On or about the first of February, 1916, and for
several days prior thereto a heavy fall of snow lay
upon the lands between Rattlesnake Hills and Yakima River in the vicinity of the station of Biggam, whereupon the temperature moderated and
chinook winds began with the result that the snow
was hurriedly melted to a certain degree and the
waters therefrom flowed down said gully and also
into Sunnyside Canal and thereby turned into said
gully, whereby and by reason of the dams aforesaid,
the lands in Section 20 aforesaid were overflowed
by said surface water and extended therefrom to
and over a portion of Sections 29 and 28, and thence
into Yakima River. The overflow of said surface
water was not caused by defendant. When said
surface water flows from Rattlesnake Hills it be-

comes impregnated with silt and soil, which silt and soil is deposited upon adjoining lands if overflowed thereby and results in great benefit to said lands, renewing the soil and increasing the quality thereof, and the foregoing is the transaction complained of in plaintiff's complaint, and not otherwise.

WHEREFORE, defendant having answered the complaint of plaintiff, prays same may be dismissed and that defendant have judgment against the plaintiff for its costs and disbursements of this action.

(Signed)   A. C. SPENCER,
C. E. COCHRAN,
Attorneys for Defendant.

United States of America,
District of Oregon,—ss.

I, A. C. Spencer, being first duly sworn, on oath deposes and say:

That I am assistant secretary and general attorney for   **[14]**   the above-named defendant; that I have read the foregoing Answer, know the contents thereof, and the same is true as I verily believe.

(Signed) . A. C. SPENCER.

Subscribed and sworn to before me this 28th day of January, 1918.

[Notarial Seal]

(Signed)   C. E. COCHRAN.
Notary Public for Oregon.

My commission expires Oct. 17, 1920.

[Endorsements]: Answer. Filed in the U. S. District Court, Eastern Dist. of Washington, Feb. 2, 1918. Wm. H. Hare, Clerk. By H. J. Dunham, Deputy.   **[15]**

*In the District Court of the United States for the
Eastern District of Washington, Southern Division.*

No. 641.

PRESTON ROYER,

Plaintiff,

vs.

OREGON–WASHINGTON RAILROAD & NAVI-
GATION COMPANY, a Corporation,

Defendant.

Reply.

Comes now the above-named plaintiff, and replying to the affirmative answer of the defendant herein, shows to the Court:

1.

That he admits the allegations and averments set
forth and contained in paragraph numbered I of
said further answer.

2.

He denies the allegations and averments contained in paragraph II of said further answer, except that plaintiff admits that near the station of
Biggam in Section 29, township 9 north, range 25
E. W. M., defendant's line of railroad passes over
a gully; that this gully or watercourse originates in
the Rattlesnake Hills and extends to the Yakima
River; and that by means of this gully or watercourse a certain area between Rattlesnake Hills and
Yakima River is drained of surface water.

3.

He denies the allegations of paragraph numbered
III of said further answer, except that plaintiff ad-

mits that Sunnyside Canal is located a short distance north of defendant's line of railroad and extends for several miles substantially parallel therewith; and the canal is owned and operated by the United States Government.   [16]

4.

He denies the allegations and averments set forth and contained in paragraph numbered IV of said further answer, except that this plaintiff admits that said gully is well defined in Section 20, twp. 9 north, range 25 E. W. M.; that the United States Government has constructed therein a dam, and a portion of the gully above the dam is used as an irrigation ditch by which water diverted from Sunnyside Canal is carried to another ditch through the lands of E. E. Starkey.

5.

He denies the allegations and averments set forth and contained in paragraph numbered V of said further answer.

WHEREFORE, plaintiff having fully replied to the allegations of defendant's answer herein, prays for the relief asked in his complaint herein.

(Signed)

    HAYDEN, LANGHORNE & METZGER
      and

        BERT LINN and
        LON BOYLES,
      Attorneys for the Plaintiff.

[Endorsements]: Reply.   Filed in the U. S. District Court, Eastern Dist. of Washington, Feb. 23, 1918. W. H. Hare, Clerk. By H. J. Dunham, Deputy.   [17]

In the District Court of the United States for the Eastern District of Washington, Southern Division.

No. 641.

PRESTON ROYER,

Plaintiff,

vs.

OREGON–WASHINGTON, RAILWAY AND NAVIGATION COMPANY,

Defendant.

Verdict.

We, the jury in the above-entitled cause, find for the plaintiff and assess the amount of recovery at the sum of Eight Hundred Seventy-five Dollars ($875.00).

(Signed) A. C. SPALDING,
Foreman.

[Endorsements]: Verdict. Filed in the U. S. District Court, Eastern Dist. of Washington, May 9, 1918. W. H. Hare, Clerk. [18]

In the District Court of the United States for the Eastern District of Washington, Southern Division.

No. 641.

PRESTON ROYER,

Plaintiff,

vs.

OREGON–WASHINGTON RAILROAD & NAVIGATION COMPANY, a Corporation,

Defendant.

Judgment.

The above matter coming on for trial, before the Hon. Frank H. Rudkin, Judge of the above-entitled court, the plaintiff appearing in person, with witnesses, and by Maurice A. Langhorne and Lon Boyle, his attorneys, the defendant corporation, appearing with witnesses and by C. E. Cochran, its attorney; the parties announcing themselves ready for trial, a jury was impanelled and sworn; and the jury having heard the testimony, listened to the arguments of counsel, and received the charge of the Court, upon their oaths do say they find the issues herein joined to be in favor of said plaintiff, and against the said defendant, and that they assess the amount of the plaintiff's damage and recovery herein against the defendant at the sum of Eight Hundred Fifty Dollars ($850.00).

On motion of the plaintiff it is therefore hereby considered by the Court that the plaintiff Preston Royer do have and recover of and from the said defendant, Oregon-Washington Railroad & Navigation Company, a corporation, said sum of Eight Hundred Fifty Dollars ($850.00), and the costs of this suit to be taxed, for the collection of which said sum and costs, execution is hereby awarded.

Done in open court this 10th day of May, A. D. 1918.

(Signed)   FRANK H. RUDKIN,

Judge.

[Endorsements]: Judgment.   Filed in the U. S. District Court, Eastern Dist. of Washington, May 10, 1918.   Wm. H. Hare, Clerk.   By H. J. Dunham, Deputy.   **[19]**

In the District Court of the United States for the Eastern District of Washington, Southern Division.

No. 641.

PRESTON ROYER,

Plaintiff,

vs.

OREGON–WASHINGTON RAILROAD & NAVIGATION COMPANY,

Defendant.

Bill of Exceptions.

BE IT REMEMBERED that the above case came regularly on for trial before Honorable Frank H. Rudkin, Judge, and a jury at Yakima, Washington; the plaintiff appearing in person and by attorneys, Maurice Langhorne, of the firm of Hayden, Langhorne & Metzger, of Tacoma, and Lon Boyle, of the firm of Linn & Boyle, Prosser, Washington, and the defendant appearing by its attorneys, Messrs. A. C. Spencer and C. E. Cochran, of Portland, Oregon, and Messrs. Richards & Fontaine, Yakima, Washington.

. Thereupon the following proceedings were had:

Testimony of Guy H. Heiberling, for Plaintiff.

GUY H. HEIBERLING, as a witness for plaintiff, testified:

Direct Examination by Mr. BOYLE.

Name, Guy H. Heiberling; occupation, County Engineer of Benton County, Washington. Plaintiff's Exhibit "A," a map of the lands of Wasson and Royer, was prepared by me. (The map was admitted in evidence for the purpose of illustration). Spring Creek originates about fifteen miles to the north and west of the Wasson and Royer land. The county road follows along the center line east and west through Section 28, and Spring Creek lies immediately east of the county road as established at the present time. The land of Mr. E. B. Starkey is shown on the map. I took levels [20] where Spring Creek crosses the line between Sections 20 and 29, and also where same crosses the O-W. R. & N. right of way, and found the fall to be about 8.6 feet in one thousand. The drain under the O-W. R. & N. tracks, where Spring Creek flows under, consisted of one 48-inch corrugated metal culvert, which was about four feet below the top of the track. At this point the line of the O-W. R. & N. Co. is on

(Testimony of Guy H. Heiberling.)

an embankment or fill, which is about eight feet deep. The fill extends from the creek six or seven hundred feet east of the county road over in Section 28, where it passes from embankment to a slight cut.

Further Examination by Mr. LANGHORNE.

With the exception of a few months I have lived in Benton County since the fall of 1908. Plaintiff's Exhibit "B," purporting to be a map of part of Benton County issued by the Department of the Interior, is shown me and I can trace from this map the course of Spring Creek. The upper limits of the head shown in Sections 25, 11 and 24, and it runs generally southeasterly at the head and bears southwesterly for three or four miles, then southeasterly into Yakima River. The topography of the land from where spring Creek has its origin is rolling, but Spring Creek is in a canyon until a short distance from the O-W. R. & N. right of way, where the ground spreads out flat. The channel is well defined and rains twenty or twenty-five thousand acres, coming down from various gulches into the Spring Creek Gulch. The fall from the source to where it crosses the right of way of the O-W. R. & N. Co. is something over two thousand feet. Where Spring Creek runs under the right of way of the O-W. R. & N. Co. there has been a fill on each side of the creek. On the east side the grade tapers gradually to nothing in about thirteen or fourteen hundred feet. The annual snowfall in the hills north of the railroad right of way varies from noth-

(Testimony of Guy H. Heiberling.)

ing to as high as 18 inches. In January, 1916, at Prosser, there were two **[21]** different snowfalls —one of these twelve and the other fifteen inches— and there is usually heavier snow in the hills. This snow generally begins to melt whenever the chinook winds come, and it melts rapidly then.

Cross-examination by Mr. COCHRAN.

Spring Creek, from the section line of 20 and 29, meanders back and forth. One standing in the bottom of Spring Creek at the O-W. R. & N. right of way, attempting to look up towards Mr. Starkey's place north, will find the creek so crooked that a straightline vision will not pass up the creek channel. The gully from which Spring Creek comes out of the Rattlesnake Hills begins to widen at point about the north line of the southeast quarter of the southeast quarter of Section 20. Mr. Starkey has quite a flat place—about ten acres or so—which would be located substantially in the southeast quarter of the southeast quarter of Section 20. The base of the bluff is about the section line between 20 and 29 on the west side of the creek.

Plaintiff's Exhibits "A" and "B" are hereto physically attached and made a part of this bill of exceptions.

Testimony of Preston Royer, for Plaintiff.

PRESTON ROYER, as plaintiff and as witness on the part of Mr. Wasson, testified:

Direct Examination by Mr. BOYLE.

Name, Preston Royer; own the lands described in

(Testimony of Preston Royer.)

my complaint, amounting to practically nineteen acres. I bought the land in the spring of 1914. I have lived along the branches of Spring Creek since the fall of 1905, and at one time lived in the Rattlesnake Country, Spring Creek passing through my homestead. The waters coming down Spring Creek is caused by the melting snow and it comes down in a series. In that country our weather goes in a circles—we will have a period of dry [22] seasons, very little moisture, poor crops, and a series of good moisture and good crops. Spring Creek runs practically every year when there are good crops and in dry seasons does not run at all. In 1907 the water down Spring Creek went through a 24-foot breach, practically four feet deep. There is no outlet other than under the O-W. R. & N. crossing. From 1906 to 1912 there was water in more or less volume running each season. This water flows to the Yakima River and the only outlet is under the O-W. R. & N. tracks. In June or July, 1914, the water crossed my ranch.

The following question was asked the witness:

Q. Just explain that to the jury.

Mr. COCHRAN.—I submit that is immaterial.

The Court overruled the objection, to which an exception was allowed.

A. In 1914, in the last of June or the first of July, there was a freshet in the Rattlesnake Hills in the watershed of Spring Creek, and water ran down this creek to where same intersects with the O-W. R. & N., where they have a 48-inch pipe. It was not suffi-

(Testimony of Preston Royer.)

cient to carry the water off and it backed the water up and it flooded straight east and west down the pit to the county road, washed out the county road to a considerable depth, and went on down where the railroad comes to the surface grade and crossed right through and ran off for five or six hours over our place.

(Witness excused temporarily. (Trans. 21.)

Testimony of Samuel H. Mason, for Plaintiff.

SAMUEL H. MASON, as a witness for plaintiff, testified as follows:

Direct Examination by Mr. LANGHORNE.

Name, Samuel H. Mason; residence, Yakima; lived here about six years all told. I homesteaded the Wasson place in 1900, owned it about ten years. I am acquainted with Spring Creek where it now leaves the O-W. R. & N. right of way to the Yakima River, approximately [23] a couple of miles. The channel is not regular—in places good and wide and other places deep. It is about four to eight feet at the bottom, the depth being irregular.

Q. Did you ever see water going down that channel?

A. Yes, the water came there in the channel in the spring when the snow would come on the Rattlesnake Hills, and melt off suddenly.

The witness proceeded:

These waters passed through the channel to the river, and at my place at the deepest time it was probably two to two and one-half feet deep, and in

(Testimony of Samuel H. Mason.)

the narrowest places deeper. While I owned the place the waters never came over the land. It generally followed the course of the creek—only time it got over was when banked up but not washed down over the land.

Cross-examination by Mr. COCHRAN.

Spring Creek carries water during the spring freshets. The time would vary. The only time I knew water to run there any time was when the snow would come on the Rattlesnake Hills and would melt and go off suddenly; would seem to absorb the water in the wintertime when it went off gradually, but when the sun and wind melted it suddenly always had these freshets in the spring. The time of the melting depends entirely on the presence or absence of these chinook winds.

Q. And where the water did go off suddenly that would be accomplished, say, within a period of ten to twenty days?

A. I never saw it last that long as a rush of waters, but when this water run down there in the creek it would be a month or so until it all went away when plenty of snow in the mountains, but a rush of waters would be generally two, three or four days.

Q. Apart from any water, if there were such coming into [24] Spring Creek from the Sunnyside Canal, how many months of the year do you say Spring Creek is dry?

A. It is dry a good deal of the time. I don't think water runs there regularly from freshets over two months of the year. (Trans. 25.)

Testimony of Preston Royer, for Plaintiff (Recalled).

Direct Examination by Mr. BOYLE.

The banks of Spring Creek vary, being well defined for probably fourteen miles above Mr. Starkey's place, there are distinct channels and have to be bridged; they expect water in these and they put in bridges. In 1916, on January 20th, there was from twelve to sixteen inches of badly drifted snow, and Spring Creek and the ditches and canals up to the top of the hill were leveled across in many places, practically no snow on the level lands but the snow was drifted into depressions. From the level lands to a distance of five or six miles up the Rattlesnake slope there was no snow. Above that there was. Also the canyons are much deeper at the top, and these were full of snow. The ground was frozen and the water could not go into the ground. The chinook winds started at 11:30 January 20th and stopped at night. January 21st, a southwest wind, mostly clear, and checked at night. January 22d southwest wind. January 23d, southwest wind. The snow melted and the high water went across my place at 5 o'clock and run about five hours in the afternoon. It destroyed the roadbed at a great distance, broke through a stretch of railroad track, went over the ties and washed a deep hole through the railroad onto the Wasson land and then to my land. On Monday following there was a cold northeast wind and it froze hard, which checked the flow of the water. Weather stayed frozen and we got some snow, probably fifteen

(Testimony of Preston Royer.)

inches, until the next chinook came. The next chinook wind started February 7th and was a clear day—with from twelve to fourteen inches badly [25] drifted snow. The wind changed and on February 9th the water started running, and on the 10th the water went over my place and over the Wasson place. The water backed up on the north side of the embankment and run down a borrow pit east and then passed across the railroad track and down over Mr. Wasson's land and my land until it met the old channel of Spring Creek.

With respect to the Wasson land, this land slopes southeast and was planted to alfalfa, and when the water came over that land would wash holes, many of them fifteen feet long and three or four feet wide, making it impossible to irrigate it and impossible to go over it with a cutting machine. The water went over my land and washed the soil somewhat. I was following the business of raising registered hogs— Tamworth hogs. I had thirteen brood sows, two boars and four gilts, and I think nine pigs, fall pigs. They were registered or eligible. The sows were heavy with pigs, due to farrow the first of March to about the 21st. The hogs were penned up. When the water came across I turned them loose in the water. The effect was that these sows had their pigs from ten days to three weeks ahead of time. The sows were worth $150 each prior to farrowing. After their experience, the market value was between 7 and 8 cents per pound. The young boar was worth $100 before the injury and the older boar was worth $250.

(Testimony of Preston Royer.)

Afterwards the young boar was valued for meat only —say, $15. The other one was damaged I would say only to the extent of $25—that is, he would be worth $225 after the injury. I had between six and seven tons of hay worth $12.50 per ton, of which four tons was rendered worthless. I lost a cow worth $100. There was a bridge across Spring Creek.

The following question was asked:

Q. What was the bridge worth?

Mr. COCHRAN.—I make the point such damages are not proper measure and the recovery cannot be made that way. It is immaterial and incompetent. [26]

The COURT.—Well, the form of the question makes very little difference one way or the other. You can answer the question and I will allow exception.

A. One hundred dollars.

Examination by Mr. LANGHORNE.

There were 40 to 45 acres of the Wasson land in alfalfa.

Q. You were acquainted somewhat with the value of land in that vicinity, were you?

A. Yes, I know when a place sells and what is is sold for.

Q. What in your opinion was the 40-acre tract of Wasson's worth before the flood?

A. I would say worth $200 per acre before the flood.

Q. After the flood, what would you say the 40-acre tract was worth, in your opinion?

(Testimony of Preston Royer.)

A. I would say $75.00 per acre.   (Trans. 47.)

Cross-examination by Mr. COCHRAN.

Between the latter part of the year 1915, up to the 23d of January, 1916, I do not know of any sales in that vicinity, nor were there any sales previously for several years.   The Wasson place was covered with water in 1916 to the extent of between 40 and 45 acres.   When the water came down on the 23d of January, it ran for five hours.   I did not turn my pigs out at that time.   Between the 23d of January and the 7th of February about fifteen inches of loose snow fell, followed by freezing weather, and no water came down until about the 7th of February.   The water would check at night and flow again in the daytime.   I have been acquainted with Spring Creek since 1905.   The creek is always dry in the summer, above the Government's canal.   It is dry in the aggregate over eleven months in the year, and sometimes it does not run that month.   There must be snow in the hills to put water in   [27]   that channel, by the chinook winds.   If it melts gradually, and no frost in the ground, you have no water in Spring Creek.   If it melts off in the winter, melts gradually, it probably runs in warm weather.   The chinook was what brought the water down.   The gully through which the water drained was practically drifted full of snow.   After January 23d, when the 15 inch snow storm came, a second chinook wind came and the snow became more dense and more dense, until it finally became water in part, and started to flow down.   The snow that had not yet congealed would

(Testimony of Preston Royer.)

hold it back for a while until the water would break through and it would come down in bunches, and the channel on the flat between the O-W. R. & N. and Starkey's place would possibly have a tendency to fill up and cause the water to spread. Spring Creek channel at my place was full of snow at that time and it had to work down gradually. I did not farm my place in 1916. (Trans. 56.)

Testimony of M. C. Williams, for Plaintiff.

M. C. WILLIAMS, Division Engineer, First Division, O-W. R. & N. Co., testified:

That the railroad track runs approximately east and west, and the grade of the track where it crosses Spring Creek is one-fifth of one per cent, ascending towards Grandview.

Testimony of Lee M. Lamson, for Plaintiff.

LEE M. LAMSON, a witness for plaintiff, testified:

Direct Examination by Mr. BOYLE.

Name, Lee M. Lamson, Kennewick, Washington; County Agricultural Agent of Benton County, have been for five years; acquainted with the Wasson and Royer land prior to January, 1916; examined the Royer land at Mr. Royer's request to give him advice whether the corn needed irrigation. There were six or seven acres of corn and probably five acres or so of a poor stand of alfalfa. The soil is a very fine sand, with a gravel subsoil. I examined [28] the land in March, 1916. The flumes were torn down,

(Testimony of Lee M. Lamson.)

the land was cut up pretty badly with little rivulets. In a good many places the surface soil was washed off entirely, so it was washed down to the gravel. The humas which was on the surface was washed off. I went over the Wasson land at the same time. The water had cut out ravines. A good many were from a foot to two feet deep—some were less. The alfalfa crown were all the way from three to ten inches above the ground. The irrigation ditches were hardly recognizable. The only practical thing to do would be to plow it up and relevel it and reseed it. In my opinion the Wasson land was worth between $160 and $175 an acre before the flood, and afterwards probably sixty to seventy-five; and the Royer land in my opinion was worth $130 per acre before and thirty to forty dollars afterwards. I received my education at the State College, specializing in animal husbandry, and am familiar with hogs. As breeders, in my opinion, the Royer sows would be worth $175 or $180 for the biggest sows he had; afterwards, as breeders, nothing at all, and for any purpose they would be worth probably four cents a pound.

Cross-examination by Mr. COCHRAN.

I never knew of Mr. Royer selling any of his breed sows for $175 to $180 each.. I never heard that he sold one to Mr. Johnson for $40. I did not measure the amount of land upon the Wasson place that the water passed over, although the line of the flow was fairly well marked with drift weeds. The water did not go over all of the land below the railroad track.

(Testimony of Lee M. Lamson.)

The Wasson place could have been leveled all right, and it would approximately cost thirty to thirty-five dollars per acre to relevel it and reseed it. I examined the land north of the railroad; nothing washed out there but some soil washed on to it. This to some extent would be a benefit, the soil will act somewhat in the nature of a fertilizer. I have known of no sales of land prior to January, [29] 1916, similar to the Wasson place, nor of any sales after the January flood in 1916. (Trans. 68.)

Testimony of Luke Powell, for Plaintiff.

LUKE POWELL, as a witness for plaintiff, testified:

Direct Examination by Mr. BOYLE.

Name, Luke Powell; residence, Prosser, Washington; District Horticulturist, State of Washington; acquainted with the Wasson and Royer land about January 1, 1916; was with Mr. Lamson and went over the land in March of that year. The soil was washed and a number of gullies washed, from six to eighteen inches and as wide as a foot to fifteen inches. Some of the alfalfa was washed but a good deal of it the crown would stand up four to ten inches. In my opinion Royer's land was worth $160 to $180 per acre, and after the flood about $25 per acre. The Wasson land about January 1st was worth $175 to $200 per acre, and afterwards from $65 to $100 per acre.

Cross-examination by Mr. COCHRAN.

I never bought or sold any land like the Wasson

(Testimony of William J. Wasson.)

and Royer land about January 1, 1916, nor for a year or so prior thereto, nor do I know of any special or general sales.   (Trans. 71.)

Testimony of William Wasson, for Plaintiff.

WILLIAM J. WASSON, plaintiff in his own case, and on behalf of Mr. Royer, plaintiff in the Royer case, testified as follows:

Direct Examination by Mr. LANGHORNE.

Name, William J. Wasson, owner of the land described in the Wasson complaint; was at Centralia, Washington, at the time of the flood in 1916; came to Prosser, March 2d, went over the land and saw the flooded area. The irrigating ditches were washed out, the rows that you irrigate with were washed and cut crossways so that you could not possibly carry water down over it and irrigate it. I should judge in the neighborhood of forty-five acres of my land was left in this condition. I placed a value of $250 per acre on the best land before the flood, and would not consider [30] it over half that value afterwards. The land was leased for the cropping season of 1915. For 1916 it was not leased. The water crossed the railroad track practically 150 feet wide and as it came down over my place it spread out. (Trans. 87.)

Testimony of L. D. Lape, for Plaintiff.

L. D. LAPE, as a witness for plaintiff, testified as follows:

Name, L. D. Lape; residence, Prosser, Washington, for 22 years; business, real estate; acquainted

(Testimony of L. D. Lape.)

. with land values in and around Prosser and vicinity; acquainted with the Wasson and Royer lands, known same for 22 years. In my opinion the Wasson tract before the overflow was worth $175 to $200 per acre, the Royer tract $160 to $185 per acre.

Testimony of M. C. Williams, for Plaintiff (Recalled).

M. C. WILLIAMS, recalled as a witness for plaintiff, testified:

Direct Examination by Mr. LANGHORNE.

The original right of way of the railroad company was forty feet on each side of the center line of the railroad. Afterwards the property owners immediately adjoining the right of way on the north added an eighty-foot strip clear across the forty acres at Biggam. That would make 120 feet on the north side and 40 feet on the south side. The 80 feet has since been deeded to the county for road purposes.

Plaintiff rests.

Mr. COCHRAN.—We desire to move for a judgment of nonsuit in each of these cases upon the following grounds.

First. The water in question is shown by the evidence as surface water and is a common enemy. In respect to surface water I think the Federal Courts follow the rule adopted in the courts of the State where the alleged cause of action arises.

Second. The complaint in each of these cases is drawn upon the theory that actual damage resulted from the flow of surface water. Under these circumstances, there is no legal liability and [31] the complaint would not state facts sufficient to constitute a cause of action.

Third. The channel called "Spring Creek" and by which it has been designated in the complaint, the evidence shows is nothing more or less than a mere drainage of surface water, resulting from melting snow or the action of chinook winds operating thereon, and that such water may be defended against, may be dammed up, the channel may be closed or open in part and closed in part and that no actionable damage results, and that the evidence shows that the railroad bridge was built for the purpose of being used by the railroad and in accordance with good railroad building, and that if surface water of the type and kind shown by the evidence overflows, it becomes a cause of damages without injury.

The COURT.—The motion will be denied. (To which ruling an exception was allowed.)

Testimony of I. J. Oder, for Defendant.

I. J. ODER, as a witness for defendant, testified as follows:

Direct Examination by Mr. COCHRAN.

Name, I. J. Oder; residence, Yakima, Washington; occupation, raising hogs, have been for two or three years. I have been on a farm most of my life, during which time handled hogs. In 1906 and 1907 I was manager of the college farm at Kingfisher, Okla., and was engaged in breeding thoroughbred Duroc hogs extensively. Since coming to Yakima Valley I have handled and bred thoroughbred hogs,

(Testimony of I. J. Oder.)

and sold and disposed of same, including the Tamworth, Hampshire and Duroc breeds. I have at the present time 208 head. I have had experience in observing the effect upon thoroughbred hogs of their being overflowed and submerged in water. During the month of December, 1917, in the Naches River, which borders my place, a flood came, in fact one of the biggest floods we have ever had in that location, and it overflowed my hog-yard. They were actually in the water part way on their bodies, five of them at least, [32] from twelve to thirty-six hours. Assuming that Mr. Royer's hogs had become submerged with water, say five hours, and then more or less for a period of three or four days, but not continuously, in my opinion, from my experience, it would have had no bad effect upon them. Three of my sows were very heavy with pig that were in the water three, twelve to thirty-six hours. Three of these sows farrowed within three weeks, and one bore ten, another twelve and another thirteen live, strong pigs. Two of these were Durocs and one Berkshire. I had two Tamworth mature sows and three Tamworth mature gilts that have farrowed since. The first Tamworth sow farrowed eleven pigs, the second nine and I think the third had seven live pigs. They were all good healthy pigs. I am acquainted with the market value of such stock in January, 1916. Gilts were worth $20 and mature sows $30, with pedigree on them for breeding purposes. According to my experience, hogs passing through a flood such as has been described are not

(Testimony of I. J. Oder.)
injured thereby in the market, any less for any of
the purposes for which they may be used.

Cross-examination by Mr. BOYLE.

Although my hogs were in the flood around the
last day of December, 1917, there was no bad effects
from it at all.   This water was snow and ice water
from the hills, through the Naches River.   (Trans.
104.)

Testimony of A. M. Cale, for Defendant.

A. M. CALE, as witness for defendant, testified as
follows:

Direct Examination by Mr. COCHRAN.

Name, A. M. Cale; residence, Yakima; occupation,
have been raising stock all my life, for sixty years;
have seen Tamworth hogs raised and know about
them, and have been familiar with that breed for
three to five years, also with the Berkshire, Duroc
and Hampshire hogs.

I am acquainted with the market value of Berkshire and Hampshire hogs, not the Tamworth.   They
are worth in the market   [33] $4 to $5.75 per hundred pounds.   They are not *worth any* other hogs,
just the same.   I never gave any more for them.   I
have seen such hogs in a flood submerged in water.
A good many years back I lived on the river and
raised a great many hogs, from five hundred to a
thousand head, and they have been in water a great
many times.   Hogs that have been bred and due to
farrow in three or four weeks I have seen such hogs

(Testimony of A. M. Cale.)

in the water, and in my experience I don't think it had any effect on them.

Cross-examination by Mr. BOYLE.

I have raised a great many Hampshire, Berkshire and Duroc hogs for breeding purposes and all I could get for them was the same as other hogs, from $4 to $5.75 per hundred pounds. A registered hog due to farrow is worth from ten to thirty dollars more for breeding purposes than in the market, owing to the size and condition of the hog. I think a good brood sow is worth from $20 to $30. (Trans. 110.)

Testimony of Christ Nelson, for Defendant.

CHRIST NELSON, a witness for defendant, testified as follows:

Direct Examination by Mr. COCHRAN.

Name, Christ Nelson; residence, Biggam, Washington, in the vicinity of where Mr. Wasson's and Mr. Royer's land is located. I was acquainted with the Royer herd of hogs in the winter of 1915 and 1916. The place where he kept the hogs was naturally damp and there was a lot of snow on the ground just before the flood. His hog pens were in a "V" shape and the pens were naturally damp and wet. Mr. Royer's hogs were not fat, they are skinny, long skinny hogs. This was their condition in the early part of January, 1916.

Cross-examination by Mr. BOYLE.

The pens were in good condition for their kind.

(Testimony of Christ Nelson.)

I saw the hogs just before Christmas.   Some of the pens had no floors in them.

Cross-examination by Mr. LANGHORNE.   [34]

I have lived at Biggam ten years; am a farmer. (Trans. 113.)

Testimony of Dr. G. W. Ridgeway, for Defendant.

Dr. G. W. RIDGEWAY, as a witness for defendant, testified as follows:

Direct examination by Mr. COCHRAN.

Name, G. W. Ridgeway; occupation, veterinary surgeon; residence, Yakima, Washington; followed this profession forty years.   I have had a little experience in treating hogs.   Pneumonia in hogs is caused from a cold.   It is not necessarily produced from wet conditions around the pens; sometimes caused by a cold draught in the open and unprotected. A cold draft is more apt to give it to them than anything else.   This cold draught operates in that respect the same as in a human being.

The COURT.—So far as pneumonia is concerned, I presume a hog is human.

A. Yes.   (Trans. 116.)

Testimony of M. C. Williams, for Defendant.

M. C. WILLIAMS, a witness for defendant, testified as follows:

Direct Examination by Mr. COCHRAN.

I am the same witness that was on the stand for plaintiff.   I was resident engineer in charge of construction.   The definite location of the railroad

(Testimony of M. C. Williams.)

across the land in controversy was made before I went on the work, but I was resident engineer when the track was building. This was in 1910 and 1911. I have been acquainted with the drain called Spring Creek since 1907. I had been back and across this territory a number of times between those dates connected with the defendant in an engineering capacity. I prescribed the size of the culvert at Biggam after inquiring as to water conditions from residents in the immediate vicinity who had lived there a number of years, and after such inquiry I put in a culvert 48 inches in diameter, circular in form. From the information received it was my opinion this 48-inch diameter was sufficient in size to carry off the normal flow of surface water that came down. The water flowage **[35]** conditions in 1916 in Yakima Valley and throughout the eastern part of Washington in January, 1916, were far greater than any since 1906. There was more run off and more snow. In the winter of 1915–1916 there were two heavy snows in the early part of the year 1916. One was twelve to fourteen inches, which all went off the ground, and was followed by a twelve to eighteen-inch snow after that, which went off in the early part of February. Plaintiff's Exhibit "B" is a topographical map of the Prosser quadrangle, including Sections 20, 21, 28 and 29, the lands in question; contains contour lines showing points of similar elevation on the natural surface of the ground. The contour distance is fifty feet. Where the lines are far apart would indicate a flat.

(Testimony of M. C. Williams.)

Am acquainted with the location of Sunnyside canal. During the winter season the spill-way has been left open, whereby melting water drains into the canal, and from that into Spring Creek. Referring to the course of Spring Creek from the county road south of Starkey's place there is a small rock dam near the fence, and as you go up the channel there are several other small obstructions, but the main dam is the one that has been put in by the Sunnyside Reclamation people, which is the outlet of the lateral that runs around the base of the hill. The dam is in the neighborhood of forty feet in height. Document marked for identification Defendant's Exhibit No. 1 is a blue-print map showing the area in controversy prepared under my direction, illustrating the land of Mr. Starkey, Mr. Wasson and Mr. Royer, Biggam station and the course of certain channels and drains made from surveys, and also showing the course of the water and the overflow, which was received in evidence and marked Defendant's Exhibit No. 1. After the water passed over the wasteway, the water came down in such volume that the original channel was so small as to be unable to carry the water, and it overflowed and spread out over the land, forming two channels in Mr. Starkey's field, one marked on the map "original channel" [36] and the other "overflow channel." It passed on down to the next forty below, which would be the southeast quarter of the southeast quarter of Section 20 and the channels came together again as a main channel with the exception the water spread out to

(Testimony of M. C. Williams.)

a considerable extent on the ground. The water overflowed the greater part of Mr. Starkey's land, running entirely out of the channel, and then as it comes to the south line of Section 20 it strikes the other dam, which had been put in just north of the county road, and again spread out, and as a matter of fact considerable amount of it has never struck that dam as the elevation of the dam has nothing to do with that just above the southeast quarter of Section twenty. The colored area on the map, Defendant's Exhibit No. 1, across the land of Mr. Wasson and part across Mr. Royer's land, illustrates the course of the water, and the map was made from notes of surveys taken shortly after February, 1916. The part colored purple illustrates the exterior areas of the flowage, and shows the overflow just as it happened.

Cross-examination by Mr. LANGHORNE.

Before I put the 48-inch pipe in I made inquiry from residents in and around Biggam as to flowage of water down Spring Creek, also made an independent investigation by going practically to the foot of the main Rattlesnake Hills, where the three branches of Spring Creek come in; also consulted a Government survey which I believe was made by the Reclamation Service, also took into consideration that the spillway from the Sunnyside canal would dump some water therein. I figured about twenty second-feet would be the flow. (Trans. 126.)

Testimony of Edward L. Short, for Defendant.

EDWARD L. SHORT, a witness for defendant, testified as follows:

Direct Examination by Mr. COCHRAN.

Name, Edward L. Short; occupation, civil engineer, five years in the employ of the defendant; headquarters, Walla Walla, [37] third district, including Yakima Branch. At request of defendant, surveyed the lands in question, first on the 21st and 22d of March, 1916; made the notes of Defendant's Exhibit No. 1 and measured the area of the overflow on the Wasson and Royer lands. The line between the area overflowed and the area not overflowed could be found and distinguished by small drifts or weeds that had lodged against the alfalfa. The map has marked upon it the different areas of land and those figures are correct.

Testimony of Alfred Gobalet, for Defendant.

ALFRED GOBALET, a witness for defendant, testified as follows:

Direct Examination by Mr. COCHRAN.

Name, Alfred Gobalet, civil engineer and draftsman; residence, Walla Walla. Was with Mr. Short on the day certain surveys were made in respect to Royer and Wasson lands. The exterior lines of the portion colored purple on Defendant's Exhibit No. 1 were arrived at by indications of sediment that was carried by the water and left on the alfalfa and by little straws that the water left on the outer edge. The areas in the map are correct. (Trans. 136.)

Testimony of W. H. Alsberry, for Defendant.

W. H. ALSBERRY, a witness on behalf of defendant, testified as follows:

Direct Examination by Mr. COCHRAN.

Name, W. H. Alsberry; residence, Zillah; occupation, fruit buyer and shipper; in respect to lands, have had eight years' experience in dealing in lands. Have bought and sold land in Yakima County and am acquainted with general land conditions in Yakima Valley from Yakima to Benton City. At defendant's request examined the Royer and Wasson land in March, 1916, with Mr. McDonald, Claim Agent, and Mr. Furman of Zillah, and the section foreman,—examined the land thoroughly. Noted some soil that washed upon the land, which is a benefit. On the Wasson land there were some little pockets washed out and holes now and then in the ground, just as I have had it in land I have been farming where a little ditch would [38] wash out. I have had experience in leveling off and know the cost of leveling places, and I estimate that it would take $58, counting $4.50 per day as the price for a Fresno scraper and teams to level it and smooth it over as good as it was before, which would include fixing the laterals. There was no soil washed off the Wasson place, only in these pockets. As to the Royer place, I could not see that any damage was done to it, other than that the dam was washed out which he had put in the old channel. I noted that cornstalks and other articles were lying loose on the

(Testimony of W. H. Alsberry.)

field, and were not washed, so the flowage could not have been very great.

Cross-examination by Mr. LANGHORNE.

Lived at Zillah, Washington, twenty years. Followed occupation of farming seven years.

Testimony of Cornelius H. Furman, for Defendant.

CORNELIUS H. FURMAN, as a witness for defendant, testified as follows:

Direct Examination by Mr. COCHRAN.

Name, Cornelius H. Furman; residence, Zillah, Washington, thirty-five miles from Prosser; acquainted with lands around Prosser; have had twenty years' experience in dealing with land in this country. Examined the Wasson and Royer lands at request of defendant. I estimate that labor to the value of $50 or $60 would put the Wasson place in good condition. The market value of the Wasson land in the year 1915 would not exceed $75 per acre and the Royer land would not exceed $60 per acre. The soil was not washed out to speak of, cornstalks were still there on the place, manure dropped in the pasture by horses and mules was undisturbed and lying on the flowage area just the same as on the area not flowed. (Trans. 149.)

Cross-examination by Mr. BOYLE.

Did not see this particular land before the flood, but without a water right the Royer land would not exceed in value Ten [39] Dollars per acre. I knew of some land four miles above the Wasson and

(Testimony of Cornelius H. Furman.)

Royer places selling for $75 an acre. The $50 to put this land in shape we figured was the cost of the team work. (Trans. 150.)

Testimony of E. E. Starkey, for Defendant.

E. E. STARKEY, as a witness for defendant, testified as follows:

Direct Examination by Mr. COCHRAN.

Name, E. E. Starkey; residence, Biggam, Washington, near Prosser. I lived on the land illustrated by Defendant's Exhibit No. 1 and marked "E. E. Starkey," which would be the southeast quarter of the southeast quarter of Section 20; lived there nine years was on the farm in January, 1916. In January, 1916, Spring Creek drain overflowed the western part of the north half of the north forty, breaking out of the natural channel, and flowed out inside the opening where it drains south and west to a limit probably 150 yards, spreading out over the land to what is known as the government dam and below the dam I had constructed a new channel to check up against it and prevent washout. Next day, when the water came, it broke over at the point where the arrows on Defendant's Exhibit No. 1 show at the point called "Plow land." The creek bed at that time was full of snow and ice. The first flow could not get through the channel because of the ice and snow. At the south line of my place I constructed a check, consisting of a rock dam, probably eighteen inches to two feet high, and I had a dike along the south side of my place to check the sediment. I have

(Testimony of E. E. Starkey.)

been acquainted with the Wasson lands for eight
years, and have been over a considerable part of it
during the time of the flood last winter a year ago,
and I have been over it several times since. I have
helped harvest crops on the land several times and
have mowed the crops of the Royer place. The water
entered Mr. Wasson's place in 1916 in two different
places, at the railroad east of the county road and at
the west side where it broke through the railway.
Where the water left the railroad right of way it was
from forty to sixty   [40]   feet wide and very shallow, and its greatest width was probably 350 feet.
Part of it turned east where there was a wagon road,
illustrated on Defendant's Exhibit No. 1 as "blown
out wagon track, northwest channel." In Mr.
Wasson's place it spread out considerably, but did
not flow deep at any point, and washed out the dirt
from the irrigation ditches and between the alfalfa
somewhat. I do not think the general width on
the Wasson place was over an average of seventy-
five feet. It did spread, however, to twice that width,
especially when this water come in from the west
side. The soil on the Wasson land is particularly
clean of rock; there is one little gravel bed not very
far from where these two streams met and there were
no washes to amount to anything. The wash covered
possibly three and a half to four acres. There was no
injury to the land except that was washed out by the
soil, possibly a quarter of an acre. I have had considerable experience in leveling ground having to meet
the tricks of that creek for the past nine years in

(Testimony of E. E. Starkey.)

leveling more or less. There was no washout in this alfalfa field, the little distance of six to twelve feet and no greater than across this room, and the longest ditch that was twelve inches deep was no longer than thirty or forty feet. To put this land in condition for working would be a very small matter, possibly a day and a half or two days work with a team. In fact, the ditches that were washed out did not injure their irrigation ditches. They were deeper and there was no alfalfa washed out except at the top at a few places, so the stumps set up, the plant would stand up a few inches above the ground and would leave the alfalfa still standing on the ground, but this did not cover an area half the size of this court-room. There was no material washed away to speak of. I do not believe a farmer estimating the use of the land could find enough washed ground to affect it in a serious way. I have kept in touch with the sales of land in this vicinity, and although there has been little selling in recent years, I have known of a few sales. [41] I would estimate Mr. Wasson's land, one lot at one hundred dollars per acre, but not to exceed eighty-five dollars per acre as a tract. The best part of the land was flooded over, and I would regard the fair market value of that before the flood to be about $150 per acre. I do not consider the value was changed a great deal after the flood, but of course, the damages to make up correction of the ditches, which I think would amount to $15 or $20. I have done a great deal of the same kind of repairing on my own place, and my experience

(Testimony of E. E. Starkey.)

convinces me that it could be very easily done.   I was over the Royer place several times.   I frequently cross it—over it first in 1910 and frequently since. The point where the water entered the Royer land was of fairly slight slope, there was from one and a half to three acres covered by the water.   In my opinion the value of the land before the flood would be about $75 per acre, and by the flood it was rendered less valuable to the extent of the repairs, which would amount in my judgment to probably twenty-five dollars in work.   I am acquainted with Mr. Royer's herd of Tamworth hogs.   At the time my boy was interested Royer gave me his prices, and the highest I remember looking at was $35, and he had some at a smaller price at that time.   (Trans. 162.)

Testimony of T. J. Good, for Defendant.

T. J. GOOD, a witness for defendant, testified as follows:

Direct Examination by Mr. COCHRAN.

Name, T. J. Good; residence, near Biggam; have been acquainted with the Royer and Wasson lands since 1910; knew about the water passing over them in 1914 and 1916.   The Royer place in 1915, in my opinion, would be worth $85 to $90 per acre, and the Wasson place from $80 to $125 per acre.   I would consider each place rendered less valuable by the water having passed over it to the amount necessary to fix them up, say about $100 for each place. (Trans. 170.)   **[42]**

Testimony of E. L. Short, for Defendant (Recalled).

E. L. SHORT, a witness for defendant, being re-called, testified as follows:

Direct Examination.

I made a survey for the purpose of determining the lay of the ground on that area bounded by the railroad track on the south and Mr. Starkeys farm on the north, the county road on the east and Spring Creek on the west, and made a map marked for iden-tification Defendant's Exhibit No. 2, which was pre-pared from my notes, which exhibit was offered and admitted in evidence and marked Defendant's Exhibit No. 2. I run levels on certain lines marked a, b, c and d. This map correctly shows the lay of the ground. Water on the southeast corner of Mr. Starkey's field, the southeast quarter of the southeast quarter of Section 20, would flow almost directly south from this point to the southeast and would not flow to the culvert. The line of levels marked C and D show the ground to be higher- than further east. Water flowing from Mr. Starkey's field would flow right across the county road. The arrows on Defend-ant's Exhibit No. 1 indicate the course of the water. (Trans. 180.)

Defendant rests.

Testimony of B. R. Sherman, for Plaintiff (In Rebuttal).

B. R. SHERMAN, as a witness for plaintiff in re-buttal, testified as follows:

(Testimony of B. R. Sherman.)

Direct Examination by Mr. BOYLE.

The waste water from Mr. Starkey's ranch in 1916 never went any further than this corner, referring to the corner caused by the county road crossing the railroad.

Plaintiff rests.

THEREUPON, the defendant requested the Court to instruct the jury in the manner following:

Instructions to the Jury Requested by Defendant.

I.

Gentlemen of the Jury, under the view the Court takes of the law in this case, your verdict should be in favor of the defendant, [43] and I therefore instruct you to that effect.

The Court refused to give the foregoing instruction, to which refusal defendant excepted, and its exception was duly allowed.

II.

I instruct you that defendant had a right to build its railroad embankment at the place and in the manner which the evidence shows the same was built.

The Court refused to give the foregoing instruction, to which refusal defendant excepted, and its exception was duly allowed.

III.

I instruct you that under the evidence in this case the so-called channel of Spring Creek was nothing more than a drain for surface water resulting from melting snow in the drainage area above the lands in question and that other than from such melting snow the channel of Spring Creek carries no water and is dry for eleven months out of the year. This surface water is a common enemy against the flowage of which every land owner must defend himself, and I instruct you that the defendant in this case did nothing in respect to such surface water other than what it had a right to do in respect to its own property and in building its own railroad embankment. It had a right to place its embankment across Spring Creek drain, leaving whatever opening its engineers decided upon, and that under the circumstances shown by the evidence in this case, the defendant is not liable to either of the plaintiffs for the overflow complained of.

The Court refused to give the foregoing instruction, to which refusal defendant excepted, and its exception was duly allowed. **[44]**

IV.

Defendant's requested instruction No. 4 was given.

V.

If you find from the evidence that any portion of the lands of Mr. Wasson and Mr. Royer was overflowed by water which passed through the defendant's culvert or which passed through the break in defendant's railroad west of the county road, then I instruct you that any flowage or damage arising by the presence of waters from that source upon those lands, the defendant would not be liable.

The Court refused to give the foregoing instruction, to which refusal defendant excepted, and its exception was duly allowed.

Thereupon, the Court instructed the jury as follows:

Instructions of Court to Jury.

GENTLEMEN OF THE JURY:

To be brief, these two actions are prosecuted by land owners to recover damages for injuries to real and personal property caused, as alleged, by the construction of a railroad embankment by the defendant over and across a natural watercourse, without making adequate provision for the flow of water running in such watercourse, whereby the water was caused to overflow the lands of the plaintiffs, thereby causing injury to the real property of the plaintiffs Wasson and to the real and personal property of the plaintiff Royer.

The law of the case is plain and simple as I view it. Of course, the railroad company had a lawful right to construct its road bed along its right of way, together with the right to make all necessary cuts and fills, but where such roadbed crossed a natural watercourse the company was bound to construct a culvert or make other adequate provision to permit of the passage of the waters flowing down the stream at times of all ordinary freshets, but was not bound to anticipate or provide against [45] unprecedented or unexpected floods.

To the giving of the foregoing instruction defendant excepted, and its exception was duly allowed.

The first question for your consideration, therefore, is, did the company in the present instance make adequate provision for the free passage of all water which might ordinarily be expected to flow through the watercourse in question? If it did not, and such failure on its part was the direct and proximate cause of the injury to the property of the plaintiffs, real or personal, the plaintiffs are entitled to a verdict at your hands.

To the giving of the foregoing instruction defendant excepted, and its exception was duly allowed.

If, on the other hand, you find from the testimony that the defendant made such adequate provision, or if you find that the Government dam in Mr. Starkey's field across the Spring Creek drain had the effect to cause the surface water to run out of the channel and to overflow a portion of Mr. Starkey's field, and that this overflow water ran directly thereon, crossing the defendant's railroad west of the county road and thence down upon the lands of Mr. Wasson, and thence to the lands of Mr. Royer, and that the flow of this particular portion of those surface waters did not at any time flow down to the railroad embankment where the culvert was located, or wherein water backed up from such culvert as located, your verdict shall be for the defendant. If you find from the evidence that any of the water which passed over the lands of Mr. Wasson and Mr. Royer was in whole or in part due to the direct flow from Mr. Starkey's field, then for any injury caused by such flowage the defendant would not be liable.

If under the instructions I have given you, you find that the company was at fault, the only remaining question will be to assess the amount of damages. The measure of damages is the difference between the fair market value of the real property immediately **[46]** before and immediately after the act or omission which caused the injury. Testimony has been offered here tending to show the cost of leveling, plowing and reseeding the property, etc., but the sole object of this testimony was to enable you to determine the correct measure of damages—that is, the actual loss sustained by the land owners. That loss, as I have already stated, is the difference between the value of the property before and after the overflow. This rule of damages applies to the real property of both of the plaintiffs. Injury is alleged to certain personal property belonging to the plaintiff Royer. Where the personal property was totally destroyed of course the measure of damages is the fair market value of the property at the time of its destruction, and where the property was only injured the measure of damages is the difference between the fair market value of the property before and immediately after the injury.

With these instructions to guide you, I apprehend you will have little difficulty in agreeing upon a verdict. Much of the testimony offered here has been expert in character. The opinions of witnesses are not binding upon you. You will give to them such weight as you deem them entitled to under all the surrounding circumstances. It is a well-known fact that the expert witness always testifies in favor of the party who calls him. He may be called because he will so testify, or he may so testify because he is called. But whatever the reason, the weight of such testimony is exclusively for your consideration, and depends in a large measure upon the ability or capacity of the witness to form a correct opinion under the circumstances of the given case, and his candor and truthfulness in expressing that opinion before the jury. Guided by these considerations you will give the opinions of such witnesses such weight as you deem them entitled to.

Testimony has been offered here tending to show the market value of certain thoroughbred hogs for breeding purposes. [47] You understand from experience that the thoroughbred hog has no fixed market value like the common hog of commerce. The price paid for such an animal depends more upon the reputation of the seller and the caprice of the buyer than upon the qualities of the animal itself. Nevertheless you must determine their value where they were destroyed, and you must determine the measure of damages where they were only injured. In fixing the market value you will fix such price as the hogs could be sold for within a reasonable time by a willing seller to a willing purchaser. If you find that the hogs were destroyed or rendered useless for the purposes for which they were kept and held, the measure of damages will be the difference between their fair market value before the injury and what was or could be realized for them after the injury.

You are the sole judges of the facts in this case and of the credibility of the witnesses. Before reaching a verdict you will carefully consider and compare all the testimony. You will observe the demeanor of the witnesses upon the stand; their interest in the result of your verdict, if any such interest is disclosed; their knowledge of the facts in relation to which they have testified; their opportunity for hearing, seeing or knowing those facts; the probability of the truth of their testimony; their intelligence or lack of intelligence; their bias or prejudice, and all the facts and circumstances given in evidence or surrounding the witnesses at the trial.

I further charge you that if you find from the testimony that any witness has wilfully testified falsely to a material fact you may disregard the testimony of such witness entirely except insofar as he is corroborated by other credible testimony or by other known facts in the case.

The burden is upon the plaintiffs in these cases to establish their claims by a preponderance of the testimony. A preponderance of the testimony does not necessarily mean the [48] greater number of witnesses because you may believe one witness in preference to many if convinced of the truthfulness of his testimony. The weight of testimony depends upon circumstances, such as the demeanor of the witnesses upon the stand; their interest; their intelligence, and other facts and circumstances which go to convince the human mind and enable the jury to say that the probabilities tend in one direction rather than in another.

Plaintiffs' Exhibits "A" and "B" and Defendant's Exhibits Nos. 1 and 2 are hereto physically attached and made a part of this Bill of Exceptions.

After the exceptions above noted were taken and allowed, the jury retired to deliberate upon their verdict, and afterwards returned into court and reported their verdict, and the same was received and filed and judgment entered thereon; and now, because the foregoing matters and things are not of record in this case, I, F. H. Rudkin, District Judge and the Judge who tried the above-entitled action in the District Court of the United States for the Eastern District of Washington, Southern Division, do hereby certify that the foregoing bill of exceptions truly states the proceedings had before me on the trial of the above-entitled action, and contains all of the evidence, both oral and written, introduced by either of said parties in said trial, and all of the instructions of the Court on the questions of law presented, and that the exceptions taken by the defendant therein were duly taken and allowed, and that said bill of exceptions was duly prepared and submitted within the time allowed by the rules and order of the court, and is now signed and settled as and for the Bill of Exceptions in the above-entitled action, and the same is ordered to be made a part of the record thereof.

(Signed)   FRANK H. RUDKIN,

Judge. **[49]**

District of Oregon.

I hereby certify that I served the within Bill of Exceptions upon Mr. Lon Boyle, by mailing a copy thereof to him in the following manner. A certified copy of said Bill of Evceptions was duly enveloped, envelope plainly and legally addressed to Mr. Lon Boyle, Prosser, Washington, and with postage prepaid the envelope was deposited in the United States Postoffice at Portland, Oregon.

Dated this 16th day of July, 1918.

(Signed)   C. E. COCHRAN,

One of the Attorneys for Defendant.

[Endorsements]: Bill of Exceptions. Filed in the U. S. District Court, Eastern Dist. of Washington. Aug. 6, 1918. Wm. H. Hare, Clerk. By C. Roy King, Deputy.   **[50]**

In the District Court of the United States for the Eastern District of Washington, Southern Division.

No. 641.

OREGON–WASHINGTON RAILROAD & NAVIGATION COMPANY, a Corporation,

Plaintiff in Error,

vs.

PRESTON ROYER,

Defendant in Error.

Assignment of Error.

Comes now the plaintiff in error above named, appearing by A. C. Spencer and C. E. Cochran, its attorneys of record, and says that the judgment and final order of this Court, made and entered in the above-entitled court on the 9th day of May, 1918, in favor of the defendant in error and against plaintiff in error, is erroneous and against the just rights of this plaintiff in error and files herein together with its petition for writ of error from said judgment and order, the following assignments of error, which it avers occurred upon the trial of said cause:

I.

The Court erred in refusing to give to the jury the following instruction requested by plaintiff in error:

Gentlemen of the Jury, under the view the Court takes of the law in this case, your verdict should be in favor of the defendant, and I therefore instruct you to that effect.

II.

The Court erred in declining to give to the Jury the following instruction requested by the defendant-plaintiff in error:

I instruct you that defendant had a right to build its railroad embankment at the place and in the manner which the evidence shows the same was built. [51]

III.

The Court erred in refusing to give to the Jury the following instruction:

I instruct you that under the evidence in this case the so-called channel of Spring Creek was nothing more than a drain for surface water resulting from melting snow in the drainage area above the lands in question and that other than from such melting snow the channel of Spring Creek carries no water and is dry for eleven months out of the year. This surface water is a common enemy against the flowage of which every land owner must defend himself, and I instruct you that the defendant in this case did nothing in respect to such surface water other than what it had a right to do in respect to its own property and in building its own railroad embankment. It had a right to place its embankment across Spring Creek drain, leaving whatever opening its engineers decided upon, and that under the circumstances shown by the evidence in this case, the defendant is not liable to either of the plaintiffs for the overflow complained of.

IV.

The Court erred in refusing to give to the jury the following instruction requested by defendant-plaintiff in error:

If you find from the evidence that any portion of the lands of Mr. Wasson and Mr. Royer was overflowed by water which passed through the defendant's culvert or which passed through the break of defendant's railroad west of the county road, then I instruct you that any flowage or damage arising by the presence of waters from that source upon those lands, the defendant would not be liable.

V.

The Court erred in giving to the jury the following instruction:

The law of the case is plain and simple as I view it. Of course, the railroad company had a lawful right to construct its roadbed along its right of way, together with the right to make all necessary cuts and fills, but where such roadbed crossed a natural watercourse the company was bound to construct a culvert or make other adequate provision to permit the passage of the waters flowing down the stream at times of all

ordinary freshets, but was not bound to anticipate or provide against unprecedented or unexpected floods.

And also the following instruction:

The first question for your consideration, therefore, is, did the company in the present instance
make adequate provision for the free passage of
all water which might ordinarily be expected to
flow through the watercourse in question? If
it did not, and such failure on its part [52]
was the direct and proximate cause of the injury
to the property of the plaintiffs, real and personal, the plaintiffs are entitled to a verdict at
your hands.

VI.

The Court erred in entering judgment in favor of
the defendant in error and against the plaintiff in
error for the sum of Eight Hundred Fifty ($850.00)
Dollars, together with the costs and disbursements
of the action, and in not dismissing said complaint,
and in refusing and declining to enter judgment in
favor of the plaintiff in error.

WHEREFORE, the plaintiff in error and defendant in the judgment, prays that said judgment of the
District Court be reversed with directions to the
District Court to enter a judgment in favor of the
defendant, plaintiff in error herein.

(Signed)   A. C. SPENCER,
C. E. COCHRAN,
Attorneys for Plaintiff in Error.

[Endorsements]: Assignment of Error. Filed in
the U. S. District Court, Eastern Dist. of Washing-

ton.   Aug. 6, 1918.   Wm. H. Hare, Clerk.   By C.
Roy King, Deputy.   **[53]**

---

*In the District Court of the United States for the
Eastern District of Washington, Southern Division.*

No. 641.

OREGON-WASHINGTON RAILROAD & NAVI-
GATION COMPANY, a Corporation,
Plaintiff in Error,

vs.

PRESTON ROYER,
Defendant in Error.

Petition for Writ of Error.

Oregon-Washington Railroad & Navigation Company, a corporation, conceiving itself aggrieved by
the final order of this Court, made and entered
against it and in favor of the defendant in error, on
the 9th day of May, 1918, and in respect to the rulings and instructions in said cause made, as set
forth in its assignments of error filed herein, petitions said Court for an order allowing said plaintiff
in error to prosecute a writ of error to the United
States Circuit Court of Appeals for the Ninth Circuit, for the reasons specified in the assignments of
error filed herewith, and also that an order be made
fixing the amount of security which the plaintiff in
error shall give upon said writ, and that upon giving
such security all further proceedings in this court
be suspended and stayed until the disposal of said

writ of error by the United States Circuit Court of Appeals, and relative thereto plaintiff in error respectfully shows:

That by reason of the premises, plaintiff in error alleges manifest error has happened, to the damage of the Oregon-Washington Railroad & Navigation Company, defendant in said cause. **[54]**

That plaintiff in error has filed herewith its assignments of error upon which it relies, and will urge in the said above-entitled court.

WHEREFORE, plaintiff in error prays that a writ of error may issue out of the United States Circuit Court of Appeals for the Ninth Circuit to this court for the correction of the errors so complained of, and that a transcript of the record of proceedings, papers and all things concerning the same, upon said judgment so made, duly authenticated, may be sent to the United States Circuit Court of Appeals for the Ninth Circuit, to the end that said judgment be reversed and that plaintiff in error recover judgment as demanded in its answer.

(Signed) A. C. SPENCER.

C. E. COCHRAN.

[Endorsements]: Petition for Writ of Error. Filed in the U. S. District Court, Eastern Dist. of Washington. Aug. 6, 1918. Wm. H. Hare, Clerk. By C. Roy King, Deputy. **[55]**

In the District Court of the United States for the Eastern District of Washington, Southern Division.

No. 641.

OREGON-WASHINGTON RAILROAD & NAVI-
GATION COMPANY, a Corporation,

Plaintiff in Error,

vs.

PRESTON ROYER,

Defendant in Error,

Order Allowing Writ of Error.

On consideration of the petition for writ of error and assignments of error attached thereto, the court does hereby allow the writ of error to the plaintiff in error, Oregon-Washington Railroad & Navigation Company, upon giving bond according to law in the sum of Two Thousand ($2,000.00) Dollars, which shall operate as a supersedeas bond.

Dated this 30 day of July, 1918.

(Signed)   FRANK H. RUDKIN,

United States District Judge, for the Eastern District of Washington, Southern Division, who tried said cause and entered said judgment.

[Endorsements]: Order Allowing Writ of Error. Filed in the U. S. District Court, Eastern Dist. of Washington, Aug. 6, 1918.   Wm. H. Hare, Clerk. By C. Roy King, Deputy.   **[56]**

In the District Court of the United States for the Eastern District of Washington, Southern Division.

No. 641.

OREGON-WASHINGTON RAILROAD & NAVI-
GATION COMPANY, a Corporation,

Plaintiff in Error,

vs.

PRESTON ROYER,

Defendant in Error.

Bond on Writ of Error.

KNOW ALL MEN BY THESE PRESENTS, that Oregon-Washington Railroad & Navigation Company, a corporation, principal, and National Surety Company of New York, a corporation, surety, are held and firmly bound unto Preston Royer, the above-named defendant in error, in the sum of Two Thousand ($2,000) Dollars, to be paid to the said defendant in error, for which payment, well and truly to be made, we bind ourselves and each of us, jointly and severally, and our and each of our successors and assigns, firmly by these presents.

Sealed with our seals this 30th day of July, 1918.

WHEREAS, the above-named plaintiff in error is prosecuting a writ of error to the United States Circuit Court of Appeals for the Ninth Circuit to reverse the judgment in the above-entitled cause by the District Court of the United States for the

Eastern District of Washington, Southern Division, entered on the 9th day of May, 1918,

NOW, THE CONDITION of this obligation is such that if the above-named Oregon-Washington Railroad & Navigation Company shall prosecute said writ of error to effect, and answer all costs and damages if it shall fail to make good its plea, then this obligation [57] to be void; otherwise to be and remain in full force and effect.

(Signed)

> OREGON-WASHINGTON RAILROAD & NAVIGATION COMPANY,
> > By A. C. SPENCER,
> > > Assistant Secretary.

(Signed)

> NATIONAL SURETY COMPANY OF NEW YORK,
> > By LESTER P. EDGE,
> > > Resident Vice-President.

Attest: (Signed) T. L. JONES,
> > Resident Assistant Secretary.

The foregoing bond is hereby approved this 5th day of Aug., 1918, and the same, when filed, shall operate as bond for costs on appeal, and as a supersedeas bond.

> (Signed) FRANK H. RUDKIN,
> > Judge.

[Endorsements]: Bond. Filed in the U. S. District Court, Eastern Dist. of Washington, Aug. 6, 1918. Wm. H. Hare, Clerk. By C. Roy King, Deputy. [58]

In the District Court of the United States for the Eastern District of Washington, Southern Division.

No. 641.

OREGON-WASHINGTON RAILROAD & NAVIGATION COMPANY, a Corporation,
Plaintiff in Error,

vs.

PRESTON ROYER,
Defendant in Error.

Writ of Error.

United States of America,
Ninth Judicial District,—ss.

The President of the United States, to the Honorable The Judge of the District Court of the United States for the Eastern District of Washington, Southern Division, GREETING:

Because in the record and proceedings, as also in the rendition of the judgment of the plea which is in the said District Court before you, between Oregon-Washington Railroad & Navigation Company, plaintiff in error, and Preston Royer, defendant in error, a manifest error hath happened, to the great damage of the said plaintiff in error, the Oregon-Washington Railroad & Navigation Company, a corporation, as by its complaint appears, we, being willing that the error, if any hath happened, should be duly corrected and full and speedy justice done to the parties aforesaid in this behalf, do command you, if judgment be therein given, that then under your seal, distinctly and openly, you send the record and proceedings aforesaid, with all things concerning the same, to the United States Circuit Court of Appeals for the Ninth Circuit, together with this writ, so that you have the same at San Francisco, California, within **[59]** thirty days from the date hereof, in the said Circuit Court of Appeals, to be then and there held; that the record and proceedings aforesaid, being then and there inspected, the said Circuit Court of Appeals may cause further to be done therein to correct that error that of right, and according to the laws and customs of the United States of America, should be done.

Witness, the Honorable EDWARD DOUGLASS WHITE, Chief Justice of the Supreme Court of the United States, this 31 day of July, 1918.

[Seal]   (Signed) W. H. HARE,

Clerk of the District Court of the United States, for the Eastern District of Washington, Southern Division.

Allowed by

(Signed) FRANK H. RUDKIN,

Judge.

[Endorsements]: Writ of Error. Filed in the U. S. District Court, Eastern Dist. of Washington, Aug. 6, 1918. Wm. M. Hare, Clerk. By C. Roy King, Deputy. **[60]**

In the District Court of the United States for the Eastern District of Washington, Southern Division.

No. 641.

OREGON–WASHINGTON RAILROAD & NAVI-
GATION COMPANY, a Corporation,
Plaintiff in Error,

vs.

PRESTON ROYER,
Defendant in Error.

Citation on Writ of Error.

To Preston Royer and Messrs. Hayden, Langhorne
& Metzger and Lon Boyle, Your Attorneys,
GREETING:

You are hereby cited and admonished to be and appear before the United States Circuit Court of Appeals for the Ninth Circuit, within thirty days from the date hereof, pursuant to writ of error filed in the clerk's office of the District Court of the United States for the Eastern District of Washington, Southern Division, wherein Oregon-Washington Railroad & Navigation Company, a corporation, is plaintiff in error, and you are defendant in error, to show cause, if any there be, why the judgment in said writ of error mentioned should not be corrected and speedy justice should not be done to the parties in this behalf.

Given under my hand at Spokane in said district, this 31 day of July, 1918.

(Signed)   FRANK H. RUDKIN,
Judge.

Service of the within citation accepted, this 19 day of August, 1918.

(Signed)   LON BOYLE and
HAYDEN, LANGHORNE & METZGER,
Attorneys for Defendant in Error.

[Endorsements]: Citation on Writ of Error. Filed in the U. S. District Court, Eastern Dist. of Washington, Aug. 6, 1918. Wm. H. Hare, Clerk. By C. Roy King, Deputy. [61]

In the District Court of the United States for the Eastern District of Washington, Southern Division.

No. 641.

OREGON-WASHINGTON RAILROAD & NAVIGATION COMPANY, a Corporation,
Plaintiff in Error,

vs.

PRESTON ROYER,
Defendant in Error.

Praecipe for Transcript of Record.

To the Clerk of the Above-entitled Court:

You will please prepare transcript of the complete record in the above-entitled case, to be filed in the office of the Clerk of the United States Circuit Court of Appeals for the Ninth Judicial Circuit, under the writ of error to be perfected to said Court, and include in said transcript the following proceedings, pleadings, papers, records and files, to wit:

1. Complaint,
2. Answer,
2-A. Reply,
2-B. Verdict,
3. Judgment,
4. Bill of Exceptions and Certificate,
5. Assignments of Error,
6. Petition for Write of Error,
7. Order Allowing Writ of Error and Fixing Bond,
8. Supersedeas Bond and Bond for Costs,
9. Citation,
10. Writ of Error,
11. Praecipe for Transcript of Record,

and any and all records, entries, pleadings, proceedings, papers and files necessary or proper to make a complete record upon said writ of error in said cause.

Said transcript to be prepared as required by law, and the rules of this Court and the rules of the United States Circuit Court of Appeals for the Ninth Judicial District.

(Signed) A. C. SPENCER,
C. E. COCHRAN,
Attorneys for Plaintiff in Error. [62]

Address of Attorneys:
510 Wells Fargo Building,
Portland, Oregon.

[Endorsements]: Praecipe for Transcript. Filed in the U. S. District Court, Eastern Dist. of Washington. August 12th, 1918. W. H. Hare, Clerk. [63]

In the District Court of the United States for the Eastern District of Washington, Southern Division.

No. 641.

PRESTON ROYER,

Plaintiff,

vs.

OREGON-WASHINGTON RAILROAD AND NAVIGATION COMPANY.

Certificate of Clerk U. S. District Court to Transcript of Record.

I, W. H. Hare, Clerk of the District Court of the United States for the Eastern District of Washington, do hereby certify that the foregoing typewritten pages constitute and are a full, true, correct and complete copy of so much of the record, pleadings, orders and other proceedings had in said action, as the same remains of record and on file in the office of the Clerk of said District Court, as called for by the defendant and plaintiff in error in its praecipe, and that the same constitutes the record on writ of error from the judgment of the District Court of the United States in and for the Eastern District of Washington, to the Circuit Court of Appeals for the Ninth Judicial Circuit, San Francisco, California, which writ of error was lodged and filed in my office on August 6th, 1918.

I further certify that I hereto attach and herewith transmit the original writ of error and the original citation issued in this cause,

I further certify that the cost of preparing, certifying and forwarding said record amounts to the sum of (26.45) twenty-six and 45/100 dollars, and that the same has been paid in full by A. C. Spencer and C. E. Cochran, Attorneys for the Defendant and Plaintiff in Error,

IN WITNESS WHEREOF, I have hereunto set my hand and affixed the seal of the said District Court, at Spokane, in said District, this 23d day of August, A. D. 1918.

[Seal]   W. H. HARE,
                                              Clerk.   [64]

[Endorsed]: No. 3203. United States Circuit Court of Appeals for the Ninth Circuit. Oregon-Washington Railroad & Navigation Company, a Corporation, Plaintiff in Error, vs. Preston Royer, Defendant in Error. Transcript of Record. Upon Writ of Error to the United States District Court of the Eastern District of Washington, Southern Division.

Filed August 26, 1918.

F. D. MONCKTON,
Clerk of the United States Circuit Court of Appeals for the Ninth Circuit.

By Paul P. O'Brien,
Deputy Clerk.

United States
Circuit Court of Appeals
For the Ninth Circuit

OREGON-WASHINGTON RAILROAD & NAVIGA-
TION COMPANY, a corporation,

  Plaintiff in Error,

v.

PRESTON ROYER,

  Defendant in Error.

No. 3203

OREGON-WASHINGTON RAILROAD & NAVIGA-
TION COMPANY, a corporation,

  Plaintiff in Error,

v.

W. J. WASSON and MABEL WASSON,

  Defendants in Error.

No. 3204

Brief of Plaintiff in Error

A. C. SPENCER and
C. E. COCHRAN,
Attorneys for Plaintiffs in Error,
Portland, Oregon.

JAMES E. FENTON,
Of Counsel,
San Francisco, California.

FILED

OCT - 191

KUBLI-HOWELL CO., PORTLAND, ORE.

United States
Circuit Court of Appeals
For the Ninth Circuit

OREGON-WASHINGTON RAILROAD & NAVIGA-
TION COMPANY, a corporation,
                    Plaintiff in Error,
            v.   No. 3203
PRESTON ROYER,
                    Defendant in Error.

OREGON-WASHINGTON RAILROAD & NAVIGA-
TION COMPANY, a corporation,
                    Plaintiff in Error,
            v.   No. 3204
W. J. WASSON and MABEL WASSON,
                    Defendants in Error.

Upon Writ of Error to the United States District Court
of the Eastern District of Washington,
Southern Division.

STATEMENT OF THE CASE.

These actions were commenced in the month of
October, 1917, by the defendants in error (who will be
referred to herein as the plaintiffs) against the plaintiff

in error (who will be referred to herein as the defendant) to recover damages from defendant for injuries to the real property of the plaintiff Wasson, and to the real and personal property of plaintiff Royer, resulting, as it is alleged, from an overflow of the lands of plaintiffs caused, as it is alleged, by the construction of an embankment by defendant on its right of way over and across an alleged water course known as Spring Creek; and by placing in the alleged bed or channel of said alleged creek a pipe or drain which, it is alleged, was insufficient to carry off the waters that flowed down through said alleged creek at certain seasons of the year. (Trans. Royer case, pp. 4-6.)

"Spring Creek is dry in the aggregate over eleven months in the year, and sometimes it does not run that month. There must be snow in the hills to put water in that channel, by the Chinook winds. The waters coming down Spring Creek is caused by the melting snow." (Testimony plaintiff Royer, Trans. Wasson case, pp. 22 and 28.)

"Spring Creek carries water only during the spring freshets; the only time the waters run there was when the snow would come on the Rattle Snake Hills and would melt and go off suddenly." (Testimony Mason, a witness for plaintiffs, Trans. Wasson case, p. 24.)

Between the 20th of January and the 10th of February in the year 1916, there were two heavy snows, one twelve to fourteen inches and the other twelve to sixteen inches in depth, in the Rattlesnake Hills, extending, gradually diminished in quantity, down to within five or six miles of the level land. There was no snow on the level land. The chinook winds started about

January 20th, melting this snow and causing an extraordinary and unexpected flood of surface waters to run in a southerly direction across the right of way of defendant; "it destroyed the roadbed at a great distance, broke through a stretch of railroad track, went over the ties, and washed a deep hole through the railroad" on to the lands of plaintiffs. (Testimony of plaintiff Royer, Trans. his case, p. 27.)

At the time of the alleged injury to the property of plaintiffs, the line of railroad of defendant ran in a westerly direction between the City of Walla Walla, Washington, and the City of North Yakima, Yakima County, Washington, and ran through Benton County, Washington, over and across a part of the land of plaintiff Wasson and north of, but near the land of plaintiff Royer.

A ravine or hollow which the plaintiffs denominate "a channel" originates in the Rattlesnake Hills in Benton County, Washington, about fifteen miles northwest of the lands of plaintiffs, and runs in a southeasterly direction towards the railroad line of defendant, spreading out into a flat some distance northerly from said railway line. (Trans. Royer case, pages 2-3 and 22.)

"The annual snowfall in the hills north of the railroad right of way varies from nothing to as high as eighteen inches." (Testimony of Heiberling, a witness for plaintiffs, Trans. Royer case, pages 22-23.)

. "Spring Creek is dry in the aggregate over eleven months in the year." "The waters coming down Spring Creek is caused by the chinook winds melting the snow."

(Testimony of plaintiff Royer, Trans. his case, pp. 24 and 30.)

The defendant constructed the embankment and drain referred to in the year 1910. The drain or culvert referred to, is circular in form, and 48 inches in diameter. Before this drain or culvert was placed in the alleged channel of Spring Creek, the engineer of defendant made inquiry from residents in and about the neighborhood as to the flowage of water, and also made an independent investigation of the climatic conditions and topography of the country, and from the information obtained, it was his opinion that a drain 48 inches in diameter was sufficient in size to carry off the normal flow of surface water that came down this alleged creek. (Trans. Royer case, pp. 41 and 43.)

The cases were tried to the Court and a jury and resulted in a verdict and judgment in favor of the plaintiff Royer in the sum of $850.00, and a verdict and judgment in favor of the plaintiff Wasson in the sum of $1000. Writs of Error were sued out for the reversal of these judgments. (Trans. Royer case, pp. 18-19.) (Trans. Wasson case, pp. 16-17.)

The questions for determination upon the Writs of Error herein are:

First: Are the rights of the respective parties to these actions to be determined by the common law relating to natural watercourses, or relating solely to surface water?

Second: If such rights are to be determined by the common law, then do the complainants herein state facts sufficient to constitute causes of action against defendant?

Third: Was the evidence herein sufficient to show: (a) that Spring Creek is a natural watercourse; or (b) that any natural watercourse was obstructed by defendant; or (c) that the flowage of water on the lands of plaintiffs was caused by any negligence of defendant?

Fourth: Was the evidence sufficient to entitle the plaintiffs to recover?

CONTENTIONS OF DEFENDANT.

The defendant contends:

(a) That the rights of the respective parties to these actions are to be determined by the rule of the common law relating to surface waters.

(b) That the complaints herein do not state facts sufficient to constitute causes of action.

(c) That Spring Creek is not a natural watercourse.

(d) That there were no natural watercourses obstructed by the defendant.

(e) That the waters which flowed upon the lands of plaintiffs were surface waters only.

(f) That the flowage of water on the lands of plaintiffs was not caused by any negligence of defendant.

(g) That plaintiffs with full knowledge of the manner of construction of said embankment and drain, and of their rights in the premises, acquiesced in the maintenance thereof.

(h) That the injury, if any, to the property of plaintiffs was the result solely of an extraordinary and unexpected flood, and the damage, if any sustained, was *damnum abseque injuria.*

. (i) That the Court should have instructed the jury to find a verdict for defendant and against each of the plaintiffs.

(j) That the Court should not have instructed the jury as a matter of law, as it did in effect, that Spring Creek was a natural watercourse, but, on the contrary, should have instructed the jury that the so-called Spring Creek was nothing more than surface water, resulting from melting snow flowing in a hollow or ravine.

The defendant upon its Writs of Error has made the following Assignments of Error:

ASSIGNMENTS OF ERROR.

I.

The Court erred in refusing to give to the jury the following instruction requested by plaintiff in error:

Gentlemen of the Jury, under the view the Court takes of the law in this case, your verdict for instruct you to that effect. (Trans. Royer case, p. 52, Wasson case, p. 50.)

II.

The Court erred in declining to give to the jury the following instruction requested by the defendant-plaintiff in error:

I instruct you that defendant had a right to build its railroad embankment at the place and in the manner which the evidence shows the same to be built. (Trans. Royer case, p. 52, Wasson case, p. 50.)

III.

The Court erred in refusing to give to the jury the following instruction:

I instruct you that under the evidence in this case the so-called channel of Spring Creek was nothing more than a drain for surface water resulting from melting snow in the drainage area above the lands in question and that other than from such melting snow the channel of Spring Creek carries no water and is dry for eleven months out of the year. This surface water is a common enemy against the flowage of which every land owner must defend himself, and I instruct you that the defendant in this case did nothing in respect to such surface water other than what it had a right to do in respect to its own property and in building its own railroad embankment. It had a right to place its embankment across Spring Creek drain. leaving whatever opening its engineers decided upon, and that under the circumstances shown by the evidence in this case, the defendant is not liable to either of the plaintiffs for the overflow complained of. (Trans. Royer case, p. 52, Wasson case, p. 51.)

IV.

The Court erred in refusing to give to the jury the following instruction requested by defendant-plaintiff in error:

If you find from the evidence that any portion of the lands of Mr. Wasson and Mr. Royer was overflowed by water which passed through the defendant's culvert or which passed through the break of defendant's railroad west of the county road, then I instruct you that any flowage or damage arising by the presence of waters from that source upon those lands, the defendant would not be liable. (Trans. Royer case, p. 53, Wasson case, p. 52.)

V.

The Court erred in giving to the jury the following instruction:

> The law of the case is plain and simple as I view it. Of course, the railroad company had a lawful right to construct its roadbed along its right of way, together with the right to make all necessary cuts and fills, but where such roadbed crossed a natural watercourse the company was bound to construct a culvert or make other adequate provision to permit the passage of the waters flowing down the stream at times of all ordinary freshets, but was not bound to anticipate or prrovide against unprecedented or unexpected floods. (Trans. Royer case p. 54, Wasson case p. 52.)

And also the following instruction:

> The first question for your consideration, therefore, is, did the company in the present instance make adequate provision for the free passage of all water which might ordinarily be expected to flow through the watercourse in question? If it did not, and such failure on its part was the direct and proximate cause of the injury to the property of the plaintiffs, real and personal, the plaintiffs are entitled to a verdict at your hands. (Trans. Royer case p. 54, Wasson case p. 53.)

VI.

The Court erred in entering judgment in favor of the defendant in error Royer and against the plaintiff in error for the sum of Eight hundred fifty ($850.00) Dollars, together with the costs and disbursements of the action, and in not dismissing the complaint and in refusing and declining to enter judgment in favor of the plaintiff in error. (Trans. Royer case, p. 19.)

And also erred in entering judgment in favor of the defendant in error Wasson and against the plaintiff in error for the sum of One thousand dollars ($1000.00), together with the costs and disbursements of the action, and in not dismissing the complaint, and in refusing and declining to enter judgment in favor of the plaintiff in error. (Trans. Wasson case, p. 17.)

(Trans. of Record, Royer case, pp. 60-63.)
(Trans. of Record, Wasson case, p. 59.)

POINTS AND AUTHORITIES.

I.

"The Common Law, so far as it is not inconsistent with the constitution and laws of the United States or of the State of Washington, nor incompatible with the institutions and condition of society in this state, shall be the rule of decision in all the courts of this state."

Remington & Ballinger's Annotated Codes and Statutes of Washington, Section 143.

This provision of the laws of the State of Washington has been construed by the Supreme Court of that state in the following cases:

Sayward v. Carlson, 1 Wash. 29.
Eisenbach v. Hatfield, 2 Wash. 236.
Wagner v. Law, 3 Wash. 500.
Cass v. Dicks, 14 Wash. 75.
Benton v. Johncox, 17 Wash. 277.
Bates v. Drake, 28 Wash. 447.
Richards v. Redelsheimer, 36 Wash. 325.
Nesalhous v. Walker, 45 Wash. 621.

Corcoran v. Postal Telegraph-Cable Co., 80
Wash. 570.

The case of Eisenbach v. Hatfield (2 Wash. 236)
was a suit in equity wherein the Court was called upon
to determine the rights of Littoral Proprietors of lands
abutting upon the shore of an arm of the sea in which the
tide ebbed and flowed. In that case the Court, at page
240, said:

> "In this state the common law is our rule of
> decision in the settlement of questions requiring
> judicial determination, when not specially provided
> for by statute."

The case of Cass v. Dicks (14 Wash. 75) was a suit
in equity to enjoin the building of a dike, and in that
case the court, at page 77, said:

> "It must be borne in mind that the water, the
> flow of which will be obstructed by the dike, is not
> the currrent of a natural stream; and therefore the
> law determinative of the rights of riparian proprie-
> tors is not at all applicable to the case in hand. The
> water which passes from the premises of appellants
> does not flow in a defined channel having a bed and
> banks, and, consequently, is to all intents and pur-
> poses surface water, and the rights of the respective
> parties in regard thereto must be determined by the
> law relating solely to surface water; and, as to these
> rights, the decisions of the courts in the various
> states are far from uniform. The courts of some
> of the states have adopted the rule of the civil law,
> by virtue of which a lower estate is held subject to
> the easement or servitude of receiving the flow of
> surface water from the upper estate. Under that
> rule, it is clear that the flow of mere surface water
> from the premises of an upper proprietor to those
> of a lower may not be obstructed or diverted to the

damage of the latter. But the contrary rule of the common law has been adopted in many of the states, and must be followed in this case, because it is neither inconsistent with the constitution and laws of the United States nor of this state, nor incompatible with the institutions and conditions of society in this state. Code Proc., Sec. 108. By that law, surface water, caused by the falling of rain or the melting of snow, and that escaping from running streams and rivers, is regarded as an outlaw and a common enemy, against which anyone may defend himself, even though by so doing injury may result to others. The rule is based upon the principle that such water is a part of the land upon which it lies, or over which it temporarily flows, and that an owner of land has a right to the free and unrestrained use of it above, upon and beneath the surface. 24 Am. & Eng. Enc. Law, pp. 906, 917; Ang. Watercourses (7th ed.) Sec. 1080.

"If one in the lawful exercise of his right to control, manage, or improve his own land, finds it necessary to protect it from surface water flowing from higher land, he may do so; and if damage thereby results to another, it is *damnum absque injuria.*"

The case of Benton v. Johncox, 17 Wash. 281, was an action by a riparian proprietor to restrain certain of the appellants from diverting the waters of a stream and conducting the same to and upon their land for the purposes of irrigation. The Court, after discussing the facts, at page 280, said:

"But it is most earnestly insisted by the learned counsel for appellants that the common-law doc-

trine touching riparian rights is not applicable to
the arid portions of the state, and especially to Yakima County; and this Court is now urged to so decide, notwithstanding anything it may heretofore
have said to the contrary. The legislature of the
territory of Washington in the year 1863 (Laws
1863, p. 68) enacted that 'the common law of England, so far as it is not repugnant to, or inconsistent
with, the constitution and laws of the United States
and the organic act and laws of Washington territory, shall be the rule of decision in all the courts of
this territory.' The language of this provision was
changed by the state legislature in 1891 by omitting
the words 'of England,' substituting the word
'state' for 'territory,' and inserting the clause, 'nor
incompatible with the institutions and condition of
society in this state.' Code Proc., Sec. 108. But
the meaning remains substantially the same. It thus
appears that the common law must be our 'rule of
decision,' unless this case falls within the exceptions
specified in the statute. Now, the common-law doctrine declaratory of riparian rights, as now generally understood by the Courts, is not, in our judgment, inconsistent with the constitution or laws of
the United States or of this state. Nor is it incompatible with the condition of society in this state,
unless it can be said that the right of an individual
to use and enjoy his own property is incompatible
with our condition—a proposition to which, we apprehend, no one would assent for a moment."

The case of Nesalhous v. Walker (45 Wash. 621),
was a suit in equity, in which the plaintiff prayed for a
decree adjudging him to be the first riparian owner of
the waters of a certain stream, and enjoining the defendant from diverting the waters of the stream. The

opinion in this case was written by Judge Rudkin, who tried the instant case. After discussing the issues in that case, Judge Rudkin in his opinion, at page 623, said:

"The Court below in its findings and conclusions, applied the doctrine of prior appropriation, and, if its ruling in that regard is correct, the decree should be affirmed, as the findings of the Court are sustained by the testimony. If, on the other hand, the rights of the parties are governed by the common-law doctrine of riparian rights, the decree is erroneous, and must be materially modified. The right to appropriate water for mining and agricultural purposes from watercourses on the public domain is sanctioned by acts of Congress, and recognized by all the Courts; but, when the government ceases to be the sole proprietor, the right of the riparian owner attaches, and cannot be subsequently invaded in those states where the common-law doctrine of riparian rights prevails. The common-law rule was recognized and adopted by this Court after full consideration in the case of Benton v. Johncox, 17 Wash. 277, 49 Pac. 495, 39 L. R. A. 107, 61 Am. St. Rep. 912, and, whether best suited to local conditions or not, the decision established a rule of property that should not now be disturbed or departed from. In the case now under consideration, all parties concerned acquired or initiated their rights to their respective tracts before any attempt was made to acquire rights in the waters of the stream by appropriation. Therefore their rights in the stream, and the waters therein flowing, must be determined by the rule announced by this Court in the case cited. It was there declared that the common law doctrine of riparian rights is not inconsistent with a reasonable use of the waters of the stream by riparian owners for the purposes of irrigation."

The case of Corcoran v. Postal Telegraph-Cable Co., 80 Wash. 570, was an action for damages for mental suffering claimed to have resulted to plaintiffs from the delay in the delivery of a telegram. The Court, in discussing the question as to whether or not there could be a recovery for mental suffering, at page 572, said:

"There is here presented the problem: Does mental suffering, independent of injury and financial loss, resulting from mere negligent delay in the transmission and delivery of a telegram, render the company, accepting such telegram for transmission and receiving pay therefor, liable in damages, measurable in money, to the sender and receiver whose mental suffering results from such negligent delay? Counsel for appellant contend that there is no such liability in this state, in view of the common law, which is in force here, in the absence of controlling statutory law. We have no statute in this state relating to damages of this nature. Since the beginning of civil government in the territory now occupied by our state, the common law has been the rule of decision in our Courts, except where other rules are prescribed by the Constitution or statutes. It has been so declared by legislative enactment. Section 143, Rem. & Bal. Code. Indeed, it would necessarily be so, even in the absence of legislative declaration, because of the source of our civilization and institutions. We have, it is true, adapted the common law and its reason to new conditions as they arose, and thereby occasionally worked what may be regarded as innovations therein, when viewed superficially, but the spirit and reason of the common law have, as understood by our Courts, always been their source of guidance when statute and Constitution were silent touching the problem in hand."

It conclusively appears from the foregoing authorities that the rights of the parties to these actions were governed by the rule of the common law relating to surface waters.

II.

The plaintiff must frame his pleading with reference to some particullar theoretical right of recovery; and the pleading must be good on the theory upon which it proceeds, or it will not be sufficient on demurrer, even though it state facts enough to be good on some other theory. Nor can the plaintiff obtain relief upon a different theory from that upon which his pleading is based.

Bremmerman v. Jennings, 101 Ind. 253.
Holderman v. Miller, 102 Ind. 356.
Whitten v. Griswold, 60 Ore. 318.

The generral scope of the complaints in these cases plainly shows that they were drawn distinctly upon the theory that the injury, if any, to the property of the plaintiffs was caused solely by an extraordinary and unexpected flood of surface water, resulting from melting snow flowing in a hollow or ravine, and that it was not the intention of the pleader to state a cause of action for injuries to property resulting from the obstruction of a natural watercourse.

To this theory plaintiffs were bound through all the stages of the trial, and upon it they must stand or fall.

III.

The complaints in these actions do not, nor does either thereof state facts sufficient to constitute a cause of action.

The complaints and each thereof are insufficient for that:

(a) It appears upon the face of each thereof that the embankment and drain, whereby it is alleged the waters from Spring Creek were caused to flow on the lands of plaintiffs, were constructed by defendant company on its own right of way.

(b) It does not appear from the complaints or either thereof that Spring Creek is a natural watercourse.

(c) It does not appear from the complaints or either thereof that the natural flow of any watercourse was obstructed by defendant.

(d) It appears from each of the complaints that the water which flowed upon the lands of plaintiffs was surface water only.

(e) It does not appear from the complaints or either thereof, that the alleged flowage of water on the lands of the plaintiffs was caused by the negligence or tortious conduct of defendant.

(f) It appears from said complaints and each thereof, that the plaintiffs with full knowledge of the manner of construct ion of said embankment and drain and of their rights, acquiesced in the maintenance thereof.

Broom's Legal Maxims, p. 265.
Cooley on Torts, p. 187.
Churchill v. Baumann, 95 Cal. 541.
Southern Marble Co. v. Darnell, 94 Ga. 231.
Groff v. Ankenbrandt, 124 Ill. 51.

Lake Erie & Western R. R. Co. v. Hilfiker, 12
Ind. App. 280.

C. C. C. & St. L. R. Co. v. Huddleston, 21 Ind.
App. 261.

Abbott v. K. C. St. J. & C. B. Ry. Co., 83 Mo.
271.

Collier v. C. & A. Ry. Co., 48 Mo. App. 398.

Koch v. Del. L. & W. R. R. Co., 54 N. J. Law,
401.

Wagner v. L. I. R. R. Co., 2 Hun. 633.

Rothschild v. Title Guaranty & Trust Co., 204
N. Y. 458.

Pa. Railroad Co. v. Washburn, 50 Fed. 335.

Post v. Beacon Vacuum Pump & Elec. Co., 89
. Fed. 1.

The case of Collier v. The C. & A. Ry. Co., 48 Mo.
App. 398, was an action to recover damages for the overflow of the plaintiff's lands caused by the backing up of
surface water from the defendant's roadbed. The Court,
in discussing the sufficiency of the complaint at page
401 said:

"The plaintiff contends that the trial Court
erred in sustaining the demurrer to the evidence
adduced in support of the first count of the petition.
There was not a *scintilla* of evidence tending in the
remotest degree to show that the defendant was
guilty of negligence in the construction of its roadbed; consequently, under the well-settled law of this
state, the injury thereby done to the plaintiff's lands
must be considered as the natural and necessary consequence of what the defendant had the right to do
under its charter, and the damage was *damnum
absque injuria*.

"There was no error in sustaining the defendant's demurrer. The defendant had the right to
construct on its right of way, except where intersected by natural waterways, a solid and continuous
roadbed for its track. No one had a right to have
the surface water flow across its right of way, but
on the contrary, it had a perfect right to prevent the
water from doing so. If the declivity of the lands
south of the defendant's road and west of that of
the plaintiff, was towards the north, and in consequence thereof the surface water at any time on
these lands occasioned either by rainfall or melting
snows flowed north until it was obstructed by the
defendant's roadbed, defendant was not required on
that account to construct drains or ditches through
its roadbed in order to allow such surface water to
continue its onward course north. Such water was
a common enemy against which the defendant had
the right to protect itself.

The case of Koch v. Del. L. & W. R. R. Co. (54
N. J. Law 401), was also an action for damages for
the overflow of plaintiff's land, and in that case the
Court said:

"The plaintiff complains that the defendant, by
certain tortious acts, has caused the waters of the
Hackensack River to be discharged upon her meadow land.

"We think it is obvious that the first count demurred to does not state facts from which the Court
can see that the plaintiff has the cause of action
alleged. The allegations and statements are, that
the meadow land in question, 'being thoroughly
drained and dry,' the defendant made 'an opening
through the causeway or roadbed of its railroad' and

thereby caused the 'tidewater from the Hackensack River' to be discharged upon the meadow lands aforesaid &c. It is impossible, from such a narration, for the Court to pronounce that a wrong in this matter has been committed by the railroad company. There is not even an averment in the count that, by reason of the natural situation or of any grant to that effect, the plaintiff has the right to require that the roadway of the defendant shall keep off this water from her land. In the natural condition of affairs, a landowner has the right to remove, either in whole or in part, any structure that he has erected upon his property, although such removal will prove detrimental to the possessions of others. The cutting complained of does not appear to be an actionable wrong.

"The fourth count we regard as also insufficient, on the same ground.

"The second and third counts are somewhat variant from the two just disposed of. They, each, in substance, aver, that the meadow land in question had been dry and drained for a number of years, and that the defendant kept and maintained a ditch alongside its roadbed, and thereby caused the water of the Hackensack River aforesaid to be discharged through said ditch last aforesaid, and through an opening through said causeway or roadbed upon the said meadow lands, etc.

"These counts, we think, are also essentially defective. Neither of them shows, with such reasonable certainty as the laws of pleading require, that, by doing the act stated, the defendant has committed a tort. The radical defect of this pleading is, that

it does not declare that the water of the Hackensack, flowing in its natural condition, would not
have inundated this meadow land to the same or to
a greater extent than is now the case by reason of
the ditch complained of. It does not appear that
this act of the defendant has, to the injury of the
plaintiff, altered the natural condition of the land.
To elucidate, let us suppose this case: That the
river water naturally would overflow this meadow;
that the defendant prevented such overflow by
building an embankment on its own land, and that
subsequently it cut a ditch along and through such
structure and thereby let in as much water as had
originally overflowed the property of the plaintiff;
it is obvious that such a course of conduct would
not have laid any ground of action, and yet, for
aught that appears in these counts, the defendant
may have done nothing more than the things above
supposed."

The case of Wagner v. Long Island R. R. Co., 2
Hun. 633, was also an action to recover damages against
a railway company for constructing an embankment for
its road along and across the adjoining land of plaintiff,
and in that case, the Court said:

"This is an action to recover damages against
the defendant for constructing the embankment for
its road along and across the adjoining land of the
plaintiff, whereby the usual flow of the water across
and off from the plaintiff's premises, was dammed
up and obstructed, and caused to accumulate, whereby the plaintiff sustained damage. It seems to be
perfectly well settled, that no action will lie against
a party for so using or changing the surface of his

own land, as to dam up and obstruct the flow of surface water, which has been accustomed to flow over and across the land of his neighbor. The question involved in the case, is precisely the same in principle, as that which came before the Supreme Court of Massachusetts, in Parks v. The City of Newburyport. In that case, the judge on the trial had instructed the jury, that if, for twenty years, the water accumulating upon the land in the rear of the lots in question, had been accustomed to find its outlet over the land of the defendants, and the same had been obstructed by the acts of the defendants, in such a way as to turn it from their own land across land of the plaintiff, and occasion substantial injury to the property of the plaintiff, without his fault, or want of care on his part, then the defendants would be liable. The plaintiff having recovered under this instruction, the verdict was set aside upon the following opinion by the Court: 'The declaration is for obstructing a watercourse, and the instruction allowed the jury to find for the plaintiff, though there was no watercourse. No action will lie for the interruption of mere surface drainage.' These principles, in the abstract, were conceded by the learned justice who tried the cause; but we think the defendant was deprived of the benefit of them by the refusal to nonsuit, and by certain instructions which were given to the jury. It was left to the jury to find, upon the evidence, whether there existed a watercourse which the defendant had obstructed. We think this was erroneous in the case, both upon the pleadings and the evidence. First, it is to be observed, that the plaintiff did not, in his complaint, claim that there had existed over this land any stream or watercourse which the defendant had obstructed. He says that 'prior to the construction of such embankment, during the winter season, large quantities of water flowed some distance above the plaintiff's premises, along and parallel with the aforesaid highway, and passed the plaintiff's premises without collecting there.' This is a statement which seems plainly to mean that such had been the natural flow of the surface water; and such, we think, the evidence on the part of the plaintiff plainly showed it to be in fact. The plaintiff's complaint was plainly founded on the theory that the defendant could not lawfully make any embankment on its own land, which would so obstruct the natural flow of surface water during thaws and freshets as to cause it to accumulate on the land of the plaintiff, but was bound, by means of sufficient culverts, or otherwise, to provide some means whereby this water should be disposed of. And the gravamen of the plaintiff's action was the alleged negligence of the defendant in constructing its embankment without providing sufficient pipes and culverts to discharge the surface water. A watercourse, according to the definitions of the authorities, 'consists of bed, banks, and water; yet, the water need not flow continually; and there are many watercourses which are sometimes dry. There is, however, a distinction to be taken, in law, between a regular, flowing stream of water, which, at certain seasons, is dried up, and those occasional bursts of water, which, in times of freshet or melting of ice and snow, descend from the hills and inundate the country. To maintain the right to a watercourse or brook, it must be made to appear that the water usually flows in a certain direction and by a regular channel, with banks or sides. It need not be shown to flow continually, as stated above; and it may at times be dry, but it must have a well-defined and

substantial existence.' * * * Flowing through a
hollow or ravine, only in times of rain or melting
of snow, is not, in contemplation of law, a watercourse.

"The plaintiff, as we think, not only failed to
allege, but also, to give any evidence tending to
show the existence of any watercourse which the
defendants had obstructed; and the motion for a
non-suit should have been granted."

The case of Churchill v. Baumann, 95 Cal 541, was
an action to recover damages for the alleged diversion
of water from a natural stream. It appears from the
facts in that case that the plaintiff participated with and
assisted the defendants in maintaining the dam and
keeping the dam and ditch in repair, and acted in connection with them in diverting some of the water from
the stream by means thereof.

The Court in discussing the doctrine of acquiescence
in that case, at page 543, said:

"Counsel for appellant make the point that no
estoppel was pleaded by defendants, and therefore
the findings of facts from which the conclusion of
an estoppel is drawn are outside of the issues. Conceding that there was no issue as to estoppel, it does
not necessarily follow that the findings of fact from
which the Court drew the conclusion that plaintiff
was estopped were not within other material issues;
nor does it follow that those findings do not warrant
the general conclusion of law that plaintiff was
not entitled to recover in this action. The facts
found necessarily imply that, from and after October, 1885, until after all the alleged injurious acts

of the defendants had been done, the plaintiff consented to those acts, and consequently was not injured thereby—*volenti non fit injuria.* In commenting upon this maxim, Mr. Broom says: 'It is a general rule of the English law that no one can maintain an action for a wrong where he has consented to the act which occasions his loss,' (Broom Leg. Max side p. 265;) and section 3515 of our Civil Code is to the same effect—"he who consents to an act is not wronged by it." Says Judge Cooley: 'Consent is generally a full and perfect shield when that is complained of as a civil injury which was consented to. A man cannot complain of a nuisance, the erection of which he concurred in or countenanced. He is not injured by a negligence which is partly chargeable to his own fault."

The case of Southern Marble Co. v. Darnell, 94 Georgia 231, was a suit in equity to enjoin the Marble Company from diverting a stream of water to the damage of the plaintiffs. The defendant Marble Company interposed a demurrer to the complaint. The Court, at page 246, said:

"It was contended on the part of defendant that the plaintiff is estopped from claiming damages, because when the ditch was being dug, he knew the purpose for which it was intended, and not only stood by and saw the work going on, but was actually employed by the defendant to assist in digging the ditch and was paid for this service. If this be true, we think the plaitniff could not afterwards complain that the ditch diverted water from his premises. It would be inequitable and unjust to allow him to recover damages for an injury resulting from this cause. He could not stand by while the ditch was being constructed at a heavy expense, or aid in the digging of the ditch, receiving compensation therefor and making no objection, and then recover damages for the diversion of the water from his premises, when he knew, or ought to have known that this would be the result of the construction of the ditch. Under these facts, he would be estopped from obtaining an injunction against the use of the ditch and the continuous diversion of water thereby."

In the case of Rothschild v. Title Guarantee & Trust Co., 204 N. Y. 458, the Court, at page 461, said:

"Where a person wronged is silent under a duty to speak, or by an act or declaration recognizes the wrong as an existing and valid transaction, and in some degree, at least, gives it effect so as to benefit himself or so as to affect the rights or relations created by it between the wrong-doer and a third person, he acquiesces in and assents to it and is equitably estopped from impeaching it. This principle is applicable to the facts found and requires the reversal of the judgment."

The complaints allege that when the defendant laid out and constructed its line of railway, "it was compelled to either bridge or fill the natural channel of said Spring Creek at the point where said line of railway and the channel of Spring Creek intersect; and that at such point, defendant railway company made a fill or embankment on its own right of way." (Paragraph 5, Royer Complaint, Trans. p. 4.)

In paragraph 3 of the Royer complaint, it is alleged

that "during certain seasons of the year, caused by the melting of snow, a large volume of water flows down, and is carried off, by the channel of said Spring Creek." (Trans. Royer case, p. 3.)

In paragraph 6 of the Royer complaint, it is alleged that "on the 23rd day of January, 1916, and between January 23d and February 17th ,1916, the waters of said Spring Creek were flowing in great quantity and volume down their natural channel, *the large volume of water therein being due to the melting of the snow,"* etc. (Paragraph 6, Royer Complaint, Trans. Royer case, p 6.)

The allegations in the complaint of Wasson and wife are identical with those in the Royer complaint, and a careful analysis of the complaints conclusively shows that the so-called Spring Creek was not a channel or natural watercouse. It was nothing more than surface water resulting from melting snow flowing in the hollow or ravine. The fact that plaintiffs in their complaints denominated it "a watercourse or creek," does not make it so, especially in view of the fact that the complaints specifically allege all through that the volume of water in this alleged creek or channel was due solely to the melting of snow. These specific allegations control the general allegations in the complaints and determine the character of the actions.

The defendant had the right to protect its property from the surface water resulting from melting snow flowing in this hollow or ravine, and if damage resulted thereby, to the property of plaintiffs, it was *damnum absque injuria.*

There is no allegation in either of the complaints that the alleged flowage of water on the lands of plaintiffs was caused by any negligence on the part of defendant. The only allegation in the complaints upon which plaintiffs can possibly predicate negligence is the following allegation:

"That said defendant company placed in the bed or channel of Spring Creek a pipe or drain 48 inches in diameter for the purpose of carrying the waters of Spring Creek under its railway bed or fill, and discharging the waters of such creek into its natural bed or channel on the south side of its fill or embankment, *which said pipe or drain was totally insufficient to carry off the waters that would flow down through the natural channel of Spring Creek at certain seasons of the year.*"

When this allegation is read in connection with the other specific allegations in the complaint to the effect that the large volume of water in Spring Creek was due to the melting of the snow, it will be readily seen that this is not a sufficient allegation of negligence.

The complaints also contain the following allegation:

The plaintiffs allege and aver the facts to be that "in the years 1912, 1914 the waters of said Spring Creek came down in such volume and quantity, the outlet for the discharge at the point herein mentioned being so totally insufficient as to cause said waters to be impounded or dammed by the embankment or fill of said railway with the west side of Spring Creek, and the raise of ground mentioned above, about the east line of the northwest quarter of the northwest quarter of Section 28 forming sides therefor, causing the said waters to back up against said fill or embankment to an unusual depth, and until such a depth had been reached as to cause the waters thus impounded to break over the fill or embankment of said railway line of the defendant company, and to flow down, over and across the lands" of plaintiffs "in great force and volume, doing great damage thereto, *but for which injury no recovery is sought in this action;* that on each of such occasions portions of the roadbed were washed away and reconstructed by said defendant company in the same manner as originally constructed, and no adequate provision being made by such company to permit the waters going down the natural channel of said Spring Creek to pass in their accustomed way, or in any other way than through the 48-inch drain pipe, as heretofore specified." (Trans. Royer case, page 5.)

It clearly appears from this and other allegations in the complaints, that although plaintiffs had resided in that community for several years, and were familiar with the climatic conditions, and had full knowledge of the manner of construction of said embankment and drain, and that the water had flowed down, over and across their lands in the years 1912 and 1914, causing, as they say, great damage thereto, they made no claim whatever for damages by reason thereof; and there is no allegation in the complaints that the plaintiffs or either of them at any time protested against, or made any objections to, the maintenance of this embankment and drain as the same was constructed; but, on the contrary, it clearly appears from the complaints, that they acquiesced in the maintenance of said drain.

The rule is well settled that no one can maintain an action for a wrong where he has consented to the act which occasioned his loss; and it is equally well settled that plaintiffs could not stand by while this embankment or drain was being reconstructed, presumably at a heavy expense, and subsequently recover damages for injuries to their property resulting, as they allege, by reason of the drain being wholly insufficient to carry off the waters that would flow down through the alleged channel of Spring Creek.

The plaintiffs with full knowledge of their rights, having made no claim for the damages which they say they sustained in 1912, 1914 by reason of the alleged faulty construction of this embankment and drain, the defendant had the right to suppose that they assented to the manner of the construction, and acquiesced in the maintenance thereof, and they were estopped by their conduct from maintaining this action.

IV.

A water course is a stream usually flowing in a particular direction, though it need not flow continually. It may sometimes be dry; it must flow in a definite channel, having beds and banks, and usually discharges itself into some other stream or body of water. It must be something more than a mere surface drainage over the entire face of the tract of land, occasioned by unusual freshets, or other extraordinary causes. It does not include the water flowing in hollows or ravines in land, which is mere surface water from rain or melting snow, and is discharged through them from a higher to a lower level, but which at all other times are destitute of water. Such hollows or ravines are not water courses.

Weil on Water Rights (3rd Ed.), page 354.

Angell on Water Courses, Sections 3-7.
Weis v. City of Madison, 75 Ind. 241.
Wagner v. L. I. R. R., 2 Hun. 633.
Thorpe v. Spokane, 78 Wash. 488.
Hagge v. Ka. City St. R. Co., 104 Fed. 391.

The case of Thorpe v. City of Spokane (78 Wash. 488), was an action to recover damages alleged to have been caused by the city so negligently grading its streets as to cause the plaintiff's premises to be flooded. The city denied that it had negligently caused the water to be cast upon the plaintiff's premises. Upon this issue the cause was tried to the Court and a jury. At the close of the evidence the Court directed a verdict to be entered in favor of the defendant. One of the questions involved was whether or not the "old channel" referred to in the case was a natural water course. Upon this question, the Court, at page 489, said:

"It is contended by the appellants that this old channel is a watercourse, and that the city was liable upon an initial grade for obstructing this watercourse. Much evidence is quoted in the appellant's brief to show that the old channel was a natural watercourse. We think it is conclusively shown by the evidence that water never flowed in this old channel, except when the ground was frozen and snows melted in the late winter or early spring upon such occasions water would flow down this old channel; but at other times there was no water therein. We are satisfied that this does not make a natural watercourse, because it is apparent that the water that flowed down this old channel was mere surface drainage over the entire face of the tract of land mentioned, occasioned by unusual freshets and nothing more."

V.

Mere surface water, or such as accumulates by rain or the melting of snow, is to be regarded as a common enemy, and the proprietor of the lower tenement or estate may, if he chooses, obstruct and hinder the flow of such water, and in doing so may turn it back upon and across lands of others without liability for injury ensuing from such obstruction.

Angell on Water Courses, Sections 4-7.

Gould on Waters, Section 267.

Chadeayne v. Robinson, 55 Conn. 345.

Robinson v. Shanks, 118 Ind. 125.

Greeley v. Maine Central Railroad, 53 Me. 200.

Morrison v. Bucksport & Bangor, 67 Me. 353.

Ashley v. Wolcott, et al., 11 Cush. 192.

Park v. City of Newburyport, 10 Gray 28.

Gannon v. Hargdon, 10 Allen 106.

Treichel v. Great N. Ry. Co., 80 Minn. 96.

Munkers v. Ka. City & St. Joe & Council Bluffs Railroad Co., 60 Mo. 334.

Abbott v. K. St. J. & C. B. R. Co., 83 Mo. 271.

Collier v. C. & A. Ry. Co., 48 Mo. App. 398

Morrissey v. Chi. B. & Q. R. R. Co., 38 Neb. 406.

Wagner v. Long I. R. R. Co., 2 Hun. 633.

Edwards v. Charlotte C. & A. R. Co., 39 S. C. 472.

Cass v. Dicks, 14 Wash. 75.

Harvey v. N. P. R. R. Co., 63 Wash. 669.

Lessard v. Stram, et al., 62 Wis. 112.

Central Trust Co. v. Wabash St. L. & P. Ry. Co., 57 Fed. 441.

Hagge v. K. C. St. Ry. Co., 104 Fed. 391.

U. P. R. R. Co. v. Campbell, 236 Fed. 708.

Walker v. N. Mex. & S. P. Ry. Co., 165 U. S. 593.

The case of Robinson v. Shanks (118 Ind. 125), was a suit to enjoin the diversion of a watercourse. In that case, the Court of its own motion gave the jury the following instruction:

"The complaint asks damages against the defendants for obstructing the flow and diverting the course of an ancient watercourse. To constitute a running stream or watercourse, for the obstruction of which an action will lie, there must be a stream usually flowing in a particular direction, though it will not flow continually; it may sometimes be dry; it must flow in a definite channel, having a bed, sides or banks, and must usually discharge itself into some other stream or body of water; it must be something more than a mere surface drainage over the entire face of a tract of land, occasioned by unusual freshets or other extraordinary cause; it does not include the water flowing in hollows or ravines in land, which is the mere surface water from rain or melting snow, and is discharged through them from higher to lower lands, but which at other times are destitute of water. Such hollows or ravines are not, in legal contemplation, watercourses, for the obstruction of which an action will lie; and if you believe from the evidence in this cause that the only flow of water in said run or ravine, described in the complaint, was rain falling upon and snow melting upon and running down from the surface of an entire tract of higher land into a hollow or ravine, and by such course carried to lower land, then said Leeper's run was not a watercourse within the meaning of the law, and then it would be your duty to find for the defendants."

It was claimed by the appellant that the instruction was erroneous. The Court, in discussing this question at page 134, said:

> "It is objected to this instruction that it is too refined and restrictive in the application made to the particular case. There is evidence, however, in the record to which it is applicable."

The case of Gannon v. Hargadon, 10 Allen 106, was an action to recover damages for the diversion of a stream of water so that it flowed upon the plaintiff's land. On the trial, the defendant requested the Court to instruct the jury as follows:

> "If the defendant placed sods in the cart ruts upon the way over his own land from time to time, as the ruts were made by the passing of the cart, and he did this merely to prevent the water from making channels of such ruts, and gullying and washing away and injuring said way and the land of the defendant, and such water was not that of a watercourse but merely surface water caused by the melting of snows and the fall of rains in the spring, and flowed on to the defendant's land from land above his own, and if in consequence of the placing of said sods the said water which would otherwise have run down said ruts was diverted upon the plaintiff's land, the defendant is not liable therefor. The plaintiff had no right that the ruts made on the defendant's land should be kept open."

The trial Court refused to give said instruction, which was assigned as error. On appeal, the Court, Bigelow, C. J., at page 109, said:

"It seems to us that the instructions for which the defendant asked should have been given, and that those under which the case was submitted to the jury were not in accordance with the principles recognized and adopted in cases recently adjudicated by this Court. The right of an owner of land to occupy and improve it in such manner and for such purposes as he may see fit, either by changing the surface or the erection of buildings or other structures thereon, is not restricted or modified by the fact that his own land is so situated with reference to that of adjoining owners that an alteration in the mode of its improvement or occupation in any portion of it will cause water which may accumulate thereon by rains and snows falling on its surface or flowing on to it over the surface of adjacent lots, either to stand in unusual quantities on other adjacent lands, or pass into and over the same in greater quantities or in other directions than they were accustomed to flow.

"The point of these decisions is, that where there is no watercourse by grant or prescription, and no stipulation exists between conterminous proprietors of land concerning the mode in which their respective parcels shall be occupied and improved, no right to regulate or control the surface drainage of water can be asserted by the owner of one lot over that of his neighbor. *Cujus est solum, ejus est usque ad caelum* is a general rule, applicable to the use and enjoyment of real property, and the right of a party to the free and unfettered control of his own land above, upon and beneath the surface cannot be interfered with or restrained by any considerations of injury to others which may be occasioned by the flow of mere surface water in consequence of the lawful appropriation of land by its owner to a particular use or mode of enjoyment. Nor is it at all material, in the application of this principle of law, whether a party obstructs or changes the direction and flow of surface water by preventing it from coming within the limits of his land, or by erecting barriers or changing the level of the soil, so as to turn it off in a new course after it has come within his boundaries. The obstruction of surface water or an alteration in the flow of it affords no cause of action in behalf of a person who may suffer loss or detriment therefrom against one who does no act inconsistent with the due exercise of dominion over his own soil. This principle seems to have been lost sight of in the instructions given to the jury. While the right of the owner of land to improve it and to change its surface so as to exclude surface water from it is fully recognized, even although such exclusion may cause the water to flow on to a neighbor's land, it seems to be assumed that he would be liable in damages, if, after suffering the water to come on his land, he obstructed it and caused it to flow in a new direction on land of a conterminous proprietor where it had not previously been accustomed to flow. But we know of no such distinction. A party may improve any portion of his land, although he may thereby cause the surface water flowing thereon, whencesoever it may come, to pass off in a different direction and in larger quantities than previously. If such an act causes damages to adjacent land, it is *damnum absque injuria.*"

The case of Munkers v. Kas. City, St. Jo. & Council Bluffs R. R. Co., 60 Mo. 334, was, among other things, an action for damages for alleged diversion from its

natural course and channel of a stream of water, causing it to flood the lands of plaintiff. In that case, the
Court, at page 339, said:

"Damages were claimed, in the second count,
for a diversion, by the defendant, in the manner
therein stated, of a certain stream of water from
its natural course and channel, whereby plaintiff's
fields were flooded. There was testimony tending
to show that no natural watercourse was interfered
with by the defendant, but that the plaintiff was
injured alone by surface water. If plaintiff's injuries were occasioned by flooding from surface
water, and not by the diversion, by the defendant,
or its predecessor, of a natural watercourse, then
there could be no recovery on the second count.
This question should have been submitted to the
jury under instructions explaining the difference
between surface water and a natural watercourse,
and defining the duties and liabilities of the defendant arising from the construction and operation of its road across or along a running stream.
This was not done."

In the case of Edwards v. Railroad Co., 39 S. C.
472, the facts which are stated in the opinion, are as
follows:

"The plaintiff who is a married woman, joining
her husband with her as co-plaintiff, brings this
action against the Charlotte, Columbia and Augus-
ta Railroad Company, to recover damages alleged
to have been done to her property, as well as to her
health, by reason of the obstruction by the defendant company of the natural flow of surface water
over and across the right of way and railroad track

of defendant. The allegations in the complaint, substantially are, that some time in the year 1867 the defendant company constructed its railway through the town of Graniteville, over and along Canal street of said town, running north and south, parallel with Horse Creek, a natural watercourse, on the west of the railway; that plaintiff is the lessee of certain premises situate at the northeast corner of Canal street and Cottage, the latter being a street running perpendicular to the former; that on the eastern side of the town of Graniteville, the land is hilly, and gradually slopes towards Horse Creek, and that the surface water which would accumulate on the eastern side was accustomed to flow, in part, down and along Cottage street, across Canal street, to said Horse Creek, previous to the construction of defendant's road, and for some time afterwards, without injury to plaintiff's premises, but that some time in the year 1878, 'the defendant negligently, unlawfully and unnecessarily' erected a large sand bank at the intersection of Canal and Cottage streets, whereby the surface water was forced back on plaintiff's premises, and has continued to maintain and increase said sand bank.

"The defendant claims that the sand bank complained of (which was constructed on defendant's right of way) was necessary to protect its roadbed and right of way from being undermined and washed away by the flow of the surface water, and, therefore, its construction was no invasion of the legal rights of the plaintiff, and the defendant is not liable for any damages which plaintiff may have sustained by reason of such obstruction of the flow of the surface water."

The Court in discussing the question as to whether

or not the water diverted was surface water or the waters
of a natural watercourse, at page 474, said:

"It is not, and cannot be, denied that the rule
in regard to interference with the flow of surface
water is wholly different from that which prevails
in regard to the waters of a natural watercourse.
We shall, therefore, confine our attention entirely
to the rule as to surface water. What that rule
is has been the subject of debate in numerous cases
in the other states, many of which we have examined
in preparing this opinion. Some of the states have
adopted what is known as the civil law rule, while
others seem to have adopted what is designated as
the intermediate rule, while others again (a majority of the states, as is said in a note to Goddard
v. Inhabitants of Harpswell, 30 Am. St. Rep., at
page 391), adhere to the rule of the common law.
In this state, so far as we are informed, there is no
ajudiciation upon the subject, for what was said
upon the subject by the late Chief Justice Simpson
was 'not intended as a final adjudication, and conclusive of said question in the future,' as he himself
expressly said in that opinion, but simply his own
opinion as to the comparative merits of the several
rules.

"But in view of the express declaration of the
law-making power, as embodied in section 2738
of the General Statutes, we feel bound to declare,
in the absence of any constitutional provision,
statute or even authoritative decision to the contrary, that the common law rule must still be recognized as controlling here, for that section expressly declares that: 'Every part of the common
law of England, not altered by this act nor incon-

sistent with the Constitution of this state, and the customs and laws thereof, is hereby continued in full force and virtue within this state in the same manner as before the passage of this act.' Under the common law rule, surface water is regarded as a common enemy, and every landed proprietor has a right to take any measures necessary to the protection of his own property from its ravages, even if in doing so, he throws it back upon a coterminous proprietor to his damage, which the law regards as a case of *damnum absque injuria,* and affording no cause of action."

The case of Walker v. New Mexico & S. P. R. Co., 165 U. S. 593, was an action to recover damages from an overflow of lands alleged to have been caused by wrongful obstructions by the company of a natural watercourse. The complaint, in substance, charged that the defendant obstructed the natural and artificial watercourses by which the waters from the north and west of the plaintiff's property, and from the Socorro and Magdalena mountains, in their natural flow and fall passed over the lands of the plaintiff and other lands, and emptied into the Rio Grande. The defendant company contended that there were no natural watercourses obstructed by the defendant's roadbed, and that the water which did the damage was simply surface water. The Court, in discussing this question, said:

"Does a lower landowner by erecting embankments or otherwise preventing the flow of surface water on to his premises render himself liable to an upper landowner for damages caused by the stopping of such flow? In this respect, the civil and common law are different, and the rules of the two laws have been recognized in different states of the Union—some accepting the doctrine of the civil law, that the lower premises are subservient to the higher, and that the latter have a qualified easement in respect to the former, an easement which gives the right to discharge all surface water upon them. The doctrine of the common law, on the other hand, is the reverse, that the lower landowner owes no duty to the upper landowner, and that each may appropriate all the surface water that falls upon his own premises, and that the one is under no obligation to receive from the other the flow of any surface water, but may in the ordinary prosecution of his business and in the improvement of his premises by embankments or otherwise, prevent any portion of the surface water coming from such upper premises. * * *

"It would be useless to cite the many authorities from the different states in which on the one side or the other these doctrines of the civil and the common law are affirmed. The divergency between the two lines of authorities is marked, springing from the difference in the foundation principle upon which the two doctrines rest, the one affirming the absolute control by the owner of his property, the other affirming a servitude, by reason of location, of the one premises to the other. * * *

"If a case came to this Court from one of the states in which the doctrine of the civil law obtains, it would become our duty, having respect to this which is a matter of local law, to follow the decisions of that state. And in like manner we should follow the adverse ruling in a case coming from one of the states in which the common law rule is recognized."

VI.

(a) Where a railroad culvert is sufficient to pass the usual amount of water resulting from melting snow, the railway company is not liable for damages to property because of the culvert being insufficient to carry off the waters of an extraordinary and unexpected flood.

> Norris v. S. F. & W. Railway Co., 23 Fla. 182.
> Cottrell v. Marshall Infirmary, 70 Hun. 495.
> B. & O. R. Co. v. Sulphur Springs Ind. School Dist., 96 Pa. St. 65.
> Central Trust Co. v. Wabash St. L. & P. R. Co., 57 Fed. 441.

The case of Central Trust Co. v. Wabash St. L. Co., 57 Fed. 441, was an action for damages for injury sustained by reason of a flood caused by an alleged insufficient culvert. The facts in that case are set out fully in the opinion.

The Court, in discussing the question of the liability of the receiver of the railway company, at page 445, said:

> "It is, however, insisted that the receiver is responsible for damages from floods occasioned by unsual and extraordinary rainfalls, because they might have been foreseen and guarded against by the exercise of ordinary and reasonable foresight, care and skill in the construction of a sufficient culvert and embankment. A railroad company, acting in pursuance of legislative authority, is only required to exercise reasonable diligence and precaution in constructing passageways for the water through its bridges and embankments, and is entitled to select a safe and massive structure, in pref-

erence to a lighter one, which would less obstruct the water. It is not liable to an action for damages if it fails to construct a culvert or bridge so as to pass extraordinary floods."

(b) A railroad company is not required to construct culverts or passageways through its embankment for the passage of surface water from the lands of others:

> Egener v. N. Y. & R. B. Ry. Co., 38 N. Y. Supp. 319.

VII.

The court should have directed the jury to find a verdict in favor of the defendant and against each of the plaintiffs in these actions, as requested by the defendant, and entered a judgment dismissing the complaints herein.

The defendant was entitled to a directed verdict and judgment against each of the plaintiffs for the following reasons:

(a) The complaints herein do not state facts sufficient to constitute causes of action.

(b) Spring Creek is not a natural watercourse.

(c) There were no natural watercourses obstructed by the defendant.

(d) The waters which flowed upon the lands of plaintiff were surface waters only.

(e) The flowage of water upon the lands of plaintiffs was not caused by any negligence of the defendant.

(f) Plaintiffs with full knowledge of the manner of construction of said embankment and drain, and of their rights in the premises, acquiesced in the maintenance thereof, and were thereby estopped from maintaining this action.

(g) The injury, if any, to the property of plaintiffs, was the result solely of an extraordinary and unexpected flood.

(h) The drain or culvert in the embankment of defendant was sufficient to pass the usual amount of water resulting from melting snow, and the company was not liable for damages to the property of plaintiffs because of the culvert being insufficient to carry off the waters of an extraordinary and unexpected flood.

(i) The defendant was not required to construct any culvert or drain through its embankment for the passage of surface water from the lands of others.

(j) The evidence in these cases is wholly insufficient to support or sustain a verdict and judgment for the plaintiffs.

VIII.

The court should have given the instructions requested in the Assignments of Error numbered I, II, III and IV. The court erred in giving the instruction set out under Assignment of Error number V for the reason that the court, in effect, instructed the jury that Spring Creek was a natural watercourse, whereas the court should have instructed the jury that the waters were surface waters only, resulting from melting snow flowing down a ravine or hollow.

The testimony in these cases is as follows:

Testimony.

GUY H. HEIBERLING,

A witness for plaintiff, testified:

Direct Examination.

County Engineer of Benton County, Washington. Plaintiff's Exhibit "A," a map of the lands of Wasson and Royer, was prepared by me. (The map was admitted in evidence for the purpose of illustration.) Spring Creek originates about fifteen miles to the north and west of the Wasson and Royer land. The county road follows along the center line east and west through Section 28, and Spring Creek lies immediately east of the county road as established at the present time. The land of Mr. E. B. Starkey is shown on the map. I took levels where Spring Creek crosses the line between Sections 20 and 29, and also where same crosses the O.-W. R. & N. right of way, and found the fall to be about 8.6 feet in one thousand. The drain under the O.-W. R. & N. tracks, where Spring Creek flows under, consisted of one 48-inch corrugated metal culvert, which was about four feet below the top of the track. At this point the line of the O.-W. R. & N. Co. is on an embankment or fill, which is about eight feet deep. The fill extends from the creek six or seven hundred feet east of the county road over in Section 28, where it passes from embankment to a slight cut.

With the exception of a few months, I have lived in Benton County since the fall of 1908. Plaintiff's Exhibit "B," purporting to be a map of part of Benton County issued by the Department of the Interior, is shown me and I can trace from this map the course of Spring Creek. The upper limits of the head show in Sections 25, 11 and 24, and it runs generally southeasterly at the head and bears southwesterly for three or four miles, then southeasterly into Yakima River.

The topography of the land from where Spring Creek has its origin is rolling, but Spring Creek is in a canyon until a short distance from the O.-W. R. & N. right of way, where the ground spreads out flat. The channel is well defined and drains twenty or twenty-five thousand acres coming down from various gulches into the Spring Creek Gulch. The fall from the source to where it crosses the right of way of the O.-W. R. & N. Co. is something over two thousand feet. Where Spring Creek runs under the right of way of the O.-W. R. & N. Co. there has been a fill on each side of the creek. On the east side the grade tapers gradually to nothing in about thirteen or fourteen hundred feet. The annual snowfall in the hills north of the railroad right of way varies from nothing to as high as 18 inches. In January, 1916, at Prosser there were two different snowfalls— one of these twelve and the other fifteen inches—and there is usually heavier snow in the hills. This snow generally begins to melt whenever the chinook winds come, and it melts rapidly then.

Cross Examination.

Spring Creek, from the section line of 20 and 29, meanders back and forth. One standing in the bottom of Spring Creek at the O.-W. R. & N. right of way, attempting to look up towards Mr. Starkey's place north, will find the creek so crooked that a straight line vision will not pass up the creek channel. The gully from which Spring Creek comes out of the Rattlesnake Hills begins to widen at point about the north line of the southeast quarter of the southeast quarter of Section 20. Mr. Starkey has quite a flat place—about ten

acres or so, which would be located substantially in the
southeast quarter of the southeast quarter of the southeast quarter of section 20. The base of the bluff is
about the section line between 20 and 29 on the west
side of the creek. (Trans. pp. 19-21.)

PRESTON ROYER,

One of plaintiffs, as a witness on the part of plaintiff
·Wasson, testified:

Direct Examination.

I own the lands described in my complaint, amounting to practicaally nineteen acres. I bought the land in
the spring of 1914. I have lived along the branches of
Spring Creek since the fall of 1905, and at one time
lived in the Rattlesnake country, Spring Creek passing
through my homestead. *The waters coming down
Spring Creek is caused by the melting snow and it
comes down in a series.* In that country our weather
goes in a circle—we will have a per iod of dry seasons,
very little moisture, poor crops, and a series of good
moisture and good crops. Spring Creek runs practically
every year, when there are good crops, and in dry seasons, does not run at all. In 1907, the water down Spring
Creek went through a 24-foot breach, practically four
feet deep. There is no outlet other than under the O.-
W. R. & N. crossing. From 1906 to 1912, there was
water in more or less volume running each season. This
water flows to the Yakima River, and the only outlet
is under the O.-W. R. & N. tracks. In June or July,
1914, the water crossed my ranch.

In 1914, in the last of June or the first of July,
there was a freshet in the Rattlesnake Hills in the water-

shed of Spring Creek, and water ran down this creek
to where same intersects with the O.-W.,R. & N., where
they have a 48-inch pipe. It was not sufficient to carry
the water off and it backed the water up and it flooded
straight east and went down the pit to the county road,
washed out the county road to a considerable depth,
and went on down where the railroad comes to the
surface grade and crossed right through and ran off for
five or six hours over our place. (Trans. pp. 22-23.)

The banks of Spring Creek vary, being well defined
for probably fourteen miles above Mr. Starkey's place,
there are distinct channels and have to be bridged; they
expect water in these, and they put in bridges. In 1916,
on January 20th, there was from twelve to sixteen inches
of badly drifted snow, and Spring Creek and the ditches
and canals up to the top of the hill were leveled across
in many places, practically no snow on the level lands
but the snow was drifted into depressions. From the
level lands to a distance of five or six miles up the
Rattlesnake slope there was no snow. Above that, there
was. Also the canyons are much deeper at the top, and
these were full of snow. The ground was frozen and
the water could not go into the ground. The chinook
winds started at 11:30 January 20th and stopped at
night. January 21st a southwest wind, mostly clear, and
checked at night. January 22d, southwest wind. The
snow melted and the high water went across my place
at 5 o'clock and run about five hours in the afternoon.
It destroyed the roadbed at a great distance, broke
through a stretch of railroad track, went over the ties
and washed a deep hole through the railroad on to the
Wasson land and then to my land. On Monday fol-

lowing there was a cold northeast wind and it froze hard, which checked the flow of the water. Weather stayed frozen and we got some snow, probably fifteen inches, until the next chinook came. The next chinook wind started February 7th and was a clear day—with from twelve to fourteen inches badly drifted snow. The wind changed and on February 9th the water started running, and on the 10th the water went over my place and over the Wasson place. The water backed up on the north side of the embankment and run down a borrow pit east and then passed across the railroad track, and down over Mr. Wasson's land and my land until it met the old channel of Spring Creek.

With respect to the Wasson land, this land slopes southeast and was planted to alfalfa, and when the water came over that land would wash holes, many of them fifteen feet lóng and three or four feet wide, making it impossible to irrigate it and impossible to go over it with a cutting machine. The water went over my land and washed the soil somewhat. (Trans. pp. 25-26.)

* * * * *

Cross Examination.

The Wasson place was covered with water in 1916 to the extent of between 40 and 45 acres. When the water came down on the 23d of January, it ran for five hours * * *. Between the 23d of January and the 7th of February about fifteen inches of loose snow fell, followed by freezing weather, and no water came down until about the 7th of February. The water would check at night and flow again in the day-time. I have been acquainted with Spring Creek since 1905. *The creek* *is always dry in the summer, above the Government canal. It is dry in the aggregate over eleven months in the year, and sometimes it does not run that month. There must be snow in the hills to put water in that channel, by the chinook winds. If it melts gradually, and no frost in the ground, you have no water in Spring Creek.* If it melts off in the winter, melts gradually, it probably runs in warm weather. *The chinook was what brought the water down.* The gully through which the water drained was practically drifted full of snow. *After January 23d, when the 15-inch snowstorm came, a second chinook wind came and the snow became more dense and more dense, until it finally became water in part, and started to flow down.* The snow that had not yet congealed would hold it back for a while until the water would break through and it would come down in bunches, and the channel on the flat between the O.-W. R. & N. and Starkey's place would possibly have a tendency to fill up and cause the water to spread. Spring Creek channel at my place was full of snow at that time and it had to work down gradually. I did not farm my place in 1916. (Trans. pp. 28-29.)

SAMUEL H. MASON,

A witness for plaintiff, testified:

Direct Examination.

I homesteaded the Wasson place in 1900, owned it about ten years. I am acquained with Spring Creek where it now leaves the O.-W. R. & N. right of way to the Yakima River, approximately a couple of miles. The channel is not regular—in places good and wide and other places deep. It is about four to eight feet at the bottom, the depth being irregular. * * * *The water came there in the channel in the spring when the snow would come on the Rattlesnake Hills, and melt off suddenly.*

These waters passed through the channel to the river, and at my place at the deepest time it was probably two to two and one-half feet deep, and in the narrower places deeper. While I owned the place the waters never came over the land. It generally followed the course of the creek—only time it got over was when banked up but not washed down over the land.

Cross Examination.

Spring Creek carries water only during the spring freshets. The time would vary. The only time I knew water to run there any time was when the snow would come on the Rattlesnake Hills and would melt and go off suddenly; would seem to absorb the water in the winter time when it went off gradually, but when the sun and wind melted it suddenly always had these freshets in the spring. The time of the melting depends entirely on the presence or absence of these chinook winds. * * * I never saw it in going off, last as long as ten to twenty days as a rush of waters, but when this water run down there in the creek it would be a month or so until it all went away when plenty of snow in the mountains, but a rush of waters would be generally two, three or four days. Spring Creek is dry a good deal of the time. *I don't think water runs there regularly from freshets over two months of the year.* (Trans. pp. 23-25.)

M. C. WILLIAMS,

A witness for the plaintiff, testified:

The railroad track runs approximately east and west, and the grade of the track where it crosses Spring Creek is one-fifth of one per cent, ascending towards Grandview. * * *

The original right of way of the railroad company was forty feet on each side of the center line of the railroad. Afterwards, the property owners immediately adjoining the right of way on the north added an eighty-foot strip clear across the forty acres at Biggam. That would make 120 feet on the north side and 40 feet on the south side. The 80 feet has since been deeded to the county for road purposes. (Trans. pp. 29-33.)

LEE M. LAMSON,

A witness for the plaintiff, testified:

Direct Examination.

County Agricultural Agent of Benton County; have been for five years; acquainted with the Wasson and Royer land prior to January, 1916; examined the Royer land at Mr. Royer's request to give him advice whether the corn needed irrigation. There were six or seven acres of corn and probably five acres or so of a poor stand of alfalfa. The soil is very fine sand, with a gravel subsoil. I examined the land in March, 1916. The flumes were torn down, the land was cut up pretty badly with little rivulets. In a good many places the surface soil was washed off entirely, so it was washed down to the gravel. The humas which was on the surface was washed off. I went over the Wasson land at the same time. The water had cut out ravines. A good many were from a foot to two feet deep—some were less. The alfalfa crown were all the way from three to ten inches above the ground. The irrigation ditches were hardly recognizable. The only practical thing to do would be to plow it up and relevel it and reseed it. (Trans. pp. 29-30.)

Cross Examination.

I did not measure the amount of land upon the Wasson place that the water passed over, although the line of the flow was fairly well marked with drift weeds. The water did not go over all of the land below the railroad track. * * * I examined the land north of the railroad; nothing washed out there but some soil washed on to it. (Trans. p. 31.)

Luke Powell,

A witness for the plaintiff, testified:

Direct Examination.

Distrct Horticulturalist, State of Washington; acquainted with the Wasson and Royer land about January 1, 1916; was with Mr. Lamson and went over the land in March of that year. The soil was washed and a number of gullies washed, from six to eighteen inches and as wide as a foot to 18 inches. (Trans. p. 31.)

William J. Wasson,

One of plaintiffs, as a witness on the part of plaintiff Royer, testified:

Direct Examination.

Owner of the land described in the Wasson complaint; was at Centralia, Washington, at the time of the flood in 1916, came to Prosser March 2d, went over the land and saw the flooded area. The irrigating ditches were washed out; the rows that you irrigate with were washed and cut crossways so that you could not possibly carry water down over it and irrigate it. I should judge in the neighborhood of forty-five acres of my land was left in this condition. * * * The water crossed the railroad track practically 150 feet wide and as it came down over my place, it spread out. (Trans. pp. 32-33.)

M. C. WILLIAMS,

A witness for defendant, testified:

Direct Examination.

I am the same witness that was on the stand for plaintiff. I was resident engineer in charge of construction. The definite location of the railroad across the land in controversy was made before I went on the work but I was resident engineer when *the track was building.* This was *in 1910 and 1911.* I have been acquainted with the drain called Spring Creek since 1907. I have been back and across this territory a number of times between those dates connected with the defendant in an engineering capacity. *I prescribed the size of the culvert at Biggam after inquiring as to water conditions from residents in the immediate vicinity who had lived there a number of years, and after such inquiry I put in a culvert 48 inches in diameter, circular in form. From the information received, it was my opinion this 48-inch diameter was sufficient in size to carry off the normal flow of surface water that came down. The water flowage conditions in 1916 in Yakima Valley and throughout the eastern part of Washington in January, 1916, were far greater than any since 1906. There was more run off and more snow. In the winter of 1915-1916, there were two heavy snows in the early part of the year 1916. One was twelve to fourteen inches, which all went off the ground, and was followed by a twelve to eighteen inch snow after that, which went off in the early part of February.* Plaintiff's Exhibit "B" is a topographical map of the Prosser quadrangle, including Sections 20, 21, 28 and 29, the lands in question; contains contour lines showing points of similar elevation on the natural surface of the ground. The contour distance is fifty feet. Am acquainted with the location of Sunnyside canal. During the winter season the spillway has been left open, whereby melting water drains into the canal, and from that into Spring Creek. Referring to the course of Spring Creek from the county road south of Starkey's place, there is a small rock dam near the fence, and as you go up the channel there are several other small obstructions, but the main dam is the one that has been put in by the Sunnyside Reclamation people, which is the outlet of the lateral that runs around the base of the hill. The dam is in the neighborhood of four feet in height. Document marked for identification, Defendant's Exhibit No. 1, is a blueprint map showing the area in controversy prepared under my direction, illustrating the land of Mr. Starkey, Mr. Wasson and Mr. Royer, Biggam Station and the course of certain channels and drains made from surveys, and also showing the course of the water and the overflow, which was received in evidence and marked Defendant's Exhibit No. 1. After the water passed over the wasteway, the water came down in such volume that the original channel was so small as to be unable to carry the water, and it overflowed and spread out over the land, forming two channels in Mr. Starkey's field, one marked on the map "original channel" and the other "overflow channel." It passed on down to the next forty below, which would be the southeast quarter of the southeast quarter of Section 20, and the channels came together again as a main channel with the exception the water spread out to a considerable extent on the ground. The water overflowed the greater part of Mr. Starkey's land, running entirely out of the channel, and then as it comes to the south line of Section 20 it strikes the other dam, which had been put in just north of the county road and again spread out, and as a matter of fact considerable amount of it has never struck that dam as the elevation of the dam has nothing to do with that just above the southeast quarter of Section twenty. The colored area on the map, Defendant's Exhibit No. 1, across the land of Mr. Wasson and part across Mr. Royer's land, illustrates the course of the water, and the map was made from notes of surveys taken shortly after February, 1916. The part colored purple illustrates the exterior areas of the flowage, and shows the overflow just as it happened.

Cross Examination.

Before I put the 48-inch pipe in, I made inquiry from residents in and around Biggam as to flowage of water down Spring Creek, also made an independent investigation by going practically to the foot of the main Rattlesnake Hills, where the three branches of Spring Creek come in; also consulted a government survey which I believe was made by the Reclamation Service, also took into consideration that the spill-way from the Sunnyside Canal would dump some water therein. I figured about twenty-second feet would be the flow. (Trans. pp. 39-42.)

EDWARD L. SHORT,

A witness for defendant, testified:
Direct Examination.

Occupation, civil engineer, five years in the employ of defendant, headquarters, Walla Walla, third district, including Yakima branch. At request of defendant surveyed the lands in questions, first on the 21st and 22d of March, 1916; made the notes of Defendant's Exhibit No. 1 and measured the area of the overflow on the Wasson and Royer lands. The line between the area overflowed and the area not overflowed could be found and distinguished by small drifts or weeds that had lodged against the alfalfa. The map has marked upon it the different areas of land and those figures are correct. (Trans. p. 42.) * * * *

I made a survey for the purpose of determining the lay of the ground on that area bounded by the railroad track on the south and Mr. Starkey's farm on the north, the county road on the east and Spring Creek on the west, and made a map marked for identification, Defendant's Exhibit No. 2, which was prepared from my notes, which exhibit was offered and admitted in evidence and marked Defendant's Exhibit No. 2. I run levels on certain lines marked a, b, c and d. This map correctly shows the lay of the ground. Water on the southeast corner of Mr. Starkey's field, the southeast quarter of the southeast quarter of Section 20, would flow almost directly south from this point to the southeast and would not flow to the culvert. The line of levels marked C and D show the ground to be higher than further east. Water flowing from Mr. Starkey's field would flow right across the county road. The arrows on Defendant's Exhibit No. 1, indicate the course of the water. (Trans. pp. 49-50.)

ALFRED GOBALET,

A witness for defendant, testified:

Direct Examination.

Civil engineer and draftsman; residence Walla Walla; was with Mr. Short on the day certain surveys were made in respect to Royer and Wasson lands. The exterior lines of the portion colored purple on Defendant's Exhibit No. 1, were arrived at by indications of sediment that was carried by the water and left on the alfalfa and by little straws that the water left on the outer edge. The areas in the map are correct. (Trans. pp. 42-43.)

E. E. STARKEY,

A witness for defendant, testified:

I lived on the land illustrated by Defendant's Exhibit No. 1 and marked "E. E. Starkey," which would be the southeast quarter of the southeast quarter of

Section 20; lived there nine years; was on the farm in January, 1916. In January, 1916, Spring Creek drain overflowed the western part of the north half of the north forty, breaking out of the natural channel, and flowed out inside the opening where it drains south and west to a limit probably 150 yards, spreading out over the land to what is known as the government dam and below the dam I·had constructed a new channel to check up against it and prevent washout. Next day when the water came, it broke over at the point where the arrows on Defendant's Exhibit No. 1 show at the point called "plow land." The creek bed at that time was full of snow and ice. The first flow could not get through the channel because of the ice and snow. At the south line of my place I constructed a check, consisting of a rock dam, probably eighteen inches to two feet high, and I had a dike along the south side of my place to check the sediment. I have been acquainted with the Wasson lands for eight years and have been over a considerable part of it during the time of the flood last winter, a year ago, and I have been over it several times since. I have helped harvest crops on the land several times and have mowed the crops of the Royer place. The water entered Mr. Wasson's place in 1916 in two different places, at the railroad east of the county road and at the west side where it broke through the railway. Where the water left the railroad right of way, it was from forty to sixty feet wide and very shallow, and its greatest width was probably 350 feet. Part of it turned east where there was a wagon road, illustrated on Defendant's Exhibit No. 1, as "blown out wagon track, northwest channel." In Mr. Wasson's place it spread out considerably but did not flow deep at any point, and washed out the dirt from the irrigation ditches and between the alfalfa somewhat. I do not think the general width on the Wasson place was over an average of seventy-five feet. It did spread, however, to twice that width, especially when this water came in from the west side. The soil on the Wasson land is particularly clean of rock; there is one little gravel bed not very far from where these two streams met and there were no washes to amount to anything. The wash covered possibly three and a half to four acres. * * * I was over the Royer place several times. I frequently cross it—over it first in 1910 and frequently since. The point where the water entered the Royer land was of fairly slight slope, there was from one and a half to three acres covered by the water. (Trans., pp. 45-47-48.)

B. R. SHERMAN,

A witness for plaintiff, testified as follows:

Direct examination.

The waste water from Mr. Starkey's ranch in 1916 never went any further than this corner, referring to the corner caused by the county road crossing the railroad. (Trans., p. 50.)

ARGUMENT.

The questions raised under points numbered IV, V, VI, VII and VIII, involving as they do practically the same questions, may be considered together.

The paramount question involved in these cases is whether or not Spring Creek is a natural watercourse, or whether it is a ravine or hollow through which mere surface water flowed resulting from rain or melting snow.

Preston Royer, one of the plaintiffs, on direct examination, testified that the waters coming down Spring Creek were caused by the melting of snow, and on cross-examination, he testified (using his own language): "The creek is always dry in the summer above the government canal. It is dry in the aggregate for eleven months in the year, and sometimes it does not run that month. There must be snow in the hills to put water in that channel by the chinook winds. If it melts gradually and no frost in the ground, you have no water in Spring Creek." "The chinook wind was what brought the water down." "After January 23d, when the 15-inch snow storm came, a second chinook wind came and the snow became more dense and more dense until it finally became water in part and started to flow down."

Samuel H. Mason, a witness for plaintiffs, on direct examination, testified (using his own language): "The water came there in the channel in the spring when the snow would come on the Rattlesnake Hills and melt off suddenly," and on cross-examination, he testified: "Spring Creek carries water only during the spring freshets. The time would vary. The only time I knew water to run there any time was when the snow would come on the Rattlesnake Hills and would melt and go off suddenly; would seem to absorb the water in the winter time when it went off gradually, but when the sun and wind melted it suddenly, always had these freshets in the spring. The time of the melting depends upon the presence or absence of these chinook winds."

"I don't think water runs there regularly from freshets over two months in the year."

It manifestly appears from the testimony of witnesses for the plaintiffs that what plaintiffs denominate as "Spring Creek" or "a natural watercourse" is nothing more than a mere surface drainage occasioned by unusual freshets or other extraordinary causes, such as melting snow from chinook winds. Under the authorities cited, the water which flowed down this ravine was merely surface water, and as such, is regarded in law as a common enemy, and the defendant had the right to obstruct and hinder the flow of such water and to turn it back, if necessary, upon and across the lands of others, without liability for injury resulting from such obstruction.

As was forcefully stated by Judge Anders in the case of Cass v. Dicks, 14 Wash. 75, "Surface water caused by the falling of rain or the melting of snow, and that escaping from running streams and rivers, is regarded as an outlaw and a common enemy, against which anyone may defend himself, even though by so doing, injury may result to others." And "If one in the lawful exercise of his right to control, manage, or improve his own land, finds it necessary to protect it from surface water flowing from higher land, he may do so; and if damage thereby results to another, it is *damnum absque injuria.*"

It further appears from the evidence in these cases that floods of the character of that which occurred in January and February, 1916, were very infrequent. The engineer of the railway company testified that:

"The water flowage conditions in 1916 in Yakima Valley and throughout the eastern part of Washington in January, 1916, were far greater than any since 1906." It appears from the testimony that there was a flood in 1912-1914, but it does not appear that these floods were periodical or were to be expected every year. The testimony also conclusivly shows that the culvert or drain constructed by the defendant was sufficient to pass the usual amount of water resulting from melting snow, and it is submitted that it is not liable for damages to the propery of plaintiffs because this drain was insufficient to carry off the water of an extraordinary and unexpected flood.

It will be noted from the engineer's testimony that before this drain or culvert was placed in the embankment of the railway, he inquired of residents in the neighborhood as to weather conditions, and made an independent examination of the topography of the country. He acted upon the information thus obtained. and no doubt was informed that the waters which passed down this ravine were merely surface waters resulting from melting snow; and in the light of testimony of witnesses for plaintiffs, he must have been informed that the alleged Spring Creek contained no water eleven months in the year, and in some years was entirely dry. Under this state of facts, it is submitted that the railroad company was not guilty of any negligence in the construction of this embankment or culvert.

It conclusively appears that the only flow of water which passed down the so-called "Spring Creek," was caused by snow melting upon and running down from the surface of the hills northwest of defendant's railway into a ravine or hollow.

The statutes of the State of Washington expressly provide that the common law, so far as it is not inconsistent with the Constitution and Laws of the United States or of the State of Washington, nor incompatible with the institutions and conditions of society of that state, shall be the rule of decision in all of its courts. There is no constitutional or statutory provision in the State of Washington governing or controlling the subject in the instant case. It therefore follows that the rights of the parties to these actions should be determined according to the rule of the common law, and under that rule surface water is regarded as a common enemy, and every owner of land has the right to take any measures necessary for the protection of his own property against surface waters, although in doing so, he may throw the same upon other landed proprietors to their damage. Such damage the law regards as *damnum absque injuria* and affording no cause of action.

As before argued by us, the complaints in these actions were drawn distinctly upon the theory that the injury sustained by the plaintiffs was the result of an overflow of surface waters. It is true that allegations are made in the complaints that "Spring Creek" is a "natural watercourse," but that allegation is qualified by the allegation that the large volume of water therein was due to the melting of the snow. The trial court, however, instructed the jury as a matter of law that Spring Creek was a natural watercourse. Our contention is that the court should have instructed the jury as a matter of law that the waters which flowed down this ravine, which plaintiffs call "Spring Creek," were nothing more than mere surface waters, resulting from melting snow which fell upon the hills in an unusual quantity. If the injury to the property of plaintiffs was occasioned by flooding from surface waters, and not by the diversion by the defendant of a natural watercourse, then it follows, under authorities, that there could be no recovery, and any damage suffered would be *damnum absque injuria.*

In any event, if there was any doubt as to whether or not the injury was occasioned by surface waters, then this question should have been submitted to the jury under proper instructions, explaining the difference between surface water and a natural watercourse. This was not done.

For the reasons assigned, the judgment of the lower court should be reversed and set aside, and it should be directed by this court to enter a judgment in favor of the defendant and against each of the plaintiffs, dismissing said actions, and awarding defendant judgment for its costs herein.

Respectfully submitted,

A. C. SPENCER and
C. E. COCHRAN,

Attorneys for Plaintiff in Error.

JAMES E. FENTON,
Of Counsel.

United States
Circuit Court of Appeals
For the Ninth Circuit

OREGON - WASHINGTON RAIL-
ROAD & NAVIGATION COM-
PANY, a corporation,

            Plaintiff in Error,

         vs.

PRESTON ROYER,

            Defendant in Error.

    No. 3203.

OREGON - WASHINGTON RAIL-
ROAD & NAVIGATION COM-
PANY, a corporation,

            Plaintiff in Error,

         vs.

W. J. WASSON and MABEL WAS-
SON,

            Defendants in Error.

    No. 3204.

Brief of Defendant in Error.

M. A. LANGHORNE,
E. M. HAYDEN,
F. D. METZGER,
        Attorneys for Defendants in Error,
                Tacoma, Washington.

United States
Circuit Court of Appeals
For the Ninth Circuit

OREGON - WASHINGTON RAIL-
ROAD & NAVIGATION COM-
PANY, a corporation,

Plaintiff in Error,

vs.

PRESTON ROYER,

Defendant in Error.

No. 3203.

OREGON - WASHINGTON RAIL-
ROAD & NAVIGATION COM-
PANY, a corporation,

Plaintiff in Error,

vs.

W. J. WASSON and MABEL WAS-
SON,

Defendants in Error.

No. 3204.

Upon Writ of Error to the United States District Court
of the Eastern District of Washington,
Southern Division.

STATEMENT OF THE CASE

As stated by counsel for the plaintiff in error,
"the paramount question involved in these cases is
whether or not Spring Creek is a natural water

course." This stream has its origin in Rattlesnake Hills, whence it flows in a general southerly direction some fifteen miles to the Yakima River (Tr. Wasson case, pp. 19-20.) It and its numerous confluents drain between twenty and twenty-five thousand acres; and while it is true that throughout its course in the hill country it flows in canyons or gullies, yet it is equally true that from the time it enters upon the flat country above the defendant's right of way until it empties into the Yakima River —a distance of some three miles or more—it flows in a well-defined if crooked and irregular channel (Tr. Wasson case, pp. 20-23.) "The channel is not regular—in places good and wide and other places deep. It is about four to eight feet at the bottom, the depth being irregular." (Testimony of Mason, Tr. Wasson case, p. 28.)

This stream does not run constantly throughout the year, but this is characteristic of the great majority of smaller water courses in similarly arid country. Nevertheless "Spring Creek runs practically every year when there are good crops and in dry seasons does not run at all. In 1907 the water down Spring Creek went through a twenty-four foot breach practically four feet deep. There is no outlet other than under the O. W. R. & N. crossing. From 1906 to 1912 there was water in more or less volume running each season. This water flows to the Yakima River and the only outlet is under the O. W. R. & N. tracks." (Testimony of Royer, Tr. Wasson case, p. 22.)

Moreover, and perhaps more illuminative of the true character of the stream, Mr. Royer on being recalled further testified as follows:

> "The banks of Spring Creek vary, being well defined for probably fourteen miles above Mr. Starkey's place, there are distinct channels and have to be bridged; they expect water in these and they put in bridges." (Tr. Wasson case, p. 25.)

Nor are the plaintiffs (to use the nomenclature adopted by counsel for the plaintiffs in error) alone in applying to their descriptions of Spring Creek terms strictly applicable to natural water courses only. The defendant's engineer refers repeatedly to the channel of Spring Creek, and testifies that "the water came down in such volume that the *original channel* was so small as to be unable to carry the water." (Tr. Wasson case, pp. 40-41); and finally admits that after making inquiry from local residents as to the flowage of water down Spring Creek, that he made an independent investigation by going practically to the foot of the main Rattlesnake Hills, where he discovered three branches uniting with Spring Creek, and as a result he figured that twenty second-feet would be the flow of water in this stream.

The damage complained of and for which jury returned verdicts for Royer in the sum of $850.00 and for the Wassons in the sum of $1000.00, resulted strictly as alleged in the complaints. The defendant's railway crosses Spring Creek on an embankment about eight feet high, and at a point approximately one-quarter of a mile east of the lands of the plaintiffs. The culvert installed by the defendant in the bed of Spring Creek proved insufficient to carry off the waters which commenced to flow about January 22d, 1916, and overran the lands in question on January 23d and again on February 10th. These waters being deprived of their natural outlet, were impounded by the defendant's embankment and followed along that embankment from the bed of Spring Creek towards the east some thirteen hundred feet, where they broke through the railroad track and washed down over the lands of the plaintiffs herein until they rejoined the natural channel of Spring Creek near the southern limits of section 28. (Testimony of Royer, Tr. Wasson case, pp. 25-26.)

Upon these facts the plaintiffs contend:

I
That Spring Creek is a natural water course.

II
That assuming the waters which did the damage complained of to be surface waters only, the defendant had no right to impound them and cast them upon the lands of the plaintiffs in increased and concentrated volume to the damage of said lands.

III

That the volume of water which resulted in the flooding of the plaintiff's lands was not due to any extraordinary and unexpected flood.

IV

That there is no claim of estoppel available to the defendant against the plaintiffs herein; and

V

That the defendant failed to preserve any sufficient exceptions to the instructions given by the court.

POINTS AND AUTHORITIES

I

*Federal courts follow the local law in determin-
ing what constitutes a water course.*

> *Chicago, B. & Q. R. Co. v. Board of Super-
> visors*, 182 Fed. 291, 31 L. R. A. (n. s.)
> 1117.
> *Walker v. New Mexico & S. P. Ry. Co.*, 165
> U. S. 593, 41 L. Ed. 837.

II

Spring Creek is a natural water course.

(a) A stream's origin in melting snow or
rain does not make it surface water.

> *Chicago, R. I. & P. R. Co. v. Groves*, 20
> Okla. 101, 93 Pac. 755, 22 L. R. A. (n. s.)
> 802.
> *McClure v. Red Wing*, 28 Minn. 186, 9
> N. W. 767.
> *Missouri Pac. R. Co. v. Wren*, 10 Kas. App.
> 408, 62 Pac. 7.
> *Gibbs v. Williams*, 25 Kas. 241, 37 Am. Rep.
> 241.
> *Simmons v. Winters*, 21 Ore. 35, 27 Pac. 7.
> *Borman v. Blackmon*, 118 Pac. 848.
> *Taylor v. Fickas*, 64 Ind. 167, 31 Am. Rep.
> 114.

Weideroder v. Mace, 111 N. E. 5.

Gould on Waters, Section 264.

(b) To be a natural water course it is not essential that the flow be continuous throughout the year.

> *Dahlgren v. Chicago, Milwaukee & P. S. Railroad Co.,* 85 Wash. 395.
>
> *Vandalia R. Co. v. Yeager,* 110 N. E. 230.
>
> *Trout v. Woodard,* 114 N. E. 467.
>
> *Missouri Pacific R. Co. v. Wren,* 10 Kas. App. 408, 62 Pac. 7.
>
> *Chamberlain v. Hemingway,* 63 Conn. 1, 27 Atl. 239, 22 L. R. A. 45.
>
> *Sanguinetti v. Pock,* 136 Cal. 466, 69 Pac. 98.
>
> *Jaquez Ditch Co. v. Garcia,* 124 Pac. 891.
>
> *Simmons v. Winters,* 21 Ore. 35, 27 Pac. 7.
>
> *Borman v. Blackmon,* 118 Pac. 848.

(c) Surface waters are waters of a casual or vagrant character, having a temporary source, and which diffuse themselves over the surface of the ground following no definite course or defined channel.

> *Dahlgren v. Chicago, Milwaukee & P. S. Railroad Co.,* 85 Wash. 395.
>
> *1 Kinney, Irrigation and Water Rights,* Section 318.
>
> *Miller v. Eastern Railroad & Lumber Co.,* 84 Wash. 31.

Harvey v. Northern Pacific Railroad Co., 63
  Wash. 669.

III

*The owner of higher land may not concentrate
at one point surface water and discharge it in a
mass upon the lower land.*

Peters v. Lewis, 28 Wash. 366.

Noyes v. Cosselman, 29 Wash. 635.

Sullivan v. Johnson, 30 Wash. 72.

Holloway v. Geck, 92 Wash. 153.

Trigg v. Timmerman, 90 Wash. 678, L. R.
  A. 1916 F, 424.

Rohsnagel v. Northern Pac. R. Co., 69
  Wash. 243.

Wood v. Tacoma, 66 Wash. at p. 270 and
  cases there cited.

Kroeger v. Twin Buttes R. Co., 127 Pac.
  735.

Keifer v. Shambaugh, 157 N. W. 634.

Gulf Sea & S. F. R. Co. v. Richardson, 141
  Pac. 1107.

Case Note, 12 L. R. A. N. S. p. 680.

IV

*Negligence is not a necessary element of the
wrong for which damages are claimed by the plaintiffs.*

*Dahlgren v. Chicago, Milwaukee & P. S.
  Railroad Co.,* 85 Wash. 395.

V

The jury's finding is conclusive that the flow of water complained of was only that "which might ordinarily be expected to flow through the water course in question."

No motion for new trial having been made, and no proper exceptions having been taken, the jury's findings settle the facts of the case.

> *Mason v. Smith*, 191 Fed. 503, 112 C. C. A. 146.
>
> *Lehnen v. Dickson*, 146 U. S. 73, 37 L. Ed. 373.
>
> *Aetna Life Ins. Co. v. Ward*, 140 U. S. 76, 35 L. Ed. 371.
>
> *Transit Development Co. v. Cheutham Co.* 194 Fed. 963.
>
> *J. W. Bishop Co. v. Shelhorse*, 72 C. C. A. 337, 141 Fed. 643.
>
> *Hamilton v. Loeb*, 108 C. C. A. 108, 186 Fed. 7.

VI.

There is no estoppel operative against the plaintiffs.

(a) Failure to plead an estoppel operates as a waiver of it.

> *Olson v. Springer*, 60 Wash. 77.

Haefel v. Brackett, 95 Wash. 625.

Jacobs v. First Natl. Bank, 15 Wash. 358.

Huggins v. Milwaukee Brewing Co., 10 Wash. 579.

Walker v. Baxter, 6 Wash. 244.

10 Cyc. 813.

10 R. C. L. 842.

(b)   The maxim is *volenti non fit injuria,* not *scienti non fit injuria.*

Drown v. New England Tel. & Tel. Co., 66 Atl. 801, at 804.

Choctaw R. Co. v. Jones, 92 S. W. 242.

VII.

A single exception to a part of a charge which embraces more than one proposition of law is not sufficient to sustain a writ of error.

Union Pacific Railroad Co. v. Thomas, 152 Fed. 372.

Chicago R. I. & Pacific Ry. Co. v. Hall, 176 Fed. 75.

City of Charlotte v. Atlantic Bitulithic Co., 228 Fed. 456.

Simkins Federal Suit at Law, pp. 114 & 116 and cases there cited.

ARGUMENT

This case comes to this court upon six assignments of error; five of which, being the principal ones, relate to instructions requested and refused or to portions of the instructions actually given. They in reality present but two questions for the consideration of this court; namely, was the damage to the plaintiffs occasioned by the obstruction of a natural water course, or was it occasioned by the impounding of surface waters and the casting of them in a concentrated volume upon and across the plaintiffs' lands.

Defendant, however, argues a number of subsidiary points, which, although we do not believe they are properly before this court, shall be first briefly discussed.

Defendant contends "that the flowage of water on the lands of plaintiffs was not caused by any negligence of defendant." (See Contentions of Defendant, Brief p. 5.) The defendant did not request the court to charge the jury that the damage for which a recovery might be had must be attributable to the negligence of the defendant, and the failure of the court to charge the jury in this particular is ordinarily to be remedied by a request for further instructions. However, the court properly eliminated negligence from its instructions; for, as said by the supreme court of the state of Washington in *Dahlgren v. Chicago, Milwaukee &*

Puget Sound Railroad Co., 85 Wash. 395—a case to which reference will be hereafter frequently made:

> "A second contention is that the instruction erroneously eliminated negligence as an element of the wrong of which complaint is made. But if it be meant by this that it was necessary for the respondent to show, in addition to the fact that the construction of the embankment caused them an injury, that the work of construction was performed in a negligent manner, we cannot agree with the contention. It is doubtless true, as the appellant argues, that it had a lawful right to construct an embankment for the use of its railway, but it does not follow that it had a lawful right to construct it in such a manner as to cause injury to the property of the respondents. It is not a case of *damnum absque injuria*. On the contrary, if the embankment impeded a natural water course, and left no sufficient vent for the escape of the water, and the water was caused thereby to overflow the premises of the respondents to their injury, the construction was negligent and wrongful as to the respondents, no matter how carefully the work of construction was performed."

The defendant next contends that the plaintiffs acquiesced in the construction of the embankment and in the maintenance thereof, and thereby either assumed the risk of injury therefrom or are estopped to claim damages resulting. (See Contentions of Defendant, Brief p. 5, and pp. 23 to 29, inc.) So far as the claim of estoppel is concerned, we believe it to be established beyond question that it is a special defense, and the failure to plead it operates as a waiver. There is no claim made that any such defense was plead or attempted to be plead; but counsel for defendant urges that the maxim *"volenti non fit injuria"* applies. It is apparent and conceded on all sides that the embankment which constituted the railroad grade across Spring Creek was constructed by the defendant upon its own right of way and as it had a lawful right to do, with the exception of the provision it made for the passage of the waters of Spring Creek. There is nothing in either complaint, and no syllable of the testimony to indicate that the plaintiffs or either of them participated in the construction or reconstruction of this grade or embankment. Conceding that they knew of its construction and that when it was last reconstructed they further knew that the forty-eight-inch culvert had previously proved insufficient, it is to be remembered that the maxim is *volenti non fit injuria*, not *scienti non fit injuria*. The maxim itself contemplates an active participation in the doing of the act or the accomplishment of the thing which is later sought to be complained of; and the cases cited by counsel for defendant corroborate this position. The person to whom the maxim is applicable is one who remains silent although under a duty to speak, or by some act or declaration "recognizes the wrong as an existing and valid transaction and in some degree at least gives it effect so as to benefit him-

self or so as to affect the rights or relations created
by it between the wrong doer and a third person."
Neither of the plaintiffs participated so far as the
record in this case is concerned in the construction
of this embankment. Neither of them was ever
under any duty to the defendant to prescribe the
character of embankment that should be built; and
neither of them has at any time recognized the
wrong as an existing and valid transaction.

Again the defendant contends that the injury
was the result solely of an extraordinary and unexpected flood, and that the damage sustained was
therefore *damnum absque injuria*. (See Contentions of Defendant, Brief p. 5.) However, the
court expressly charged the jury:

> "Of course, the railroad company had a
> lawful right to· construct its roadbed along
> its right of way, together with the right
> to make all necessary cuts and fills, but
> where such roadbed crossed a natural water-
> course the company was bound to construct
> a culvert or make other adequate provision
> to permit of the passage of the waters
> flowing down the stream at times of all or-
> dinary freshets, *but was not bound to an-
> ticipate or provide against unprecedented or
> unexpected floods.*
> "The first question for your considera-
> tion, therefore, is, did the company in the
> present instance make adequate provision
> for the free passage of all water *which might
> ordinarily be expected to flow* through the
> watercourse in question? If it did not, and

such failure on its part was the direct and proximate cause of the injury to the property of the plaintiffs, real or personal, the plaintiffs are entitled to a verdict at your hands." (Tr. Wasson case, pp. 52 & 53, Italics ours.)

It is evident, therefore, from the jury's findings in favor of the plaintiffs that they found that this volume of water did not result from an unprecedented or unexpected flood, but was such volume as might ordinarily be expected to flow through Spring Creek. Defendants, moreover, preserved no exception to this finding, and both they and this court are bound by it.

A discussion of the requested instructions which were refused by the court cannot be separated from that dealing with the concrete question as to whether or not Spring Creek is a natural water course, and the second question involved in this appeal whether the defendant caused surface waters impounded by it to be released in concentrated volume upon the plaintiffs' lands to their material damage; but the defendant's exceptions to the portions of the charge given are insufficient because those particular portions of the charge involve and state more than one proposition of law, and one of those propositions, at least, is correct. At any rate it does not lie in the mouth of defendant to urge the contrary as it itself requested the court to charge the jury in practically the identical language used. (Compare defendant's requested instruction 2, Tr. Wasson case, p. 50, with the second paragraph of the instructions given by the court, Tr. Wasson case, pp. 52 & 53.)

In the Dahlgren case, 85 Wash. 395, the court instructed the jury as follows:

"In this connection you are instructed that any drain provided by the defendant to take care of the waters of the stream, if you shall find there was one, as above, must have been sufficient to take care of and dispose of the waters flowing down the stream at times of any ordinary freshet, but need not have been sufficient to provide against any unprecedented flow of high water."

This instruction was objected to upon the ground that it invaded the province of the jury. The supreme court of Washington answered this objection as follows:

"But clearly the court here determined no question of fact. It but stated the measure of duty the law imposed upon the appellant with regard to the drain. And we think it correctly stated the rule. If it has fault at all, the fault lies in the fact that it is not sufficiently full to cover the entire evidence on the particular subject. But the remedy for this defect is to ask for further instructions, not to object to the instruction given."

Spring Creek is a natural water course.

The time available to us for the preparation of

this brief has not sufficed for a minute consideration of the vast number of cases cited on behalf of
the defendant. It is apparent, however, that many
of them are early decisions, and that the great
majority of them are from states differing wholly
in the natural conditions as to rainfall and waters
from those found in Benton County, Washington.
To all of these early decisions, Chief Justice Beasley
in *Bowlsby v. Speer*, 31 N. J. L. 351, 353, 86 Am.
Dec. 216, suggested an exception in these words:

> "How far it may be necessary to modify
> this general proposition in cases in which, in
> a hilly region, from the natural formation
> of the surface of the ground, large quan
> tities of water, in times of excessive rains
> or from the melting of heavy snows, are
> forced to seek a channel through gorges or
> narrow valleys, will probably require con
> sideration when the facts of the case shall
> present the question."

That exception has been now many times considered and has become as well established as the
original rule; so well established indeed that argument in aid thereof must be a superfluity. We
purpose therefore merely to call this court's attention to what we believe to be the more modern
definitions of a water course, and to point out their
applicability to the facts of this case.

The Dahlgren case, 85 Wash. 395, was brought
to recover damages for the alleged wrongful obstruction of a water course, causing injury to the

plaintiff's real property, which was bottom land sloping slightly to the southwest. West and north-west of it is a hill "which for a considerable distance from the property gathers drainage waters which flow in a natural channel or gully at the base of the hill, making a flowing stream throughout the year except in the driest months." In holding this stream a natural water course, and incidentally in passing upon the sufficiency of the pleadings in that particular, the supreme court said:

"Surface waters, in a technical sense, are waters of a casual or vagrant character having a temporary source, and which diffuse themselves over the surface of the ground, following no definite course or defined channel, while here the waters are described as coming from the vicinity of a large area to the north of the respondents' premises and flowing naturally and without hindrance through a natural water course and channel which crossed such premises. The description is that of a natural and regular water course, rather than that of a mere casual overflow. * * * But if the pleadings be obscure on the particular question, the testimony introduced thereunder without objection was not so. The testimony showed a stream flowing in a well defined channel, continuous for some nine months of the year, and that it was this particular channel that the appellant closed to the injury of the respondents. Where evidence is introduced without objection, the court may properly base its instructions thereon, even though the evi-

dence be broader than the pleadings."
(Opinion, p. 405.)

Again, and notwithstanding the decision in
Robinson v. Shanks, 118 Ind. 125, (Appellant's
Brief, p. 32), the appellat ecourt of that state in
the recent case of *Vandalia Railroad Co. v. Yeager*,
60 Ind. App. 118, defined a water course as follows:

> "An origin from rains and melting snow
> is by no means an infallible guide in determ-
> ining that a certain flow of water is mere
> surface water that may be damned with im-
> punity. The Supreme Court states the fol-
> lowing as the true rule:
> " 'If the face of the country is such
> as necessarily collects in one body so large a
> quantity of water, after heavy rains and
> the melting of large boies of snow, as to
> require an outlet to some common reservoir,
> and if such water is regularly discharged
> through a well-defined channel, which the
> force of the water has made for itself, and
> which is the accustomed channel through
> which it flows, and has flowed from time
> immemorial, such channel is an ancient
> natural water course.' *Taylor v. Fickas*, 64
> Ind. 167, 31 Am. Rep. 114."

And following upon that decision, the supreme
court of Indiana, in *Weideroder v. Mace*, 184 Ind.
242, 111 N. E. 5, held that language of an answer
as follows:

> "that the face of the country in the
> vicinity of appellant's said land is such as

necessarily collects on said land in one
body, so large a body of water, after heavy
rains and the melting of large bodies of
snow, as to require an outlet to some reservoir; that such water is now and has been
from time to time immemorial regularly
discharged through a 'well-defined channel'
which the force of the water has made
for it."

described a natural water course.

The standard definition of "water course" in
Oregon is to be found in *Simmons v. Winters*, 21
Ore. 35, 27 Pac. 7, quoted with approval in the
recent case of *Borman v. Blackmon*, 60 Ore. 304,
118 Pac. 848, as follows:

" 'That a water course is a stream of
water usually flowing in a particular direction, with well-defined banks and channel,
but that the water need not flow continuously—the channel may sometimes be dry;
that the term "water course" does not include water descending from the hills down
the hollows and ravines, without any definite channel, only in times of rain and melting snow, but that, where water, owing to
the hilly or mountainous configuration of
the country, accumulates in large quantities from rain and melting snow, and at
regular seasons descends through long, deep
gullies or ravines upon the lands below, and
in its onward flow carves out a distinct and
well-defined channel, which even to the
casual glance bears the unmistakable impress of the frequent action of running
water, and through which it has flowed

from time immemorial, such a stream is to be considered a water course and to be governed by the same rules.' "

We believe it must be apparent that these definitions fit the case now before the court, for here the face of the country is such that there is necessarily collected in the Rattlesnake Hills a large quantity of water which for years past has irresistibly sought an outlet for itself until it has made a well-defined channel in which water is expected to flow and which is bridged wherever the roads of the vicinity have occasion to cross it. We desire, however, to call the court's attention particularly to two other cases in this connection; namely, *Jaquez Ditch Co.* v. *Garcia*, 124 Pac. 891, and *Kroeger* v. *Twin Buttes Railroad Co.*, 127 Pac. 735. In the first case the supreme court of New Mexico examines a large number of definitions of natural water course as promulgated by the various states of the Union; and then after remarking that "the only case that seems to be in conflict with these definitions is the case of *Walker* v. *New Mexico & Sourthern Pacific R. Co.*, 165 U. S. 593, 14 Lawyers Edition 837," (cited in defendant's brief, pp. 31, 39-40), proceeds to distinguish that case in the following language:

"But a careful examination of this case (the Walker case) shows that the obstruction or embankment complained of was four miles from the mouths of the arroyo, and that the water after leaving the arroyo spread out, and became surface or flood water. It is obvious that this case rests on a different state of facts, and it appears from the evidence that the arroyo in question came out of the hills in a well-defined channel a few rods from where the obstruction was erected."

So in the present case, although the point where the defendant's embankment crossed the channel of Spring Creek was several miles from where that creek emerged from the hills, nevertheless throughout that distance the creek flowed in a well-defined channel to which its waters were wholly confined except where they were spread out by the government's dam and that made by Mr. Starkey; but that even then, they came together again and before reaching the defendant's track once more flowed in a single well-defined channel. (Testimony of Williams, Defendant's Engineer, Tr. Wasson case, pp. 40-41.)

The second of the two cases last above cited is important in that it points out another ground of distinction from the Walker case in this, that in the Walker case the waters passed over the plaintiff's land in their natural flow and fall and were then dammed by the defendant's embankment and thereby cast back from the defendant's lower lands onto the plaintiff's higher lands. "The Walker case was dealing with surface water flowing from plaintiff's lands onto defendant's lands;" while in the Kroeger case, as well as in the instant case, the waters complained of were cast from the defendant's lands onto the plaintiff's lands over which in their natural state they were not accustomed to flow.

Defendant in collecting the water behind its embankment, and discharging it in a concentrated body upon the lands of the plaintiffs to their damage, became liable to them for such damage.

The foregoing statement is of a rule so firmly established in the United States, and particularly in the state of Washington, that we do not believe it will be contested. It applies equally to the obstruction of a natural water course as to the impounding of surface water; and that it is applicable to the facts here must be apparent. The waters of Spring Creek, unable to follow their natural and accustomed channel, were dammed back by the railroad company's embankment on its right of way and followed the slight grade toward the east down a borrow pit until they reached a point on the lands of the plaintiff Wasson where they broke through the defendant's grade, washing away the roadbed and across the plaintiff's land. The exhibits in the case clearly point out the course the waters took and their discharge in destructive concentration upon the plaintiff's fields.

The supreme court of Washington in the early case of *Peters* v. *Lewis,* 28 Wash. 366, 68 Pac.

869, adopted the rule hereinabove stated in this language:

> "When surface water is collected and discharged upon adjoining lands in quantities greater than or in a manner different from the natural flow, a liability accrues for the injury occasioned thereby."

This general rule has been applied in varying circumstances in the long line of cases hereinabove cited.

Thus in *Noyes* v. *Cosselman*, 29 Wash. 635, 70 Pac. 61, the plaintiffs brought an action to restrain the defendants from digging a ditch whereby the waters resulting from rains and melted snows, which commonly accumulated in a natural depression on their lands, should be drained off and cast upon plaintiffs' lands. The lower court found for the plaintiffs, issued the injunction, and the defendants appealed, placing their main reliance upon the case of *Cass* v. *Dicks*, 14 Wash. 75, 44 Pac. 113, which case is likewise one of the main props of the defendant's argument (See Brief, pp. 9-10, 31.) The supreme court of Washington in commenting upon that case says that it "was a case where lands lying along a river were subject to inundation at times of high water unless protected by means of dikes. The defendants in that case were lower proprietors, and were proceeding to erect a large dike for the purpose of preventing their lands from being flooded during extraordinary freshets. The plaintiffs brought the action to restrain the erection of the dikes upon the ground that the same would prevent the seepage, surface water, and overflow from flowing from their premises, as it was accustomed to do, and ·thus destroy their crops and render their farm valueless."

Continuing, and still referring to that case, the court further said:

"It was therefore held that the lower proprietor had a right to construct the dike in order to protect his own land. And it is argued in this case that the appellants here have a right to drain the water which accumulates in Long Lake from rains and melting snows through an artificial ditch built for that purpose through a natural barrier upon their own land, and cast the same upon lower lands of their own, from whence it is cast upon respondents' lands, and that the damage thus caused to respondents is *damnum absque injuria;* that the only remedy of respondents is to dike against the flow of water, and thereby keep it upon the lands of appellants, or to construct ditches to carry off the increased water. If the position of appellants that respondents may dike against the water thus turned upon them is correct, under the rule announced in *Cass* v. *Dicks, supra,* still we do not think it necessarily follows that the appellants may by artificial means turn the water from Long Lake upon other parts of their own lands, to the injury of respondents. The rule that an owner of land has no right to rid his land of surface water by collecting it in artificial channels, and discharging it upon the land of an adjoining proprietor, to his injury, is followed alike in the states which have adopted the common law as well as those which have adopted the rule of the civil law." (Citing cases.)

In *Rohsnagel* v. *Northern Pacific Railroad Co.*, the plaintiffs sought to recover damages from the defendant railway company under allegations showing that the defendant company's roadbed where it passed plaintiff's lands was upon a solid embankment from four to eight feet above the natural level of the ground, so that in times of flood the waters of the Snohomish river, which flowed on the opposite side of this roadbed from the plaintiffs' land, were from two to three feet above the level of the plaintiffs' ground. In November, 1906, the defendant's roadbed was washed out at a point immediately opposite plaintiffs' land; and following upon that, the defendant installed a culvert at the place where the washout had occurred, with the result that during each succeeding annual high water after the installation of this culvert, the water impounded by the defendant's embankment was forced through this culvert and discharged upon the lands of the plaintiffs to their damage in the sum of six thousand dollars. To this complaint a demurrer was sustained upon the case of *Harvey* v. *Northern Pacific Railway Co.*, cited in defendant's brief, page 31.

The supreme court held this action to be erroneous, and reversed the lower court. The supreme court, after pointing out the true nature of the Harvey case, proceeds with its opinion as follows:

"In this action, the surface water does not meet the embankment and then proceed with the natural course of the stream, but respondent has collected the water on its right of way and has discharged it upon appellants' land through a culvert constructed for that purpose. It has not raised its own premises for the sole purpose of diking against and preventing the flow of surface water thereon, but has also created a new, unnatural, and destructive current through its embankment, to appellants' damage. In the *Harvey* case, we observed that, as a result of the embankment there constructed, the surface water was returned to the stream; that all the defendant did was to protect its property from overflow water which would otherwise leave the natural channel of the stream. To construct the embankment and thereby raise the water to an unnatural height on respondent's right of way, and then force it through the culvert upon appellants' land with destructive force and in a larger volume that its natural flow, is not a protection of respondent's right of way from surface water, as held in the *Harvey* case; but is an attempt to control and dispose of the water in a manner to suit the respondent's pleasure and convenience without returning it to the stream and without regard to appellants' rights. A property owner cannot gather surface water on his land, discharge it in an unusual volume and with excessive force through an artificial ditch or culvert upon the land of another, and then be relieved from liability on the theory that the injury resulting to his neighbor is *damnum absque injuria.* Gould, Waters (3d ed.), 271; *Peters* v. *Lewis,* 28 Wash. 366, 68 Pac. 869; *Livingston* v. *McDonald,* 21 Iowa 160, 89 Am. Dec. 563."

A continued citation of authority would be a work of supererogation. This court is bound in passing upon the issues presented to apply the law as laid down by the supreme court of the state of Washington. That court has in no uncertain terms, in cases presenting facts so nearly identical with those of the instant cases as to be wholly indistinguishable from them so far as the legal principles which are to be applied are concerned, enunciated the rules hereinbefore set out. Those rules were with his usual force and clarity of expression adopted and applied by the Honorable Judge Rudkin in the trial of these cases. We therefore respectfully submit that no error has been committed and that the judgments should be affirmed.

Respectfully submitted,

M. A. LANGHORNE,
E. M. HAYDEN,
F. D. METZGER,
Attorneys for Defendants in Error.

United States
Circuit Court of Appeals
For the Ninth Circuit

OREGON - WASHINGTON RAIL-
ROAD & NAVIGATION COM-
PANY, a corporation,

Plaintiff in Error,

vs.

PRESTON ROYER,

Defendant in Error.

No. 3203

OREGON - WASHINGTON RAIL-
ROAD & NAVIGATION COM-
PANY, a corporation,

Plaintiff in Error,

vs.

W. J. WASSON and MABEL WAS-
SON,

Defendants in Error.

No. 3204

Reply Brief of Plaintiff in Error

A. C. SPENCER and
C. E. COCHRAN,
Attorneys for Plaintiffs in Error,
Portland, Oregon.

JAMES E. FENTON,
Of Counsel,
San Francisco, Cal.

Ivy Press, 382 Stark Street. Portland, Oregon

United States
Circuit Court of Appeals
For the Ninth Circuit

OREGON - WASHINGTON RAIL-
ROAD & NAVIGATION COM-
PANY, a corporation,

Plaintiff in Error,

vs.

PRESTON ROYER,

Defendant in Error.

No. 3203

OREGON - WASHINGTON RAIL-
ROAD & NAVIGATION COM-
PANY, a corporation,

Plaintiff in Error,

vs.

W. J. WASSON and MABEL WAS-
SON,

Defendants in Error.

No. 3204

Reply Brief of Plaintiff in Error

The brief of the defendants in error, who are hereinafter referred to as plaintiffs, proceeds in the main as
an answer to the one filed by us, and in this reply we
will endeavor to avoid a repetition of contentions made
in our opening brief.

CASES CITED BY PLAINTIFFS IN SUP-
PORT OF THEIR CONTENTION THAT
SPRING CREEK IS A NATURAL WATER
COURSE.

These cases are collected under the second division of counsel's Points and Authorities, and embraced under sub-heads a, b and c. These cases are so numerous that a dicussion of each would not be justified, indeed we feel like apologizing for the excessive number of citations on the same subject assembled in our own brief. We all appreciate that each case depends upon its own facts, and it is extremely difficult to formulate a definition or a number of definitions which will cover and dispose of every conceivable case. The fallacy of attempting to do this is illustrated when we turn to the citations of counsel under Subdivision II, and note what a large percentage of them discuss cases wherein a water course is accepted as a fact, or wherein there could, under the facts stated, be no serious contention urged against the proposition that a natural water course was involved.

Let us refer to all of the Washington cases cited by counsel under heading II, in support of his contention that Spring Creek is a natural water course.

Dahlgren v. C. M. & Puget Sound R. R. Co., 85 Wash. 395-405.

We quote from the opinion in this case, Page 405:

"The description is that of a natural and regular water course, rather than that of a mere casual overflow. * * * The testimony showed a stream flowing in a well defined channel, continuous for some nine months of the year, and that it was this particular channel that the appellant closed, to the injury of the respondents."

Miller v. Eastern R. R. & Lbr. Co., 84 Wash. 31.

In this case it appears that there was so much water and constant flow that the stream had formed more or less of a marsh in spreading out over the land, and the defendant was proceeding to avail itself of the waters by constructing a mill pond. The contention in that case that the waters were surface waters, is disposed of as follows:

> "Nor can it be said that the waters of which respondent complains are surface waters. Surface waters which may become vagrant and subject to outlawry are waters accumulating and spreading in consequence of heavy rains and storms. Cass v. Dicks, 14 Wash. 75, 44 Pac. 113, 53 Am. St. 859; 40 Cyc. 639.
>
> " 'Surface' water may be defined as water on the surface of the ground, the course of which is so temporary or limited as not to be able to maintain for any considerable time a stream or body of water having a well defined and substantial existence."
> 1 Kinney, Irrigation & Water Rights, Sec. 318.

We call this Court's attention, in passing, that the law with respect to surface waters in the State of Washington was the same in 1915, when this decision in the Miller case was rendered, as announced by the Washington Court in its leading case of *Cass v. Dicks,* 14 Wash. 75.

Harvey v. Northern Pacific Ry., 63 Wash. 669.

By this case a landowner was located in a triangle formed by a crossing of the Great Northern and Northern Pacific railways. The lands involved, and a large area immediately to the south of them, were subject to overflow from the waters of the Snohomish River. These waters had passed around and upon some of the lands of the plaintiff without interference by the Northern Pacific's construction and operation, because its railroad was supported over these lowlands on trestles, until the Northern Pacific filled same except for a small space immediately south of its crossing with the Great Northern, and in this open space the overflow waters, running with the current of the river, surged through and upon the lands of the plaintiff, causing substantial damage. The Court found that these overflow waters were surface waters, and that on the authority of this same leading case of *Cass v. Dicks,* recovery could not be sustained.

We find in the authorities cited by counsel under this Subdivision II, a number from semi-arid states. Naturally in these jurisdictions the people want to think they have water courses, whether they do or not, and if physical conditions are such that a water course could be established upon their maps, or found by their courts or juries by the application of a little imagination, the conceived water course would become an established fact, if judicial precedent could make it such.

Illustrative of these cases is *Jaquez Ditch Co. v. Garcia* (New Mexico), 124 Pac. 891, wherein we find a state of facts reported, not substantially different from those in the leading case of Walker v. New Mexico & S. P. R. R. Co., 165 U. S. 593. We leave to the Court to determine whether the New Mexico court has succeeded in distinguishing the Garcia case from the Walker case. The case was reversed because of alleged error of the trial court in its definition of a natural water course, and while the facts are not sufficiently stated to determine whether a natural water course was involved, yet from the definitions assembled in the opinion it appears that in each and all of the instances cited there is presented not only the arroyo, the defined channel, the gully, the ditch, the banks, the gorge, or the ravine, but we also fined a flow of water during some period or season *of each year*. In other words, this case is *not* authority for the contention that onrushing waters originating with a cloud-burst, or suddenly produced by the influence of a Chinook wind upon mountains of snow, will turn the physical conditions described into natural water courses if the depressions, gorges, etc., are parched or dry from one season into another, and one year into another.

THIS IS NOT A CASE WHEREIN THE DEFENDANT HAS CONCENTRATED SURFACE WATER AT ONE POINT AND DISCHARGED IT IN A DESTRUCTIVE VOLUME UPON THE LANDS OF ANOTHER, WHERE SUCH WATERS ARE NOT WONT TO FLOW.

Under Subdivision III of their brief, plaintiffs have collected a considerable number of cases which deal with surface waters, and which present a contention in line with the theory advanced in their complaint, but in entire variance with the theory upon which the case was tried, over the objection of defendants' counsel. A casual reading of these cases might lead to the hasty conclusion that they are in conflict or tend to modify the doctrine announced in *Cass v. Dicks,* 14 Wash. 75 and in *Walker v. New Mexico, etc., R. R. Co.,* 165 U. S. 593, but as we analyze them we find that they are as remote from application to the facts presented in this case, as are the authorities cited by counsel under his Subdivision II, some of which we have discussed above.

Take the first case cited,

Peters v. Lewis, 28 Wash. 366.

It appears from the opinion in this case that the defendant owned improved property in Seattle, and that the water from the roofs of the buildings was carried by gutters onto adjoining premises. Clearly surface water was involved, but the defendant owner diverted same to premises where they *were not wont to flow.* The case is analogous to one where a property owner might cut down a natural barrier and thereby divert surface water from his premises onto lands that would not, under the conditions established by nature, be reached or affected by such surface water at all. The distinction as made in this very case of Peters v. Lewis is made by the Supreme Court of Washington in *Harvey v. Northern Pacific R. R.,* 63 Wash. 669-676. And the second case of *Noyes v. Cosselman,* 29 Wash. 635, cited by counsel, is, we think, far afield from this discussion, it appearing in that case that the defendant owning land in which there was a natural depression known as Long Lake, proceeded to cut through natural barriers and drain this water in a course where it was not wont to flow, and thereby shifted it upon the lands of the plaintiff where it did not belong. The Court, in the very opinion in question, refers to the decision of *Cass v. Dicks,* reaffirms it, and says (Page 642):

"When the waters are confined by natural barriers so that the same do not run from such confinement naturally the appellant may not construct a ditch on his own land so as to cast the waters which do not naturally pass therefrom, onto his neighbor, to the material injury of such neighbor."

This Noyes case is also well distinguished by the Supreme Court of the State of Washington in the Harvey case, 63 Wash. 676.

Sullivan v. Johnson, 30 Wash. 72.

This is a case wherein the defendant owned low, marshy unimproved land surrounded by natural barriers which prevented it from draining upon the land of plaintiff. The defendant proceeded to cut a ditch through these natural barriers for the purpose of draining his land onto that of his neighbor. The Court disposed of the case upon the authority of the Noyes decision, and said (Page 73):

> "It was there held that where surface waters are confined by natural barriers so that the same do not run from such confinement *naturally,* the upper proprietor may not construct a ditch so as to cast such waters upon his neighbor, to the material injury of such neighbor."

Holloway v. Geck, 92 Wash. 153.

This is also a case wherein surface water was diverted from its natural flow. The quotation from the opinion indicates how entirely dissimilar the case is presented than in the one here under consideration.

> "When the defendants constructed their ditch from the center marsh, they followed the natural course of drainage as far as the center of Adams' forty, and there turned the ditch directly west, casting the water against the lands of the plaintiffs at a point some 500 feet south of where such waters would naturally drain."

The Court classified this Holloway case with the

Peters, the Noyes, and the Sullivan cases, in all of which surface water was drained away from its natural course.

Trigg v. Timmerman, 90 Wash. 678.

This is the next case cited, and illustrates the distinction we have been endeavoring to make. In this Trigg case the plaintiff proceeded to drain his wet, marshy land onto his neighbor, but he directed the flow of the water in its natural drainage by constructing ditches and apparently somewhat confining it, and the Court sustained him in doing so, upon the ground that he had removed no natural barrier. 19 L. R. A. (n. s.) 167 is quoted to the effect that

"It is established by the great weight of authority that the flow of surface water along such depressions or drainways may be hastened and incidentally increased by artificial means so long as the water is *not diverted from its natural flow.*"

The doctrine announced by the Washington Court in the case of *Cass v. Dicks,* supra, has been approved and reiterated repeatedly and as late as February, 1916, in *Bonthuis v. Great Northern Railroad,* 89 Wash. 442, and we submit that it should control and dispose of this case in favor of the defendant. If there could be any question as to the attitude of the Washington Court, to our minds it is set at rest by the opinion in this case of *Trigg v. Timmerman,* supra, wherein the rule announced by the Supreme Court of Wisconsin with respect to surface waters, is cited with approval. (Page 682.) In this connection we would cite from the Supreme Court of Wisconsin the opinion in *Johnson v. Chicago, St. Paul, M. & O. R. Co.,* 80 Wis. 641, 14 L. R. A. 495, 27 Am. St. Rep. 76, 50 N. W. 771, from which we quote:

"The true rule in respect to surface waters, as gathered from the cases, is that 'the owner of an estate, for the purpose of securing or protecting its reasonable use and enjoyment, may obstruct or divert surface waters thereon, and which have come down from higher levels, by embankments, ditches, drains, and culverts, and other constructions; and, in doing so, may lawfully hinder the natural flow of such waters and turn the same back upon, or off, onto, or over the lands of other proprietors, without liability for injuries ensuing from such obstruction or diversion.' * * * One proprietor may turn and divert surface water from his own land onto the land of another, and such other proprietor may turn and divert the same waters onto the land of his adjacent neighbor, and so on. Each proprietor may thus pass on surface water, and there is no remedy except in doing so. The cases sanctioning this doctrine are too numerous to be cited."

Rohsnagel v. Northern Pacific R. Co., 69 Wash. 243.

This presents a case wherein overflow waters of the Snohomish River were involved. It seems that the water at the point in question runs north and south. Parallel with it and on its west bank the railroad was constructed. Immediately west of the railroad, Rohsnagel's premises are located. The river runs out of its banks in freshet seasons, and the railroad company proceeded to fill its roadbed between the premises of the plaintiff, and the river, with solid material, causing the water in the river, in ordinary floods, to rise from two to three feet higher on the easterly side of the railroad grade, than on the side where plaintiff's property was located. In November, 1906, the railroad embankment washed out at a point opposite plaintiff's land and buildings, and the railroad company proceeded to construct a culvert about 50 feet in width immediately opposite the buildings of the plaintiff, through which culvert the flood waters of the river rushed with great current on plaintiff's land, and with great resulting damage to his premises. The Court permitted a recovery, stating that the railroad company "has not raised its own premises for the sole purpose of diking against and preventing the flow of surface water thereon, but has also created a new, unnatural, and destructive current through its embankment."

Wood v. Tacoma, 66 Wash. 270.

This, to our mind, is an extreme case, but it stands unchallenged as the law in the State of Washington, and why it should be cited as an authority in support of plaintiffs' contention in this case, we are at a loss to understand. If we read the case correctly, the City of Tacoma impounded surface water into a sewer and discharged it through a manhole onto lots owned by the plaintiff. It is true that the water was carried in the direction of its natural drainage, but it would seem to us to be so collected and cast upon the plaintiff's lands as to have warranted relief. The Court, however, (Page 270) says:

"But *even if there was an increase in the amount of water, it has been held not to create a liability unless the water be cast in a concentrated and destructive body upon the land.*"

The Arizona case of Kroeger v. Twin Butte R. Co., 127 Pac. 735, is another case wherein surface water is accumulated, diverted from its natural course, and cast upon premises which it would not ordinarily reach but for the action of the defendant complained of, and further discussion of the case would, therefore, seem unnecessary.

Keifer v. Schambaugh (Nebr.), 157 N. W. 634.

The facts in this case impress us that it is not properly classified under the discussion of surface water. It appears to involve the question as to whether a property owner was warranted in constructing a dam across a natural water course, diverting the water out of its natural channel onto the lands of another, the defendant in the case claiming and pleading an alleged oral agreement with the plaintiff under which, as he claimed, he had a right to so divert the waters in question.

The last case cited by counsel under this Subdivision, *Gulf Sea & S. F. R. Co. v. Richardson,* 141 Pac. 1107, is not an authority for either side in this case. It is admitted that the common law rule with respect to surface waters obtains in the State of Washington with full force and effect, and it is stated in this Oklahoma decision that the common law rule in Oklahoma has been restricted and modified. A further discussion of the case would therefore seem unnecessary.

THE COMPLAINT AND TESTIMONY BRIEFLY SUMMARIZED.

The complaints in these cases are substantially the same. We will refer to the record in the Royer case, wherein it appears (Page 4) that the railroad company constructed its grade across Section 29, in Township 9 North of Range 25 E. W. M. in a general easterly direction; that upon crossing Spring Creek, so-called, it made a fill or embankment for a distance of some 700 feet, establishing its grade 5 feet above the actual surface of the ground at the crossing in question, and proceeded easterly with the grade gradually decreasing in height until it reached surface grade in about 700 feet. To the north of the railroad it appears (page 3) that there are mountains or hills known as the Rattlesnake Hills, and in these hills is a *"valley"* or *"channel"* comprising some twenty thousand acres, an average of about ten miles in width. The gorge known as Spring Creek is alleged to have its source at the top of the Rattlesnake Hills some eighteen or twenty miles away, and it is alleged in substance that it proceeds in a southeasterly direction through this "channel" to the Yakima River. It is charged that in its construction the defendant railroad company placed a drain pipe in Spring Creek, 48 inches in diameter, under its grade, and that during certain seasons of the year, caused by the melting of snow, a large volume of water flows down, and is carried off by the "channel" of Spring Creek, and the contention is made that this 48 inch drain being insufficient to accommodate the waters of the so-called Spring Creek, same were backed up by the railroad fill and broke *over* the fill or embankment onto the lower lands of the plaintiffs, etc.

The witness, Heiberling, states that this creek, so-called, is in a canyon until a short distance from the O.-W. R. & N. right of way, where the ground spreads out flat. The plaintiff, Royer, testified (Page 24) that the water coming down Spring Creek is caused by the melting snow, and *it comes down in a series.* Spring Creek runs practically every year when there are good crops *and in dry seasons does not run at all.* In 1907, the water went down Spring Creek through a 24-foot breach, practically 4 feet deep. The channel, so-called, of the creek, is not regular, it being about 4 to 8 feet

at the bottom, the depth being irregular. (Page 25.)
The witness, Mason, testified that he homesteaded the
Wasson place in 1900, and owned it about ten years,
and that the water at his place passed through the
channel to the river (Yakima) at a maximum depth of
two to two and one-half feet. On Page 26 the witness
testified that the only time he knew water to run in
Spring Creek was when the snow would come on the
Rattlesnake Hills and melt and go off suddenly. "It
would seem to absorb the water in the winter time when
it went off gradually, but when the sun and wind melted
it suddenly always had these freshets in the spring. The
time of the melting depends entirely on the presence or
absence of these Chinook winds. * * * I never
saw it last that long as a rush of waters, but when this
water run down there in the creek it would be a month
or so until it all went away when plenty of snow in the
mountains, but a rush of waters would be generally two,
three, or four days."

The plaintiff Royer is then recalled, and proceeds
to narrate conditions as they developed at the time of
the damage complained of. (Page 27.) He states that
on the 20th of January, 1916, there was from 12 to 16
inches of badly drifted snow, and Spring Creek and the
ditches and canals up to the top of the hill were leveled
across in many places, with the snow drifted into depressions; that the canyons are much deeper at the top
of the hills, and these were full of snow; that the ground
was frozen and the water could not go into the ground.
The Chinook winds started at 11:30 January 20th, and
stopped at night. The water was checked on the night
of the 21st, but it came down on January 23rd and ran
five hours. (Page 30.) Between January 23rd and
February 7th about 15 inches of loose snow fell followed
by freezing weather until the 7th of February. The

water was checked at night and flowed again in the daytime. The Creek is always dry in summer, above the Government's canal. "It is dry over *eleven months of the year, and sometimes it does not run that month. There must be snow in the hills to put water in that channel, by the Chinook winds. If it melts gradually, and no frost in the ground, you have no water in Spring Creek. If it melts off in the winter, melts gradually, it probably runs in warm weather* The Chinook was what brought the water down. The gully through which the water drained was practically drifted full of snow. After January 23rd, when the 15-inch snow storm came, a second Chinook wind came and the snow became more dense, until it finally became water in part, and started to flow down. *The snow that had not yet congealed would hold it back for a while until the water would break through* and it would come down in bunches, and the channel on the flat between the O.-W. R. & N. and Starkey's place would possibly have a tendency to fill up and cause the water to spread. ·*Spring Creek channel at my place was full of snow at that time and it had to work down gradually.*"

DEFENDANT ENTITLED TO DIRECTED VERDICT.

If, with this undisputed testimony, we consider the laws of nature, we can see these hills heavily covered with snow, which suddenly yielded water and surged over a great area and in great volume with the coming of the winter cloudbursts—the Chinook winds. With a condition of that kind presented it is unreasonable to submit to a jury the question of whether or not an adequate culvert was built by the railroad company under its grade. It is equally unreasonable to permit them to assume that the so-called channel of Spring Creek, a few feet wide and a few feet deep, would accommodate this great rush of waters and melting snow. It is equally unreasonable to contend that these waters came upon the lower lands of these plaintiffs because they were impounded by railroad grade with a maximum height of 5 feet, tapering to nothing in a distance of a few hundred feet, and it seems to us equally unreasonable to contend that these waters were anything else than surface waters.

With this record counsel for the defendant interposed at the conclusion of the plaintiffs' case, the following motion:

"We desire to move for a judgment of nonsuit in each of these cases upon the following grounds:

"*First.* The water in question is shown by the evidence as surface water and is a common enemy. In respect to surface water I think the Federal Courts follow the rule adopted in the courts of the State where the alleged cause of action arises.

"*Second.* The complaint in each of these cases is drawn upon the theory that actual damage resulted from the flow of surface water. Under these circumstances, there is no legal liability and the complaint would not state facts sufficient to constitute a cause of action.

"*Third.* The channel called "Spring Creek" and by which it has been designated in the complaint, the evidence shows is nothing more or less than a mere drainage of surface water, resulting from melting snow or the action of Chinook winds operating thereon, and that such water may be defended against, may be dammed up, the channel may be closed or open in part and closed in part and that no actionable damage results, and that the evidence shows that the railroad bridge was built for the purpose of being used by the railroad and in accordance with good railroad building, and that if surface water of the type and kind shown by the evidence overflows, it becomes a cause of damages without injury."

(Page 35, Transcript)

At the conclusion of the taking of testimony, defendant applied to the Court to instruct the jury to return a verdict in favor of the defendant. (Page 61.)

Upon the authority of *Cass v. Dicks,* 14 Wash. 75, *Walker v. S. P. R. Co.,* 165 U. S. 593, *Wood v. Tacoma,* 66 Wash. 270, and *Johnson v. Chicago, St. Paul, etc., R. Co.,* 80 Wis. 641, the case should have been taken from the jury and a verdict directed in favor of the defendant. The Court, however, proceeded to instruct the jury that where the railroad crossed a natural water course the company was bound to construct a culvert or make other adequate provision to permit of the passage of the waters flowing down the stream at times of all ordinary freshets, and then presents the question, did the company, in the present instance, make adequate provision for the free passage of all water which might ordinarily be expected to flow through the water course in question. If it did not, an injury resulted, and plaintiffs are entitled to a verdict.

It is therefore assumed, and in effect stated by the Court, that this was a natural water course, and the question is submitted to the jury as to whether or not the defendant should have made necessary provision to accommodate a volume of water that was moving en masse from several thousand acres of frozen area, down a precipitous hillside.

SUFFICIENCY OF EXCEPTIONS CHALLENGED.

The instructions in question were separately excepted to and appropriate requests for submission to the jury were timely presented, and yet counsel for plaintiffs challenge the sufficiency of the exceptions upon the theory that more than one proposition of law was involved and but a single exception taken. We are familiar with the rule announced in the cases cited by counsel, but fail to see their application to the record as presented in this case. The office of an exception is to challenge the correctness of the rulings or decisions of the trial court, promptly, when made, to the end that such rulings or decisions may be corrected by the court itself, if deemed erroneous, and to lay the foundation for their review, if necessary, by the appropriate appellate tribunal. 3 *Corpus Juris,* 895. There was certainly no misunderstanding in view of the objections made during the trial, and the very specific motion for a nonsuit presented by defendant's counsel. This record supports the assertion that the exceptions are sufficiently definite and specific to point out clearly the rulings which are relied upon as erroneous. 3 *Corpus Juris* 900.

We respectfully submit that the judgment in these cases should be reversed and proper order made for the entry of a judgment in the lower court as against each of the plaintiffs, in favor of the defendant.

A. C. SPENCER and
C. E. COCHRAN,
Attorneys for Plaintiff in Error.

JAMES E. FENTON,
of Counsel.

No. 3204

United States

Circuit Court of Appeals

For the Ninth Circuit.

OREGON-WASHINGTON RAILROAD & NAVI-
GATION COMPANY, a Corporation,
Plaintiff in Error,

vs.

W. J. WASSON and MABEL WASSON,
Defendants in Error.

Transcript of Record.

Upon Writ of Error to the United States District Court of the
Eastern District of Washington, Southern Division.

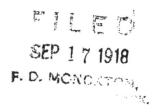

FILED

SEP 1 7 1918

F. D. MONCKTON,

Filmer Bros Co. Print, 330 Jackson St., S. F., Cal.

No. 3204

United States

Circuit Court of Appeals

For the Ninth Circuit.

OREGON–WASHINGTON RAILROAD & NAVI-
GATION COMPANY, a Corporation,
                                        Plaintiff in Error,

vs.

W. J. WASSON and MABEL WASSON,
                                        Defendants in Error.

Transcript of Record.

Upon Writ of Error to the United States District Court of the
Eastern District of Washington, Southern Division.

Filmer Bros Co Print, 330 Jackson St., S. F., Cal.

INDEX TO THE PRINTED TRANSCRIPT OF RECORD.

[Clerk's Note: When deemed likely to be of an important nature, errors or doubtful matters appearing in the original certified record are printed literally in italic; and, likewise, cancelled matter appearing in the original certified record is printed and cancelled herein accordingly. When possible, an omission from the text is indicated by printing in italic the two words between which the omission seems to occur.]

Names and Addresses of Attorneys of Record.

HAYDEN, LANGHORNE & METZGER, 617 Tacoma Building, Tacoma, Washington,

LINN & BOYLE, Prosser, Washington,

Attorneys for Plaintiff, and Defendants in Error,

and

A. C. SPENCER and C. E. COCHRAN, 510 Wells Fargo Building, Portland, Oregon,

RICHARDS & FONTAINE, Yakima, Washington,

Attorneys for Defendants, and Plaintiffs in Error. [2*]

———

In the Superior Court of the State of Washington for Benton County.

No. 2404.

W. J. WASSON and MABLE WASSON, His Wife,

Plaintiffs,

vs.

OREGON–WASHINGTON RAILROAD & NAVIGATION COMPANY, a Corporation,

Defendant.

Complaint.

Come now the plaintiffs, by Hayden, Langhorne & Metzger, and Linn & Boyle, their attorneys, and for cause of action against the above-named defendant, show to the Court as follows:

———

*Page-number appearing at foot of page of original certified Transcript of Record.

1.

That during all of the times hereinafter mentioned, and for a long time prior thereto, the plaintiffs W. J. Wasson and Mabel Wasson were and now are husband and wife doing business as a community and as such community were the owners in fee of the following described tracts of land situate in Benton County, Washington, to wit:

The south half of the northwest quarter of the northwest quarter (S. ½ of N. W. ¼ of N. W. ¼) less the right of way of the Oregon-Washington Railroad & Navigation Company; and the southwest quarter of the northwest quarter (S. W. ¼ of N. W. ¼); less the right of way of the Northern Pacific Company; and the south half of the northeast quarter of the northwest quarter (S. ½ of N. E. ¼ of N. W. ¼), less the right of way of the Oregon-Washington Railroad & Navigation Company; and the northeast quarter of the northwest quarter of the northwest quarter (N. E. ¼ of N. W. ¼ of N. W. ¼); all of the foregoing parcels being in Section twenty-eight (28), township nine (9) north, range **[3]** twenty-five (25) east W. M.

2.

That now, and during all of the times hereinafter mentioned, the defendant Oregon-Washington Railroad & Navigation Company, is and was a corporation organized and existing under and in virtue of the laws of the State of Oregon, at all of said times doing business in the State of Washington, to wit: a railway business and was running and operating a line of railway between the city of North Yakima, Yakima County, Washington, and Walla Walla, Walla Walla County, Washington, and its said line of railway so extending between the City of North Yakima and the City of Walla Walla runs through Benton County, Washington, and over and across the South half of the northwest quarter of the northwest quarter (S. ½ of N. W. ¼ of N. W. ¼), of the lands described in the first paragraph of this complaint; the right of way of said railway company over and across said described lands being One Hundred (100) feet in width.

3.

That that certain creek or watercourse known as Spring Creek has its source at the top of Rattlesnake Hills in Benton County, Washington, and runs in a general southeasterly direction for a distance of some eighteen or twenty miles and drains an area of land comprising more than twenty thousand acres, and the valley through which said creek runs and has its course, averages from one to ten miles in width and discharges its waters in the Yakima River. That during certain seasons of the year, caused by the melting of the snow a large volume of water flows through the channel of said Spring Creek.

4.

That the channel of Spring Creek enters Section twenty-nine (29) in township nine (9) north, range twenty-five (25) east, W. M. on the north line of said Section and near the west line of [4] the east half of the northeast quarter of said Section

twenty-nine (29) continuing in a generally southeasterly direction across said east half of the northeast quarter of such section, and the southwest quarter of the northwest quarter of Section 28, township
9 north, range 25 E. W. M., to a point near the southwest corner of said southwest quarter of the northwest quarter, continuing thence easterly across and
near the south line of the southwest quarter of the
northwest quarter, and across and near the south
line of the west half of the southeast quarter of the
northwest quarter of said Section 28, township and
range aforesaid.

5.

Some years prior to the commencement of this action the defendant Oregon-Washington Railroad &
Navigation Company laid out and constructed a line
of railway extending between the points and places
mentioned in paragraph 2 of this complaint, and
that said line of railway runs over and across the
lands and premises of the plaintiffs also described
in paragraph numbered 2 of this complaint. That
the channel of Spring Creek intersects the line of
railway so constructed across the bed or channel of
Spring Creek at a point in or near the east half of
the northeast quarter of Section 29, township 9
north, range 25 east W. M.; and such channel extends and its waters flow over and across the southwest quarter of the northwest quarter, near the
south line thereof.

6.

When said defendant Railroad Company laid out
and constructed its line of railway over and across

the lands of said section twenty-nine (29), as well
as across other lands directly adjacent thereto, it
was compelled to either bridge or fill the natural
channel of said Spring Creek at the point where said
line of railway and the channel of Spring Creek
intersect; that at such point defendant railway company made a fill or embankment on its own right of
way for a distance of some seven hundred feet, [5]
establishing its grade five feet above the actual surface of the grade, which said grade gradually decreased in height as it proceeded easterly until it
reached a surface grade near or about the east line
of the northwest quarter of the northwest quarter
of section twenty-eight (28) as aforesaid, and at
such latter point the land to the north of the right
of way starts to raise as it proceeds eastward; that
said defendant company placed in the bed or channel of Spring Creek a pipe or drain 48 inches in
diameter for the purpose of carrying the waters of
Spring Creek under its railway bed or fill and discharging the waters of such creek in its natural bed
or channel on the south side of its fill or embankment, which said pipe or drain was totally insufficient to carry off the waters that would flow down
through the natural channel of Spring Creek at certain seasons of the year, as defendant well knew;
and these plaintiffs allege and aver the fact to be
that in the years 1912 and 1914 the waters of said
Spring Creek came down in such volume and quantity the outlet for their discharge at the point herein
mentioned being so totally insufficient as to cause
said waters to be impounded or dammed by the em-

bankment or fill of said railway, with the west side
of Spring Creek and the raise of ground mentioned
above about the east line of the northwest quarter
of the northwest quarter of section twenty-eight
forming sides therefor, causing said waters to back
up against said fill or embankment to an unusual
depth, and until such a depth had been reached as
to cause the waters thus impounded to break over
the fill or embankment of said railway line of the
defendant company and to flow down, over and
across the lands of these plaintiffs in great force
and volume doing great damage thereto, but for
which injury no recovery is sought in this action;
that on each of such occasions portions of the roadbed were washed away, and reconstructed by said defendant company in the same manner as originally
constructed, and no adequate provision being made
by [6] such company to permit the waters going
down the natural channel of said Spring Creek to
pass in their accustomed way, or in any other way
than through the 48-inch drain pipe as heretofore
alleged.

7.

That on the 23d day of January, 1916, and between
January 23d and February 17th, 1916, the waters
of said Spring Creek were flowing in great quantity
and volume down their natural channel, the large
volume of water therein being due to the melting
of the snow; and said waters so flowing down the
channel of Spring Creek were impounded and
backed up by the embankment or fill of the defendant company across said Spring Creek, causing a

large volume or reservoir of water extending from
the west bank of said Spring Creek to a point near
the east line of the northwest quarter of the northwest quarter of said section twenty-eight (28), and
no adequate outlet being provided therefor the same
broke over such fill or embankment at or near the
east line of said *northwest quarter* of the northwest
quarter of the northwest quarter of such section, and
the waters thus released again swept down in great
volume over and across the lands of this plaintiff,
washing away the surface soil of the lands of these
plaintiffs, totally destroying all crops growing
thereon, washing away and filling up with debris
the system of ditches which has been constructed on
said lands, and also cutting great gulleys or holes
in said lands, to the damage of the plaintiffs in the
sum of $7,500.

WHEREFORE, plaintiffs pray judgment against
the defendant Oregon-Washington Railroad & Navigation Company, a corporation, for the sum of
$7,500, together with their costs and disbursements
herein.

(Signed)   LINN & BOYLE and
HAYDEN, LANGHORNE & METZGER,
Attorneys for the Plaintiffs.   [7]

State of Washington,
County of Lewis,—ss.

Mabel Wasson being first duly sworn, on her oath
deposes and says: I am one of the plaintiffs above-
named and make this verification for myself and for
and on behalf of my coplaintiff; that I have read

the foregoing complaint, know the contents thereof,
and that the same is true as I verily believe.

(Signed)   MABEL WASSON.

Subscribed and sworn to before me this 15th day
of September, A. D. 1917.

(Signed)   GEO. C. ELLSBURY,

Notary Public for Washington, Residing at Centralia, Washington.

[Seal—Geo. C. Ellsbury, Notary Public, State of Washington.]

Commission expires June 20, 1919.

Filed Oct. 15, 1917.

[Endorsements] : Complaint.   Filed in the United
States District Court, Eastern Dist. of Washington,
Oct. 26, 1917. W. H. Hare, Clerk. By E. E.
Wright, Deputy.   **[8]**

---

*In the District Court of the United States for the
Eastern District of Washington, Southern Division.*

No. 644.

W. J. WASSON and MABEL WASSON, His Wife,
Plaintiffs,

vs.

OREGON-WASHINGTON RAILROAD & NAVIGATION COMPANY, a Corporation,
Defendant.

Answer.

Defendant for answer to plaintiffs' complaint,
says:

I.

Denies any knowledge or information as to whether or not the allegations of paragraph 1 of the complaint are true or otherwise, and therefore denies the same.

II.

Admits the allegations contained in paragraph II of the complaint.

III.

Denies each and every allegation contained in paragraph III of the complaint except that defendant admits that a certain gully or depression extends from Rattlesnake Hills in Benton County, Washington, in a generally southerly and southeasterly direction to Yakima River, which upon occasions of melting snow, but not otherwise, carries water drained from an area tributary thereto to Yakima River.

IV.

Denies each and every allegation contained in paragraph IV, except that defendant admits that the gully or depression, but which is not a channel of a creek, enters section 29, twp. **[9]** 9 north, range 25, E. W. M., in Benton County, Washington, and continues in a generally southeasterly direction through a portion of section 28 to Yakima River, but defendant will further allege the facts in respect thereto in its further answer.

V.

Admits the allegations contained in paragraph V of the Complaint, except that part designating the gully as the channel of Spring Creek, which defendant denies, and further excepting where the lands are designated to be the premises of the plaintiff, and as to such defendant has no knowledge or information sufficient to form a belief.

VI.

Denies each and every allegation contained in paragraph VI of the complaint, except that defendant admits that in the gully or drain which entered section 29 and other lands adjacent thereto defendant filled the same, except there was retained therein a drain pipe 48 inches in diameter passing through and under the defendant's railroad grade.

VII.

Denies each and every allegation contained in paragraph VII of the complaint, except as hereinafter alleged.

Defendant further answering said complaint, alleges:

I.

Defendant is a corporation organized under and by virtue of the laws of the State of Oregon, with its principal office and place of business in said state, but it has taken all the steps necessary and has been authorized to transact its business in the State of Washington. It is the owner of a line of railroad as alleged in paragraph II of the complaint, extending from Wallula to North Yakima, Washington, passing through Benton County and along the north side of the Yakima River. [10]

II.

Near the station of Biggam in Section 29, Twp. 9, north of range 25, E. W. M., defendant's line of rail-

road passes over a gully or drain. This gully or
drain originates at Rattlesnake Hills five or six
miles north of said point, extends in a general southerly direction until it reaches the substantially level
ground in Sections 28 and 29, where same turns in
an easterly direction and extends to Yakima River.
By means of this gully a certain area between
Rattlesnake Hills and Yakima River is drained of
surface waters formed by the occasional accumulation of snow and the speedy melting thereof, and except for such drainage the gully is dry during all the
year.

III.

Sunnyside Canal is located a short distance north
of defendant's line of Railroad and extends for several miles substantially parallel therewith. It is a
large canal and so situated whereby surface water
resulting from melting snow and the like between
Grandview, Washington, and the gully or depression referred to herein and the surface water from
the territory north thereof, is empounded and run
down to said gully, where there is constructed a
waste-way which in the winter season is left open so
that the canal operates to increase the surface water
occasionally flowing in said gully and depression.
This canal is owned and operated by the Government of the United States.

IV.

In Section 20, Twp. 9, south, range 25, E. W. M.,
in Benton County, Washington, the gully has become somewhat well defined, and the United States
Government has constructed therein a dam, and a

portion of the gully above the dam is used as an irrigation ditch, by which water diverted from Sunnyside Canal is carried to another ditch extending northerly through the lands of Mr. E. E. Starkey. Also a short distance south of the Government [11] dam Mr. Starkey had placed in said channel a dam so that the surface water, if any should come down said gully, would overflow his premises, which are located in the southeast quarter of Section 20, aforesaid.

V.

On or about the first of February, 1916, and for several days prior thereto, a heavy fall of snow lay upon the lands between Rattlesnake Hills and Yakima River in the vicinity of the station of Biggam, whereupon the temperature moderated and chinook winds began with the result that the snow was hurriedly melted to a certain degree and the waters therefrom flowed down said gully and also into Sunnyside Canal and thereby turned into said gully whereby and by reason of the dams aforesaid, the lands in Section 20 aforesaid were overflowed by said surface water and extended therefrom to and over a portion of Sections 29 and 28, and thence into Yakima River. The overflow of said surface water was not caused by defendant. When said surface water flows from Rattlesnake Hills it becomes impregnated with silt and soil, which silt and soil is deposited upon adjoining lands if overflowed there by and results in great benefit to said lands, renewing the soil and increasing the quality thereof, and the foregoing is the transaction complained of in plaintiff's complaint, and not otherwise.

WHEREFORE, defendant having answered the complaint of plaintiff, prays same may be dismissed, and that defendant have judgment against the plaintiff for its costs and disbursements of this action.

(Signed)   A. C. SPENCER,
C. E. COCHRAN,
Attorneys for Defendant.

United States of America,

District of Oregon,—ss.

I, A. C. Spencer, being first duly sworn, on oath depose **[12]** and say:

That I am assistant secretary and general attorney for the above-named defendant; that I have read the foregoing Answer, know the contents thereof, and the same is true as I verily believe.

(Signed)   A. C. SPENCER.

Subscribed and sworn to before me this 28th day of January, 1918.

[Notarial Seal] (Signed)   C. E. COCHRAN,

Notary Public for Oregon.

My commission expires Oct. 17, 1920.

[Endorsements]: Answer. Filed in the U. S. District Court, Eastern Dist. of Washington, Feb. 2, 1918. Wm. H. Hare, Clerk. By H. J. Dunham, Deputy. **[13]**

In the District Court of the United States for the Eastern District of Washington, Southern Division.

No. 644.

W. J. WASSON and MABEL WASSON, His Wife,

Plaintiffs,

vs.

OREGON-WASHINGTON RAILROAD & NAVIGATION COMPANY, a Corporation,

Defendant.

Reply.

Come now the plaintiffs above-named, and replying to the further and affirmative answer of the defendant herein, state:

1.

That they admit the allegations of paragraph numbered 1 of such further answer.

2.

That they deny the allegations of paragraph II of said further answer, except that these plaintiffs admit that near the Station of Biggam in Section 29, township 9 north, range 25 E. W. M., the defendant's line of railroad passes over a gully; that this gully or watercourse originates in the Rattlesnake Hills and extends to the Yakima River; and that by means of this gully or water course a certain area between Rattlesnake Hills and Yakima River is drained of surface water.

3.

That they deny the allegations of paragraph numbered III of said further answer, except that plaintiff admits that Sunnyside Canal is located a short distance north of defendant's line of railroad and extends for several miles substantially parallel therewith; and the canal is owned and operated by the United States. **[14]**

4.

That they deny the allegations of paragraph numbered IV of said further answer, except that plaintiffs admit that said gully is well defined in Section 20, Twp. 9 north, range 25 E. W. M.; that the United States Government has constructed therein a dam, and a portion of the gully above the dam is used as an irrigation ditch by which water diverted from Sunnyside Canal is carried to another ditch through the lands of E. E. Starkey.

5.

That they deny the allegations and averments set forth and contained in paragraph numbered V of said further answer.

WHEREFORE, plaintiff having fully replied to the allegations of defendant's answer herein, prays for the relief asked in the complaint herein.

(Signed) HAYDEN, LANGHORNE & METZGER and

LON BOYLE,
Attorneys for the Plaintiffs.

State of Washington,
County of Pierce,—ss.

W. J. Wasson, being first duly sworn, upon oath deposes and says: I am one of the Plaintiffs named in the attached and foregoing Reply, and action; that I have read such Reply, know the facts therein stated, and the same are true, as I verily believe.

(Signed)   W. J. WASSON.

Subscribed and sworn to before me this 14 day of February, A. D. 1918.

(Signed)   M. A. LANGHORNE,
Notary Public for Washington, Residing at ——.

[Endorsements]: Reply.   Filed in the U. S. District Court, Eastern Dist. of Washington, March 3, 1918.   Wm. H. Hare, Clerk.   By H. J. Dunham, Deputy   **[15]**

———

In the District Court of the United States for the Eastern District of Washington, Southern Division.

No. 644.

W. J. WASSON et ux.,

Plaintiffs,

vs.

OREGON–WASHINGTON RAILROAD & NAVIGATION COMPANY,

Defendant.

Verdict.

We, the jury in the above-entitled cause, find for the plaintiffs and assess the amount of recovery at the sum of One Thousand Dollars ($1,000).

(Signed)   A. C. SPALDING,

Foreman.

[Endorsements]: Verdict.   Filed in the U. S. District Court, Eastern Dist. of Washington, May 9th, 1918.   W. H. Hare, Clerk.   **[16]**

In the District Court of the United States for the Eastern District of Washington, Southern Division.

No. 644.

W. J. WASSON and MABEL WASSON, His Wife,
Plaintiffs,

vs.

OREGON-WASHINGTON RAILROAD & NAVIGATION COMPANY, a Corporation,
Defendant.

Judgment.

The above matter coming on for trial, before the Hon. Frank Rudkin, Judge of the above-entitled Court, the Plaintiff appearing in person, with witnesses, and by Maurice A. Langhorne and Lon Boyle, his attorneys, the defendant corporation, appearing with witnesses and by C. E. Cochran, its attorney; the parties announcing themselves ready for trial, a jury was impanelled and sworn; and the jury having heard the testimony, listened to the arguments of counsel, and received the charge of the Court, upon their oaths do say they find the issues herein joined to be in favor of said Plaintiff, and against the said defendant,, and that they assess the amount of the plaintiffs' damage and recovery herein against the defendant at the sum of One Thousand Dollars ($1,000).

On motion of the plaintiffs it is therefore hereby considered by the Court that the plaintiffs, W. J. Wasson and Mabel Wasson his wife, do have and recover of and from the defendant Oregon-Washington Railroad & Navigation Company, a corporation, said sum of One Thousand Dollars ($1,000), and the costs of this suit to be taxed, for the collection of which said sum and costs, execution is hereby awarded. **[17]**

Done in open court this 10 day of May A .D. 1918.

(Signed)   FRANK H. RUDKIN,

Judge.

[Endorsements]: Judgment.   Filed in the U. S. District Court, Eastern Dist. of Washington, May 10, 1918. Wm. H. Hare, Clerk.   By H. J. Dunham, Deputy. **[18]**

In the District Court of the United States for the Eastern District of Washington, Southern Division.

No. 644.

W. J. WASSON and MABEL WASSON, Husband and Wife,

Plaintiffs,

vs.

OREGON–WASHINGTON RAILROAD & NAVIGATION COMPANY,

Defendant.

Bill of Exceptions.

BE IT REMEMBERED that the above case came regularly on for trial before Honorable FRANK H. RUDKIN, Judge, and a jury at Yakima, Washington; the plaintiff appearing in person and by attorneys, Maurice Langhorne, of the firm of Hayden, Langhorne & Metzger, of Tacoma, and Lon Boyle, of the firm of Linn & Boyle, Prosser, Washington, and the defendant appearing by its attorneys, Messrs. A. C. Spencer and C. E. Cochran, of Portland, Oregon, and Messrs. Richards & Fontaine, Yakima, Washington.

Thereupon the following proceedings were had:

Testimony of Guy H. Heiberling, for Plaintiff.

GUY H. HEIBERLING, as a witness for plaintiff, testified:

Direct Examination by Mr. BOYLE.

Name, Guy H. Heiberling; occupation, County Engineer of Benton County, Washington. Plaintiff's Exhibit "A," a map of the lands of Wasson and Royer, was prepared by me. (The map was admitted in evidence for the purpose of illustration.) Spring Creek originates about fifteen miles to the north and west of the Wasson and Royer land. The county road follows along the center line east and west through Section 28, and Spring Creek lies immediately east of the county road as established at the present time. The land of Mr. E. B. Starkey is shown on the map. I took levels **[19]** where Spring Creek crosses the line between Sections 20 and 29, and also where same crosses the O.-W. R. & N. right of way, and found the fall to be about 8.6 feet in one thousand. The drain under the O.-W. R. & N. tracks, where Spring Creek flows under, consisted of one 48-inch corrugated metal culvert, which was about four feet below the top of the track.

(Testimony of Guy H. Heiberling.)

At this point the line of the O.-W. R..& N. Co. is on an embankment or fill, which is about eight feet deep. The fill extends from the creek six or seven hundred feet east of the county road over in Section 28, where it passes from embankment to a slight cut.

Further Examination by Mr. LANGHORNE.

With the exception of a few months I have lived in Benton County since the fall of 1908. Plaintiff's Exhibit "B," purporting to be a map of part of Benton County issued by the Department of the Interior, is shown me and I can trace from this map the course of Spring Creek. The upper limits of the head show in Section 25, 11 and 24, and it runs generally southeasterly at the head and bears southwesterly for three or four miles, then southeasterly into Yakima River. The topography of the land from where Spring Creek has its origin is rolling, but Spring Creek is in a canyon until a short distrance from the O.-W. R. & N. right of way, where the ground spreads out flat. The channel is well defined and drains twenty or twenty-five thousand acres, coming down from various gulches into the Spring Creek Gulch. The fall from the source to where it crosses the right of way of the O.-W. R. & N. Co. is something over two thousand feet. Where Spring Creek runs under the right of way of the O.-W. R. & N. Co. there has been a fill on each side of the creek. On the east side the grade tapers gradually to nothing in about thirteen or fourteen hundred feet. The annual snowfall in the hills north of

(Testimony of Guy H. Heiberling.)

the railroad right of way varies from nothing to as high as 18 inches. In January, 1916, at Prosser there were two different snowfalls—one of these twelve and the **[20]** other fifteen inches—and there is usually heavier snow in the hills. This snow generally begins to melt whenever the chinook winds come, and it melts rapidly then.

Cross-examination by Mr. COCHRAN.

Spring Creek, from the section line of 20 and 29, meanders back and forth. One standing in the bottom of Spring Creek at the O.-W. R. & N. right of way, attempting to look up towards Mr. Starkey's place north, will find the creek so crooked that a straight line vision will not pass up the creek channel. The gully from which Spring Creek comes out of the Rattlesnake Hills begins to widen at point about the north line of the southeast quarter of the southeast quarter of Section 20. Mr. Starkey has quite a flat place—about ten acres or so—which would be located substantially in the southeast quarter of the southeast quarter of the southeast quarter of Section 20. The base of the bluff is about the section line between 20 and 29 on the west side of the creek.

Plaintiff's Exhibits "A" and "B" are hereto physically attached and made a part of this bill of exceptions.

Testimony of Preston Royer, for Plaintiff.

PRESTON ROYER, as plaintiff and as witness on the part of Mr. Wasson, testified:

Direct Examination by Mr. BOYLE.

Name, Preston Royer; own the lands described in my complaint, amounting to practically nineteen acres. I bought the land in the spring of 1914. I have lived along the branches of Spring Creek since the fall of 1905, and at one time lived in the Rattlesnake Country, Spring Creek passing through my homestead. The waters coming down Spring Creek is caused by the melting snow and it comes down in a series. In that country our weather goes in a circle—we will have a period of dry seasons, very little moisture, poor crops, and a series of good moisture and good crops. Spring Creek runs practically every year when there are good crops and in dry seasons does not run at all. In 1907 the water down [21] Spring Creek went through a 24-foot breach, practically four feet deep. There is no outlet other than under the O.-W. R. & N. crossing. From 1906 to 1912 there was water in more or less volume running each season. This water flows to the Yakima River and the only outlet is under the O.-W. R. & N. tracks. In June or July, 1914, the water crossed my ranch.

The following question was asked the witness:

Q. Just explain that to the jury.

Mr. COCHRAN.—I submit that is immaterial. ·

The Court overruled the objection, to which an exception was allowed.

(Testimony of Preston Royer.)

A. In 1914, in the last of June or the first of July, there was a freshet in the Rattlesnake Hills in the watershed of Spring Creek, and water ran down this creek to where same intersects with the O.-W. R. & N., where they have a 48-inch pipe. It was not sufficient to carry the water off and it backed the water up and it flooded straight east and went down the pit to the county road, washed out the county road to a considerable depth, and went on down where the railroad comes to the surface grade and crossed right through and ran off for five or six hours over our place.

Witness excused temporarily. (Trans. 21.)

Testimony of Samuel H. Mason, for Plaintiff.

SAMUEL H. MASON, as a witness for plaintiff, testified as follows:

Direct Examination by Mr. LANGHORNE.

Name, Samuel H. Mason; residence, Yakima; lived here about six years all-told. I homesteaded the Wasson place in 1900, owned it about ten years. I am acquainted with Spring Creek where it now leaves the O.-W. R. & N. right of way to the Yakima River, approximately a couple of miles. The channel is not regular—in places good and wide and other places deep. It is about four to eight feet at the bottom, the depth being irregular.

Q. Did you ever see water going down that channel? [22]

A. Yes, the water came there in the channel in the

(Testimony of Samuel H. Mason.)

spring when the snow would come on the Rattlesnake Hills, and melt off suddenly.

The witness proceeded:

These waters passed through the channel to the river, and at my place at the deepest time it was probably two to two and one-half feet deep, and in the narrower places deeper. While I owned the place the waters never came over the land. It generally followed the course of the creek—only time it got over was when banked up but not washed down over the land.

Cross-examination by Mr. COCHRAN.

Spring Creek carries water only during the spring freshets. The time would vary. The only time I knew water to run there any time was when the snow would come on the Rattlesnake Hills and would melt and go off suddenly; would seem to absorb the water in the wintertime when it went off gradually, but when the sun and wind melted it suddenly always had these freshets in the spring. The time of the melting depends entirely on the presence or absence of these chinook winds.

Q. And where the water did go off suddenly that would be accomplished, say, within a period of ten to twenty days?

A. I never saw it last that long as a rush of waters, but when this water run down there in the creek it would be a month or so until it all went away when plently of snow in the mountains, but a rush of waters would be generally two, three or four days.

(Testimony of Preston Royer.)

Q. Apart from any water, if there were such coming into Spring Creek from the Sunnyside Canal, how many months of the year do you say Spring Creek is dry?

A. It is dry a good deal of the time. I don't think water runs there regularly from freshets over two months of the year. (Trans. 25.) [23]

Testimony of Preston Royer, for Plaintiff (Recalled).

PRESTON ROYER (Recalled).

Direct Examination by Mr. BOYLE.

The banks of Spring Creek vary, being well defined for probably fourteen miles above Mr. Starkey's place, there are distinct channels and have to be bridged; they expect water in these and they put in bridges. In 1916, on January 20th, there was from twelve to sixteen inches of badly drifted snow, and Spring Creek and the ditches and canals up to the top of the hill were leveled across in many places, practically no snow on the level lands but the snow was drifted into depressions. From the level lands to a distance of five or six miles up the Rattlesnake slope there was no snow. Above that there was. Also the canyons are much deeper at the top, and these were full of snow. The ground was frozen and the water could not go into the ground. The chinook winds started at 11:30 January 20th and stopped at night. January 21st a southwest wind, mostly clear, and checked at night. January 22d southwest wind. January 23d, southwest wind.

(Testimony of Preston Royer.)

The snow melted and the high water went across my place at 5 o'clock and run about five hours in the afternoon.   It destroyed the roadbed at a great distance, broke through a stretch of railroad track, went over the ties and washed a deep hole through the railroad on to the Wasson land and then to my land. On Monday following there was a cold northeast wind and it froze hard, which checked the flow of the water.   Weather stayed frozen and we got some snow, probably fifteen inches, until the next chinook came.   The next chinook wind started February 7th and was a clear day—with from twelve to fourteen inches badly drifted snow.   The wind changed and on February 9th the water started running, and on the 10th the water went over my place and over the Wasson place.   The water backed up on the north side of the embankment and run down a borrow pit east and then passed across the railroad track and down over Mr. Wasson's land and my land until it met the old channel of Spring Creek.   [24]

With respect to the Wasson land, this land slopes southeast and was planted to alfalfa, and when the water came over that land would wash holes, many of them fifteen feet long and three or four feet wide, making it impossible to irrigate it and impossible to go over it with a cutting machine.   The water went over my land and washed the soil somewhat.   I was following the business of raising registered hogs—Tamworth hogs.   I had thirteen brood sows, two boars and four gilts, and I think nine pigs, fall pigs, due to farrow from the first of March to about

(Testimony of Preston Royer.)

the 21st. The hogs were penned up. When the water came across I turned them loose in the water. The effect was that these sows had their pigs from ten days to three weeks ahead of time. The sows were worth $150 each prior to farrowing. After their experience, the market value was between 7 and 8 cents per pound. The young boar was worth $100 before the injury and the older boar was worth $250. Aftewards the young boar was valued for meat only —say, $15. The other one was damaged I would say only to the extent of $25—that is, he would be worth $225 after the injury. I had between six and seven tons of hay worth $12.50 per ton, of which four tons was rendered worthless. I lost a cow worth $100. There was a bridge across Spring Creek.

The following question was asked:

Q. What was the bridge worth?

Mr. COCHRAN.—I make the point such damages are not proper measure and the recovery cannot be made that way. It is immaterial and incompetent.

The COURT.—Well, the form of the question makes very little difference one way or the other. You can answer the question and I will allow exception.

A. One hundred dollars.

Examination by Mr. LANGHORNE.   [25]

There were 40 to 45 acres of the Wasson land in alfalfa.

Q. You are acquainted somewhat with the value of land in that vicinity, were you?

(Testimony of Preston Royer.)

A. Yes, I know when a piece sells and what it is sold for.

Q. What in your opinion was the 40-acre tract of Wasson's worth before the flood?

A. I would say worth $200 per acre before the flood.

Q. After the flood, what would you say the 40-acre tract was worth, in your opinion?

A. I would say $75.00 per acre.   (Trans. 47.)

Cross-examination by Mr. COCHRAN.

Between the latter part of the year 1915, up to the 23d of January, 1916, I do not know of any sales in that vicinity, nor were there any sales previously for several years. The Wasson place was covered with water in 1916 to the extent of between 40 and 45 acres. When the water came down on the 23d of January, it ran for five hours. I did not turn my pigs out at that time. Between the 23d of January and the 7th of February about fifteen inches of loose snow fell, followed by freezing weather, and no water came down until about the 7th of February. The water would check at night and flow again in the day-time. I have been acquainted with Spring Creek since 1905. The creek is always dry in the summer, above the Government canal. It is dry in the aggregate over eleven months in the year, and sometimes it does not run that month. There must be snow in the hills to put water in that channel, by the chinook winds. If it melts gradually, and no frost in the ground, you have no water in Spring Creek. If it melts off in the winter, melts grad-

(Testimony of Preston Royer.)

ually, it probably runs in warm weather. The chinook was what brought the water down. The gully through which the water drained was practically drifted full of snow. After January 23d, when the 15-inch snowstorm came, a [26] second chinook wind came and the snow became more dense and more dense, until it finally became water in part, and started to flow down. The snow that had not yet congealed would hold it back for a while until the water would break through and it would come down in bunches, and the channel on the flat between the O.-W. R. & N. and Starkey's place would possibly have a tendency to fill up and cause the water to spread. Spring Creek channel at my place was full of snow at that time and it had to work down gradually. I did not farm my place in 1916. (Trans. 56.)

Testimony of M. C. Williams, for Plaintiff.

M. C. WILLIAMS, Division Engineer, First Division, O.-W. R. & N. Co., testified:

That the railroad track runs approximately east and west, and the grade of the track where it crosses Spring Creek is one-fifth of one per cent, ascending towards Grandview.

Testimony of Lee M. Lamson, for Plaintiff.

LEE M. LAMSON, a witness for plaintiff, testified:

Direct Examination by Mr. BOYLE.

Name, Lee M. Lamson, Kennewick, Washington; County Agricultural Agent of Benton County, have

(Testimony of Lee M. Lamson.)

been for five years; acquainted with the Wasson and Royer land prior to January, 1916; examined the Royer land at Mr. Royer's request to give him advice whether the corn needed irrigation. There were six or seven acres of corn and probably five acres or so of a poor stand of alfalfa. The soil is very fine sand, with a gravel subsoil. I examined the land in March, 1916. The flumes were torn down, the land was cut up pretty badly with little rivulets. In a good many places the surface soil was washed off entirely, so it was washed down to the gravel. The humas which was on the surface was washed off. I went over the Wasson land at the same time. The water had cut out ravines. A good many were from a foot to two feet deep—some were less. The alfalfa crown were all the way from three to ten inches above the ground. The irrigation ditches were hardly [27] recognizable. The only practical thing to do would be to plow it up and relevel it and reseed it. In my opinion the Wasson land was worth between $160 and $175 an acre before the flood, and afterwards probably sixty to seventy-five; and the Royer land in my opinion was worth $130 per acre before and thirty to forty dollars afterwards. I received my education at the State College, specializing in animal husbandry, and am familiar with hogs. As breeders, in my opinion, the Royer sows would be worth $175 or $180 for the biggest sows he had; afterwards, as breeders, nothing at all, and for any purpose they would be worth probably four cents a pound.

(Testimony of Lee M. Lamson.)

Cross-examination by Mr. COCHRAN.

I never knew of Mr. Royer selling any of his breed sows for $175 or $180 each. I never heard that he sold one to Mr. Johnson for $40. I did not measure the amount of land upon the Wasson place that the water passed over, although the line of the flow was fairly well marked with drift weeds. The water did not go over all of the land below the railroad track. The Wasson place could have been leveled all right, and it would approximately cost thirty to thirty-five dollars per acre to relevel it and reseed it. I examined the land north of the railroad; nothing washed out there but some soil washed on to it. This to some extent would be a benefit, the soil will act somewhat in the nature of a fertilizer. I have known of no sales of land prior to January, 1916, similar to the Wasson place, nor of any sales after the January flood in 1916. (Trans. 68.)

Testimony of Luke Powell, for Plaintiff.

LUKE POWELL, as a witness for plaintiff, testified:

Direct Examination by Mr. BOYLE.

Name, Luke Powell; residence, Prosser, Washington; District Horticulturist, State of Washington; acquainted with the Wasson and Royer land about January 1, 1916; was with Mr. Lamson and went over the land in March of that year. The soil was washed and a number of [28] gullies washed, from six to eighteen inches and as wide as a foot to fifteen inches. Some of the alfalfa was washed

(Testimony of Luke Powell.)

but a good deal of it the crown would stand up four to ten inches. In my opinion Royer's land was worth $160 to $180 per acre, and after the flood about $25 per acre. The Wasson land about January 1st was worth $175 to $200 per acre, and afterwards from $65 to $100 per acre.

Cross-examination by Mr. COCHRAN.

I never bought or sold any land like the Wasson and Royer land about January 1, 1916, nor for a year or so prior thereto, nor do I know of any special or general sales. (Trans. 71.)

Testimony of William J. Wasson, for Plaintiff.

WILLIAM J. WASSON, plaintiff in his own case, and on behalf of Mr. Royer, plaintiff in the Royer case, testified as follows:

Direct Examination by Mr. LANGHORNE.

Name, William J. Wasson, owner of the land described in the Wasson complaint; was at Centralia, Washington, at the time of the flood in 1916; came to Prosser March 2d, went over the land and saw the flooded area. The irrigating ditches were washed out, the rows that you irrigate with were washed and cut crossways so that you could not possibly carry water down over it and irrigate it. I should judge in the neighborhood of forty-five acres of my land was left in this condition. I placed a value of $250 per acre on the best land before the flood, and would not consider it over half that value afterwards. The land was leased for the cropping season of 1915. For 1916 it was not leased. The

(Testimony of William J. Wasson.)
water crossed the railroad track practically 150 feet wide and as it came down over my place it spread out. (Trans. 87.)

Testimony of L. D. Lape, for Plaintiff.

L. D. LAPE, as a witness for plaintiff, testified as follows:

Name, L. D. Lape; residence, Prosser, Washington, for 22 years; business, real estate; acquainted with land values in and around Prosser and vicinity; acquainted with the Wasson and Royer [29] lands, known same for 22 years. In my opinion the Wasson tract before the overflow was worth $175 to $200 per acre, the Royer tract $160 to $185 per acre.

Testimony of M. C. Williams, for Plaintiff (Recalled).

M. C. WILLIAMS, recalled as a witness for plaintiff, testified:

Direct Examination by Mr. LANGHORNE.

The original right of way of the railroad company was forty feet on each side of the center line of the railroad. Afterwards the property owners immediately adjoining the right of way on the north added an eighty-foot strip clear across the forty acres at Biggam. That would make 120 feet on the north side and 40 feet on the south side. The 80 feet has since been deeded to the county for road purposes.

Plaintiff rests.

Mr. COCHRAN.—We desire to move for a judgment of nonsuit in each of these cases upon the following grounds.

First. The water in question is shown by the evidence as surface water and is a common enemy. In respect to surface water I think the Federal courts follow the rule adopted in the courts of the State where the alleged cause of action arises.

Second. The complaint in each of these cases is drawn upon the theory that actual damage resulted from the flow of surface water. Under these circumstances, there is no legal liability and the complaint would not state facts sufficient to constitute a cause of action.

Third. The channel called "Spring Creek" and by which it has been designated in the complaint, the evidence shows is nothing more or less than a mere drainage of surface water, resulting from melting snow or the action of chinook winds operating thereon, and that such water may be defended against, may be dammed up, the channel may be closed or open in part and closed in part and that no actionable damage results, and that the evidence shows that the [30] railroad bridge was built for the purpose of being used by the railroad and in accordance with good railroad building, and that if surface water of the type and kind shown by the evidence overflows, it becomes a cause of damages without injury.

The COURT.—The motion will be denied. (To which ruling an exception was allowed.)

Testimony of I. J. Oder, for Defendant.

I. J. ODER, as a witness for defendant, testified as follows:

Direct Examination by Mr. COCHRAN.

Name, I. J. Oder; residence, Yakima, Washington; occupation, raising hogs, have been for two or three years. I have been on a farm most of my life, during which time handled hogs. In 1906 and 1907 I was manager of the college farm at Kingfisher, Okla., and was engaged in breeding thoroughbred Duroc hogs extensively. Since coming to Yakima Valley I have handled and bred thoroughbred hogs, and sold and disposed of same, including the Tamworth, Hampshire and Duroc breeds. I have at the present time 208 head. I have had experience in observing the effect upon thoroughbred hogs of their being overflowed and submerged in water. During the month of December, 1917, in the Naches River, which borders my place, a flood came, in fact one of the biggest floods we have ever had in that location, and it overflowed my hog yard. They were actually in the water part way on their bodies, five of them at least, from twelve to thirty-six hours. Assuming that Mr. Royer's hogs had become submerged with water, say five hours, and then more or less for a period of three or four days, but not continuously, in my opinion, from my experience, it would have had no bad effect upon them. Three of my sows were very heavy with pigs that were in the water, three, twelve to thirty-six hours. Three of these sows farrowed within three weeks, and one

(Testimony of I. J. Oder.)

bore ten, another twelve and another thirteen live, strong pigs. Two of these were Durocs and one Berkshire. I had two Tamworth mature [31] sows and three Tamworth mature gilts that have farrowed since. The first Tamworth sow farrowed eleven pigs, the second nine and I think the third had seven live pigs. They were all good, healthy pigs. I am acquainted with the market value of such stock in January, 1916. Gilts were worth $20 and mature sows $30, with pedigree on them for breeding purposes. According to my experience, hogs passing through a flood such as has been described are not injured thereby in the market, any less for any of the purposes for which they may be used.

Cross-examination by Mr. BOYLE.

Although my hogs were in the flood around the last day of December, 1917, there was no bad effects from it at all. This water was snow and ice water from the hills, through the Naches River. (Trans. 104.)

Testimony of A. M. Cale, for Defendant.

A. M. CALE, as a witness for defendant, testified as follows:

Direct Examination by Mr. COCHRAN.

Name, A. M. Cale; residence, Yakima; occupation, have been raising stock all my life, for sixty years; have seen Tamworth hogs raised and know about them, and have been familiar with that breed for three to five years, also with the Berkshire, Duroc and Hampshire hogs.

(Testimony of A. M. Cale.)

I am acquainted with the market value of Berkshire and Hampshire hogs, not the Tamworth. They are worth in the market $4 to $5.75 per hundred pounds. They are not worth *any other* hogs, just the same. I never gave any more for them. I have seen such hogs in a flood submerged in water. A good many years back I lived on the river and raised a great many hogs, from five hundred to a thousand head, and they have been in water a great many times. Hogs that have been bred and due to farrow in three or four weeks I have seen such hogs in the water, and in my experience I don't think it had any effect on them. [32]

Cross-examination by Mr. BOYLE.

I have raised a great many Hampshire, Berkshire and Duroc hogs for breeding purposes and all I could get for them was the same as other hogs, from $4 to $5.75 per hundred pounds. A registered hog due to farrow is worth from ten to thirty dollars more for breeding purposes than in the market, owing to the size and condition of the hog. I think a good brood sow is worth from $20 to $30. (Trans. 110).

Testimony of Christ Nelson, for Defendant.

CHRIST NELSON, a witness for defendant, testified as follows:

Direct Examination by Mr. COCHRAN.

Name, Christ Nelson; residence, Biggam, Washington, in the vicinity of where Mr. Wasson's and Mr. Royer's land is located. I was acquainted with

(Testimony of Christ Nelson.)

the Royer herd of hogs in the winter of 1915 and 1916. The place where he kept the hogs was naturally damp and there was a lot of snow on the ground just before the flood. His hog pens were in a "V" shape and the pens were naturally damp and wet. Mr. Royer's hogs were not fat, they are skinny, long skinny hogs. This was their condition in the early part of January, 1916.

Cross-examination by Mr. BOYLE.

The pens were in good condition for their kind. I saw the hogs just before Christmas. Some of the pens had no floors in them.

Cross-examination by Mr. LANGHORNE.

I have lived at Biggam ten years; am a farmer. (Trans. 113).

Testimony of Dr. G. W. Ridgeway, for Defendant.

Dr. G. W. RIDGEWAY, as a witness for defendant, testified as follows:

Direct Examination by Mr. COCHRAN.

Name, G. W. Ridgeway, occupation, veterinary surgeon; residence, Yakima, Washington; followed this profession forty years. I have had a little experience in treating hogs. Pneumonia in hogs is caused from a cold. It is not necessarily produced from wet conditions around the pens; sometimes caused by a cold draught in the **[33]** open and unprotected. A cold draft is more apt to give it to them than anything else. This cold draught operates in that respect the same as in a human being.

(Testimony of M. C. Williams.)

The COURT.—So far as pneumonia is concerned, I presume a hog is human.

A. Yes. (Trans. 116).

Testimony of M. C. Williams, for Defendant.

M. C. WILLIAMS, a witness for defendant, testified as follows:

Direct Examination by Mr. COCHRAN.

I am the same witness that was on the stand for plaintiff. I was resident engineer in charge of construction. The definite location of the railroad across the land in controversy was made before I went on the work but I was resident engineer when the track was building. This was in 1910 and 1911. I have been acquainted with the drain called Spring Creek since 1907. I had been back and across this territory a number of times between those dates connected with the defendant in an engineering capacity. I prescribed the size of the culvert at Biggam after inquiring as to water conditions from residents in the immediate vicinity who had lived there a number of years, and after such inquiry I put in a culvert 48 inches in diameter, circular in form. From the information received, it was my opinion this 48-inch diameter was sufficient in size to carry off the normal flow of surface water that came down. The water flowage conditions in 1916 in Yakima Valley and throughout the eastern part of Washington in January, 1916, were far greater than any since 1906. There was more run off and more snow. In the winter of 1915–1916 there were two heavy snows

(Testimony of M. C. Williams.)

in the early part of the year 1916. One was twelve
to fourteen inches, which all went off the ground,
and was followed by a twelve to eighteen inch snow
after that, which went off in the early part of February. Plaintiff's Exhibit "B" is a topographical
map of the Prosser quadrangle, including **[34]**
Sections 20, 21, 28 and 29, the lands in question; contains contour lines showing points of similar elevation on the natural surface of the ground. The contour distance is fifty feet. Am acquainted with the
location of Sunnyside canal. During the winter season the spill-way has been left open, whereby melting water drains into the canal, and from that into
Spring Creek. Referring to the course of Spring
Creek from the county road south of Starkey's place
there is a small rock dam near the fence, and as you
go up the channel there are several other small obstructions, but the main dam is the one that has been
put in by the Sunnyside Reclamation people, which
is the outlet of the lateral that runs around the base
of the hill. The dam is in the neighborhood of four
feet in height. Document marked for identification
Defendant's Exhibit No. 1 is a blue-print map showing the area in controversy prepared under my
direction, illustrating the land of Mr. Starkey, Mr.
Wasson and Mr. Royer, Biggam station and the
course of certain channels and drains made from
surveys, and also showing the course of the water
and the overflow, which was received in evidence
and marked Defendant's Exhibit No. 1. After the
water passed over the wasteway, the water came

(Testimony of M. C. Williams.)

down in such volume that the original channel was so small as to be unable to carry the water, and it overflowed and spread out over the land, forming two channels in Mr. Starkey's field, one marked on the map "original channel" and the other "overflow channel." It passed on down to the next forty below, which would be the southeast quarter of the southeast quarter of Section 20 and the channels came together again as a main channel with the exception the water spread out to a considerable extent on the ground. The water overflowed the greater part of Mr. Starkey's land, running entirely out of the channel, and then as it comes to the south line of Section 20 it strikes the other dam, which had been put in just north of the county road, and again spread out, and as a matter **[35]** of fact considerable amount of it has never struck that dam as the elevation of the dam has nothing to do with that just above the southeast quarter of Section twenty. The colored area on the map, Defendant's Exhibit No. 1, across the land of Mr. Wasson and part across Mr. Royer's land, illustrates the course of the water, and the map was made from notes of surveys taken shortly after February, 1916. The part colored purple illustrates the exterior areas of the flowage, and shows the overflow just as it happened.

Cross-examination by Mr. LANGHORNE.

Before I put the 48-inch pipe in I made inquiry from residents in and around Biggam as to flowage of water down Spring Creek, also made an independent investigation by going practically to the

(Testimony of M. C. Williams.)

foot of the main Rattlesnake Hills, where the three branches of Spring Creek come in; also consulted a government survey which I believe was made by the Reclamation Service, also took into consideration that the spillway from the Sunnyside canal would dump some water therein. I figured about twenty second-feet would be the flow.   (Trans. 126).

Testimony of Edward L. Short, for Defendant.

EDWARD L. SHORT, a witness for defendant, testified as follows:

Direct Examination by Mr. COCHRAN.

Name, Edward L. Short; occupation, civil engineer, five years in the employ of defendant, headquarters, Walla Walla, third district, including Yakima Branch. At request of defendant surveyed the lands in question, first on the 21st and 22d of March, 1916; made the notes of Defendant's Exhibit No. 1 and measured the area of the overflow on the Wasson and Royer lands. The line between the area overflowed and the area not overflowed could be found and distinguished by small drifts or weeds that had lodged against the alfalfa. The map has marked upon it the different areas of land and those figures are correct. **[36]**

Testimony of Alfred Gobalet, for Defendant.

ALFRED GOBALET, a witness for defendant, testified as follows:

Direct Examination by Mr. COCHRAN:

Name, Alfred Gobalet, civil engineer and drafts-

(Testimony of Alfred Gobalet.)

man; residence Walla Walla. Was with Mr. Short on the day certain surveys were made in respect to Royer and Wasson lands. The exterior lines of the portion colored purple on Defendant's Exhibit No. 1 were arrived at by indications of sediment that was carried by the water and left on the alfalfa and by little straws that the water left on the outer edge. The areas in the map are correct. (Trans. 136).

Testimony of W. H. Alsberry, for Defendant.

W. H. ALSBERRY, a witness on behalf of defendant, testified as follows:

Direct Examination by Mr. COCHRAN.

Name, W. H. Alsberry; residence, Zillah; occupation fruit buyer and shipper; in respect to lands have had eight years experience in dealing in lands. Have bought and sold lands in Yakima County and am acquainted with general land conditions in Yakima Valley from Yakima to Benton City. At defendant's request examined the Boyer and Wasson land in March 1916 with Mr. McDonald, Claim Agent, and Mr. Furman of Zillah, and the section foreman—examined the land thoroughly. Noted some soil that had washed upon the land, which is a benefit. On the Wasson land there were some little pockets washed out and holes now and then in the ground, just as I have had it in land I have been farming where a little ditch would wash out. I have had experience in leveling off and know the cost of leveling places, and I estimate that it would take $58, counting $4.50 per day as the price for a Fresno

(Testimony of W. H. Alsberry.)

scraper and teams to level it and smooth it over as good as it was before, which would include fixing the laterals. There was no soil washed off the Wasson place, only in these pockets. As to the Royer place, I could not see that any damage was done to it, other than that the dam was washed out which he had put [37] in the old channel. I noted that corn stalks and other articles were lying loose on the field, and were not washed, so the flowage could not have been very great.

Cross-examination by Mr. LANGHORNE.

Lived at Zillah, Washington, twenty years. Followed occupation of farming seven years.

Testimony of Cornelius H. Furman, for Defendant.

CORNELIUS H. FURMAN, as a witness for defendant, testified as follows:

Direct Examination by Mr. COCHRAN.

Name, Cornelius H. Furman; residence, Zillah, Washington, thirty-five miles from Prosser; acquainted with lands around Prosser; have had twenty years experience in dealing with land in this country. Examined the Wasson and Royer lands at request of defendant. I estimate that labor to the value of $50 or $60 would put the Wasson place in good condition. The market value of the Wasson land in the year 1915 would not exceed $75 per acre and the Royer land would not exceed $60 per acre. The soil was not washed out to speak of, corn stalks were still there on the place, manure dropped in the pasture by horses and mules was undisturbed and

(Testimony of Cornelius H. Furman.)

lying on the flowage area just the same as on the area not flowed. (Trans. 149,)

Cross-examination by Mr. BOYLE.

Did not see this particular land before the flood, but without a water right the Royer land would not exceed in value Ten dollars per acre. I knew of some land four miles above the Wasson and Royer places selling for $75 an acre. The $50 to put this land in shape we figured was the cost of the team work. (Trans. 150.)

Testimony of E. E. Starkey, for Defendant.

E. E. STARKEY, as a witness for defendant, testified as follows:

Direct Examination by Mr. COCHRAN.

Name, E. E. Starkey; residence, Biggam, Washington, near **[38]** Prosser. I lived on the land illustrated by defendant's Exhibit No. 1 and marked "E. E. Starkey," which would be the southeast quarter of the southeast quarter of Section 20; lived there nine years; was on the farm in January, 1916. In January 1916 Spring Creek drain overflowed the western part of the north half of the north forty, breaking out of the natural channel, and flowed out inside the opening where it drains south and west to a limit probably 150 yards, spreading out over the land to what is known as the government dam and below the dam I had constructed a new channel to check up against it and prevent wash out. Next day, when the water came, it broke over at the point where the arrows on

(Testimony of E. E. Starkey.)

Defendant's Exhibit No. 1 show at the point called "Plow land." The creek bed at that time was full of snow and ice. The first flow could not get through the channel because of the ice and snow. At the south line of my place I constructed a check, consisting of a rock dam, probably eighteen inches to two feet high, and I had a dike along the south side of my place to check the sediment. I have been acquainted with the Wasson lands for eight years, and have been over a considerable part of it during the time of the flood last winter, a year ago, and I have been over it several times since. I have helped harvest crops on the land several times and have mowed the crops of the Royer place. The water entered Mr. Wasson's place in 1916 in two different places, at the railroad east of the county road and at the west side where it broke through the railway. Where the water left the railroad right of way it was from forty to sixty feet wide and very shallow, and its greatest width was probably 350 feet. Part of it turned east where there was a wagon road, illustrated on Defendant's Exhibit No. 1 as "blown out wagon track, northwest channel." In Mr. Wasson's place it spread out considerably but did not flow deep at any point, and washed out the dirt from the irrigation ditches and between the alfalfa somewhat. I do not think the general width on the Wasson [39] place was over an average of seventy-five feet. It did spread, however, to twice that width, especially when this water came in from the west side. The soil on the Wasson land is par-

(Testimony of E. E. Starkey.)

ticularly clean of rock; there is one little gravel bed not very far from where these two streams met and there were no washes to amount to anything. The wash covered possibly three and a half to four acres. There was no injury to the land except that was washed out by the soil, possibly a quarter of an acre. I have had considerable experience in leveling ground, having to meet the tricks of that creek for the past nine years in leveling more or less. There was no washout in this alfalfa field, the little distance of six to twelve feet and no greater than across this room, and the longest ditch that was twelve inches deep was no longer than thirty or forty feet. To put this land in condition for working would be a very small matter, possibly a day and a half or two days work with a team. In fact, the ditches that were washed out did not injure their irrigation ditches. They were deeper and there was no alfalfa washed out, except at the top at a few places, so the stumps set up, the plant would stand up a few inches above the ground and would leave the alfalfa still standing on the ground, but this did not cover an area half the size of this courtroom. There was no material washed away to speak of. I do not believe a farmer estimating the use of the land could find enough washed ground to affect it in a serious way. I have kept in touch with the sales of land in this vicinity, and though there has been little selling in recent years I have known of a few sales. I would estimate Mr. Wasson's land, one lot at one hundred dollars per acre, but not to exceed eighty-five dollars

(Testimony of E. E. Starkey.)

per acre as a tract. The best part of the land was flooded over, and I would regard the fair market value of that before the flood to be amout $150 per acre. I do not consider the value was changed a great deal after the flood, but of course, the damages to make up correction of the **[40]** ditches, which I think would amount to $15 or $20. I have done a great deal of the same kind of repairing on my own place, and my experience convinces me that it could be very easily done. I was over the Royer place several times. I frequently cross it—over it first in 1910 and frequently since. The point where the water entered the Royer land was of fairly slight slope, there was from one and a half to three acres covered by the water. In my opinion the value of the land before the flood would be about $75 per acre, and by the flood it was rendered less valuable to the extent of the repairs, which would amount in my judgment to probably twenty-five dollars in work. I am acquainted with Mr. Royer's herd of Tamworth hogs. At the time my boy was interested Royer gave me his price, and the highest I remember looking at was $35 and he had some at a smaller price at that time. (Trans. 162.)

Testimony of T. J. Good, for Defendant.

T. J. GOOD, a witness for defendant, testified as follows:

Direct Examination by Mr. COCHRAN.

Name, T. J. Good; residence, near Biggam; have been acquainted with the Royer and Wasson lands

(Testimony of T. J. Good.)

since 1910; knew about the water passing over them in 1914 and in 1916. The Royer place in 1915, in my opinion, would be worth $85 to $90 per acre, and the Wasson place from $80 to $125 per acre. I would consider each place rendered less valuable by the water having passed over it to the amount necessary to fix them up, say about $100 for each place. (Trans. 170.)

Testimony of E. L. Short, for Defendant (Recalled).

E. L. SHORT, a witness for defendant, being recalled, testified as follows:

Direct Examination.

I made a survey for the purpose of determining the lay of the ground on that area bounded by the railroad track on the south and Mr. Starkey's farm on the north, the county road on the **[41]** east and Spring Creek on the west, and made a map marked for identification Defendant's Exhibit No. 2, which was prepared from my notes, which exhibit was offered and admitted in evidence and marked Defendant's Exhibit No. 2. I run levels on certain lines marked a, b, c and d. This map correctly shows the lay of the ground. Water on the southeast corner of Mr. Starkey's field, the southeast quarter of the southeast quarter of Section 20, would flow almost directly south from this point to the southeast and would not flow to the culvert. The line of levels marked C and D show the ground to be higher than further east. Water flowing from Mr. Starkey's field would flow right across the county

(Testimony of E. L. Short).

road.   The arrows on Defendant's Exhibit No. 1 indicate the course of the water.   (Trans. 180.)

Defendant rests.

Testimony of B. R. Sherman, for Plaintiff (In Rebuttal).

B. R. SHERMAN, as a witness for plaintiff in rebuttal, testified as follows:

Direct Examination by Mr. BOYLE.

The waste water from Mr. Starkey's ranch in 1916 never went any further than this corner, referring to the corner caused by the county road crossing the railroad.

Plaintiff rests.

THEREUPON, the defendant requested the Court to instruct the jury in the manner following:

Instructions of Court to Jury Requested by Defendant.

I.

Gentlemen of the Jury, under the view the Court takes of the law in this case, your verdict should be in favor of the defendant, and I therefore instruct you to that effect.

The Court refused to give the foregoing instruction, to which refusal defendant excepted, and its exception was duly allowed.   [42]

II.

I instruct you that defendant had a right to build its railroad embankment at the place and in the manner which the evidence shows the same was built.

The Court refused to give the foregoing instruction, to which refusal defendant excepted, and its exception was duly allowed.

III.

I instruct you that under the evidence in this case the so-called channel of Spring Creek was nothing more than a drain for surface water resulting from melting snow in the drainage area above the lands in question and that other than from such melting snow the channel of Spring Creek carries no water and is dry for eleven months of the year. This surface water is a common enemy against the flowage of which every land owner must defend himself, and I instruct you that the defendant in this case did nothing in respect to such surface water other than what it had a right to do in respect to its own property and in building its own railroad embankment. It had a right to place its embankment across Spring Creek drain, leaving whatever opening its engineers decided upon, and that under the circumstances shown by the evidence in this case, the defendant is not liable to either of the plaintiffs for the overflow complained of.

The Court refused to give the foregoing instruction, to which refusal defendant excepted, and its exception was duly allowed.

IV.

Defendant's requested Instruction No. 4 was given.

V.

If you find from the evidence that any portion of the lands of Mr. Wasson and Mr. Royer was overflowed by water which passed through the defendant's culvert or which passed through the break in defendant's railroad west of the county road, then I instruct you that any flowage or damage arising by the presence **[43]** of waters from that source upon those lands, the defendant would not be liable.

The Court refused to give the foregoing instruction, to which refusal defendant excepted, and its exception was duly allowed.

Thereupon the Court instructed the jury as follows:

Instructions of Court to Jury.

GENTLEMEN OF THE JURY:

To be brief, these two actions are prosecuted by land owners to recover damages for injuries to real and personal property caused as alleged, by the construction of a rairoad embankment by the defendant over and across a natural watercourse, without making adequate provision for the flow of water running in such watercourse, whereby the water was caused to overflow the lands of the plaintiffs, thereby causing injury to the real property of the plaintiffs Wasson and to the real and personal property of the plaintiff Royer.

The law of the case is plain and simple as I view it. Of course, the railroad company had a lawful right to construct its roadbed along its right of way, together with the right to make all necessary cuts and fills, but where such roadbed crossed a natural watercourse the company was bound to construct a culvert or make other adequate provision to permit of the passage of the waters flowing down the stream at times of all ordinary freshets, but was not bound to anticipate or provide against unprecedented or unexpected floods.

To the giving of the foregoing instruction defendant excepted, and its exception was duly allowed.

The first question for your consideration, therefore, is, did the company in the present instance make adequate provision for the free passage of all water which might ordinarily be expected to flow through the watercourse in question? If it did not, and such failure on its part was the direct and proximate cause [44] of the injury to the property of the plaintiffs, real or personal, the plaintiffs are entitled to a verdict at your hands.

To the giving of the foregoing instruction defendant excepted, and its exception was duly allowed.

If, on the other hand you find from the testimony that the defendant made such adequate provision, or if you find that the government dam in Mr. Starkey's field across the Spring Creek drain had the effect to cause the surface water to run out of the channel and to overflow a portion of Mr. Starkey's field, and that this overflow ran directly thereon, crossing the defendant's railroad west of the county road and thence down upon the lands of Mr. Wasson, and thence to the lands of Mr. Royer, and that the flow of this particular portion of those surface waters did not at any time flow down to the railroad

embankment where the culvert was located, or wherein water backed up from such culvert as located,
your verdict shall be for the defendant. If you
find from the evidence that any of the water which
passed over the lands of Mr. Wasson and Mr. Royer
was in whole or in part due to the direct flow from
Mr. Starkey's field, then for any injury caused by
such flowage the defendant would not be liable.

If under the instructions I have given you, you
find that the company was at fault, the only remaining question will be to assess the amount of damages. The measure of damages is the difference between the fair market value of the real property
immediately before and immediately after the act
or omission which caused the injury. Testimony
has been offered here tending to show the cost of
leveling, plowing and reseeding the property etc.,
but the sole object of this testimony was to enable
you to determine the correct measure of damages—
that is, the actual loss sustained by the land owners.
That loss, as I have already stated, is the difference
between the value of the property before and after
the overflow. This rule of damages applies to the
real [45] property of both of the plaintiffs. Injury is alleged to certain personal property belonging to the plaintiff Royer. Where the personal
property was totally destroyed of course the measure of damages is the fair market value of the property at the time of its destruction, and where the
property was only injured the measure of damages
is the difference between the fair market value of

the property before and immediately after the injury.

With these instructions to guide you, I apprehend
you will have little difficulty in agreeing upon a verdict. Much of the testimony offered here has been
expert in character. The opinions of witnesses are
not binding upon you. You will give to them such
weight as you deem them entitled to under all the
surrounding circumstances. It is a well-known fact
that the expert witness always testifies in favor of
the party who calls him. He may be called because
he will so testify or he may so testify because he is
called. But whatever the reason, the weight of such
testimony is exclusively for your consideration, and
depends in a large measure upon the ability or capacity of the witness to form a correct opinion under the circumstances of a given case, and his candor and truthfulness in expressing that opinion
before the jury. Guided by these considerations
you will give the opinions of such witnesses such
weight as you deem them entitled to.

Testimony has been offered here tending to show
the market value of certain thoroughbred hogs for
breeding purposes. You understand from experience that the thoroughbred hog has no fixed market
value like the common hog of commerce. The price
paid for such an animal depends more upon the
reputation of the seller and the caprice of the buyer
than upon the qualities of the animal itself. Nevertheless you must determine their value where they
were destroyed, and you must determine the measure
of damages where they were only injured. In fixing

the market value you will fix such price as the hogs
could be sold for within a **[46]** reasonable time
by a willing seller to a willing purchaser. If you
find that the hogs were destroyed or rendered useless for the purpose for which they were kept and
held, the measure of damages will be the difference
between their fair market value before the injury
and what was or could be realized for them after
the injury.

You are the sole judges of the facts in this case:
and of the credibility of the witnesses. Before reaching a verdict you will carefully consider and compare all the testimony. You will observe the demeanor of the witnesses upon the stand; their interest in the result of your verdict, if any such interest is disclosed; their knowledge of the facts in
relation to which they have testified; their opportunity for hearing, seeing or knowing those facts;
the probability of the truth of their testimony; their
intelligence or lack of intelligence; their bias or
prejudice, and all the facts and circumstances given
in evidence or surrounding the witnesses at the trial.

I further charge you, that if you find from the
testimony that any witness has willfully testified
falsely to a material fact you may disregard the testimony of such witness entirely except insofar as he
is corroborated by other credible testimony or by
other known facts in the case.

The burden is upon the plaintiffs in these cases to
establish their claims by a preponderance of the testimony. A preponderance of the testimony does
not necessarily mean the greater number of wit-

nesses because you may believe one witness in preference to many if convinced of the truthfulness of
his testimony. The weight of testimony depends
upon many circumstances; such as the demeanor of
the witnesses upon the stand; their interest; their
intelligence, and other facts and circumstances which
go to convince the human mind and enable the jury
to say that the probabilities tend in one direction
rather than in another. [47]

Plaintiffs' Exhibits "A" and "B" and Defendant's Exhibits Nos. 1 and 2 are hereto physically attached and made a part of this Bill of Exceptions.

After the exceptions above noted were taken and
allowed, the jury retired to deliberate upon their
verdict and afterwards returned into court and
reported their verdict, and the same was received
and filed and judgment entered thereon; and now,
because the foregoing matters and things are not of
record in this case, I, F. H. Rudkin, District Judge
and the Judge who tried the above-entitled action
in the District Court of the United States for the
Eastern District of Washington, Southern Division,
do hereby certify that the foregoing bill of exceptions truly states the proceedings had before me on
the trial of the above-entitled action, and contains
all of the evidence, both oral and written, introduced
by either of said parties in said trial, and all of the
instructions of the court on the questions of law
presented, and that the exceptions taken by the defendant therein were duly taken and allowed, and
that said Bill of Exceptions was duly prepared and
submitted within the time allowed by the rules and

order of the court, and is now signed and settled as and for the Bill of Exceptions in the above-entitled action, and the same is ordered to be made a part of the record thereof.

(Signed) FRANK H. RUDKIN,

Judge.

District of Oregon.

I hereby certify that I served the within Bill of Exceptions upon Messrs. Hayden, Langhorne & Metzger, by mailing a copy thereof to them in the following manner: A certified copy of said bill of exceptions was duly enveloped, the envelope plainly and legibly addressed to Messrs. Hayden, Langhorne & Metzger, Tacoma Building, Tacoma, Washington, and with postage [48] fully prepaid, the envelope was deposited in the United States Postoffice at Portland, Oregon.

Dated this 16th day of July, 1918.

(Signed) C. E. COCHRAN,
One of Attorneys for Defendant.

[Endorsements]: Bill of Exceptions. Filed in the U. S. District Court, Eastern Dist. of Washington, Aug. 6, 1918. Wm. H. Hare Clerk. By C. Roy King, Deputy. [49]

In the District Court of the United States for the Eastern District of Washington, Southern Division.

No. 644.

OREGON-WASHINGTON RAILROAD & NAVIGATION COMPANY, a Corporation,
Plaintiff in Error,

vs.

W. J. WASSON and MABLE WASSON, Husband and Wife,
Defendants in Error.

Assignment of Error.

Comes now the plaintiff in error above-named appearing by A. C. Spencer and C. E. Cochran, its attorneys of record, and says that the judgment and final order of this court made and entered in the above-entitled court on the 9th day of May, 1918, in favor of the defendants in error and against plaintiffs in error, is erroneous and against the just rights of this plaintiff in error and files herein together with its petition for writ of error from said judgment and order, the following assignments of error which it avers occurred upon the trial of said cause:

I.

The Court erred in refusing to give to the jury the following instruction requested by plaintiff in error:

Gentlemen of the Jury, under the view the Court takes of the law in this case, your verdict should be in favor of the defendant, and I therefore instruct you to that effect.

II.

The Court erred in declining to give to the jury the following instruction requested by the defendant, plaintiff in error:

I instruct you that defendant had a right to build its railroad embankment at the place and in the manner which the evidence shows the same was built. [50]

III.

The Court erred in refusing to give the jury the following instruction:

I instruct you that under the evidence in this case the so-called channel of Spring Creek was nothing more than a drain for surface water resulting from melting snow in the drainage area above the lands in question and that other than from such melting snow the channel of Spring Creek carries no water and is dry for eleven months out of the year. This surface water is a common enemy, against the flowage of which every land owner must defend himself, and I instruct you that the defendant in this case did nothing in respect to such surface water other than what it had a right to do in respect to its own property and in building its own railroad embankment. It had a right to place its embankment across Spring Creek drain, leaving whatever opening its Engineers decided upon, and that under the circumstances shown by the evidence in this case, the defendant is not liable to either of the plaintiffs for the overflow complained of.

IV.

The Court erred in refusing to give to the jury the following instruction requested by defendant, plaintiff in error:

If you find from the evidence that any portion of the lands of Mr. Wasson and Mr. Royer was overflowed by water which passed through the defendant's culvert or which passed through the break of defendant's railroad west of the county road, then I instruct you that any flowage or damage arising by the presence of waters from that source upon those lands, the defendant would not be liable.

V.

The Court erred in giving to the jury the following instruction:

The law of the case is plain and simple as I view it. Of course, the railroad company had a lawful right to construct its roadbed along its right of way, together with the right to make all necessary cuts and fills, but where such roadbed crossed a natural watercourse the company was bound to construct a culvert or make other adequate provision to permit of the passage of the waters flowing down the stream at times of all ordinary freshets, but was not bound to anticipate or provide against unprecedented or unexpected floods.

and also the following instruction:

The first question for your consideration therefore is, did the company in the present instance make adequate provision for the free passage of all water which might ordinarily be expected to flow through the watercourse in question? If it did not, and such failure on its part was the direct and proximate cause of the injury to the property of the plaintiffs, real or personal, the plaintiffs are entitled to a verdict at your hands. [51]

The Court erred in entering a judgment in favor of the defendants in error and against the plaintiff in error for the sum of One Thousand ($1,000.00) Dollars, together with the costs and disbursements of the action, and in not dismissing said complaint, and in refusing and declining to enter judgment in favor of the plaintiff in error.

WHEREFORE, the plaintiff in error and defendant in the judgment, prays that said judgment of the District Court be reversed with directions to the District Court to enter a judgment in favor of the defendant, plaintiff in error herein.

(Signed) A. C. SPENCER,

C. E. COCHRAN,

Attorneys for Plaintiff in Error.

[Endorsements]: Assignment of Error. Filed in the U. S. District Court, Eastern Dist. of Washington, Aug. 6, 1918. Wm. H. Hare, Clerk. By C. Roy King, Deputy. [52]

In the District Court of the United States for the Eastern District of Washington, Southern Division.

No. 644.

OREGON–WASHINGTON RAILROAD & NAVI-
GATION COMPANY, a Corporation,
Plaintiff in Error,

vs.

W. J. WASSON and MABEL WASSON, Husband
and Wife,
Defendants in Error.

Petition for Writ of Error.

Oregon-Washington Railroad & Navigation Company, a corporation, conceiving itself aggrieved by the final order of this Court, made and entered against it and in favor of the defendants in error, on the 9th day of May, 1918, and in respect to the rulings and instructions in said cause made, as set forth in its assignments of error filed herein, petitions said Court for an order allowing said plaintiff in error to prosecute a writ of error to the United States Circuit Court of Appeals for the Ninth Circuit, for the reasons specified in the assignments of error filed herewith, and also that an order be made fixing the amount of security which the plaintiff in error shall give upon said writ, and that upon giving such security all further proceedings in this court be suspended and stayed until the disposal of said writ of error by the United States Circuit Court of

Appeals, and relative thereto plaintiff in error respectfully shows:

That by reason of the premises, plaintiff in error alleges manifest error has happened, to the damage of the Oregon-Washington Railroad & Navigation Company, defendant in said cause.

That plaintiff in error has filed herewith its assignments [53] of error upon which it relies, and will urge in the said above-entitled court.

WHEREFORE, plaintiff in error prays that a writ of error may issue out of the United States Circuit Court of Appeals for the Ninth Circuit to this court for the correction of the errors so complained of, and that a transcript of the records of proceedings, papers and all things concerning same, upon said judgment so made, duly authenticated, may be sent to the United States Circuit Court of Appeals for the Ninth Circuit, to the end that said judgment be reversed and that plaintiff in error recover judgment as demanded in its answer.

(Signed)   A. C. SPENCER,
C. E. COCHRAN,
Attorneys for Plaintiff in Error.

[Endorsements]: Petition for Writ of Error. Filed in the U. S. District Court, Eastern Dist. of Washington. Aug. 6, 1918. Wm. H. Hare, Clerk. C. Roy King, Deputy. [54]

In the District Court of the United States for the Eastern District of Washington, Southern Division.

No. 644.

OREGON–WASHINGTON RAILROAD & NAVI-
GATION COMPANY, a Corporation,
Plaintiff in Error,

vs.

W. J. WASSON and MABEL WASSON, Husband
and Wife,
Defendants in Error.

Order Allowing Writ of Error.

On consideration of the petition for writ of error and assignments of error attached thereto, the Court does hereby allow the writ of error to the plaintiff in error, Oregon-Washington Railroad & Navigation Company, upon giving bond according to law in the sum of Two Thousand ($2,000) Dollars, which shall operate as a supersedeas bond. —

Dated this 30 day of July, 1918.

(Signed)   FRANK H. RUDKIN,
United States District Judge, for the Eastern Dis-
trict of Washington, Southern Division, Who
Tried Said Cause and Entered Said Judgment.

[Endorsements]: Order Allowing Writ of Error. Filed in the U. S. District Court, Eastern Dist. of Washington. Aug. 6, 1918. W. H. Hare, Clerk. By C. Roy King, Deputy. **[55]**

In the District Court of the United States for the Eastern District of Washington, Southern Division.

No. 644.

OREGON-WASHINGTON RAILROAD & NAVIGATION COMPANY, a Corporation,

Plaintiff in Error,

vs.

W. J. WASSON and MABEL WASSON, Husband and Wife,

Defendants in Error.

Bond on Writ of Error.

KNOW ALL MEN BY THESE PRESENTS, that Oregon-Washington Railroad & Navigation Company, a Corporation, principal, and National Surety Company of New York, a corporation, surety, are held and firmly bound unto W. J. Wasson and Mabel Wasson the above-named defendants in error, in the sum of Two Thousand ($2,000) Dollars, to be paid to the said defendants in error, for which payment, well and truly to be made, we bind ourselves and each of us, jointly and severally, and our and each of our successors and assigns, firmly by these presents.

Sealed with our seals this 30th day of July, 1918.

WHEREAS, the above-named plaintiff in error is prosecuting a writ of error to the United States District Court of Appeals for the Ninth Circuit to reverse the judgment in the above-entitled cause by the District Court of the United States for the

Eastern District of Washington, Southern Division, entered on the 9th day of May, 1918.

NOW, THE CONDITION of this obligation is such that if the above-named Oregon-Washington Railroad & Navigation Company shall prosecute said writ of error to effect, and answer all costs and damages if it shall fail to make good its plea, then this [56] obligation to be void; otherwise to be and remain in full force and effect.

(Signed) OREGON–WASHINGTON RAIL-
ROAD & NAVIGATION COMPANY,
By A. C. SPENCER,
Assistant Secretary.
NATIONAL SURETY COMPANY OF
NEW YORK,
By LESTER P. EDGE,
Resident Vice-president.
[Seal] Attest: F. J. JONES,
Resident Assistant Secretary.

The foregoing bond is hereby approved this 5th day of August, 1918, and the same, when filed, shall operate as bond for costs on appeal, and as a super-sedeas bond.

(Signed) FRANK H. RUDKIN,
Judge.

[Endorsements]: Bond. Filed in the U. S. District Court, Eastern Dist. of Washington. Aug. 6, 1918. Wm. H. Hare, Clerk. By C. Roy King, Deputy. [57]

In the District Court of the United States for the Eastern District of Washington, Southern Division.

No. 644.

OREGON-WASHINGTON RAILROAD & NAVI-
GATION COMPANY, a Corporation,

Plaintiff in Error,

vs.

W. J. WASSON and MABEL WASSON, Husband
and Wife,

Defendants in Error.

Writ of Error.

United States of America,

Ninth Judicial District,—ss.

The President of the United States, to the Honor-
able, the Judge of the District Court of the
United States for the Eastern District of
Washington, Southern Division, GREETING:

Because in the record and proceedings, as also in
the rendition of the judgment of the plea which is in
the said District Court before you, between Oregon-
Washington Railroad & Navigation Company,
plaintiff in error, and W. J. Wasson and Mabel
Wasson, defendants in error, a manifest error hath
happened, to the great damage of the said plaintiff
in error, the Oregon-Washington Railroad & Navigation Company, a corporation, as by its complaint
appears, we, being willing that the error, if any, hath
happened, should be duly corrected and full and

speedy justice done to the parties aforesaid in this behalf, do command you, if judgment be therein given, that then under your seal, distinctly and openly, you send the record and proceedings aforesaid, with all things concerning the same, to the United States Circuit Court of Appeals for the Ninth Circuit, together with this writ, so that you have [58] the same at San Francisco, California, within thirty days from the date hereof, in the said Circuit Court of Appeals, to be then and there held; that the record and proceedings aforesaid, being then and there inspected, the said Circuit Court of Appeals may cause further to be done therein to correct that error that of right, and according to the laws and customs of the United States of America, should be done.

Witness, the Honorable EDWARD DOUGLAS WHITE, Chief Justice of the Supreme Court of the United States, this 31 day of July, 1918.

(Signed)   W. H. HARE,

Clerk of the District Court of the United States for the Eastern District of Washington, Southern Division.

Allowed by

(Signed)   FRANK H. RUDKIN,

Judge.

[Endorsements]: Writ of Error. Filed in the U. S. District Court, Eastern Dist. of Washington. Aug. 6, 1918. Wm. H. Hare, Clerk. By C. Roy King, Deputy.   [59]

In the District Court of the United States for the Eastern District of Washington, Southern Division.

No. 644.

OREGON-WASHINGTON RAILROAD & NAVI-
GATION COMPANY, a Corporation,

Plaintiff in Error,

vs.

W. J. WASSON and MABEL WASSON, Husband
and Wife,

Defendants in Error.

Citation on Writ of Error.

To W. J. Wasson and Mabel Wasson, and Messrs.
Hayden, Langhorne & Metzger and Lon Boyle,
Your Attorneys, GREETING:

You are hereby cited and admonished to be and
appear before the United States Circuit Court of
Appeals for the Ninth Circuit, within thirty days
from the date hereof, pursuant to writ of error filed
in the clerk's office of the District Court of the
United States for the Eastern District of Washington, Southern Division, wherein Oregon-Washington Railroad & Navigation Company, a corporation,
is plaintiff in error, and you are defendants in error,
to show cause, if any there be, why the judgment in
said writ of error mentioned should not be corrected
and speedy justice should not be done to the parties
in this behalf.

Given under my hand at Spokane in said district, this 30 day of July, 1918.

(Signed)   FRANK H. RUDKIN,
Judge.

Service of the within citation accepted, this 19 day of August, 1918.

(Signed)   LON BOYLE and
HAYDEN, LANGHORNE & METZGER,
Attorneys for Defendants in Error.

[Endorsements]: Citation on Writ of Error. Filed in the U. S. District Court, Eastern Dist. of Washington. Aug. 6, 1918. Wm. H. Hare, Clerk. By C. Roy King, Deputy. **[60]**

———

In the District Court of the United States for the Eastern District of Washington, Southern Division.

No. 644.

OREGON–WASHINGTON RAILROAD & NAVI-
GATION COMPANY, a Corporation,
Plaintiff in Error,

vs.

W. J. WASSON and MABEL WASSON,
Defendants in Error.

Praecipe for Transcript of Record.

To the Clerk of the Above-entitled Court:

You will please prepare transcript of the complete record in the above-entitled case, to be filed in the office of the Clerk of the United States Circuit Court of Appeals for the Ninth Judicial Circuit, under the writ of error to be perfected to said court, and include in said transcript the following proceedings, pleadings, papers, records and files, to wit:

1. Complaint.
2. Answer.
2a. Reply.
2b. Verdict.
3. Judgment.
4. Bill of exceptions and certificate.
5. Assignments of error.
6. Petition for writ of error.
7. Order allowing writ of error and fixing bond.
8. Supersedeas bond and bond for costs.
9. Citation.
10. Writ of error.
11. Praecipe for transcript of record.

—and any and all records, entries, pleadings, proceedings, papers, and filings necessary or proper to make a complete record upon said writ of error in said cause.

Said transcript to be prepared as required by law, and the rules of this court and the rules of the United States Circuit Court of Appeals for the Ninth Judicial District. [61]

(Signed) A. C. SPENCER,
C. E. COCHRAN,
Attorneys for Plaintiff in Error.

Address of Attorneys:

510 Wells Fargo Building,
Portland, Oregon.

[Endorsements] : Praecipe for Transcript. Filed in the U. S. District Court, Eastern Dist. of Washington. August 12th, 1918. W. H. Hare, Clerk. [62]

In the District Court of the United States for the Eastern District of Washington, Southern Division.

No. 644.

W. J. WASSON and MABEL WASSON,

vs.

OREGON-WASHINGTON RAILROAD and NAVIGATION COMPANY.

Certificate of Clerk U. S. District Court to Transcript of Record.

I. W. H. Hare, Clerk of the District Court of the United States for the Eastern District of Washington, do hereby certify that the foregoing typewritten pages constitute and are a full, true and complete copy of so much of the record, pleadings, orders and other proceedings had in said action, as the same remains of record and on file in the office of the Clerk of said District Court, as called for by the defendant and plaintiff in error in its praecipe, and that the same constitutes the record on writ of error from the judgment of the District Court of the United States in and for the Eastern District of Washington, to the Circuit Court of Appeals for the Ninth Circuit at San Francisco, California, which writ of error was lodged and filed in my office on August 6th, 1918.

I further certify that I hereto attach and herewith transmit the original writ of error and the original citation issued in the cause.

I further certify that the cost of preparing, certifying and transmitting said record amounts to the sum of ($26.60) twenty-six and 60/100 dollars, and that the same has been paid in full by A. C. Spencer, and C. E. Cochran, Attorneys for Defendants, and Plaintiff in error.

In witness whereof, I have hereunto set my hand and affixed the seal of said District Court, at Spokane, Washington, in said District, this 23 day of August, A. D. 1918.

[Seal]   W. H. HARE,
                                      Clerk.   [63]

[Endorsed]: No. 3204. United States Circuit Court of Appeals for the Ninth Circuit. Oregon-Washington Railroad & Navigation Company, a Corporation, Plaintiff in Error, vs. W. J. Wasson and Mabel Wasson, Defendants in Error. Transcript of Record. Upon Writ of Error to the United States District Court of the Eastern District of Washington, Southern Division.

Filed August 26, 1918.

F. D. MONCKTON,
Clerk of the United States Circuit Court of Appeals for the Ninth Circuit.

By Paul P. O'Brien,
Deputy Clerk.

United States
Circuit Court of Appeals
For the Ninth Circuit

O_REGON-WASHINGTON RAILROAD & NAVIGA-
TION COMPANY, a corporation,

Plaintiff in Error,

v.

PRESTON ROYER,

Defendant in Error.

No. 3203

OREGON-WASHINGTON RAILROAD & NAVIGA-
TION COMPANY, a corporation,

Plaintiff in Error,

v.

W. J. WASSON and MABEL WASSON,

Defendants in Error.

No. 3204

Brief of Plaintiff in Error

A. C. SPENCER and
C. E. COCHRAN,
Attorneys for Plaintiffs in Error,
Portland, Oregon.

JAMES E. FENTON,
Of Counsel,
San Francisco, California.

FILED

OCT 1 - 1918

KUBLI HOWELL CO., PORTLAND, ORE

United States
Circuit Court of Appeals
For the Ninth Circuit

OREGON-WASHINGTON RAILROAD & NAVIGA-
TION COMPANY, a corporation,
Plaintiff in Error,

v.

PRESTON ROYER,
Defendant in Error.

No. 3203

OREGON-WASHINGTON RAILROAD & NAVIGA-
TION COMPANY, a corporation,
Plaintiff in Error,

v.

W. J. WASSON and MABEL WASSON,
Defendants in Error.

No. 3204

Upon Writ of Error to the United States District Court
of the Eastern District of Washington,
Southern Division.

STATEMENT OF THE CASE.

These actions were commenced in the month of
October, 1917, by the defendants in error (who will be
referred to herein as the plaintiffs) against the plaintiff

in error (who will be referred to herein as the defend- ᐟ
ant) to recover damages from defendant for injuries
to the real property of the plaintiff Wasson, and to the
real and personal property of plaintiff Royer, resulting, as it is alleged, from an overflow of the lands of
plaintiffs caused, as it is alleged, by the construction of
an embankment by defendant on its right of way over
and across an alleged water course known as Spring
Creek; and by placing in the alleged bed or channel of
said alleged creek a pipe or drain which, it is alleged,
was insufficient to carry off the waters that flowed
down through said alleged creek at certain seasons of
the year. (Trans. Royer case, pp. 4-6.)

"Spring Creek is dry in the aggregate over eleven
months in the year, and sometimes it does not run that
month. There must be snow in the hills to put water in
that channel, by the Chinook winds. The waters coming down Spring Creek is caused by the melting snow."
(Testimony plaintiff Royer, Trans. Wasson case, pp.
22 and 28.)

"Spring Creek carries water only during the spring
freshets; the only time the waters run there was when
the snow would come on the Rattle Snake Hills and
would melt and go off suddenly." (Testimony Mason,
a witness for plaintiffs, Trans. Wasson case, p. 24.)

Between the 20th of January and the 10th of February in the year 1916, there were two heavy snows, one
twelve to fourteen inches and the other twelve to sixteen inches in depth, in the Rattlesnake Hills, extending, gradually diminished in quantity, down to within
five or six miles of the level land. There was no snow
on the level land. The chinook winds started about

January 20th, melting this snow and causing an extra-ordinary and unexpected flood of surface waters to run in a southerly direction across the right of way of de-fendant; "it destroyed the roadbed at a great distance, broke through a stretch of railroad track, went over the ties, and washed a deep hole through the railroad" on to the lands of plaintiffs. (Testimony of plaintiff Royer, Trans. his case, p. 27.)

At the time of the alleged injury to the property of plaintiffs, the line of railroad of defendant ran in a westerly direction between the City of Walla Walla, Washington, and the City of North Yakima, Yakima County, Washington, and ran through Benton County, Washington, over and across a part of the land of plaintiff Wasson and north of, but near the land of plaintiff Royer.

A ravine or hollow which the plaintiffs denominate "a channel" originates in the Rattlesnake Hills in Ben-ton County, Washington, about fifteen miles north-west of the lands of plaintiffs, and runs in a south-easterly direction towards the railroad line of defend-ant, spreading out into a flat some distance northerly from said railway line. (Trans. Royer case, pages 2-3 and 22.)

"The annual snowfall in the hills north of the rail-road right of way varies from nothing to as high as eighteen inches." (Testimony of Heiberling, a witness for plaintiffs, Trans. Royer case, pages 22-23.)

"Spring Creek is dry in the aggregate over eleven months in the year." "The waters coming down Spring Creek is caused by the chinook winds melting the snow."

(Testimony of plaintiff Royer, Trans. his case, pp. 24 and 30.)

The defendant constructed the embankment and drain referred to in the year 1910. The drain or culvert referred to, is circular in form, and 48 inches in diameter. Before this drain or culvert was placed in the alleged channel of Spring Creek, the engineer of defendant made inquiry from residents in and about the neighborhood as to the flowage of water, and also made an independent investigation of the climatic conditions and topography of the country, and from the information obtained, it was his opinion that a drain 48 inches in diameter was sufficient in size to carry off the normal flow of surface water that came down this alleged creek. (Trans. Royer case, pp. 41 and 43.)

The cases were tried to the Court and a jury and resulted in a verdict and judgment in favor of the plaintiff Royer in the sum of $850.00, and a verdict and judgment in favor of the plaintiff Wasson in the sum of $1000. Writs of Error were sued out for the reversal of these judgments. (Trans. Royer case, pp. 18-19.) (Trans. Wasson case, pp. 16-17.)

The questions for determination upon the Writs of Error herein are:

First: Are the rights of the respective parties to these actions to be determined by the common law relating to natural watercourses, or relating solely to surface water?

Second: If such rights are to be determined by the common law, then do the complainants herein state facts sufficient to constitute causes of action against defendant?

Third: Was the evidence herein sufficient to show: (a) that Spring Creek is a natural watercourse; or (b) that any natural watercourse was obstructed by defendant; or (c) that the flowage of water on the lands of plaintiffs was caused by any negligence of defendant?

Fourth: Was the evidence sufficient to entitle the plaintiffs to recover?

CONTENTIONS OF DEFENDANT.

The defendant contends:

(a) That the rights of the respective parties to these actions are to be determined by the rule of the common law relating to surface waters.

(b) That the complaints herein do not state facts sufficient to constitute causes of action.

(c) That Spring Creek is not a natural watercourse.

(d) That there were no natural watercourses obstructed by the defendant.

(e) That the waters which flowed upon the lands of plaintiffs were surface waters only.

(f) That the flowage of water on the lands of plaintiffs was not caused by any negligence of defendant.

(g) That plaintiffs with full knowledge of the manner of construction of said embankment and drain, and of their rights in the premises, acquiesced in the maintenance thereof.

(h) That the injury, if any, to the property of plaintiffs was the result solely of an extraordinary and unexpected flood, and the damage, if any sustained, was *damnum abseque injuria.*

(i) That the Court should have instructed the jury to find a verdict for defendant and against each of the plaintiffs.

(j) That the Court should not have instructed the jury as a matter of law, as it did in effect, that Spring Creek was a natural watercourse, but, on the contrary, should have instructed the jury that the so-called Spring Creek was nothing more than surface water, resulting from melting snow flowing in a hollow or ravine.

The defendant upon its Writs of Error has made the following Assignments of Error:

ASSIGNMENTS OF ERROR.

I.

The Court erred in refusing to give to the jury the following instruction requested by plaintiff in error:

Gentlemen of the Jury, under the view the Court takes of the law in this case, your verdict for instruct you to that effect. (Trans. Royer case, p. 52, Wasson case, p. 50.)

II.

The Court erred in declining to give to the jury the following instruction requested by the defendant-plaintiff in error:

I instruct you that defendant had a right to build its railroad embankment at the place and in the manner which the evidence shows the same to be built. (Trans. Royer case, p. 52, Wasson case, p. 50.)

III.

The Court erred in refusing to give to the jury the following instruction:

I instruct you that under the evidence in this case the so-called channel of Spring Creek was nothing more than a drain for surface water resulting from melting snow in the drainage area above the lands in question and that other than from such melting snow the channel of Spring Creek carries no water and is dry for eleven months out of the year. This surface water is a common enemy against the flowage of which every land owner must defend himself, and I instruct you that the defendant in this case did nothing in respect to such surface water other than what it had a right to do in respect to its own property and in building its own railroad embankment. It had a right to place its embankment across Spring Creek drain, leaving whatever opening its engineers decided upon, and that under the circumstances shown by the evidence in this case, the defendant is not liable to either of the plaintiffs for the overflow complained of. (Trans. Royer case, p. 52, Wasson case, p. 51.)

IV.

The Court erred in refusing to give to the jury the following instruction requested by defendant-plaintiff in error:

If you find from the evidence that any portion of the lands of Mr. Wasson and Mr. Royer was overflowed by water which passed through the defendant's culvert or which passed through the break of defendant's railroad west of the county road, then I instruct you that any flowage or damage arising by the presence of waters from that source upon those lands, the defendant would not be liable. (Trans. Royer case, p. 53, Wasson case, p. 52.)

V.

The Court erred in giving to the jury the following instruction:

The law of the case is plain and simple as I view it. Of course, the railroad company had a lawful right to construct its roadbed along its right of way, together with the right to make all necessary cuts and fills, but where such roadbed crossed a natural watercourse the company was bound to construct a culvert or make other adequate provision to permit the passage of the waters flowing down the stream at times of all ordinary freshets, but was not bound to anticipate or prrovide against unprecedented or unexpected floods. (Trans. Royer case p. 54, Wasson case p. 52.)

And also the following instruction:

The first question for your consideration, therefore, is, did the company in the present instance make adequate provision for the free passage of all water which might ordinarily be expected to flow through the watercourse in question? If it did not, and such failure on its part was the direct and proximate cause of the injury to the property of the plaintiffs, real and personal, the plaintiffs are entitled to a verdict at your hands. (Trans. Royer case p. 54, Wasson case p. 53.)

VI.

The Court erred in entering judgment in favor of the defendant in error Royer and against the plaintiff in error for the sum of Eight hundred fifty ($850.00) Dollars, together with the costs and disbursements of the action, and in not dismissing the complaint and in refusing and declining to enter judgment in favor of the plaintiff in error. (Trans. Royer case, p. 19.)

And also erred in entering judgment in favor of the defendant in error Wasson and against the plaintiff in error for the sum of One thousand dollars ($1000.00), together with the costs and disbursements of the action, and in not dismissing the complaint, and in refusing and declining to enter judgment in favor of the plaintiff in error. (Trans. Wasson case, p. 17.)

(Trans. of Record, Royer case, pp. 60-63.)
(Trans. of Record, Wasson case, p. 59.)

POINTS AND AUTHORITIES.

I.

"The Common Law, so far as it is not inconsistent with the constitution and laws of the United States or of the State of Washington, nor incompatible with the institutions and condition of society in this state, shall be the rule of decision in all the courts of this state."

Remington & Ballinger's Annotated Codes and Statutes of Washington, Section 143.

This provision of the laws of the State of Washington has been construed by the Supreme Court of that state in the following cases:

Sayward v. Carlson, 1 Wash. 29.
Eisenbach v. Hatfield, 2 Wash. 236.
Wagner v. Law, 3 Wash. 500.
Cass v. Dicks, 14 Wash. 75.
Benton v. Johncox, 17 Wash. 277.
Bates v. Drake, 28 Wash. 447.
Richards v. Redelsheimer, 36 Wash. 325.
Nesalhous v. Walker, 45 Wash. 621.

Corcoran v. Postal Telegraph-Cable Co., 80 Wash. 570.

The case of Eisenbach v. Hatfield (2 Wash. 236) was a suit in equity wherein the Court was called upon to determine the rights of Littoral Proprietors of lands abutting upon the shore of an arm of the sea in which the tide ebbed and flowed. In that case the Court, at page 240, said:

"In this state the common law is our rule of decision in the settlement of questions requirin⸗ judicial determination, when not specially provided for by statute."

The case of Cass v. Dicks (14 Wash. 75) was a suit in equity to enjoin the building of a dike, and in that case the court, at page 77, said:

"It must be borne in mind that the water, the flow of which will be obstructed by the dike, is not the currrent of a natural stream; and therefore the law determinative of the rights of riparian proprietors is not at all applicable to the case in hand. The water which passes from the premises of appellants does not flow in a defined channel having a bed and banks, and, consequently, is to all intents and purposes surface water, and the rights of the respective parties in regard thereto must be determined by the law relating solely to surface water: and, as to these rights, the decisions of the courts in the various states are far from uniform. The courts of some of the states have adopted the rule of the civil law. by virtue of which a lower estate is held subject to the easement or servitude of receiving the flow of surface water from the upper estate. Under that rule, it is clear that the flow of mere surface water from the premises of an upper proprietor to those of a lower may not be obstructed or diverted to the damage of the latter. But the contrary rule of the common law has been adopted in many of the states, and must be followed in this case, because it is neither inconsistent with the constitution and laws of the United States nor of this state, nor incompatible with the institutions and conditions of society in this state. Code Proc., Sec. 108. By that law, surface water, caused by the falling of rain or the melting of snow, and that escaping from running streams and rivers, is regarded as an outlaw and a common enemy, against which anyone may defend himself, even though by so doing injury may result to others. The rule is based upon the principle that such water is a part of the land upon which it lies, or over which it temporarily flows, and that an owner of land has a right to the free and unrestrained use of it above, upon and beneath the surface. 24 Am. & Eng. Enc. Law, pp. 906, 917; Ang. Watercourses (7th ed.) Sec. 1080.

"If one in the lawful exercise of his right to control, manage, or improve his own land, finds it necessary to protect it from surface water flowing from higher land, he may do so; and if damage thereby results to another, it is *damnum absque injuria.*"

The case of Benton v. Johncox, 17 Wash. 281, was an action by a riparian proprietor to restrain certain of the appellants from diverting the waters of a stream and conducting the same to and upon their land for the purposes of irrigation. The Court, after discussing the facts, at page 280, said:

"But it is most earnestly insisted by the learned counsel for appellants that the common-law doctrine touching riparian rights is not applicable to the arid portions of the state, and especially to Yakima County; and this Court is now urged to so decide, notwithstanding anything it may heretofore have said to the contrary. The legislature of the territory of Washington in the year 1863 (Laws 1863, p. 68) enacted that 'the common law of England, so far as it is not repugnant to, or inconsistent with, the constitution and laws of the United States and the organic act and laws of Washington territory, shall be the rule of decision in all the courts of this territory.' The language of this provision was changed by the state legislature in 1891 by omitting the words 'of England,' substituting the word 'state' for 'territory,' and inserting the clause, 'nor incompatible with the institutions and condition of society in this state.' Code Proc., Sec. 108. But the meaning remains substantially the same. It thus appears that the common law must be our 'rule of decision,' unless this case falls within the exceptions specified in the statute. Now, the common-law doctrine declaratory of riparian rights, as now generally understood by the Courts, is not, in our judgment, inconsistent with the constitution or laws of the United States or of this state. Nor is it incompatible with the condition of society in this state, unless it can be said that the right of an individual to use and enjoy his own property is incompatible with our condition—a proposition to which, we apprehend, no one would assent for a moment."

The case of Nesalhous v. Walker (45 Wash. 621), was a suit in equity, in which the plaintiff prayed for a decree adjudging him to be the first riparian owner of the waters of a certain stream, and enjoining the defendant from diverting the waters of the stream. The opinion in this case was written by Judge Rudkin, who tried the instant case. After discussing the issues in that case, Judge Rudkin in his opinion, at page 623, said:

"The Court below in its findings and conclusions, applied the doctrine of prior appropriation, and, if its ruling in that regard is correct, the decree should be affirmed, as the findings of the Court are sustained by the testimony. If, on the other hand, the rights of the parties are governed by the common-law doctrine of riparian rights, the decree is erroneous, and must be materially modified. The right to appropriate water for mining and agricultural purposes from watercourses on the public domain is sanctioned by acts of Congress, and recognized by all the Courts; but, when the government ceases to be the sole proprietor, the right of the riparian owner attaches, and cannot be subsequently invaded in those states where the common-law doctrine of riparian rights prevails. The common-law rule was recognized and adopted by this Court after full consideration in the case of Benton v. Johncox, 17 Wash. 277, 49 Pac. 495, 39 L. R. A. 107, 61 Am. St. Rep. 912, and, whether best suited to local conditions or not, the decision established a rule of property that should not now be disturbed or departed from. In the case now under consideration, all parties concerned acquired or initiated their rights to their respective tracts before any attempt was made to acquire rights in the waters of the stream by appropriation. Therefore their rights in the stream, and the waters therein flowing, must be determined by the rule announced by this Court in the case cited. It was there declared that the common law doctrine of riparian rights is not inconsistent with a reasonable use of the waters of the stream by riparian owners for the purposes of irrigation."

The case of Corcoran v. Postal Telegraph-Cable Co., 80 Wash. 570, was an action for damages for mental suffering claimed to have resulted to plaintiffs from the delay in the delivery of a telegram. The Court, in discussing the question as to whether or not there could be a recovery for mental suffering, at page 572, said:

"There is here presented the problem: Does mental suffering, independent of injury and financial loss, resulting from mere negligent delay in the transmission and delivery of a telegram, render the company, accepting such telegram for transmission and receiving pay therefor, liable in damages, measurable in money, to the sender and receiver whose mental suffering results from such negligent delay? Counsel for appellant contend that there is no such liability in this state, in view of the common law, which is in force here, in the absence of controlling statutory law. We have no statute in this state relating to damages of this nature. Since the beginning of civil government in the territory now occupied by our state, the common law has been the rule of decision in our Courts, except where other rules are prescribed by the Constitution or statutes. It has been so declared by legislative enactment. Section 143, Rem. & Bal. Code. Indeed, it would necessarily be so, even in the absence of legislative declaration, because of the source of our civilization and institutions. We have, it is true, adapted the common law and its reason to new conditions as they arose, and thereby occasionally worked what may be regarded as innovations therein, when viewed superficially, but the spirit and reason of the common law have, as understood by our Courts, always been their source of guidance when statute and Constitution were silent touching the problem in hand."

It conclusively appears from the foregoing authorities that the rights of the parties to these actions were governed by the rule of the common law relating to surface waters.

II.

The plaintiff must frame his pleading with reference to some particullar theoretical right of recovery; and the pleading must be good on the theory upon which it proceeds, or it will not be sufficient on demurrer, even though it state facts enough to be good on some other theory. Nor can the plaintiff obtain relief upon a different theory from that upon which his pleading is based.

Bremmerman v. Jennings, 101 Ind. 253.
Holderman v. Miller, 102 Ind. 356.
Whitten v. Griswold, 60 Ore. 318.

The genrral scope of the complaints in these cases plainly shows that they were drawn distinctly upon the theory that the injury, if any, to the property of the plaintiffs was caused solely by an extraordinary and unexpected flood of surface water, resulting from melting snow flowing in a hollow or ravine, and that it was not the intention of the pleader to state a cause of action for injuries to property resulting from the obstruction of a natural watercourse.

To this theory plaintiffs were bound through all the stages of the trial, and upon it they must stand or fall.

III.

The complaints in these actions do not, nor does either thereof state facts sufficient to constitute a cause of action.

The complaints and each thereof are insufficient for that:

(a) It appears upon the face of each thereof that the embankment and drain, whereby it is alleged the waters from Spring Creek were caused to flow on the lands of plaintiffs, were constructed by defendant company on its own right of way.

(b) It does not appear from the complaints or either thereof that Spring Creek is a natural watercourse.

(c) It does not appear from the complaints or either thereof that the natural flow of any watercourse was obstructed by defendant.

(d) It appears from each of the complaints that the water which flowed upon the lands of plaintiffs was surface water only.

(e) It does not appear from the complaints or either thereof, that the alleged flowage of water on the lands of the plaintiffs was caused by the negligence or tortious conduct of defendant.

(f) It appears from said complaints and each thereof, that the plaintiffs with full knowledge of the manner of construction of said embankment and drain and of their rights, acquiesced in the maintenance thereof.

Broom's Legal Maxims, p. 265.
Cooley on Torts, p. 187.
Churchill v. Baumann, 95 Cal. 541.
Southern Marble Co. v. Darnell, 94 Ga. 231.
Groff v. Ankenbrandt, 124 Ill. 51.

Lake Erie & Western R..R. Co. v. Hilfiker, 12 Ind. App. 280.

C. C. C. & St. L. R. Co. v. Huddleston, 21 Ind. App. 261.

Abbott v. K. C. St. J.'& C. B. Ry. Co., 83 Mo. 271.

Collier v. C. & A. Ry. Co., 48 Mo. App. 398.

Koch v. Del. L. & W. R. R. Co., 54 N. J. Law, 401.

Wagner v. L. I. R. R. Co., 2 Hun. 633.

Rothschild v. Title Guaranty & Trust Co., 204 N. Y. 458.

Pa. Railroad Co. v. Washburn, 50 Fed. 335.

Post v. Beacon Vacuum Pump & Elec. Co., 89 Fed. 1.

The case of Collier v. The C. & A. Ry. Co., 48 Mo. App. 398, was an action to recover damages for the overflow of the plaintiff's lands caused by the backing up of surface water from the defendant's roadbed. The Court, in discussing the sufficiency of the complaint at page 401 said:

"The plaintiff contends that the trial Court erred in sustaining the demurrer to the evidence adduced in support of the first count of the petition. There was not a *scintilla* of evidence tending in the remotest degree to show that the defendant was guilty of negligence in the construction of its roadbed; consequently, under the well-settled law of this state, the injury thereby done to the plaintiff's lands must be considered as the natural and necessary consequence of what the defendant had the right to do under its charter, and the damage was *damnum absque injuria.*

"There was no error in sustaining the defendant's demurrer. The defendant had the right to construct on its right of way, except where intersected by natural waterways, a solid and continuous roadbed for its track. No one had a right to have the surface water flow across its right of way, but on the contrary, it had a perfect right to prevent the water from doing so. If the declivity of the lands south of the defendant's road and west of that of the plaintiff, was towards the north, and in consequence thereof the surface water at any time on these lands occasioned either by rainfall or melting snows flowed north until it was obstructed by the defendant's roadbed, defendant was not required on that account to construct drains or ditches through its roadbed in order to allow such surface water to continue its onward course north. Such water was a common enemy against which the defendant had the right to protect itself.

The case of Koch v. Del. L. & W. R. R. Co. (54 N. J. Law 401), was also an action for damages for the overflow of plaintiff's land, and in that case the Court said:

"The plaintiff complains that the defendant, by certain tortious acts, has caused the waters of the Hackensack River to be discharged upon her meadow land.

"We think it is obvious that the first count demurred to does not state facts from which the Court can see that the plaintiff has the cause of action alleged. The allegations and statements are, that the meadow land in question, 'being thoroughly drained and dry,' the defendant made 'an opening through the causeway or roadbed of its railroad' and thereby caused the 'tidewater from the Hackensack River' to be discharged upon the meadow lands aforesaid &c. It is impossible, from such a narration, for the Court to pronounce that a wrong in this matter has been committed by the railroad company. There is not even an averment in the count that, by reason of the natural situation or of any grant to that effect, the plaintiff has the right to require that the roadway of the defendant shall keep off this water from her land. In the natural condition of affairs, a landowner has the right to remove, either in whole or in part, any structure that he has erected upon his property, although such removal will prove detrimental to the possessions of others. The cutting complained of does not appear to be an actionable wrong.

"The fourth count we regard as also insufficient, on the same ground.

"The second and third counts are somewhat variant from the two just disposed of. They, each, in substance, aver, that the meadow land in question had been dry and drained for a number of years, and that the defendant kept and maintained a ditch alongside its roadbed, and thereby caused the water of the Hackensack River aforesaid to be discharged through said ditch last aforesaid, and through an opening through said causeway or roadbed upon the said meadow lands, etc.

"These counts, we think, are also essentially defective. Neither of them shows, with such reasonable certainty as the laws of pleading require, that, by doing the act stated, the defendant has committed a tort. The radical defect of this pleading is, that it does not declare that the water of the Hackensack, flowing in its natural condition, would not have inundated this meadow land to the same or to a greater extent than is now the case by reason of the ditch complained of. It does not appear that this act of the defendant has, to the injury of the plaintiff, altered the natural condition of the land. To elucidate, let us suppose this case: That the river water naturally would overflow this meadow; that the defendant prevented such overflow by building an embankment on its own land, and that subsequently it cut a ditch along and through such structure and thereby let in as much water as had originally overflowed the property of the plaintiff; it is obvious that such a course of conduct would not have laid any ground of action, and yet, for aught that appears in these counts, the defendant may have done nothing more than the things above supposed."

The case of Wagner v. Long Island R. R. Co., 2 Hun. 633, was also an action to recover damages against a railway company for constructing an embankment for its road along and across the adjoining land of plaintiff, and in that case, the Court said:

"This is an action to recover damages against the defendant for constructing the embankment for its road along and across the adjoining land of the plaintiff, whereby the usual flow of the water across and off from the plaintiff's premises, was dammed up and obstructed, and caused to accumulate, whereby the plaintiff sustained damage. It seems to be perfectly well settled, that no action will lie against a party for so using or changing the surface of his own land, as to dam up and obstruct the flow of surface water, which has been accustomed to flow over and across the land of his neighbor. The question involved in the case, is precisely the same in principle, as that which came before the Supreme Court of Massachusetts, in Parks v. The City of Newburyport. In that case, the judge on the trial had instructed the jury, that if, for twenty years, the water accumulating upon the land in the rear of the lots in question, had been accustomed to find its outlet over the land of the defendants, and the same had been obstructed by the acts of the defendants, in such a way as to turn it from their own land across land of the plaintiff, and occasion substantial injury to the property of the plaintiff, without his fault, or want of care on his part, then the defendants would be liable. The plaintiff having recovered under this instruction, the verdict was set aside upon the following opinion by the Court: 'The declaration is for obstructing a watercourse, and the instruction allowed the jury to find for the plaintiff, though there was no watercourse. No action will lie for the interruption of mere surface drainage.' These principles, in the abstract, were conceded by the learned justice who tried the cause; but we think the defendant was deprived of the benefit of them by the refusal to nonsuit, and by certain instructions which were given to the jury. It was left to the jury to find, upon the evidence, whether there existed a watercourse which the defendant had obstructed. We think this was erroneous in the case, both upon the pleadings and the evidence. First, it is to be observed, that the plaintiff did not, in his complaint, claim that there had existed over this land any stream or watercourse which the defendant had obstructed. He says that 'prior to the

construction of such embankment, during the winter
season, large quantities of water flowed some distance above the plaintiff's premises, along and parallel with the aforesaid highway, and passed the
plaintiff's premises without collecting there.' This
is a statement which seems plainly to mean that
such had been the natural flow of the surface water;
and such, we think, the evidence on the part of the
plaintiff plainly showed it to be in fact. The plaintiff's complaint was plainly founded on the theory
that the defendant could not lawfully make any embankment on its own land, which would so obstruct
the natural flow of surface water during thaws and
freshets as to cause it to accumulate on the land
of the plaintiff, but was bound, by means of sufficient culverts, or otherwise, to provide some means
whereby this water should be disposed of. And the
gravamen of the plaintiff's action was the alleged
negligence of the defendant in constructing its embankment without providing sufficient pipes and
culverts to discharge the surface water. A watercourse, according to the definitions of the authorities, 'consists of bed, banks, and water; yet, the
water need not flow continually; and there are many
watercourses which are sometimes dry. There is,
however, a distinction to be taken, in law, between
a regular, flowing stream of water, which, at certain
seasons, is dried up, and those occasional bursts of
water, which, in times of freshet or melting of ice
and snow, descend from the hills and inundate the
country. To maintain the right to a watercourse
or brook, it must be made to appear that the water
usually flows in a certain direction and by a regular
channel, with banks or sides. It need not be shown
to.flow continually, as stated above; and it may at
times be dry, but it must have a well-defined and

substantial existence.' * * * Flowing through a hollow or ravine, only in times of rain or melting of snow, is not, in contemplation of law, a watercourse.

"The plaintiff, as we think, not only failed to allege, but also, to give any evidence tending to show the existence of any watercourse which the defendants had obstructed; and the motion for a non-suit should have been granted."

The case of Churchill v. Baumann, 95 Cal 541, was an action to recover damages for the alleged diversion of water from a natural stream. It appears from the facts in that case that the plaintiff participated with and assisted the defendants in maintaining the dam and keeping the dam and ditch in repair, and acted in connection with them in diverting some of the water from the stream by means thereof.

The Court in discussing the doctrine of acquiescence in that case, at page 543, said:

"Counsel for appellant make the point that no estoppel was pleaded by defendants, and therefore the findings of facts from which the conclusion of an estoppel is drawn are outside of the issues. Conceding that there was no issue as to estoppel, it does not necessarily follow that the findings of fact from which the Court drew the conclusion that plaintiff was estopped were not within other material issues; nor does it follow that those findings do not warrant the general conclusion of law that plaintiff was not entitled to recover in this action. The facts found necessarily imply that, from and after October, 1885, until after all the alleged injurious acts of the defendants had been done, the plaintiff consented to those acts, and consequently was not injured thereby—*volenti non fit injuria.* In commenting upon this maxim, Mr. Broom says: 'It is a general rule of the English law that no one can maintain an action for a wrong where he has consented to the act which occasions his loss,' (Broom Leg. Max side p. 265;) and section 3515 of our Civil Code is to the same effect—"he who consents to an act is not wronged by it." Says Judge Cooley: 'Consent is generally a full and perfect shield when that is complained of as a civil injury which was consented to. A man cannot complain of a nuisance, the erection of which he concurred in or countenanced. He is not injured by a negligence which is partly chargeable to his own fault."

The case of Southern Marble Co. v. Darnell, 94 Georgia 231, was a suit in equity to enjoin the Marble Company from diverting a stream of water to the damage of the plaintiffs. The defendant Marble Company interposed a demurrer to the complaint. The Court, at page 246, said:

"It was contended on the part of defendant that the plaintiff is estopped from claiming damages, because when the ditch was being dug, he knew the purpose for which it was intended, and not only stood by and saw the work going on, but was actually employed by the defendant to assist in digging the ditch and was paid for this service. If this be true, we think the plaitniff could not afterwards complain that the ditch diverted water from his premises. It would be inequitable and unjust to allow him to recover damages for an injury resulting from this cause. He could not stand by while the ditch was being constructed at a heavy expense, or aid in the digging of the ditch, receiving compensation therefor and making no objection, and then recover damages for the diversion of the water from his premises, when he knew, or ought to have known that this would be the result of the construction of the ditch. Under these facts, he would be estopped from obtaining an injunction against the use of the ditch and the continuous diversion of water thereby."

In the case of Rothschild v. Title Guarantee & Trust Co., 204 N. Y. 458, the Court, at page 461, said:

"Where a person wronged is silent under a duty to speak, or by an act or declaration recognizes the wrong as an existing and valid transaction, and in some degree, at least, gives it effect so as to benefit himself or so as to affect the rights or relations created by it between the wrong-doer and a third person, he acquiesces in and assents to it and is equitably estopped from impeaching it. This principle is applicable to the facts found and requires the reversal of the judgment."

The complaints allege that when the defendant laid out and constructed its line of railway, "it was compelled to either bridge or fill the natural channel of said Spring Creek at the point where said line of railway and the channel of Spring Creek intersect; and that at such point, defendant railway company made a fill or embankment on its own right of way." (Paragraph 5, Royer Complaint, Trans. p. 4.)

In paragraph 3 of the Royer complaint, it is alleged

that "during certain seasons of the year, caused by the melting of snow, a large volume of water flows down, and is carried off, by the channel of said Spring Creek." (Trans. Royer case, p. 3.)

· In paragraph 6 of the Royer complaint, it is alleged that "on the 23rd day of January, 1916, and between January 23d and February 17th ,1916, the waters of said Spring Creek were flowing in great quantity and volume down their natural channel, *the large volume of water therein being due to the melting of the snow,*" etc. (Paragraph 6, Royer Complaint, Trans. Royer case, p 6.)

The allegations in the complaint of Wasson and wife are identical with those in the Royer complaint, and a careful analysis of the complaints conclusively shows that the so-called Spring Creek was not a channel or natural watercouse. It was nothing more than surface water resulting from melting snow flowing in the hollow or ravine. The fact that plaintiffs in their complaints denominated it "a watercourse or creek," does not make it so, especially in view of the fact that the complaints specifically allege all through that the volume of water in this alleged creek or channel was due solely to the melting of snow. These specific allegations control the general allegations in the complaints and determine the character of the actions.

The defendant had the right to protect its property from the surface water resulting from melting snow flowing in this hollow or ravine, and if damage resulted thereby, to the property of plaintiffs, it was *damnum absque injuria.*

There is no allegation in either of the complaints that the alleged flowage of water on the lands of plaintiffs was caused by any negligence on the part of defendant. The only allegation in the complaints upon which plaintiffs can possibly predicate negligence is the following allegation:

"That said defendant company placed in the bed or channel of Spring Creek a pipe or drain 48 inches in diameter for the purpose of carrying the waters of Spring Creek under its railway bed or fill, and discharging the waters of such creek into its·natural bed or channel on the south side of its fill or embankment, *which said pipe or drain was totally insufficient to carry off the waters that would flow down through the natural channel of Spring Creek at certain seasons of the year.*"

When this allegation is read in connection with the other specific allegations in the complaint to the effect that the large volume of water in Spring Creek was due to the melting of the snow, it will be readily seen that this is not a sufficient allegation of negligence.

The complaints also contain the following allegation:

The plaintiffs allege and aver the facts to be that "in the years 1912, 1914 the waters of said Spring Creek came down in such volume and quantity, the outlet for the discharge at the point herein mentioned being so totally insufficient as to cause said waters to be impounded or dammed by the embankment or fill of said railway with the west side of Spring Creek, and the raise of ground mentioned above, about the east line of the northwest quarter of the northwest quarter of Section 28 forming sides therefor, causing the said waters to back up against said fill or embankment to an unusual depth, and until such a depth had been reached as to cause the waters thus impounded to break over the fill or embankment of said railway line of the defendant company, and to flow down, over and across the lands" of plaintiffs "in great force and volume, doing great damage thereto, *but for which injury no recovery is sought in this action;* that on each of such occasions portions of the roadbed were washed away and reconstructed by said defendant company in the same manner as originally constructed, and no adequate provision being made by such company to permit the waters going down the natural channel of said Spring Creek to pass in their accustomed way, or in any other way than through the 48-inch drain pipe, as heretofore specified." (Trans. Royer case, page 5.)

It clearly appears from this and other allegations in the complaints, that although plaintiffs had resided in that community for several years, and were familiar with the climatic conditions, and had full knowledge of the manner of construction of said embankment and drain, and that the water had flowed down, over and across their lands in the years 1912 and 1914, causing, as they say, great damage thereto, they made no claim whatever for damages by reason thereof; and there is no allegation in the complaints that the plaintiffs or either of them at any time protested against, or made any objections to, the maintenance of this embankment and drain as the same was constructed; but, on the contrary, it clearly appears from the complaints, that they acquiesced in the maintenance of said drain.

The rule is well settled that no one can maintain an action for a wrong where he has consented to the act which occasioned his loss; and it is equally well settled that plaintiffs could not stand by while this embankment or drain was being reconstructed, presumably at a heavy expense, and subsequently recover damages for injuries to their property resulting, as they allege, by reason of the drain being wholly insufficient to carry off the waters that would flow down through the alleged channel of Spring Creek.

The plaintiffs with full knowledge of their rights, having made no claim for the damages which they say they sustained in 1912, 1914 by reason of the alleged faulty construction of this embankment and drain, the defendant had the right to suppose that they assented to the manner of the construction, and acquiesced in the maintenance thereof, and they were estopped by their conduct from maintaining this action.

IV.

A water course is a stream usually flowing in a particular direction, though it need not flow continually. It may sometimes be dry; it must flow in a definite channel, having beds and banks, and usually discharges itself into some other stream or body of water. It must be something more than a mere surface drainage over the entire face of the tract of land, occasioned by unusual freshets, or other extraordinary causes. It does not include the water flowing in hollows or ravines in land, which is mere surface water from rain or melting snow, and is discharged through them from a higher to a lower level, but which at all other times are destitute of water. Such hollows or ravines are not water courses.

Weil on Water Rights (3rd Ed.), page 354.

Angell on Water Courses, Sections 3-7.
Weis v. City of Madison, 75 Ind. 241.
Wagner v. L. I. R. R., 2 Hun. 633.
Thorpe v. Spokane, 78 Wash. 488.
Hagge v. Ka. City St. R. Co., 104 Fed. 391.

· The case of Thorpe v. City of Spokane (78 Wash. 488), was an action to recover damages alleged to have been caused by the city so negligently grading its streets as to cause the plaintiff's premises to be flooded. The city denied that it had negligently caused the water to be cast upon the plaintiff's premises. Upon this issue the cause was tried to the Court and a jury. At the close of the evidence the Court directed a verdict to be entered in favor of the defendant. One of the questions involved was whether or not the "old channel" referred to in the case was a natural water course. Upon this question, the Court, at page 489, said:

"It is contended ·by the appellants that this old channel is a watercourse, and that the city was liable upon an initial grade for obstructing this watercourse. Much evidence is quoted in the appellant's brief to show that the old channel was a natural watercourse. We think it is conclusively shown by the evidence that water never flowed in this old channel, except when the ground was frozen and snows melted in the late winter or early spring upon such occasions water would flow down this old channel; but at other times there was no water therein. We are satisfied that this does not make a natural watercourse, because it is apparent that the water that flowed down this old channel was mere surface drainage over the entire face of the tract of land mentioned, occasioned by unusual freshets and nothing more."

V.

Mere surface water, or such as accumulates by rain or the melting of snow, is to be regarded as a common enemy, and the proprietor of the lower tenement or estate may, if he chooses, obstruct and hinder the flow of such water, and in doing so may turn it back upon and across lands of others without liability for injury ensuing from such obstruction.

Angell on Water Courses, Sections 4-7.

Gould on Waters, Section 267.

Chadeayne v. Robinson, 55 Conn. 345.

Robinson v. Shanks, 118 Ind. 125.

Greeley v. Maine Central Railroad, 53 Me. 200.

Morrison v. Bucksport & Bangor, 67 Me. 353.

Ashley v. Wolcott, et al., 11 Cush. 192.

Park v. City of Newburyport, 10 Gray 28.

Gannon v. Hargdon, 10 Allen 106.

Treichel v. Great N. Ry. Co., 80 Minn. 96.

Munkers v. Ka. City & St. Joe & Council Bluffs Railroad Co., 60 Mo. 334.

Abbott v. K. St. J. & C. B. R. Co., 83 Mo. 271.

Collier v. C. & A. Ry. Co., 48 Mo. App. 398

Morrissey v. Chi. B. & Q. R. R. Co., 38 Neb. 406.

Wagner v. Long I. R. R. Co., 2 Hun. 633.

Edwards v. Charlotte C. & A. R. Co., 39 S. C. 472.

Cass v. Dicks, 14 Wash. 75.

Harvey v. N. P. R. R. Co., 63 Wash. 669.

Lessard v. Stram, et al., 62 Wis. 112.

Central Trust Co. v. Wabash St. L. & P. Ry. Co., 57 Fed. 441.

Hagge v. K. C. St. Ry. Co., 104 Fed. 391.

U. P. R. R. Co. v. Campbell, 236 Fed. 708.

Walker v. N. Mex. & S. P. Ry. Co., 165 U. S. 593.

The case of Robinson v. Shanks (118 Ind. 125), was a suit to enjoin the diversion of a watercourse. In that case, the Court of its own motion gave the jury the following instruction:

"The complaint asks damages against the defendants for obstructing the flow and diverting the course of an ancient watercourse. To constitute a running stream or watercourse, for the obstruction of which an action will lie, there must be a stream usually flowing in a particular direction, though it will not flow continually; it may sometimes be dry; it must flow in a definite channel, having a bed, sides or banks, and must usually discharge itself into some other stream or body of water; it must be something more than a mere surface drainage over the entire face of a tract of land, occasioned by unusual freshets or other extraordinary cause; it does not include the water flowing in hollows or ravines in land, which is the mere surface water from rain or melting snow, and is discharged through them from higher to lower lands, but which at other times are destitute of water. Such hollows or ravines are not, in legal contemplation, watercourses, for the obstruction of which an action will lie; and if you believe from the evidence in this cause that the only flow of water in said run or ravine, described in the complaint, was rain falling upon and snow melting upon and running down from the surface of an entire tract of higher land into a hollow or ravine, and by such course carried to lower land, then said Leeper's run was not a watercourse within the meaning of the law, and then it would be your duty to find for the defendants."

It was claimed by the appellant that the instruction was erroneous. The Court, in discussing this question at page 134, said:

"It is objected to this instruction that it is too refined and restrictive in the application made to the particular case. There is evidence, however, in the record to which it is applicable."

The case of Gannon v. Hargadon, 10 Allen 106, was an action to recover damages for the diversion of a stream of water so that it flowed upon the plaintiff's land. On the trial, the defendant requested the Court to instruct the jury as follows:

"If the defendant placed sods in the cart ruts upon the way over his own land from time to time, as the ruts were made by the passing of the cart, and he did this merely to prevent the water from making channels of such ruts, and gullying and washing away and injuring said way and the land of the defendant, and such water was not that of a watercourse but merely surface water caused by the melting of snows and the fall of rains in the spring, and flowed on to the defendant's land from land above his own, and if in consequence of the placing of said sods the said water which would otherwise have run down said ruts was diverted upon the plaintiff's land, the defendant is not liable therefor. The plaintiff had no right that the ruts made on the defendant's land should be kept open."

The trial Court refused to give said instruction, which was assigned as error. On appeal, the Court, Bigelow, C. J., at page 109, said:

"It seems to us that the instructions for which the defendant asked should have been given, and that those under which the case was submitted to the jury were not in accordance with the principles recognized and adopted in cases recently adjudicated by this Court. The right of an owner of land to occupy and improve it in such manner and for such purposes as he may see fit, either by changing the surface or the erection of buildings or other structures thereon, is not restricted or modified by the fact that his own land is so situated with reference to that of adjoining owners that an alteration in the mode of its improvement or occupation in any portion of it will cause water which may accumulate thereon by rains and snows falling on its surface or flowing on to it over the surface of adjacent lots, either to stand in unusual quantities on other adjacent lands, or pass into and over the same in greater quantities or in other directions than they were accustomed to flow.

"The point of these decisions is, that where there is no watercourse by grant or prescription, and no stipulation exists between conterminous proprietors of land concerning the mode in which their respective parcels shall be occupied and improved, no right to regulate or control the surface drainage of water can be asserted by the owner of one lot over that of his neighbor. *Cujus est solum, ejus est usque ad caelum* is a general rule, applicable to the use and enjoyment of real property, and the right of a party to the free and unfettered control of his own land above, upon and beneath the surface cannot be interfered with or restrained by any considerations of injury to others which may be occasioned by the flow of mere surface water in consequence of the lawful appropriation of land by its owner to a particular use or mode of enjoyment. Nor is it at all material, in the application of this principle of law, whether a party obstructs or changes the direction and flow of surface water by preventing it from coming within the limits of his land, or by erecting barriers or changing the level of the soil, so as to turn it off in a new course after it has come within his boundaries. The obstruction of surface water or an alteration in the flow of it affords no cause of action in behalf of a person who may suffer loss or detriment therefrom against one who does no act inconsistent with the due exercise of dominion over his own soil. This principle seems to have been lost sight of in the instructions given to the jury. While the right of the owner of land to improve it and to change its surface so as to exclude surface water from it is fully recognized, even although such exclusion may cause the water to flow on to a neighbor's land, it seems to be assumed that he would be liable in damages, if, after suffering the water to come on his land, he obstructed it and caused it to flow in a new direction on land of a conterminous proprietor where it had not previously been accustomed to flow. But we know of no such distinction. A party may improve any portion of his land, although he may thereby cause the surface water flowing thereon, whencesoever it may come, to pass off in a different direction and in larger quantities than previously. If such an act causes damages to adjacent land, it is *damnum absque injuria.*"

The case of Munkers v. Kas. City, St. Jo. & Council Bluffs R. R. Co., 60 Mo. 334, was, among other things, an action for damages for alleged diversion from its

natural course and channel of a stream of water, causing it to flood the lands of plaintiff. In that case, the
Court, at page 339, said:

> "Damages were claimed, in the second count,
> for a diversion, by the defendant, in the manner
> therein stated, of a certain stream of water from
> its natural course and channel, whereby plaintiff's
> fields were flooded. There was testimony tending
> to show that no natural watercourse was interfered
> with by the defendant, but that the plaintiff was
> injured alone by surface water. If plaintiff's in-
> juries were occasioned by flooding from surface
> water, and not by the diversion, by the defendant,
> or its predecessor, of a natural watercourse, then
> there could be no recovery on the second count.
> This question should have been submitted to the
> jury under instructions explaining the difference
> between surface water and a natural watercourse,
> and defining the duties and liabilities of the de-
> fendant arising from the construction and opera-
> tion of its road across or along a running stream.
> This was not done."

In the case of Edwards v. Railroad Co., 39 S. C.
472, the facts which are stated in the opinion, are as
follows:

> "The plaintiff who is a married woman, joining
> her husband with her as co-plaintiff, brings this
> action against the Charlotte, Columbia and Augus-
> ta Railroad Company, to recover damages alleged
> to have been done to her property, as well as to her
> health, by reason of the obstruction by the defend-
> ant company of the natural flow of surface water
> over and across the right of way and railroad track

of defendant. The allegations in the complaint,
substantially are, that some time in the year 1867
the defendant company constructed its railway
through the town of Graniteville, over and along
Canal street of said town, running north and south,
parallel with Horse Creek, a natural watercourse,
on the west of the railway; that plaintiff is the lessee
of certain premises situate at the northeast corner
of Canal street and Cottage, the latter being a street
running perpendicular to the former; that on the
eastern side of the town of Graniteville, the land is
hilly, and gradually slopes towards Horse Creek,
and that the surface water which would accumulate
on the eastern side was accustomed to flow, in part,
down and along Cottage street, across Canal street,
to said Horse Creek, previous to the construction
of defendant's road, and for some time afterwards,
without injury to plaintiff's premises, but that some
time in the year 1878, 'the defendant negligently,
unlawfully and unnecessarily' erected a large sand
bank at the intersection of Canal and Cottage
streets, whereby the surface water was forced back
on plaintiff's premises, and has continued to maintain and increase said sand bank.

"The defendant claims that the sand bank complained of (which was constructed on defendant's
right of way) was necessary to protect its roadbed
and right of way from being undermined and
washed away by the flow of the surface water, and,
therefore, its construction was no invasion of the
legal rights of the plaintiff, and the defendant is
not liable for any damages which plaintiff may have
sustained by reason of such obstruction of the flow
of the surface water."

The Court in discussing the question as to whether

or not the water diverted was surface water or the waters
of a natural watercourse, at page 474, said:

"It is not, and cannot be, denied that the rule
in regard to interference with the flow of surface
water is wholly different from that which prevails
in regard to the waters of a natural watercourse.
We shall, therefore, confine our attention entirely
to the rule as to surface water. What that rule
is has been the subject of debate in numerous cases
in the other states, many of which we have examined
in preparing this opinion. Some of the states have
adopted what is known as the civil law rule, while
others seem to have adopted what is designated as
the intermediate rule, while others again (a majority of the states, as·is said in a note to Goddard
v. Inhabitants of Harpswell, 30 Am. St. Rep., at
page 391), adhere to the rule of the common law.
In this state, so far as we are informed, there is no
ajudiciation upon the subject, for what was said
upon the subject by the late Chief Justice Simpson
was 'not intended as a final adjudication, and conclusive of said question in the future,' as he himself
expressly said in that opinion, but simply his own
opinion as to the comparative merits of the several
rules.

"But in view of the express declaration of the
law-making power, as embodied in section 2738
of the General Statutes, we feel bound to declare,
in the absence of any constitutional provision,
statute or even authoritative decision to the contrary, that the common law rule must still be recognized as controlling here, for that section expressly declares that: 'Every part of the common
law of England, not altered by this act nor incon-

sistent with the Constitution of this state, and the customs and laws thereof, is hereby continued in full force and virtue within this state in the same manner as before the passage of this act.' Under the common law rule, surface water is regarded as a common enemy, and every landed proprietor has a right to take any measures necessary to the protection of his own property from its ravages, even if in doing so, he throws it back upon a coterminous proprietor to his damage, which the law regards as a case of *damnum absque injuria,* and affording no cause of action."

The case of Walker v. New Mexico & S. P. R. Co., 165 U. S. 593, was an action to recover damages from an overflow of lands alleged to have been caused by wrongful obstructions by the company of a natural watercourse. The complaint, in substance, charged that the defendant obstructed the natural and artificial watercourses by which the waters from the north and west of the plaintiff's property, and from the Socorro and Magdalena mountains, in their natural flow and fall passed over the lands of the plaintiff and other lands, and emptied into the Rio Grande. The defendant company contended that there were no natural watercourses obstructed by the defendant's roadbed, and that the water which did the damage was simply surface water. The Court, in discussing this question, said:

"Does a lower landowner by erecting embankments or otherwise preventing the flow of surface water on to his premises render himself liable to an upper landowner for damages caused by the stopping of such flow? In this respect, the civil and common law are different, and the rules of the two laws have been recognized in different states of the Union—some accepting the doctrine of the civil law, that the lower premises are subservient to the higher, and that the latter have a qualified easement in respect to the former, an easement which gives the right to discharge all surface water upon them. The doctrine of the common law, on the other hand, is the reverse, that the lower landowner owes no duty to the upper landowner, and that each may appropriate all the surface water that falls upon his own premises, and that the one is under no obligation to receive from the other the flow of any surface water, but may in the ordinary prosecution of his business and in the improvement of his premises by embankments or otherwise, prevent any portion of the surface water coming from such upper premises. * * *

"It would be useless to cite the many authorities from the different states in which on the one side or the other these doctrines of the civil and the common law are affirmed. The divergency between the two lines of authorities is marked, springing from the difference in the foundation principle upon which the two doctrines rest, the one affirming the absolute control by the owner of his property, the other affirming a servitude, by reason of location, of the one premises to the other. * * *

"If a case came to this Court from one of the states in which the doctrine of the civil law obtains, it would become our duty, having respect to this which is a matter of local law, to follow the decisions of that state. And in like manner we should follow the adverse ruling in a case coming from one of the states in which the common law rule is recognized."

VI.

(a) **Where a railroad culvert is sufficient to pass the usual amount of water resulting from melting snow, the railway company is not liable for damages to property because of the culvert being insufficient to carry off the waters of an extraordinary and unexpected flood.**

> Norris v. S. F. & W. Railway Co., 23 Fla. 182.
> Cottrell v. Marshall Infirmary, 70 Hun. 495.
> B. &' O. R. Co. v. Sulphur Springs Ind. School Dist., 96 Pa. St. 65.
> Central Trust Co. v. Wabash St. L. & P. R. Co., 57 Fed. 441.

The case of Central Trust Co. v. Wabash St. L. Co., 57 Fed. 441, was an action for damages for injury sustained by reason of a flood caused by an alleged insufficient culvert. The facts in that case are set out fully. in the opinion.

The Court, in discussing the question of the liability of the receiver of the railway company, at page 445, said:

> "It is, however, insisted that the receiver is responsible for damages from floods occasioned by unsual and extraordinary rainfalls, because they might have been foreseen and guarded against by the exercise of ordinary and reasonable foresight, care and skill in the construction of a sufficient culvert and embankment. A railroad company, acting in pursuance of legislative authority, is only required to exercise reasonable diligence and precaution in constructing passageways for the water through its bridges and embankments, and is entitled to select a safe and massive structure, in pref-

erence to a lighter one, which would less obstruct the water. It is not liable to an action for damages if it fails to construct a culvert or bridge so as to pass extraordinary floods."

(b) A railroad company is not required to construct culverts or passageways through its embankment for the passage of surface water from the lands of others:

Egener v. N. Y. & R. B. Ry. Co., 38 N. Y. Supp. 319.

VII.

The court should have directed the jury to find a verdict in favor of the defendant and against each of the plaintiffs in these actions, as requested by the defendant, and entered a judgment dismissing the complaints herein.

The defendant was entitled to a directed verdict and judgment against each of the plaintiffs for the following reasons:

(a) The complaints herein do not state facts sufficient to constitute causes of action.

(b) Spring Creek is not a natural water-course.

(c) There were no natural watercourses obstructed by the defendant.

(d) The waters which flowed upon the lands of plaintiff were surface waters only.

(e) The flowage of water upon the lands of plaintiffs was not caused by any negligence of the defendant.

(f) Plaintiffs with full knowledge of the manner of construction of said embankment and drain, and of their rights in the premises, acquiesced in the maintenance thereof, and were thereby estopped from maintaining this action.

(g) The injury, if any, to the property of plaintiffs, was the result solely of an extraordinary and unexpected flood.

(h) The drain or culvert in the embankment of defendant was sufficient to pass the usual amount of water resulting from melting snow, and the company was not liable for damages to the property of plaintiffs because of the culvert being insufficient to carry off the waters of an extraordinary and unexpected flood.

(i) The defendant was not required to construct any culvert or drain through its embankment for the passage of surface water from the lands of others.

(j) The evidence in these cases is wholly insufficient to support or sustain a verdict and judgment for the plaintiffs.

VIII.

The court should have given the instructions requested in the Assignments of Error numbered I, II, III and IV. The court erred in giving the instruction set out under Assignment of Error number V for the reason that the court, in effect, instructed the jury that Spring Creek was a natural watercourse, whereas the court should have instructed the jury that the waters were surface waters only, resulting from melting snow flowing down a ravine or hollow.

The testimony in these cases is as follows:

Testimony.

GUY H. HEIBERLING,

A witness for plaintiff, testified:

Direct Examination.

County Engineer of Benton County, Washington. Plaintiff's Exhibit "A," a map of the lands of Wasson and Royer, was prepared by me. (The map was admitted in evidence for the purpose of illustration.) Spring Creek originates about fifteen miles to the north and west of the Wasson and Royer land. The county road follows along the center line east and west through Section 28, and Spring Creek lies immediately east of the county road as established at the present time. The land of Mr. E. B. Starkey is shown on the map. I took levels where Spring Creek crosses the line between Sections 20 and 29, and also where same crosses the O.-W. R. & N. right of way, and found the fall to be about 8.6 feet in one thousand. The drain under the O.-W. R. & N. tracks, where Spring Creek flows under, consisted of one 48-inch corrugated metal culvert, which was about four feet below the top of the track. At this point the line of the O.-W. R. & N. Co. is on an embankment or fill, which is about eight feet deep. The fill extends from the creek six or seven hundred feet east of the county road over in Section 28, where it passes from embankment to a slight cut.

With the exception of a few months, I have lived in Benton County since the fall of 1908. Plaintiff's Exhibit "B," purporting to be a map of part of Benton County issued by the Department of the Interior, is shown me and I can trace from this map the course of Spring Creek. The upper limits of the head show in Sections 25, 11 and 24, and it runs generally southeasterly at the head and bears southwesterly for three or four miles, then southeasterly into Yakima River.

The topography of the land from where Spring Creek has its origin is rolling, but Spring Creek is in a canyon until a short distance from the O.-W. R. & N. right of way, where the ground spreads out flat. The channel is well defined and drains twenty or twenty-five thousand acres coming down from various gulches into the Spring Creek Gulch. · The fall from the source to where it crosses the right of way of the O.-W. R. & N. Co. is something over two thousand feet. Where Spring Creek runs under the right of way of the O.-W. R. & N. Co. there has been a fill on each side of the creek. On the east side the grade tapers gradually to nothing in about thirteen or fourteen hundred feet. The annual snowfall in the hills north of the railroad right of way varies from nothing to as high as 18 inches. In January, 1916, at Prosser there were two different snowfalls— one of these twelve and the other fifteen inches—and there is usually heavier snow in the hills. This snow generally begins to melt whenever the chinook winds come, and it melts rapidly then.

Cross Examination.

Spring Creek, from the section line of 20 and 29, meanders back and forth. One standing in the bottom of Spring Creek at the O.-W. R. & N. right of way, attempting to look up towards Mr. Starkey's place north, will find the creek so crooked that a straight line vision will not pass up the creek channel. The gully from which Spring Creek comes out of the Rattlesnake Hills begins to widen at point about the north line of the southeast quarter of the southeast quarter of Section 20. Mr. Starkey has quite a flat place—about ten acres or so, which would be located substantially in the southeast quarter of the southeast quarter of the southeast quarter of section 20. The base of the bluff is about the section line between 20 and 29 on the west side of the creek. (Trans. pp. 19-21.)

PRESTON ROYER,

One of plaintiffs, as a witness on the part of plaintiff Wasson, testified:

Direct Examination.

I own the lands described in my complaint, amounting to practicaally nineteen acres. I bought the land in the spring of 1914. I have lived along the branches of Spring Creek since the fall of 1905, and at one time lived in the Rattlesnake country, Spring Creek passing through my homestead. *The waters coming down Spring Creek is caused by the melting snow and it comes down in a series.* In that country our weather goes in a circle—we will have a per iod of dry seasons, very little moisture, poor crops, and a series of good moisture and good crops. Spring Creek runs practically every year, when there are good crops, and in dry seasons, does not run at all. In 1907, the water down Spring Creek went through a 24-foot breach, practically four feet deep. There is no outlet other than under the O.-W. R. & N. crossing. From 1906 to 1912, there was water in more or less volume running each season. This water flows to the Yakima River, and the only outlet is under the O.-W. R. & N. tracks. In June or July, 1914, the water crossed my ranch.

In 1914, in the last of June or the first of July, there was a freshet in the Rattlesnake Hills in the watershed of Spring Creek, and water ran down this creek to where same intersects with the O.-W. R. & N., where they have a 48-inch pipe. It was not sufficient to carry the water off and it backed the water up and it flooded straight east and went down the pit to the county road, washed out the county road to a considerable depth, and went on down where the railroad comes to the surface grade and crossed right through and ran off for five or six hours over our place. (Trans. pp. 22-23.)

The banks of Spring Creek vary, being well defined for probably fourteen miles above Mr. Starkey's place, there are distinct channels and have to be bridged; they expect water in these, and they put in bridges. In 1916, on January 20th, there was from twelve to sixteen inches of badly drifted snow, and Spring Creek and the ditches and canals up to the top of the hill were leveled across in many places, practically no snow on the level lands but the snow was drifted into depressions. From the level lands to a distance of five or six miles up the Rattlesnake slope there was no snow. Above that, there was. Also the canyons are much deeper at the top, and these were full of snow. The ground was frozen and the water could not go into the ground. The chinook winds started at 11:30 January 20th and stopped at night. January 21st a southwest wind, mostly clear, and checked at night. January 22d, southwest wind. The snow melted and the high water went across my place at 5 o'clock and run about five hours in the afternoon. It destroyed the roadbed at a great distance, broke through a stretch of railroad track, went over the ties and washed a deep hole through the railroad on to the Wasson land and then to my land. On Monday following there was a cold northeast wind and it froze hard, which checked the flow of the water. Weather stayed frozen and we got some snow, probably fifteen inches, until the next chinook came. The next chinook wind started February 7th and was a clear day—with from twelve to fourteen inches badly drifted snow. The wind changed and on February 9th the water started running, and on the 10th the water went over my place and over the Wasson place. The water backed up on the north side of the embankment and run down a borrow pit east and then passed across the railroad track, and down over Mr. Wasson's land and my land until it met the old channel of Spring Creek.

With respect to the Wasson land, this land slopes southeast and was planted to alfalfa, and when the water came over that land would wash holes, many of them fifteen feet long and three or four feet wide, making it impossible to irrigate it and impossible to go over it with a cutting machine. The water went over my land and washed the soil somewhat. (Trans. pp. 25-26.)
* * * * *

Cross Examination.

The Wasson place was covered with water in 1916 to the extent of between 40 and 45 acres. When the water came down on the 23d of January, it ran for five hours * * *. Between the 23d of January and the 7th of February about fifteen inches of loose snow fell, followed by freezing weather, and no water came down until about the 7th of February. The water would check at night and flow again in the day-time. I have been acquainted with Spring Creek since 1905. *The creek* *is always dry in the summer, above the Government canal. It is dry in the aggregate over eleven months in the year, and sometimes it does not run that month. There must be snow in the hills to put water in that channel, by the chinook winds. If it melts gradually, and no frost in the ground, you have no water in Spring Creek.* If it melts off in the winter, melts gradually, it probably runs in warm weather. *The chinook was what brought the water down.* The gully through which the water drained was practically drifted full of snow. *After January 23d, when the 15-inch snowstorm came, a second chinook wind came and the snow became more dense and more dense, until it finally became water in part, and started to flow down.* The snow that had not yet congealed would hold it back for a while until the water would break through and it would come down in bunches, and the channel on the flat between the O.-W. R. & N. and Starkey's place would possibly have a tendency to fill up and cause the water to spread. Spring Creek channel at my place was full of snow at that time and it had to work down gradually.—I did not farm my place in 1916. (Trans. pp. 28-29.)

SAMUEL H. MASON,

A witness for plaintiff, testified:

Direct Examination.

I homesteaded the Wasson place in 1900, owned it about ten years. I am acquained with Spring Creek where it now leaves the O.-W. R. & N. right of way to the Yakima River, approximately a couple of miles. The channel is not regular—in places good and wide and other places deep. It is about four to eight feet at the bottom, the depth being irregular. * * * *The water came there in the channel in the spring when the snow would come on the Rattlesnake Hills, and melt off suddenly.*

These waters passed through the channel to the river, and at my place at the deepest time it was probably two to two and one-half feet deep, and in the narrower places deeper. While I owned the place the waters never came over the land. It generally followed the course of the creek—only time it got over was when banked up but not washed down over the land.

Cross Examination.

Spring Creek carries water only during the spring freshets. The time would vary. The only time I knew water to run there any time was when the snow would come on the Rattlesnake Hills and would melt and go off suddenly; would seem to absorb the water in the winter time when it went off gradually, but when the sun and wind melted it suddenly always had these freshets in the spring. The time of the melting depends entirely on the presence or absence of these chinook winds. * * * I never saw it in going off, last as long as ten to twenty days as a rush of waters, but when this water run down there in the creek it would be a month or so until it all went away when plenty of snow in the mountains, but a rush of waters would be generally two, three or four days. Spring Creek is dry a good deal of the time. *I don't think water runs there regularly from freshets over two months of the year.* (Trans. pp. 23-25.)

M. C. WILLIAMS,

A witness for the plaintiff, testified:

The railroad track runs approximately east and west, and the grade of the track where it crosses Spring Creek is one-fifth of one per cent, ascending towards Grandview. * * *

The original right of way of the railroad company was forty feet on each side of the center line of the railroad. Afterwards, the property owners immediately adjoining the right of way on the north added an eighty-foot strip clear across the forty acres at Biggam. That would make 120 feet on the north side and 40 feet on the south side. The 80 feet has since been deeded to the county for road purposes. (Trans. pp. 29-33.)

LEE M. LAMSON,

A witness for the plaintiff, testified:

Direct Examination.

County Agricultural Agent of Benton County; have been for five years; acquainted with the Wasson and Royer land prior to January, 1916; examined the Royer land at Mr. Royer's request to give him advice whether the corn needed irrigation. There were six or seven acres of corn and probably five acres or so of a poor stand of alfalfa. The soil is very fine sand, with a gravel subsoil. I examined the land in March, 1916. The flumes were torn down, the land was cut up pretty badly with little rivulets. In a good many places the surface soil was washed off entirely, so it was washed down to the gravel. The humas which was on the surface was washed off. I went over the Wasson land at the same time. The water had cut out ravines. A good many were from a foot to two feet deep—some were less. The alfalfa crown were all the way from three to ten inches above the ground. The irrigation ditches were hardly recognizable. The only practical thing to do would be to plow it up and relevel it and reseed it. (Trans. pp. 29-30.)

Cross Examination.

I did not measure the amount of land upon the Wasson place that the water passed over, although the line of the flow was fairly well marked with drift weeds. The water did not go over all of the land below the railroad track. * * * I examined the land north of the railroad; nothing washed out there but some soil washed on to it. (Trans. p. 31.)

Luke Powell,

A witness for the plaintiff, testified:

Direct Examination.

Distrct Horticulturalist, State of Washington; acquainted with the Wasson and Royer land about January 1, 1916; was with Mr. Lamson and went over the land in March of that year. The soil was washed and a number of gullies washed, from six to eighteen inches and as wide as a foot to 18 inches. (Trans. p. 31.)

William J. Wasson,

One of plaintiffs, as a witness on the part of plaintiff Royer, testified:

Direct Examination.

Owner of the land described in the Wasson complaint; was at Centralia, Washington, at the time of the flood in 1916, came to Prosser March 2d, went over the land and saw the flooded area. The irrigating ditches were washed out; the rows that you irrigate with were washed and cut crossways so that you could not possibly carry water down over it and irrigate it. I should judge in the neighborhood of forty-five acres of my land was left in this condition. * * * The water crossed the railroad track practically 150 feet wide and as it came down over my place, it spread out. (Trans. pp. 32-33.)

M. C. WILLIAMS,

A witness for defendant, testified :

Direct Examination.

I am the same witness that was on the stand for plaintiff. I was resident engineer in charge of construction. The definite location of the railroad across the land in controversy was made before I went on the work but I was resident engineer when *the track was building*. This was *in 1910 and 1911*. I have been acquainted with the drain called Spring Creek since 1907. I have been back and across this territory a number of times between those dates connected with the defendant in an engineering capacity. *I prescribed the size of the culvert at Biggam after inquiring as to water conditions from residents in the immediate vicinity who had lived there a number of years, and after such inquiry I put in a culvert 48 inches in diameter, circular in form. From the information received, it was my opinion this 48-inch diameter was sufficient in size to carry off the normal flow of surface water that came down. The water flowage conditions in 1916 in Yakima Valley and throughout the eastern part of Washington in January, 1916, were far greater than any since 1906. There was more run off and more snow. In the winter of 1915-1916, there were two heavy snows in the early part of the year 1916. One was twelve to fourteen inches, which all went off the ground, and was followed by a twelve to eighteen inch snow after that, which went off in the early part of February.* Plaintiff's Exhibit "B" is a topographical map of the Prosser quadrangle, including Sections 20, 21, 28 and 29, the lands in question; contains contour lines showing points of similar elevation on the natural surface of the ground. The contour distance is fifty feet. Am acquainted with the location of Sunnyside canal. During the winter season the spillway has been left open, whereby melting water drains into the canal, and from that into Spring Creek. Referring to the course of Spring Creek from the county road south of Starkey's place, there is a small rock dam near the fence, and as you go up the channel there are several other small obstructions, but the main dam is the one that has been put in by the Sunnyside Reclamation people, which is the outlet of the lateral that runs around the base of the hill. The dam is in the neighborhood of four feet in height. Document marked for identification, Defendant's Exhibit No. 1, is a blueprint map showing the area in controversy prepared under my direction, illustrating the land of Mr. Starkey, Mr. Wasson and Mr. Royer, Biggam Station and the course of certain channels and drains made from surveys, and also showing the course of the water and the overflow, which was received in evidence and marked Defendant's Exhibit No. 1. After the water passed over the wasteway, the water came down in such volume that the original channel was so small as to be unable to carry the water, and it overflowed and spread out over the land, forming two channels in Mr. Starkey's field. one marked on the map "original channel" and the other "overflow channel." It passed on down to the next forty below, which would be the southeast quarter of the southeast quarter of Section 20, and the channels came together again as a main channel with the exception the water spread out to a considerable extent on the ground. The water overflowed the greater part of Mr. Starkey's land, running entirely out of the channel, and then as it comes to the south line of Section 20 it strikes the other dam, which had been put in just north of the county road and again spread out, and as a matter of fact considerable amount of it has never struck that dam as the elevation of the dam has nothing to do with that just above the southeast quarter of Section twenty. The colored area on the map, Defendant's Exhibit No. 1, across the land of Mr. Wasson and part across Mr. Royer's land, illustrates the course of the water, and the map was made from notes of surveys taken shortly after February, 1916. The part colored purple illustrates the exterior areas of the flowage, and shows the overflow just as it happened.

Cross Examination.

Before I put the 48-inch pipe in, I made inquiry from residents in and around Biggam as to flowage of water down Spring Creek, also made an independent *investigation by going practically to the foot of the main` Rattlesnake Hills, where the three branches of Spring Creek come in; also consulted a government survey which I believe was made by the Reclamation Service, also took into consideration that the spill-way from the Sunnyside Canal would dump some water therein. I figured about twenty-second feet would be the flow.* (Trans. pp. 39-42.)

EDWARD L. SHORT,

A witness for defendant, testified:

Direct Examination.

Occupation, civil engineer, five years in the employ of defendant, headquarters, Walla Walla, third district, including Yakima branch. At request of defendant surveyed the lands in questions, first on the 21st and 22d of March, 1916; made the notes of Defendant's Exhibit No. 1 and measured the area of the overflow oh the Wasson and Royer lands. The line between the area overflowed and the area not overflowed could be found and distinguished by small drifts or weeds that had lodged against the alfalfa. The map has marked upon it the different areas of land and those figures are correct. (Trans. p. 42.) * * * *

I made a survey for the purpose of determining the lay of the ground on that area bounded by the railroad track on the south and Mr. Starkey's farm on the north, the county road on the east and Spring Creek on the west, and made a map marked for identification, Defendant's Exhibit No. 2, which was prepared from my notes, which exhibit was offered and admitted in evidence and marked Defendant's Exhibit No. 2. I run levels on certain lines marked a, b, c and d. This map correctly shows the lay of the ground. Water on the southeast corner of Mr. Starkey's field, the southeast quarter of the southeast quarter of Section 20, would flow almost directly south from this point to the southeast and would not flow to the culvert. The line of levels marked C and D show the ground to be higher than further east. Water flowing from Mr. Starkey's field would flow right across the county road. The arrows on Defendant's Exhibit No. 1, indicate the course of the water. (Trans. pp. 49-50.)

ALFRED GOBALET,

A witness for defendant, testified:

Direct Examination.

Civil engineer and draftsman; residence Walla Walla; was with Mr. Short on the day certain surveys were made in respect to Royer and Wasson lands. The exterior lines of the portion colored purple on Defendant's Exhibit No. 1, were arrived at by indications of sediment that was carried by the water and left on the alfalfa and by little straws that the water left on the outer edge. The areas in the map are correct. (Trans. pp. 42-43.)

E. E. STARKEY,

A witness for defendant, testified:

I lived on the land illustrated by Defendant's Exhibit No. 1 and marked "E. E. Starkey," which would be the southeast quarter of the southeast quarter of

Section 20; lived there nine years; was on the farm in January, 1916. In January, 1916, Spring Creek drain overflowed the western part of the north half of the north forty, breaking out of the natural channel, and flowed out inside the opening where it drains south and west to a limit probably 150 yards, spreading out over the land to what is known as the government dam and below the dam I had constructed a new channel to check up against it and prevent washout. Next day when the water came, it broke over at the point where the arrows on Defendant's Exhibit No. 1 show at the point called "plow land." The creek bed at that time was full of snow and ice. The first flow could not get through the channel because of the ice and snow. At the south line of my place I constructed a check, consisting of a rock dam, probably eighteen inches to two feet high, and I had a dike along the south side of my place to check the sediment. I have been acquainted with the Wasson lands for eight years and have been over a considerable part of it during the time of the flood last winter, a year ago, and I have been over it several times since. I have helped harvest crops on the land several times and have mowed the crops of the Royer place. The water entered Mr. Wasson's place in 1916 in two different places, at the railroad east of the county road and at the west side where it broke through the railway. Where the water left the railroad right of way, it was from forty to sixty feet wide and very shallow, and its greatest width was probably 350 feet. Part of it turned east where there was a wagon road, illustrated on Defendant's Exhibit No. 1, as "blown out wagon track, northwest channel." In Mr. Wasson's place it spread out considerably but did not flow deep at any point, and washed out the dirt

from the irrigation ditches and between the alfalfa somewhat. I do not think the general width on the Wasson
place was over an average of seventy-five feet. It did
spread, however, to twice that width, especially when
this water came in from the west side. The soil on the
Wasson land is particularly clean of rock; there is one
little gravel bed not very far from where these two
streams met and there were no washes to amount to
anything. The wash covered possibly three and a half
to four acres. * * * I was over the Royer place several times. I frequently cross it—over it first in 1910
and frequently since. The point where the water entered the Royer land was of fairly slight slope, there
was from one and a half to three acres covered by the
water. (Trans., pp. 45-47-48.)

B. R. SHERMAN,

A witness for plaintiff, testified as follows:

Direct examination.

The waste water from Mr. Starkey's ranch in 1916
never went any further than this corner, referring to the
corner caused by the county road crossing the railroad.
(Trans., p. 50.)

ARGUMENT.

The questions raised under points numbered IV, V,
VI, VII and VIII, involving as they do practically the
same questions, may be considered together.

The paramount question involved in these cases is
whether or not Spring Creek is a natural watercourse,
or whether it is a ravine or hollow through which mere

surface water flowed resulting from rain or melting snow.

Preston Royer, one of the plaintiffs, on direct examination, testified that the waters coming down Spring Creek were caused by the melting of snow, and on cross-examination, he testified (using his own language): "The creek is always dry in the summer above the government canal. It is dry in the aggregate for eleven months in the year, and sometimes it does not run that month. There must be snow in the hills to put water in that channel by the chinook winds. If it melts gradually and no frost in the ground, you have no water in Spring Creek." "The chinook wind was what brought the water down." "After January 23d, when the 15-inch snow storm came, a second chinook wind came and the snow became more dense and more dense until it finally became water in part and started to flow down."

Samuel H. Mason, a witness for plaintiffs, on direct examination, testified (using his own language): "The water came there in the channel in the spring when the snow would come on the Rattlesnake Hills and melt off suddenly," and on cross-examination, he testified: "Spring Creek carries water only during the spring freshets. The time would vary. The only time I knew water to run there any time was when the snow would come on the Rattlesnake Hills and would melt and go off suddenly; would seem to absorb the water in the winter time when it went off gradually, but when the sun and wind melted it suddenly, always had these freshets in the spring. The time of the melting depends upon the presence or absence of these chinook winds."

"I don't think water runs there regularly from freshets over two months in the year."

It manifestly appears from the testimony of witnesses for the plaintiffs that what plaintiffs denominate as "Spring Creek" or "a natural watercourse" is nothing more than a mere surface drainage occasioned by unusual freshets or other extraordinary causes, such as melting snow from chinook winds. Under the authorities cited, the water which flowed down this ravine was merely surface water, and as such, is regarded in law as a common enemy, and the defendant had the right to obstruct and hinder the flow of such water and to turn it back, if necessary, upon and across the lands of others, without liability for injury resulting from such obstruction.

As was forcefully stated by Judge Anders in the case of Cass v. Dicks, 14 Wash. 75, "Surface water caused by the falling of rain or the melting of snow, and that escaping from running streams and rivers, is regarded as an outlaw and a common enemy, against which anyone may defend himself, even though by so doing, injury may result to others." And "If one in the lawful exercise of his right to control, manage, or improve his own land, finds it necessary to protect it from surface water flowing from higher land, he may do so; and if damage thereby results to another, it is *damnum absque injuria.*"

It further appears from the evidence in these cases that floods of the character of that which occurred in January and February, 1916, were very infrequent. The engineer of the railway company testified that:

"The water flowage conditions in 1916 in Yakima Valley and throughout the eastern part of Washington in January, 1916, were far greater than any since 1906." It appears from the testimony that there was a flood in 1912-1914, but it does not appear that these floods were periodical or were to be expected every year. The testimony also conclusivly shows that the culvert or drain constructed by the defendant was sufficient to pass the usual amount of water resulting from melting snow, and it is submitted that it is not liable for damages to the propery of plaintiffs because this drain was insufficient to carry off the water of an extraordinary and unexpected flood.

It will be noted from the engineer's testimony that before this drain or culvert was placed in the embankment of the railway, he inquired of residents in the neighborhood as to weather conditions, and made an independent examination of the topography of the country. He acted upon the information thus obtained, and no doubt was informed that the waters which passed down this ravine were merely surface waters resulting from melting snow; and in the light of testimony of witnesses for plaintiffs, he must have been informed that the alleged Spring Creek contained no water eleven months in the year, and in some years was entirely dry. Under this state of facts, it is submitted that the railroad company was not guilty of any negligence in the construction of this embankment or culvert.

It conclusively appears that the only flow of water which passed down the so-called "Spring Creek," was caused by snow melting upon and running down from the surface of the hills northwest of defendant's railway into a ravine or hollow.

The statutes of the State of Washington expressly provide that the common law, so far as it is not inconsistent with the Constitution and Laws of the United States or of the State of Washington, nor incompatible with the institutions and conditions of society of that state, shall be the rule of decision in all of its courts. There is no constitutional or statutory provision in the State of Washington governing or controlling the subject in the instant case. It therefore follows that the rights of the parties to these actions should be determined according to the rule of the common law, and under that rule surface water is regarded as a common enemy, and every owner of land has the right to take any measures necessary for the protection of his own property against surface waters, although in doing so, he may throw the same upon other landed proprietors to their damage. Such damage the law regards as *damnum absque injuria* and affording no cause of action.

As before argued by us, the complaints in these actions were drawn distinctly upon the theory that the injury sustained by the plaintiffs was the result of an overflow of surface waters. It is true that allegations are made in the complaints that "Spring Creek" is a "natural watercourse," but that allegation is qualified by the allegation that the large volume of water therein was due to the melting of the snow. The trial court, however, instructed the jury as a matter of law that Spring Creek was a natural watercourse. Our contention is that the court should have instructed the jury as a matter of law that the waters which flowed down this ravine, which plaintiffs call "Spring Creek," were nothing more than mere surface waters, resulting from melting snow which fell upon the hills in an unusual quantity. If the injury to the property of plaintiffs was occasioned by flooding from surface waters, and not by the diversion by the defendant of a natural watercourse, then it follows, under authorities, that there could be no recovery, and any damage suffered would be *damnum absque injuria*.

In any event, if there was any doubt as to whether or not the injury was occasioned by surface waters, then this question should have been submitted to the jury under proper instructions, explaining the difference between surface water and a natural watercourse. This was not done.

For the reasons assigned, the judgment of the lower court should be reversed and set aside, and it should be directed by this court to enter a judgment in favor of the defendant and against each of the plaintiffs, dismissing said actions, and awarding defendant judgment for its costs herein.

Respectfully submitted,

A. C. SPENCER and
C. E. COCHRAN,

Attorneys for Plaintiff in Error.

JAMES E. FENTON,
Of Counsel.

United States
Circuit Court of Appeals
For the Ninth Circuit

OREGON - WASHINGTON RAIL-
ROAD & NAVIGATION COM-
PANY, a corporation,

> Plaintiff in Error,

vs.

PRESTON ROYER,

> Defendant in Error.

No. 3203.

OREGON - WASHINGTON RAIL-
ROAD & NAVIGATION COM-
PANY, a corporation,

> Plaintiff in Error,

vs.

W. J. WASSON and MABEL WAS-
SON,

> Defendants in Error.

No. 3204.

Brief of Defendant in Error

M. A. LANGHORNE,
E. M. HAYDEN,
F. D. METZGER,
> Attorneys for Defendants in Error,
> Tacoma, Washington.

United States
Circuit Court of Appeals
For the Ninth Circuit

OREGON - WASHINGTON RAIL-
ROAD & NAVIGATION COM-
PANY, a corporation,

              Plaintiff in Error,   } No. 3203.

              vs.

PRESTON ROYER,

              Defendant in Error.

OREGON - WASHINGTON RAIL-
ROAD & NAVIGATION COM-
PANY, a corporation,

              Plaintiff in Error,   } No. 3204.

              vs.

W. J. WASSON and MABEL WAS-
SON,

              Defendants in Error.

Upon Writ of Error to the United States District Court
of the Eastern District of Washington,
Southern Division.

STATEMENT OF THE CASE

As stated by counsel for the plaintiff in error,
"the paramount question involved in these cases is
whether or not Spring Creek is a natural water

course." This stream has its origin in Rattlesnake
Hills, whence it flows in a general southerly direction some fifteen miles to the Yakima River (Tr.
Wasson case, pp. 19-20.) It and its numerous confluents drain between twenty and twenty-five thous-
and acres; and while it is true that throughout its
course in the hill country it flows in canyons or
gullies, yet it is equally true that from the time it
enters upon the flat country above the defendant's
right of way until it empties into the Yakima River
—a distance of some three miles or more—it flows
in a well-defined if crooked and irregular channel
(Tr. Wasson case, pp. 20-23.) "The channel is not
regular—in places good and wide and other places
deep. It is about four to eight feet at the bottom,
the depth being irregular." (Testimony of Mason,
Tr. Wasson case, p. 23.)

This stream does not run constantly throughout
the year, but this is characteristic of the great majority of smaller water courses in similarly arid
country. Nevertheless "Spring Creek runs practically every year when there are good crops and in
dry seasons does not run at all. In 1907 the water
down Spring Creek went through a twenty-four
foot breach practically four feet deep. There is no
outlet other than under the O. W. R. & N. crossing.
From 1906 to 1912 there was water in more or less
volume running each season. This water flows to
the Yakima River and the only outlet is under the
O. W. R. & N. tracks." (Testimony of Royer, Tr.
Wasson case, p. 22.)

Moreover, and perhaps more illuminative of the true character of the stream, Mr. Royer on being recalled further testified as follows:

> "The banks of Spring Creek vary, being well defined for probably fourteen miles above Mr. Starkey's place, there are distinct channels and have to be bridged; they expect water in these and they put in bridges." (Tr. Wasson case, p. 25.)

Nor are the plaintiffs (to use the nomenclature adopted by counsel for the plaintiffs in error) alone in applying to their descriptions of Spring Creek terms strictly applicable to natural water courses only. The defendant's engineer refers repeatedly to the channel of Spring Creek, and testifies that "the water came down in such volume that the *original channel* was so small as to be unable to carry the water." (Tr. Wasson case, pp. 40-41); and finally admits that after making inquiry from local residents as to the flowage of water down Spring Creek, that he made an independent investigation by going practically to the foot of the main Rattlesnake Hills, where he discovered three branches uniting with Spring Creek, and as a result he figured that twenty second-feet would be the flow of water in this stream.

The damage complained of and for which jury returned verdicts for Royer in the sum of $850.00 and for the Wassons in the sum of $1000.00, resulted strictly as alleged in the complaints. The defendant's railway crosses Spring Creek on an embankment about eight feet high, and at a point approximately one-quarter of a mile east of the lands of the plaintiffs. The culvert installed by the defendant in the bed of Spring Creek proved insufficient to carry off the waters which commenced to flow about January 22d, 1916, and overran the lands in question on January 23d and again on February 10th. These waters being deprived of their natural outlet, were impounded by the defendant's embankment and followed along that embankment from the bed of Spring Creek towards the east some thirteen hundred feet, where they broke through the railroad track and washed down over the lands of the plaintiffs herein until they rejoined the natural channel of Spring Creek near the southern limits of section 28. (Testimony of Royer, Tr. Wasson case, pp. 25-26.)

Upon these facts the plaintiffs contend:

I

That Spring Creek is a natural water course.

II

That assuming the waters which did the damage

complained of to be surface waters only, the defendant had no right to impound them and cast them upon the lands of the plaintiffs in increased and concentrated volume to the damage of said lands.

III

That the volume of water which resulted in the flooding of the plaintiff's lands was not due to any extraordinary and unexpected flood.

IV

That there is no claim of estoppel available to the defendant against the plaintiffs herein; and

V

That the defendant failed to preserve any sufficient exceptions to the instructions given by the court.

POINTS AND AUTHORITIES

I

Federal courts follow the local law in deter~nin-ing what constitutes a water course.

> *Chicago, B. & Q. R. Co. v. Board of Supervisors,* 182 Fed. 291, 31 L. R. A. (n. s.) 1117.
>
> *Walker v. New Mexico & S. P. Ry. Co.,* 165 U. S. 593, 41 L. Ed. 837.

II

Spring Creek is a natural water course.

(a) A stream's origin in melting snow or rain does not make it surface water.

> *Chicago, R. I. & P. R. Co. v. Groves,* 20 Okla. 101, 93 Pac. 755, 22 L. R. A. (n. s.) 802.
>
> *McClure v. Red Wing,* 28 Minn. 186, 9 N. W. 767.
>
> *Missouri Pac. R. Co. v. Wren,* 10 Kas. App. 408, 62 Pac. 7.
>
> *Gibbs v. Williams,* 25 Kas. 241, 37 Am. Rep. 241.
>
> *Simmons v. Winters,* 21 Ore. 35, 27 Pac. 7.
>
> *Borman v. Blackmon,* 118 Pac. 848.
>
> *Taylor v. Fickas,* 64 Ind. 167, 31 Am. Rep. 114.

Weideroder v. Mace, 111 N. E. 5.
Gould on Waters, Section 264.

(b) To be a natural water course it is not essential that the flow be continuous throughout the year.

> *Dahlgren v. Chicago, Milwaukee & P. S.*
>   *Railroad Co.*, 85 Wash. 395.
> *Vandalia R. Co. v. Yeager*, 110 N. E. 230.
> *Trout v. Woodard*, 114 N. E. 467.
> *Missouri Pacific R. Co. v. Wren*, 10 Kas.
>   App. 408, 62 Pac. 7.
> *Chamberlain v. Hemingway*, 63 Conn. 1, 27
>   Atl. 239, 22 L. R. A. 45.
> *Sanguinetti v. Pock*, 136 Cal. 466, 69 Pac. 98.
> *Jaquez Ditch Co. v. Garcia*, 124 Pac. 891.
> *Simmons v. Winters*, 21 Ore. 35, 27 Pac. 7.
> *Borman v. Blackmon*, 118 Pac. 848.

(c) Surface waters are waters of a casual or vagrant character, having a temporary source, and which diffuse themselves over the surface of the ground following no definite course or defined channel.

> *Dahlgren v. Chicago, Milwaukee & P. S.*
>   *Railroad Co.*, 85 Wash. 395.
> 1 *Kinney, Irrigation and Water Rights*,
>   Section 318.
> *Miller v. Eastern Railroad & Lumber Co.*,
>   84 Wash. 31.

Harvey v. Northern Pacific Railroad Co., 63 Wash. 669.

III

The owner of higher land may not concentrate at one point surface water and discharge it in a mass upon the lower land.

Peters v. Lewis, 28 Wash. 366.

Noyes v. Cosselman, 29 Wash. 635.

Sullivan v. Johnson, 30 Wash. 72.

Holloway v. Geck, 92 Wash. 153.

Trigg v. Timmerman, 90 Wash. 678, L. R. A. 1916 F, 424.

Rohsnagel v. Northern Pac. R. Co., 69 Wash. 243.

Wood v. Tacoma, 66 Wash. at p. 270 and cases there cited.

Kroeger v. Twin Buttes R. Co., 127 Pac. 735.

Keifer v. Shambaugh, 157 N. W. 634·

Gulf Sea & S. F. R. Co. v. Richardson, 141 Pac. 1107.

Case Note, 12 L. R. A. N. S. p. 680.

IV

Negligence is not a necessary element of the wrong for which damages are claimed by the plaintiffs.

Dahlgren v. Chicago, Milwaukee & P. S. Railroad Co., 85 Wash. 395.

V

The jury's finding is conclusive that the flow of water complained of was only that "which might ordinarily be expected to flow through the water course in question."

No motion for new trial having been made, and no proper exceptions having been taken, the jury's findings settle the facts of the case.

> *Mason v. Smith,* 191 Fed. 503, 112 C. C. A. 146.
>
> *Lehnen v. Dickson,* 146 U. S. 73, 37 L. Ed. 373.
>
> *Aetna Life Ins. Co. v. Ward,* 140 U. S. 76, 35 L. Ed. 371.
>
> *Transit Development Co. v. Cheutham Co.* 194 Fed. 963.
>
> *J. W. Bishop Co. v. Shelhorse,* 72 C. C. A. 337, 141 Fed. 643.
>
> *Hamilton v. Loeb,* 108 C. C. A. 108, 186 Fed. 7.

VI.

There is no estoppel operative against the plaintiffs.

(a) Failure to plead an estoppel operates as a waiver of it.

> *Olson v. Springer,* 60 Wash. 77.

Haefel v. Brackett, 95 Wash. 625.

Jacobs v. First Natl. Bank, 15 Wash. 358.

Huggins v. Milwaukee Brewing Co., 10 Wash. 579.

Walker v. Baxter, 6 Wash. 244.

10 Cyc. 813.

10 R. C. L. 842.

(b)   The maxim is *volenti non fit injuria*, not *scienti non fit injuria*.

Drown v. New England Tel. & Tel. Co., 66 Atl. 801, at 804.

Choctaw R. Co. v. Jones, 92 S. W. 242.

VII.

A single exception to a part of a charge which embraces more than one proposition of law is not sufficient to sustain a writ of error.

Union Pacific Railroad Co. v. Thomas, 152 Fed. 372.

Chicago R. I. & Pacific Ry. Co. v. Hall, 176 Fed. 75.

City of Charlotte v. Atlantic Bitulithic Co., 228 Fed. 456.

Simkins Federal Suit at Law, pp. 114 & 116 and cases there cited.

ARGUMENT

This case comes to this court upon six assignments of error; five of which, being the principal ones, relate to instructions requested and refused or to portions of the instructions actually given. They in reality present but two questions for the consideration of this court; namely, was the damage to the plaintiffs occasioned by the obstruction of a natural water course, or was it occasioned by the impounding of surface waters and the casting of them in a concentrated volume upon and across the plaintiffs' lands.

Defendant, however, argues a number of subsidiary points, which, although we do not believe they are properly before this court, shall be first briefly discussed.

Defendant contends "that the flowage of water on the lands of plaintiffs was not caused by any negligence of defendant." (See Contentions of Defendant, Brief p. 5.) The defendant did not request the court to charge the jury that the damage for which a recovery might be had must be attributable to the negligence of the defendant, and the failure of the court to charge the jury in this particular is ordinarily to be remedied by a request for further instructions. However, the court properly eliminated negligence from its instructions; for, as said by the supreme court of the state of Washington in *Dahlgren v. Chicago, Milwaukee &*

Puget Sound Railroad Co., 85 Wash. 395—a case to which reference will be hereafter frequently made:

> "A second contention is that the instruction erroneously eliminated negligence as an element of the wrong of which complaint is made. But if it be meant by this that it was necessary for the respondent to show, in addition to the fact that the construction of the embankment caused them an injury, that the work of construction was performed in a negligent manner, we cannot agree with the contention. It is doubtless true, as the appellant argues, that it had a lawful right to construct an embankment for the use of its railway, but it does not follow that it had a lawful right to construct it in such a manner as to cause injury to the property of the respondents. It is not a case of *damnum absque injuria.* On the contrary, if the embankment impeded a natural water course, and left no sufficient vent for the escape of the water, and the water was caused thereby to overflow the premises of the respondents to their injury, the construction was negligent and wrongful as to the respondents, no matter how carefully the work of construction was performed."

The defendant next contends that the plaintiffs acquiesced in the construction of the embankment and in the maintenance thereof, and thereby either assumed the risk of injury therefrom or are estopped to claim damages resulting. (See Contentions of Defendant, Brief p. 5, and pp. 23 to 29, inc.) So far as the claim of estoppel is concerned, we believe it to be established beyond question that it is a special defense, and the failure to plead it operates as a waiver. There is no claim made that any such defense was plead or attempted to be plead; but counsel for defendant urges that the maxim *"volenti non fit injuria"* applies. It is apparent and conceded on all sides that the embankment which constituted the railroad grade across Spring Creek was constructed by the defendant upon its own right of way and as it had a lawful right to do, with the exception of the provision it made for the passage of the waters of Spring Creek. There is nothing in either complaint, and no syllable of the testimony to indicate that the plaintiffs or either of them participated in the construction or reconstruction of this grade or embankment. Conceding that they knew of its construction and that when it was last reconstructed they further knew that the forty-eight-inch culvert had previously proved insufficient, it is to be remembered that the maxim is *volenti non fit injuria*, not *scienti non fit injuria*. The maxim itself contemplates an active participation in the doing of the act or the accomplishment of the thing which is later sought to be complained of; and the cases cited by counsel for defendant corroborate this position. The person to whom the maxim is applicable is one who remains silent although under a duty to speak, or by some act or declaration "recognizes the wrong as an existing and valid transaction and in some degree at least gives it effect so as to benefit himself or so as to affect the rights or relations created by it between the wrong doer and a third person." Neither of the plaintiffs participated so far as the record in this case is concerned in the construction of this embankment. Neither of them was ever under any duty to the defendant to prescribe the character of embankment that should be built; and neither of them has at any time recognized the wrong as an existing and valid transaction.

Again the defendant contends that the injury was the result solely of an extraordinary and unexpected flood, and that the damage sustained was therefore *damnum absque injuria*. (See Contentions of Defendant, Brief p. 5.) However, the court expressly charged the jury:

> "Of course, the railroad company had a lawful right to construct its roadbed along its right of way, together with the right to make all necessary cuts and fills, but where such roadbed crossed a natural watercourse the company was bound to construct a culvert or make other adequate provision to permit of the passage of the waters flowing down the stream at times of all ordinary freshets, *but was not bound to anticipate or provide against unprecedented or unexpected floods.*
>
> "The first question for your consideration, therefore, is, did the company in the present instance make adequate provision for the free passage of all water *which might ordinarily be expected to flow* through the watercourse in question? If it did not, and

such failure on its part was the direct and proximate cause of the injury to the property of the plaintiffs, real or personal, the plaintiffs are entitled to a verdict at your hands." (Tr. Wasson case, pp. 52 & 53, Italics ours.)

It is evident, therefore, from the jury's findings in favor of the plaintiffs that they found that this volume of water did not result from an unprecedented or unexpected flood, but was such volume as might ordinarily be expected to flow through Spring Creek. Defendants, moreover, preserved no exception to this finding, and both they and this court are bound by it.

A discussion of the requested instructions which were refused by the court cannot be separated from that dealing with the concrete question as to whether or not Spring Creek is a natural water course, and the second question involved in this appeal whether the defendant caused surface waters impounded by it to be released in concentrated volume upon the plaintiffs' lands to their material damage; but the defendant's exceptions to the portions of the charge given are insufficient because those particular portions of the charge involve and state more than one proposition of law, and one of those propositions, at least, is correct. At any rate it does not lie in the mouth of defendant to urge the contrary as it itself requested the court to charge the jury in practically the identical language used. (Compare defendant's requested instruction 2, Tr. Wasson case, p. 50, with the second paragraph of the instructions given by the court, Tr. Wasson case, pp. 52 & 53.)

In the Dahlgren case, 85 Wash. 395, the court instructed the jury as follows:

"In this connection you are instructed that any drain provided by the defendant to take care of the waters of the stream, if you shall find there was one, as above, must have been sufficient to take care of and dispose of the waters flowing down the stream at times of any ordinary freshet, but need not have been sufficient to provide against any unprecedented flow of high water."

This instruction was objected to upon the ground that it invaded the province of the jury. The supreme court of Washington answered this objection as follows:

"But clearly the court here determined no question of fact. It but stated the measure of duty the law imposed upon the appellant with regard to the drain. And we think it correctly stated the rule. If it has fault at all, the fault lies in the fact that it is not sufficiently full to cover the entire evidence on the particular subject. But the remedy for this defect is to ask for further instructions, not to object to the instruction given."

Spring Creek is a natural water course.

The time available to us for the preparation of

this brief has not sufficed for a minute consideration of the vast number of cases cited on behalf of the defendant. It is apparent, however, that many of them are early decisions, and that the great majority of them are from states differing wholly in the natural conditions as to rainfall and waters from those found in Benton County, Washington. To all of these early decisions, Chief Justice Beasley in *Bowlsby v. Speer*, 31 N. J. L. 351, 353, 86 Am. Dec. 216, suggested an exception in these words:

> "How far it may be necessary to modify this general proposition in cases in which, in a hilly region, from the natural formation of the surface of the ground, large quantities of water, in times of excessive rains or from the melting of heavy snows, are forced to seek a channel through gorges or narrow valleys, will probably require consideration when the facts of the case shall present the question."

That exception has been now many times considered and has become as well established as the original rule; so well established indeed that argument in aid thereof must be a superfluity. We purpose therefore merely to call this court's attention to what we believe to be the more modern definitions of a water course, and to point out their applicability to the facts of this case.

The Dahlgren case, 85 Wash. 395, was brought to recover damages for the alleged wrongful obstruction of a water course, causing injury to the plaintiff's real property, which was bottom land sloping slightly to the southwest. West and northwest of it is a hill "which for a considerable distance from the property gathers drainage waters which flow in a natural channel or gully at the base of the hill, making a flowing stream throughout the year except in the driest months." In holding this stream a natural water course, and incidentally in passing upon the sufficiency of the pleadings in that particular, the supreme court said:

> "Surface waters, in a technical sense, are waters of a casual or vagrant character having a temporary source, and which diffuse themselves over the surface of the ground, following no definite course or defined channel, while here the waters are described as coming from the vicinity of a large area to the north of the respondents' premises and flowing naturally and without hindrance through a natural water course and channel which crossed such premises. The description is that of a natural and regular water course, rather than that of a mere casual overflow. * * * But if the pleadings be obscure on the particular question, the testimony introduced thereunder without objection was nqot so. The testimony showed a stream flowing in a well defined channel, continuous for some nine months of the year, and that it was this particular channel that the appellant closed to the injury of the respondents. Where evidence is introduced without ob. jection, the court may properly base its instructions thereon, even though the evi-

dence be broader than the pleadings."
(Opinion, p. 405.)

Again, and notwithstanding the decision in
Robinson v. Shanks, 118 Ind. 125, (Appellant's
Brief, p. 32), the appellat ecourt of that state in
the recent case of *Vandalia Railroad Co. v. Yeager*,
60 Ind. App. 118, .defined a water course as follows:

> "An origin from rains and melting snow
> is by no means an infallible guide in determ-
> ining that a certain flow of water is mere
> surface water that may be damned with im-
> punity. The Supreme Court states the fol-
> lowing as the true rule:
> " 'If the face of the country is such
> as necessarily collects in one body so large a
> quantity of water, after heavy rains and
> the melting of large boies of snow, as to
> require an outlet to some common reservoir,
> and if such water is regularly discharged
> through a well-defined channel, which the
> force of the water has made for itself, and
> which is the accustomed channel through
> which it flows, and has flowed from time
> immemorial, such channel is an ancient
> natural water course.' *Taylor v. Fickas*, 64
> Ind. 167, 31 Am. Rep. 114."

And following upon that decision, the supreme
court of Indiana, in *Weideroder v. Mace*, 184 Ind.
242, 111 N. E. 5, held that language of an answer
as follows:

> "that the face of the country in the
> vicinity of appellant's said land is such as

necessarily collects on said land in one
body, so large a body of water, after heavy
rains and the melting of large bodies of
snow, as to require an outlet to some reservoir; that such water is now and has been
from time to time immemorial regularly
discharged through a 'well-defined channel'
which the force of the water has made
for it."

described a natural water course.

The standard definition of "water course" in
Oregon is to be found in *Simmons v. Winters*, 21
Ore. 35, 27 Pac. 7, quoted with approval in the
recent case of *Borman v. Blackmon*, 60 Ore. 304,
118 Pac. 848, as follows:

"'That a water course is a stream of
water usually flowing in a particular direction, with well-defined banks and channel,
but that the water need not flow continuously—the channel may sometimes be dry;
that the term "water course" does not include water descending from the hills down
the hollows and ravines, without any definite channel, only in times of rain and melting snow, but that, where water, owing to
the hilly or mountainous configuration of
the country, accumulates in large quantities from rain and melting snow, and at
regular seasons descends through long, deep
gullies or ravines upon the lands below, and
in its onward flow carves out a distinct and
well-defined channel, which even to the
casual glance bears the unmistakable impress of the frequent action of running
water, and through which it has flowed

from time immemorial, such a stream is to be considered a water course and to be governed by the same rules.' "

We believe it must be apparent that these definitions fit the case now before the court, for here the face of the country is such that there is necessarily collected in the Rattlesnake Hills a large quantity of water which for years past has irresistibly sought an outlet for itself until it has made a well-defined channel in which water is expected to flow and which is bridged wherever the roads of the vicinity have occasion to cross it. We desire, however, to call the court's attention particularly to two other cases in this connection; namely, *Jaquez Ditch Co.* v. *Garcia*, 124 Pac. 891, and *Kroeger* v. *Twin Buttes Railroad Co.*, 127 Pac. 735. In the first case the supreme court of New Mexico examines a large number of definitions of natural water course as promulgated by the various states of the Union; and then after remarking that "the only case that seems to be in conflict with these definitions is the case of *Walker* v. *New Mexico & Sourthern Pacific R. Co.*, 165 U. S. 593, 14 Lawyers Edition 837," (cited in defendant's brief, pp. 31, 39-40), proceeds to distinguish that case in the following language:

> "But a careful examination of this case (the Walker case) shows that the obstruction or embankment complained of was four miles from the mouths of the arroyo, and that the water after leaving the arroyo

spread out, and became surface or flood
water. It is obvious that this case rests on
a different state of facts, and it appears
from the evidence that the arroyo in question came out of the hills in a well-defined
channel a few rods from where the obstruction was erected."

So in the present case, although the point where
the defendant's embankment crossed the channel
of Spring Creek was several miles from where that
creek emerged from the hills, nevertheless throughout that distance the creek flowed in a well-defined
channel to which its waters were wholly confined
except where they were spread out by the government's dam and that made by Mr. Starkey; but
that even then, they came together again and before
reaching the defendant's track once more flowed
in a single well-defined channel. (Testimony of
Williams, Defendant's Engineer, Tr. Wasson case,
pp. 40-41.)

The second of the two cases last above cited
is important in that it points out another ground
of distinction from the Walker case in this, that in
the Walker case the waters passed over the plaintiff's land in their natural flow and fall and were
then dammed by the defendant's embankment and
thereby cast back from the defendant's lower lands
onto the plaintiff's higher lands. "The Walker
case was dealing with surface water flowing from
plaintiff's lands onto defendant's lands;" while
in the Kroeger case, as well as in the instant case,

the waters complained of were cast from the defendant's lands onto the plaintiff's lands over which in their natural state they were not accustomed to flow.

Defendant in collecting the water behind its embankment, and discharging it in a concentrated body upon the lands of the plaintiffs to their damage, became liable to them for such damage.

The foregoing statement is of a rule so firmly established in the United States, and particularly in the state of Washington, that we do not believe it will be contested. It applies equally to the obstruction of a natural water course as to the impounding of surface water; and that it is applicable to the facts here must be apparent. The waters of Spring Creek, unable to follow their natural and accustomed channel, were dammed back by the railroad company's embankment on its right of way and followed the slight grade toward the east down a borrow pit until they reached a point on the lands of the plaintiff Wasson where they broke through the defendant's grade, washing away the roadbed and across the plaintiff's land. The exhibits in the case clearly point out the course the waters took and their discharge in destructive concentration upon the plaintiff's fields.

The supreme court of Washington in the early case of *Peters* v. *Lewis*, 28 Wash. 366, 68 Pac.

869, adopted the rule hereinabove stated in this language:

> "When surface water is collected and discharged upon adjoining lands in quantities greater than or in a manner different from the natural flow, a liability accrues for the injury occasioned thereby."

This general rule has been applied in varying circumstances in the long line of cases hereinabove cited.

Thus in *Noyes* v. *Cosselman,* 29 Wash. 635, 70 Pac. 61, the plaintiffs brought an action to restrain the defendants from digging a ditch whereby the waters resulting from rains and melted snows, which commonly accumulated in a natural depression on their lands, should be drained off and cast upon plaintiffs' lands. The lower court found for the plaintiffs, issued the injunction, and the defendants appealed, placing their main reliance upon the case of *Cass* v. *Dicks,* 14 Wash. 75, 44 Pac. 113, which case is likewise one of the main props of the defendant's argument (See Brief, pp. 9-10, 31.) The supreme court of Washington in commenting upon that case says that it "was a case where lands lying along a river were subject to inundation at times of high water unless protected by means of dikes. The defendants in that case were lower proprietors, and were proceeding to erect a large dike for the purpose of preventing their lands from being flooded during extraordinary freshets. The plaintiffs brought the action to restrain the erection of the dikes upon the ground that the same would prevent the seepage, surface water, and overflow from flowing from their premises, as it was accustomed to do, and thus destroy their crops and render their farm valueless."

Continuing, and still referring to that case, the court further said:

"It was therefore held that the lower proprietor had a right to construct the dike in order to protect his own land. And it is argued in this case that the appellants here have a right to drain the water which accumulates in Long Lake from rains and melting snows through an artificial ditch built for that purpose through a natural barrier upon their own land, and cast the same upon lower lands of their own, from whence it is cast upon respondents' lands, and that the damage thus caused to respondents is *damnum absque injuria;* that the only remedy of respondents is to dike against the flow of water, and thereby keep it upon the lands of appellants, or to construct ditches to carry off the increased water. If the position of appellants that respondents may dike against the water thus turned upon them is correct, under the rule announced in *Cass* v. *Dicks, supra,* still we do not think it necessarily follows that the appellants may by artificial means turn the water from Long Lake upon other parts of their own lands, to the injury of respondents. The rule that an owner of land has no right to rid his land of surface water by collecting it in artificial channels, and discharging it upon the land of an adjoining proprietor, to his injury, is followed alike in the states which have adopted the common law as well as those which have adopted the rule of the civil law." (Citing cases.)

In *Rohsnagel* v. *Northern Pacific Railroad Co.*, the plaintiffs sought to recover damages from the defendant railway company under allegations showing that the defendant company's roadbed where it passed plaintiff's lands was upon a solid embankment from four to eight feet above the natural level of the ground, so that in times of flood the waters of the Snohomish river, which flowed on the opposite side of this roadbed from the plaintiffs' land, were from two to three feet above the level of the plaintiffs' ground. In November, 1906, the defendant's roadbed was washed out at a point immediately opposite plaintiffs' land; and following upon that, the defendant installed a culvert at the place where the washout had occurred, with the result that during each succeeding annual high water after the installation of this culvert, the water impounded by the defendant's embankment was forced through this culvert and discharged upon the lands of the plaintiffs to their damage in the sum of six thousand dollars. To this complaint a demurrer was sustained upon the case of *Harvey* v. *Northern Pacific Railway Co.*, cited in defendant's brief, page 31.

The supreme court held this action to be erroneous, and reversed the lower court. The supreme court, after pointing out the true nature of the Harvey case, proceeds with its opinion as follows:

"In this action, the surface water does not meet the embankment and then proceed with the natural course of the stream, but respondent has collected the water on its right of way and has discharged it upon appellants' land through a culvert constructed for that purpose. It has not raised its own premises for the sole purpose of diking against and preventing the flow of surface water thereon, but has also created a new, unnatural, and destructive current through its embankment, to appellants' damage. In the *Harvey* case, we observed that, as a result of the embankment there constructed, the surface water was returned to the stream; that all the defendant did was to protect its property from overflow water which would otherwise leave the natural channel of the stream. To construct the embankment and thereby raise the water to an unnatural height on respondent's right of way, and then force it through the culvert upon appellants' land with de-destructive force and in a larger volume that its natural flow, is not a protection of respondent's right of way from surface water, as held in the *Harvey* case; but is an attempt to control and dispose of the water in a manner to suit the respondent's pleasure and convenience without returning it to the stream and without regard to appellants' rights. A property owner cannot gather surface water on his land, discharge it in an unusual volume and with excessive force through an artificial ditch or culvert upon the land of another, and then be relieved from liability on the theory that the injury resulting to his neighbor is *damnum absque injuria.* Gould, Waters (3d ed.), 271; *Peters* v. *Lewis*, 28 Wash. 366, 68 Pac. 869; *Livingston* v. *McDonald*, 21 Iowa 160, 89 Am. Dec. 563.''

A continued citation of authority would be a work of supererogation. This court is bound in passing upon the issues presented to apply the law as laid down by the supreme court of the state of Washington. That court has in no uncertain terms, in cases presenting facts so nearly identical with those of the instant cases as to be wholly indistinguishable from them so far as the legal principles which are to be applied are concerned, enunciated the rules hereinbefore set out. Those rules were with his usual force and clarity of expression adopted and applied by the Honorable Judge Rudkin in the trial of these cases. We therefore respectfully submit that no error has been committed and that the judgments should be affirmed.

Respectfully submitted,

M. A. LANGHORNE,
E. M. HAYDEN,
F. D. METZGER,
Attorneys for Defendants in Error.